EARLY CHILDHOOD EDUCATION 96/97

Seventeenth Edition

Editor

Karen Menke Paciorek
Eastern Michigan University

Karen Menke Paciorek is an associate professor of Early Childhood Education at Eastern Michigan University in Ypsilanti. She has degrees in early childhood education from the University of Pittsburgh, George Washington University, and Peabody College of Vanderbilt University. Currently, she is president of the 4,500-member Michigan Association for the Education of Young Children. Dr. Paciorek presents at local and national conferences on a variety of topics, including curriculum planning, establishing a quality learning environment, and guiding young children's behavior.

Joyce Huth Munro
Centenary College

Joyce Munro is director of Teacher Education at Centenary College. In addition to administration and teaching, she oversees The Children's Center at Centenary, which serves 200 children in a variety of programs ranging from toddler care to full-day kindergarten. Regionally and nationally, she presents seminars on curriculum design and teacher education. Currently, she is the early childhood education editor for a teaching cases data bank. She also serves on the Professional Development Advisory Panel of the National Association for the Education of Young Children. Dr. Munro holds an M.Ed. from the University of South Carolina and a Ph.D. from Peabody College at Vanderbilt University.

D1402736

Annual Editions

A Library of Information from the Public Press

Cover illustration by Mike Eagle

Dushkin Publishing Group/
Brown & Benchmark Publishers
Sluice Dock, Guilford, Connecticut 06437

The Annual Editions Series

Annual Editions is a series of over 65 volumes designed to provide the reader with convenient, low-cost access to a wide range of current, carefully selected articles from some of the most important magazines, newspapers, and journals published today. Annual Editions are updated on an annual basis through a continuous monitoring of over 300 periodical sources. All Annual Editions have a number of features designed to make them particularly useful, including topic guides, annotated tables of contents, unit overviews, and indexes. For the teacher using Annual Editions in the classroom, an Instructor's Resource Guide with test questions is available for each volume.

Printed on Recycled Paper

VOLUMES AVAILABLE

Abnormal Psychology
Africa
Aging
American Foreign Policy
American Government
American History, Pre-Civil War
American History, Post-Civil War
American Public Policy
Anthropology
Archaeology
Biopsychology
Business Ethics
Child Growth and Development
China
Comparative Politics
Computers in Education
Computers in Society
Criminal Justice
Developing World
Deviant Behavior
Drugs, Society, and Behavior
Dying, Death, and Bereavement
Early Childhood Education
Economics
Educating Exceptional Children
Education
Educational Psychology
Environment
Geography
Global Issues
Health
Human Development
Human Resources
Human Sexuality

India and South Asia
International Business
Japan and the Pacific Rim
Latin America
Life Management
Macroeconomics
Management
Marketing
Marriage and Family
Mass Media
Microeconomics
Middle East and the Islamic World
Multicultural Education
Nutrition
Personal Growth and Behavior
Physical Anthropology
Psychology
Public Administration
Race and Ethnic Relations
Russia, the Eurasian Republics, and Central/Eastern Europe
Social Problems
Sociology
State and Local Government
Urban Society
Western Civilization, Pre-Reformation
Western Civilization, Post-Reformation
Western Europe
World History, Pre-Modern
World History, Modern
World Politics

Cataloging in Publication Data
Main entry under title: Annual editions: Early Childhood Education. 1996/97.
    1. Education, Preschool—Periodicals. 2. Child development—Periodicals. 3 Child rearing—United Stats—Periodicals. I. Paciorek, Karen Menke, comp.; Munro, Joyce Huth, comp. II. Title: Early Childhood Education.
ISBN 0–697–31550–9   372.21'05   77–640114

Seventeenth Edition

Printed in the United States of America

Editors/ Advisory Board

EDITOR

Karen Menke Paciorek
Eastern Michigan University

Joyce Huth Munro
Centenary College

ADVISORY BOARD

Members of the Advisory Board are instrumental in the final selection of articles for each edition of Annual Editions. Their review of articles for content, level, currentness, and appropriateness provides critical direction to the editor and staff. We think you'll find their careful consideration well reflected in this volume.

STAFF

To the Reader

In publishing ANNUAL EDITIONS we recognize the enormous role played by the magazines, newspapers, and journals of the *public press* in providing current, first-rate educational information in a broad spectrum of interest areas. Within the articles, the best scientists, practitioners, researchers, and commentators draw issues into new perspective as accepted theories and viewpoints are called into account by new events, recent discoveries change old facts, and fresh debate breaks out over important controversies.

Many of the articles resulting from this enormous editorial effort are appropriate for students, researchers, and professionals seeking accurate, current material to help bridge the gap between principles and theories and the real world. These articles, however, become more useful for study when those of lasting value are carefully *collected, organized, indexed,* and *reproduced* in a *low-cost format,* which provides easy and permanent access when the material is needed. That is the role played by ANNUAL EDITIONS. Under the direction of each volume's *Editor,* who is an expert in the subject area, and with the guidance of an *Advisory Board,* we seek each year to provide in each ANNUAL EDITION a current, well-balanced, carefully selected collection of the best of the public press for your study and enjoyment. We think you'll find this volume useful, and we hope you'll take a moment to let us know what you think.

Early childhood education is an interdisciplinary field that includes child development, family issues, educational practices, behavior guidance, and curriculum. *Annual Editions: Early Childhood Education 96/97* brings you the latest information on the field from a wide variety of recent journals, newspapers, and magazines. In making the selections of articles, we were careful to provide the reader with a well-balanced look at the issues and concerns facing teachers, families, society, and children. This edition begins with some startling information on today's young children in the first two selections. How knowledgeable are you about the issues facing the children you work with or know?

As we prepare for another presidential election, it is important for all of us to keep issues facing young children and their families on the front line. Ask politicians questions about what they have done to improve the lives of young children in their community, or what programs they see as most beneficial to the health and well-being of children and families. Be active, write letters, and make calls to current and prospective legislators and leaders. Children are depending on us to speak for them.

The three themes found in articles chosen for this seventeenth edition of *Annual Editions: Early Childhood Education* are (1) the condition of America's families; (2) appropriate educational practices; and (3) the cost and availability of quality care for children in America.

The articles in unit 6, "Reflections," are almost all new. We are pleased to bring you the article "Movers and Shapers of Early Childhood Education." Have you heard any of their names, listened to one of their speeches, or read an article any one of them has written? It is important for us to be familiar with those who have gone before us and are continuing to make major contributions to our profession. Next time you are in the library, seek out more information on these outstanding individuals. Many of them have touched our lives and continue to serve as inspiration to work even harder.

Given the wide range of topics it includes, *Annual Editions: Early Childhood Education 96/97* may be used with several groups: undergraduate or graduate students studying early childhood education, professionals pursuing further development, or parents seeking to improve their skills.

The selection of articles for this edition has been a cooperative effort between the two editors. We meet each year with members of our advisory board who share with us in the selection process. The production and editorial staff of the Dushkin Publishing Group/Brown & Benchmark Publishers ably support and coordinate our efforts.

We are grateful to readers who have corresponded with us about the selection and organization of previous editions. Your comments and articles for consideration are welcomed and will serve to modify future volumes. Please take the time to fill out and return the postage-paid *article rating form* on the last page. You may also contact either one of us online at: ted_paciorek@emuvax.emich.edu or jhmunro@aol.com.

We look forward to hearing from you.

Karen Menke Paciorek

Karen Menke Paciorek

Joyce Huth Munro

Joyce Huth Munro
Editors

Contents

Unit

1

Perspectives

Seven selections consider both the national and international development of early childhood education.

The concepts in bold italics are developed in the article. For further expansion please refer to the Topic Guide and the Index.

Unit 2

Child Development and Families

Nine selections consider the effects of family life on the growing child and the importance of parent education.

The concepts in bold italics are developed in the article. For further expansion please refer to the Topic Guide and the Index.

Unit
3

Educational Practices

Nine selections examine various educational programs, assess the effectiveness of some teaching methods, and consider some of the problems faced by students with special needs.

The concepts in bold italics are developed in the article. For further expansion please refer to the Topic Guide and the Index.

Unit 4

Guiding and Supporting Young Children

Six selections examine the importance of establishing
self-esteem in the child and consider the effects of
stressors and stress reduction on behavior.

Unit 5

Curricular Issues

Eight selections consider various curricular choices. The areas covered include creating, inventing, emergent literacy, motor development, and conceptualizing curriculum.

The concepts in bold italics are developed in the article. For further expansion please refer to the Topic Guide and the Index.

Unit

6

Reflections

Seven selections consider the present and future of early childhood education.

The concepts in bold italics are developed in the article. For further expansion please refer to the Topic Guide and the Index.

The concepts in bold italics are developed in the article. For further expansion please refer to the Topic Guide and the Index.

Topic Guide

This topic guide suggests how the selections in this book relate to topics of traditional concern to students and professionals involved with early childhood education. It is useful for locating articles that relate to each other for reading and research. The guide is arranged alphabetically according to topic. Articles may, of course, treat topics that do not appear in the topic guide. In turn, entries in the topic guide do not necessarily constitute a comprehensive listing of all the contents of each selection.

TOPIC AREA	TREATED IN	TOPIC AREA	TREATED IN
Abuse	12. Why Leave Children with Bad Parents? 30. Breaking the Cycle of Violence 31. Supporting Victims of Child Abuse	**Developmentally Appropriate Practice**	17. DAP Message to Kindergarten and Primary Teachers 18. Teaching Young Children 19. Essentials of Developmentally Appropriate Practice 21. Fourth-Grade Slump 22. Teaching Children in Multiage Classrooms 23. Nurturing Kids: Seven Ways of Being Smart 24. Assessing Young Children Appropriately 25. Aiming for New Outcomes 37. Framework for Literacy 39. Early Childhood Physical Education
Advocacy	2. Call to Action 4. World's 5 Best Ideas 12. Aiding Families with Referrals 31. Supporting Victims of Child Abuse		
Assessment	18. Teaching Young Children 23. Nurturing Kids: Seven Ways of Being Smart 24. Challenges of Assessing Young Children Appropriately 25. Aiming for New Outcomes		
Child Care: Full Day/Half Day	5. It's Hard to Do Day Care Right—and Survive 7. Companies Help Solve Day-Care Problems 11. Keeping Kids Healthy in Child Care 45. Choosing Child Care 46. Cost, Quality, and Child Outcomes in Child Care Centers	**Discipline**	26. Misbehavior or Mistaken Behavior? 27. Behavior Management and "The Five C's" 28. Encouraging Positive Social Development
		Diversity	32. Diversity 33. Project Work with Diverse Students
		Divorce	1. Portrait of the American Child, 1995 13. Life without Father
Child Development	8. Educational Implications of Developmental Transitions 9. Amazing Minds of Infants 10. Creativity and the Child's Social Development 11. Keeping Kids Healthy in Child Care 43. Mrs. Paley's Lessons	**Drugs**	1. Portrait of the American Child, 1995 6. Helping Crack-Affected Children Succeed
		Emergent Literacy	37. Framework for Literacy
		Emotions	31. Supporting Victims of Child Abuse 36. All about Me
Collaboration	4. World's 5 Best Ideas 7. Companies Help Solve Day-Care Problems 14. Aiding Families with Referrals 40. Starting Points 44. Families and Children	**Employer Supported**	7. Companies Help Solve Day-Care Problems
		Families	3. Next Baby Boom 12. Why Leave Children with Bad Parents? 13. Life without Father 14. Aiding Families with Referrals 15. Homeless Families 16. How Families are Changing . . . for the Better! 20. Infants and Toddlers with Special Needs 40. Starting Points 44. Families and Children
Creativity	10. Creativity and the Child's Social Development 33. Project Work with Diverse Students		
Curriculum	25. Aiming for New Outcomes 32. Diversity 33. Project Work with Diverse Students 34. Curriculum Webs 35. Voice of Inquiry 37. Framework for Literacy 38. Read Me a Story 39. Early Childhood Physical Education		
		Federal Government	44. Families and Children

Perspectives

Not surprisingly, children and children's issues have never had much influence on the political agenda in this country. Young children are at the mercy of politicians who have little worry that these young constituents will get angry at budget cuts that affect them or at the lack of policies for their protection and vote their legislators out of office in the next election. The lead article, "Portrait of The American Child, 1995" by Camille Sweeney, paints a grim picture of life in America, especially for the over one-fourth of our children under the age of six who live in poverty.

If we are to prosper as a society, we must find ways to improve the lives of children and their families. As Cornell University Professor Urie Bronfenbrenner stated in 1970, "A society that does well by its children and parents is basically sound." When we have over 16 million children living in poverty and denied access to medical care, proper nutrition, shelter, and educational opportunities, we are not a sound society. How has the face of the American child changed over the years? Why is the poverty of today deeper and more irreversible than 35 years ago? We have a new generation of young children called the babies of the post–World War II baby boomers. These 72 million children are living in a world vastly different from that of their parents. One in 35 is multiracial, 27 percent live with a single parent, 5 percent live in a grandparent's home, and 46 percent of black children live in poverty. These are just some of the statistics that describe the children of the baby boomers.

With many political leaders talking of welfare reform, the key message to remember is this: Welfare reform will work only if child care works. Most people on welfare are children, and most of the adults on welfare are the mothers of those children. The current push to reform

welfare and return mothers to the workforce will only be successful if the mothers have affordable, quality, regulated, or licensed care for their children. Families who receive reimbursements that only allow them to pay for low-quality, unstimulating care will not be contributing members of the workforce. In California, parents were twice as likely to drop out of a welfare-to-work program during the first year if their children were in unlicensed and poor-quality care. Many welfare reform proponents want to skimp on the funding available for quality child care to make their reforms work. This is unwise. Quality early care and education should be the cornerstone of successful welfare reform.

In this unit are two of the three articles on child care that appeared in the *Wall Street Journal* in July 1994. Not only did the series focus on such old problems as low wages and high staff turnover, but it concluded with some possible solutions. Providing quality child care while keeping costs affordable for families and adequately compensating staff are the key problems. There are solutions, however.

The vast numbers of young children being born into and raised in environments where poverty, drugs, abuse, homelessness, and lack of medical care are prevalent pose special challenges for early childhood educators. The 26 percent of American children under the age of 6 living in poverty (Children's Defense Fund, 1993) are denied medical care, proper nutrition, shelter, and educational opportunities necessary for survival in America today. Families living in poverty are faced with a multitude of concerns, but few resources. A 1990 report (Chasnoff et al.) notes that approximately 400,000 cocaine-exposed children are born each year. After their birth, these children live in environments where drugs are an everyday part of their lives. Within a few years, they enter preschool and public school settings, and very few professionals are ready to meet their special needs. Teachers are looking for ways to help crack-affected children succeed in their classrooms. Specific suggestions for teachers working with children affected by drugs are included in this unit.

Difficult times lie ahead for our nation's young children, their families, and those who care for them. One-third of the youth of America live in Texas, California, New York, and Florida, and one-half of the minority youth live in those four states. Increased advocacy efforts are required if we are to maintain and attempt to increase awareness of, and commitment to, our young children. Many teachers are beginning to see themselves as not only educators, but as strong advocates for children who can be vocal and vote. The poor, uneducated, homeless, unemployed, and uninsured depend on individuals who view programs with overall benefits to society as wise investments of our resources.

Looking Ahead: Challenge Questions

How can quality preschool programs benefit children?

In what ways are other countries addressing the needs of families with young children?

What strategies can employers offer to assist employees in dealing with child care?

What factors have led to the increase in child poverty and abuse?

What separates the haves from the have-nots in this new generation of baby boomers?

Portrait of the American Child, 1995

Camille Sweeney

THERE ARE ABOUT 57 million children under 15, about 22 percent of the population. About 79 percent are white, 16 percent black and 5 percent Asian or Pacific Islander, American Indian, Eskimo or Aleutian. About 12 percent of the population is of Hispanic origin.

IN 1994, THERE were an estimated 3,949,000 births. This was the first time since 1989 that the total has fallen under four million. The decline indicates an echo effect, as the outsize number of baby-boom mothers start to pass out of their childbearing years.

THE NUMBER OF children per woman has decreased from 3.6 in 1960 to 2.0 today. Nearly 1 potential mother in 10 now says she never expects to bear a child.

THE AVERAGE AGE of a first-time mother is 23.7, only slightly higher than the average age of first-time mothers in 1940 but nearly two years higher than in 1960. First-time fathers then and now are typically three or four years older.

THE INFANT MORTALITY rate decreased from 10.6 per 1,000 births in 1985 to 8.5 in 1992. This has been attributed to expanded Medicaid coverage, better nutrition and better medical technology. Even so, a recent report found that the rate is still lower in 22 other developed countries.

AMERICA RANKS 31ST in the percentage of low-birth-weight babies, behind Turkey, Iran and even Romania. Washington, D.C., had the highest U.S. concentration of low-birth-weight births, 14.3 percent as of 1991, compared with 10 percent for New York City and 7.1 percent for the country.

THE PROPORTION OF multiple births to all births in America is still very small, 2.4 percent in 1992. Nonetheless, since the early 70's the multiple-birth rate has increased by a third. The increase is attributable to an increase in births to older women, an increase in infertility service seekers and new drugs and treatments.

RECENT DATA SHOW that 42 percent of families with children under 18 have only one child in the household. In 1960, the figure was only 32 percent. Now, 6 percent have four or more children. Then, the figure was 17 percent.

SINCE 1950, THE number of American children living in mother-only families has quadrupled, from about 5 million to nearly 20 million, and since 1970 the number of single parents has tripled, from about 4 million to about 12 million. About 26 percent of households with children under 18 now have only a mother at home, and another 4 percent have only a father. The highest concentrations of such single-parent households are in Louisiana, Mississippi, Tennessee and Washington, D.C.

ONE OF EVERY six children is a stepchild. One of every eleven adults is divorced, three times the proportion in 1970.

IN 1991, OF the total amount of child support supposed to be paid, only 67 percent was actually paid.

AS OF 1992, the median income of families with children was $35,100. The official poverty level for a family of four was $14,763. There are more than 14 million children living in poverty in the U.S. In a recent study, the U.S. ranked worst among 18 Western industrialized nations for the percentage of children living in poverty.

AN ESTIMATED 464,000 children were in foster homes, group homes or residential treatment centers on any single day in 1993. That's only 0.5 percent of all children, but it represents an increase of 77 percent since 1982.

ABOUT 200,000 WOMEN a year are trying to adopt a child.

IN RECENT YEARS, about 200,000 children 14 and under immigrate to the United States annually. Nearly a quarter of the children come from Mexico, with high concentrations from the former Soviet Union, Vietnam, India and China. New York City's public-school student body represents children from 188 countries.

IN CONSTANT DOLLARS, in 1959-60 public schools spent $1,765 per student in average daily attendance. By 1980, that amount had more than doubled. By 1990, it had more than tripled.

STUDENT-TEACHER RATIOS in public schools have been decreasing steadily nationwide. In 1940, there were 29 students per teacher; in 1950, 27; in 1960, 25.8; in 1970, 22.3; in 1980, 18.7; and in 1990, 17.2. New York City's ratio of 18 is only slightly higher than the national average, but with current budget cuts, the number of students per classroom in the city is on the rise.

OVER 25 YEARS, national averages for reading and math at the grade-school level have not changed significantly. The most recent report indicates that 42 percent of fourth graders scored below the basic reading level, and 41 percent scored below the basic math level.

AVERAGE COMBINED SCORES on the Scholastic Aptitude Test have dropped 78 points since 1963. The latest national average S.A.T. scores are 424 in verbal and 478 in math.

THE NO. 1 foreign language studied in public schools is Spanish, with 443,000 students in 1948 and more than 2.5 million by the early 90's. Only French has come close.

SINCE 1978, THE number of children receiving home schooling has jumped from 12,500 to 1 million.

FROM 1985 TO 1994, the number of reported cases of child abuse nationwide increased 64 percent. More than three million cases were reported in 1993. It's estimated that a third of all cases reported are substantiated. It is also estimated that three children died each day in the U.S. in 1994 as a result of maltreatment.

IN A RECENT study, the U.S. ranked in the lower half of Western industrialized countries in providing services for family support.

PUBLIC CONCERN ABOUT teen-age pregnancy appears to be having an effect. The Government reported last month that the birthrate among teen-agers dropped 2 percent in 1993. That followed a drop of 2 percent in 1992. Even so, teen pregnancy rates are significantly higher in the U.S. than in many developed countries — twice as high as in England, France and Canada, and nine times as high as in the Netherlands and Japan. Every day in America, 1,340 teen-agers give birth.

THE PERCENTAGE OF first births to American teen-agers that occur out of wedlock has increased over 30 years from 33 percent to 81 percent. The percentage of teen-age first-time mothers in America nearly equals the percentages in Jordan, the Philippines and Thailand.

IN 1991, MORE teen-agers and young adults died from suicide than from cancer, heart disease, H.I.V. infection or AIDS, birth defects, pneumonia, influenza, stroke and chronic lung disease combined.

IN 1994, ABOUT one in five high-school seniors smoked. In 1975, it was about one in four. More than half the three million adolescent smokers are male. Another one million use smokeless tobacco.

EVERY DAY, 135,000 children take guns to school.

EVERY DAY, 1,200,000 latchkey children go home to a house in which there is a gun.

THE PERCENTAGE OF mothers using organized day care for children under 5 rose from 13 percent in 1977 to 30 percent in 1993.

ALTHOUGH REPORTED CRIMES of violence have decreased nationwide in the past 10 years, arrest rates for violent crimes committed by juveniles ages 10 to 17 doubled between 1983 and 1992. The majority of juvenile violent crimes are committed between 3 P.M. and 6 P.M.

IN 1994, 99 PERCENT of the 850,000 children reported missing were found.

A CALL TO ACTION
Improving
the Situation
of Children
WORLDWIDE

**Judith Evans
and Robert G. Myers**

Judith Evans and Robert Myers are codirectors of the Secretariat of the Consultative Group on Early Childhood Care and Development, an international interagency group dedicated to improving the condition of young children at risk. The Consultative Group was begun by Robert Myers in 1984. Judith Evans joined the Secretariat in 1992. Prior to that, she worked with the Aga Khan Foundation and was vice-president of programs at High/Scope Foundation.

The High/Scope Foundation has always supported international care and education program development, implementation, and research. Therefore, High/Scope supports the Consultative Group in its work of strengthening programs benefiting young children and their families. This article provides important information on the inroads being made by the Group throughout the world. The Group's major objective is to foster communication among international agencies and their national counterparts—among decision-makers, funders, researchers, program providers, parents, and communities.

According to UNICEF estimates, more than 1.5 billion children will have been born during the 1990s. While many of the births will be in the United States, the majority will be in what are commonly referred to as "developing countries," in Africa, Latin America, and Asia. This means that increasing numbers of children will be born into poverty and will live in conditions that threaten their chances for optimal human growth and development. Over the past 10 years, significant efforts have been made to improve the situation of such children by providing a variety of early childhood programs that support their development. The purpose of this article is to review the latest advances in the field of early childhood care and development at the international level, in terms of present accomplishments and future challenges.

A Focus on Children

Worldwide, the environments in which millions of children are growing up are inadequate by any number of criteria; shortcomings include overcrowding, absence of potable water and sewage facilities, lack of sufficient food, and inadequate caretaking. Not surprisingly, frequent infection (most commonly diarrhea) and malnutrition account for over 50 percent of infant deaths in developing countries. These statistics are likely to worsen as the numbers of people living in urban areas increase, which they will. It is estimated that by the year 2000, urban populations in the developing countries will have increased from 1 billion

(in 1980) to 2.1 billion. This represents a 110 percent increase—which is almost 3 times the rate of increase predicted for the world's population during that same period. Thus, a further expansion of urban slums and squatter settlements is inevitable.

This situation is of concern to many, including those of us at High/Scope. Recent years have witnessed an attempt, through various international, regional, and national conferences, to focus the world's attention on the needs of children. It is notable that the *Convention of the Rights of the Child*, brought to the General Assembly of the United Nations in 1989, set universal standards for children in relation to survival, development and protection.

There is growing international concern not only about protecting children's rights but also about meeting their educational needs. In March 1990, as a result of a joint UNICEF/UNESCO initiative, the World Conference on Education for All (WCEFA) was held in Bangkok, Thailand. While for many, *basic education* has denoted education in the primary grades, the WCEFA expanded this definition to include *meeting a child's basic learning needs even in the earliest years*. This redefinition was a recognition that early development provides children with a firm foundation for learning in primary school and for productive social contributions in later life. As a result of this recognition, the WCEFA Framework for Action included, as the first target for the 1990s, **expansion of early childhood care and development activities, including family and community interventions, especially for poor, disadvantaged, and disabled children.**

WCEFA spurred among many governments and some international organizations a new interest in creating and strengthening programs for the early childhood years. **Indeed, it is probably fair to say that attention to children during the preschool years is now the fastest growing part of the educational sector internationally.**

This international climate in support of programs addressing the young child has attracted new funding sources. For instance, the World Bank, which had virtually no loans in this area 5 years ago, has since responded to national requests with at least a dozen loans in support of health, nutrition, and education programs for young children. These loans support such diverse initiatives as parent-education programs, formal and nonformal preschool programs, and home day care in countries like India, Brazil, Bolivia,

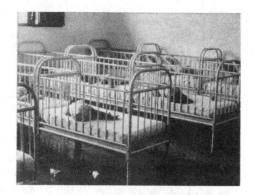

and Colombia. Also, comprehensive child health, nutrition, and education programs are being developed in Thailand and the Philippines. In addition, UNICEF and UNESCO have established a variety of early childhood programs within the last decade. Thus there is increasing awareness of the needs of young children and the necessity of meeting those needs during the early years. How did this come about?

Looking at the Evidence

The action taken at WCEFA was in response to overwhelming evidence that appropriate support for children's growth and development during the first years of life is a sound social investment. It is now well established that the rapid growth and early acquisition of motor and cognitive skills typical of infancy and early childhood make children vulnerable to a variety of health, nutritional, psychosocial, and other environmental conditions. Those living in poverty are particularly at risk of

poor physical and psychosocial development. Thus it is being argued that a critical time to assure survival and sustained development is during the early years.

Scientific findings from a variety of fields have demonstrated that support of early development yields rich benefits not only in immediate ways for the child and parents but also over time in terms of the child's ability to contribute to the community. Interventions in the early childhood years offer an extraordinary opportunity to avoid or moderate learning problems and to bring lasting benefits to individuals and society.

For INDIVIDUALS, there are several areas where early intervention can have an impact:

1. **Brain development.** During the first 2 years of life, critical brain structures develop that affect children's ability to learn. If the brain develops well, learning potential is increased, and the chances of failure in school and life are decreased. It is only when programs provide proper nutrition and pro-

mote stimulation of a child's senses that the structure and organization of the brain is enhanced.

2. Nutrition, care, health, and learning ability. Nutritional supplementation (simply giving children more food) is not sufficient to stimulate brain development. The feeding process itself is an important part of what contributes to a child's nutritional well-being. When children have access to food, those children with consistent, caring attention are better nourished, healthier, and more able to learn than children who do not receive such care. Neglected children are more prone to sickness and malnutrition, and they are less equipped and motivated to learn. Programs that support families and teach them how to provide consistent, healthful care—care that includes stimulation and support for cognitive development—are helping children develop the readiness to participate productively in school and the community.

For SOCIETY there are many benefits of early childhood interventions:

1. Increased economic productivity. In many countries of the world only about 80 percent of the school-aged population enter first grade (of girls, there are countries where fewer than 50 percent even begin school). About half the children who enroll in school either drop out at the end of the year or have to repeat the grade. Early childhood programs of high quality that support young children's physical and mental capacities make a difference in these statistics. To begin with, children from these programs are more likely to go to school, are likely to remain in school longer, and do better in school than children without the early childhood experience. Over time, school performance is linked to increased economic productivity.

2. Cost savings. Early childhood intervention investments can reduce costs and improve the efficiency of primary schooling. Children who are better prepared physically, mentally, and socially for school have an easier transition from home to school and do better than their peers who lack this preparation. As a result, dropout and repetition rates are lower, and the need for remedial programs is reduced, cutting costs. But it is not only education costs that are reduced. Effective early childhood programs can also bring savings in health care costs when preventive measures have been built into programs, reducing disease and accidents; the social costs of delinquency and related problems are also cut when children stay in school

longer; and work absenteeism is reduced when parents, assured of proper care for their children, can devote their time to the job.

3. Reductions in social and economic inequalities. Investments in early childhood development have been shown to modify inequalities rooted in poverty and social discrimination by giving children from "disadvantaged" backgrounds a fair start in school and in life. Studies suggest that these children benefit more from early intervention programs than do their more privileged peers.

4. Benefits to girls. Through early childhood programs, girls have an opportunity both to improve their abilities and to show what they are capable of doing. Studies from diverse cultures show that girls who participate in early childhood programs are more likely to attend and continue in school. They are first of all better prepared for school, and their parents, having increased expectations for them, allow them to continue their education longer. Further, when there are child care programs for younger siblings, school-aged girls are freed of child care responsibilities and thus more available to go to school.

5. Strengthened values. Transmission of the social and moral values that will guide all of us in the future begins in the earliest months of life. In societies where there is concern that crucial values are being eroded, a strong incentive exists to find ways to strengthen those values. Early childhood programs can assist in that effort by strengthening the resolve and actions of parents and by providing environments in which children can give attention to culturally desirable values.

6. Social mobilization. In many locations, political and social tensions make it extremely difficult to mobilize people for actions that will be to their own benefit. In such circumstances, one way to begin working with the community is to provide a point of common interest. The needs of young children often provide this focus. An early childhood program can be an effective strategy for developing community action.

7. Community and family benefits. The various components included in early childhood programs—improvements in health, sanitation, and nutrition—are also likely to benefit parents, families, and the community at large. Besides the direct benefits, such as better health and sanitation in the community, there are some indirect benefits. If the parents and community have been involved in creating the early childhood program and have ongoing responsibility for sustaining it, then parents develop self-confidence, leaders emerge from the community, and there is increased community organization and social action. Early childhood programs can also benefit families by freeing women and older siblings from constant child care responsibilities, so they can learn and seek better employment and earnings.

It is evident from these examples that support for young children does not merely refer to establishing preschools. **Support refers to all the activities and interventions that address the needs of young children and help strengthen the environments in which they live, including the family and community, and the physical, social, and economic environments.** This is a very unconventional way of thinking about education and the basic educational strategies relating to preschool and the needs of primary and secondary students. But one of the important findings from international early childhood programs has been that a very broad definition needs to be embraced if an early childhood education intervention is to be effective over time. There are other things that have been learned as well, so let's consider them next.

Building on Knowledge and Experience

The benefits of early childhood programs mentioned earlier in this article, coupled with the World Conference call to meet basic learning

---

Early Childhood Development Programs
AROUND THE WORLD

Nepal—Project "Entry Point"

Taking its name from the Nepali word meaning "first door into an important place," the Entry Point program is unusual for its joint attention to the child care needs of working women (families) and the developmental needs of young children. The setting for the project is rural Nepal, where more than 42 percent of the population live below the poverty line and where the infant mortality rate is above the (1991) national average of 102 per 1000 (the U.S. rate was 10 per 1000).. Women play a major role in the sustenance of the family farms, which produce approximately 80 percent of families' average annual incomes. They also engage in a range of informal income-generating activities.

Recognizing women's important economic role and their need for credit, the government initiated a program of Production credit for Rural Women. The goal of the credit scheme was to support activities that would simultaneously generate income and improve community conditions, including levels of health, nutrition, and literacy. As the project took shape, it became clear that working women needed an alternative arrangement for child care. Thus Entry Point was born, both to free women's time for economic activities and to improve the well-being of their children.

To obtain and guarantee repayment of credit, the credit program asked that the women organize themselves into small groups of five or six members. These groups of women also became the unit for organizing day care. Within the group, women agree to share rotating responsibility for taking care of one another's young children, with each woman taking the children into her home for one day of each week. In 1989, approximately 54 groups of mothers in 11 districts were in operation, and an estimated 1,700 children were participating in these home day care arrangements.

All women in the group receive an intensive course at the village level. Each group is provided with a basic kit of materials containing cooking utensils, plates, cups, a bucket, a jug, personal hygiene products, a rug, two dolls, three puppets, a ball, and a drum. Besides this basic kit, nine different kits are now in use. Neighboring groups exchange materials periodically, so children can be exposed to a wide variety of toys and play materials. Since the majority of the women are illiterate, pictures of different activities are used in the curriculum and training that has been provided by an innovative Nepalese nongovernmental organization. Training emphasizes the importance of mothers as caregivers and teachers and aims at building up women's confidence in their ability to manage and run the program regularly. The quality of the mother-child interaction improves because of increased knowledge and confidence that both gain from the program.

A pressing demand for training suggests that the project is successful. Contributing to this success are a variety of factors, including the power of group support, a decentralized planning process involving community definition of needs, a comprehensive curriculum, and on-site training that respects traditional practices while incorporating new information. Success has occurred in spite of problems related to Nepal's challenging geography, the need to follow-up initial training, and occasional conflicts between traditional and child-centered approaches to childrearing. Furthermore, because the day care is provided by local women on a rotating basis, the operating costs for this project are very low.

Reference: Arnold, C. (1992, February). Nepal: Project Entry Point, in C. Landers and A. Leonard (Eds.), *Women, work, and the need for child care, a review of UNICEF-supported programs in Nepal, Ecuador, and Ethiopia.* New York: UNICEF.

needs of young children, are not just elements of a theoretical wish list. We know enough to take action. Consider the following points.

1. **A great deal is known about how young children develop and learn and about what causes delays.** It is not necessary to wait for further research to provide new knowledge:

■ It has been amply proved that development and learning occur as children interact with people and objects in the environment. Therefore, adults can foster learning and development by making the environment more supportive. That involves creating a healthy setting and providing space, materials, and opportunities to help children learn through play, whether at home or else-

where. It involves enabling parents as well as other caregivers to encourage, nurture, stimulate, talk to, and play with their children.

■ Children learn and develop better if they are actively involved in the learning process. It is important for children to have opportunities to construct their own knowledge through exploration, interaction with materials, and imitation of role models.

■ It is now well understood that physical, mental, social, and emotional development and learning are interrelated and that progress in one area affects progress in all the others, so programs need to have a holistic approach.

Thailand—Integrated Nutrition and Community Development Project

Analyses by the Ministry of Health in Thailand pointed to three major constraints to significant reduction in the level of protein energy malnutrition (PEM) in infants and preschool children: (1) the inadequate coverage of the health system, (2) the lack of community awareness of the problem, and (3) the inadequate multisectorial input into the nutrition program. Studies have shown also that by themselves, income-generating projects do not necessarily have an impact on the problem. Accordingly, in 1979 the government introduced a program of community-based primary health care together with a program of growth monitoring, accompanied by a supplementary food program and nutrition education, all within a national plan for poverty alleviation.

Within this broad framework, the Institute of Nutrition at Mahidol University carried out a nutrition education project that was directed toward families with the most vulnerable infants and preschoolers. An important part of that nutrition education was a psychosocial component focusing on caregiver-child interactions and on improvements in the physical and social environment surrounding the child.

As a basis for the project, childrearing attitudes and practices were studied. A number of nutritional and social taboos were discovered that were not beneficial to the child. For instance, a misbelief about colostrum and early suckling was associated with failure to begin breastfeeding immediately following birth. In addition, it was found that few mothers recognized the visual or auditory abilities of a baby at birth. Mothers displayed little awareness of their own capacity to make a difference in their child's development by making use of existing resources to create a more nurturing environment.

With these practices in mind, a series of five interactive videos was created. One of the five was specifically oriented toward child development. It aimed at creating maternal awareness of (1) the child as an individual with early perceptual ability and (2) the importance of play and of mother-child interaction in play and supplementary feeding. A second video compared two 15-month-old boys—one malnourished, the other normal—identifying behavioral as well as nutritional differences. Health communicators in each village, who served as distributors of supplementary food, were trained in the use of the videos, which were presented several times in each village.

Based on home observations and interviews with mothers of children under age 2, evaluators of the project concluded that maternal knowledge about and attitudes toward infants' ability to see were significantly more positive after seeing the videos. More open cradles were found during home visits. More colostrum was given. The results suggest that visual messages, when they are provided in a way that permits discussion, can bring about significant changes in childrearing beliefs and practices.

This project illustrates how both nutrition and psychosocial education components can be incorporated, with good results, into a national program of growth monitoring and targeted supplementary feeding. The method of incorporation does not depend on literacy and takes into account local practices.

Reference: Kotchabhakdi, N. (1958, January 12–14). *A case study: The integration of psychosocial components of early childhood development into a nutrition education program of Northeast Thailand.* Paper prepared for the Third Inter-Agency Meeting of the Consultative Group on Early Childhood Care and Development, Washington, DC.

These accounts are adapted from the Consultative Group's document *Meeting Basic Learning Needs Through Programs of Early Childhood Care and Development.*

These principles of learning have been embodied successfully in many early childhood programs.

2. There is a wealth of early childhood program experience. Over the last 20 years a wide range of effective and financially feasible model programs from countries all around the world have demonstrated their ability to promote integrated care, development, and learning in the early years. These programs embrace a range of approaches, some of them complementary.

■ *Attending to children:* The immediate goal of this center-based, direct approach—focusing on **the child**—is to enhance child development and learning by attending to the immediate needs of children in centers organized outside the home. These centers serve as "alternative" environments for both care and development.

■ *Supporting and educating caregivers:* This approach focuses on the **family members** and is intended to educate and enable parents and other family members in ways that improve their care for and interaction with the child. This enriches the immediate environment in which the child is developing.

■ *Promoting community development:* Here, emphasis is on working to change **community** conditions that may adversely affect child development. This strategy stresses community initiative, organization, and participation in a range of interrelated activities that are directed toward improving the physical environment, knowledge, and practices of community members and toward improving the organizational base, to allow common action and "empower" the community.

■ *Strengthening institutional resources and capabilities:* The many **institutions** involved in the early childhood field need adequate financial, material, and human resources to do a proper job. Programs within this complementary strategy might involve building institutions, training, providing materials, or experimenting with innovative techniques and models (improving the available "technology"). This strategy should include attention to nongovernmental as well as governmental organizations.

■ *Strengthening national commitment:* National commitment is expressed in the **legal, regulatory, and policy frameworks** provided for dealing with young children and families, as well as in the processes established to plan and implement programs. Accordingly, commitment can be strengthened through such activities as reforming a national constitution, passing new laws, establishing national committees, and incorporating an early childhood dimension into regular planning processes.

■ *Strengthening demand and awareness:* This program approach concentrates on the production and distribution of **knowledge** to create awareness and demand in the population at large and to promote social participation. This approach is directed toward affecting the broad cultural ethos that affects child development.

Lessons learned from these and other program approaches provide guidelines to help in adapting programs to local conditions, in a variety of settings.

3. Simple and proven approaches to providing services for young children and their families can be applied in a variety of settings. Many approaches for working with young children have been codified, tested, and proved to be effective. The preschool model developed by High/Scope is an example of such an approach. Training models incorporating these tried and true early childhood approaches have been developed and used successfully in a variety of settings. Many of these are easy to use and inexpensive, and they make a dramatic difference in the health and welfare of young children.

In most countries there is no need to reinvent the wheel or start from zero to promote the development of young children. Many efforts to support children and families exist, sometimes in small grassroots projects, sometimes in the context of health or other services, sometimes as part of private, nongovernmental efforts to improve community life. Often what is needed is the effort and willingness to strengthen existing services; to disseminate or publicize the lessons learned from small-scale, successful programs; and to promote and support the integration of services between governmental departments and nongovernmental organizations.

Resource materials are available that offer plentiful information on working with young children and understanding their developmental needs, training caregivers, addressing health needs, promoting parent involvement, stimulating grassroots community involvement, coordinating efforts between agencies and sectors, and identifying support networks and financial resources locally and nationally. Often these materials can be provided by in-country, nongovernmental agencies already working to promote the welfare of young children. In addition, many international funding agencies can serve as resources to national groups wishing to stimulate their early childhood care and development activities.

Responding to the WCEFA Call for Early Childhood Programs

In response to the Education for All call to action, each country is first assessing what is already done within the country to support families and young children and then looking at ways to strengthen and supplement those resources. Though WCEFA focused on improving basic education in developing countries, the challenge presented by WCEFA is equally applicable in the United States. Some of the challenges are as follows:

1. We need to reach children and families who are most at risk. In most countries, identifiable, organized programs for preschool children (including parental and child-center community programs) still cover a relatively low percentage of the population. Though the distribution of programs, particularly institutionalized programs, is improving, it usually continues to favor the cities. This is particularly true in Sub-Saharan African countries. Reaching the children and families living in conditions that put them at risk is a major challenge for programs of early childhood development and learning. Embedded in this challenge is a need to develop appropriate diagnostic and assessment systems to identify children at risk, a need to create appropriate interventions to help these children, and then a need to follow the progress of the children to assess the effectiveness of the support efforts.

2. Parental and community participation is needed to ensure program quality and to bring benefits to parents and communities as well as children. Programs that educate and enable parents have grown dramatically in some countries but are virtually nonexistent in others, particularly with respect to the psychosocial components of early development and the role that parents play in that development. In creating programs, it is important to recognize and acknowledge the role parents can play. They should be involved in the development of the program, beginning with the planning process and extending to the evaluation as well as the financing and operation of the program. This will ensure programs that are culturally sensitive, meaningful, and sustainable.

3. We need to improve attention to the development and learning of children during their first two years. Reaching children before the age of 3, and particularly between the ages of 1 and 3, continues to be a challenge, particularly in situations where children are at risk of malnutrition and life-threatening diseases. The importance of supporting learning and development during the early years is not fully appreciated. During these crucial years, development is closely tied to health and nutrition, and children are usually at home. Early childhood programs for children in the first two years must take a holistic approach, including attention to mental, social, and physical development, and should address parent education more than center-based programs for children.

4. We must create multisectoral programs. Given the integral nature of early development and learning, a piecemeal approach to early development does not work well. Programs of child care are often purely custodial and fail to include an education component, and nutrition programs may provide supplementary food but little else. Moreover, early education programs may fail to take into account parents' needs for child care. Combining the elements of *nutrition, care,* and *education* remains a challenge. Although governments and other institutions are often organized by sectors, making integration difficult, there are program examples that demonstrate how to provide a holistic experience. Some programs integrate a learning and psychosocial development component into primary health care and into programs of supplementary feeding and growth monitoring. Others incorporate health and nutrition components into preschool, child care, parent education, and community-based programs.

5. The diverse learning environments of home and school should be brought into greater compatibility. The school learning environments usually differ from those in homes or in early education programs. For some children in the United States and many children in developing countries, the radical shift from the native language or idiom used at home to the national language used at school or the radical home/school shifts in activities, expectations, level of formality, and rules of conduct make the home-to-school transition difficult. To support young children in moving from home to school, it is important that early childhood programs continue to work with young children in a way that recognizes and responds to their developmental needs and readiness; programs must resist the temptation to "prepare" children for the academics of formal schooling.

It is not just homes and children that need

to be made ready for school; schools also need to adjust to the children they receive. In light of what is known about the developmental processes of young children, it would seem appropriate for primary schools to adopt some of the informal, flexible, and active child-centered teaching methods used in early education.

6. We need to assure quality while working with limited resources and largely "volunteer" efforts. When program quality is poor, the benefits for children are minimal. There are many reasons for poor-quality programs. Poor quality may reflect the fact that there is heavy reliance on paraprofessional teachers who do not receive adequate training or ongoing support. Poor quality may also be due to inadequate attention to methods and content; poor organization; an inability to combine education, health, and nutrition components; or weak monitoring and evaluation. In situations where the resources are limited, it is particularly important to develop cost-effective programs that do not compromise quality.

7. Program coverage should be extended to large-scale. Often successful models are found in small, grassroots, experimental projects. Many projects and programs continue as pilot or demonstration activities that are innovative, effective, and feasible to replicate but have not been extended in a significant way. Sometimes difficulties are encountered when these successful initiatives are adopted for nationwide application. However, there is an alternative way to "go to scale." National coverage can also be achieved by linking a range of local and regional efforts that have a common goal but different strategies for reaching that goal. At the same time, it is a challenge to devise ways to monitor and evaluate diverse efforts, to ensure that certain baseline goals and standards of implementation are achieved.

8. Program costs must remain manageable. Many low-cost and effective alternatives are available. One option is to incorporate early childhood development actions into ongoing programs of adult education, regional development, child care, health, nutrition, and so on. This strategy avoids the need for expensive new infrastructure. Although this is not without cost, experience shows that such integration can be efficient and produce a synergism that benefits

the original program. Perhaps the most important strategy for meeting costs and extending the financing base is to develop partnerships among parents, communities, governments, nongovernmental organizations, and donor organizations. Such collaboration appears to be the key to sustainability as well as to financing.

A Call to Action

Early childhood development is the first point on a continuum that represents basic education across the life span. Acceptance of the fact that early childhood care and education is the foundation stone for all further development means it should be a high priority for citizens and policymakers worldwide. For a relatively small investment of effort and funds, programs that meet children's basic learning needs can be expanded or increased, yielding significant long-term benefits. Responding to these challenges will require new attention on the part of us all—to the knowledge base on which actions are built, to the state of technology serving the field, to methods of planning and organization, to the quality and availability of human resources, to various forms of collaboration, and to the sources and soundness of program financing. What is called for now? Enough political will and financial commitment to assure that the 21st century avoids the waste of human potential that has tragically characterized the 20th century.

References

Consultative Group on Early Childhood Care and Development. (1993, September). *Meeting basic learning needs through programs for early childhood care and development.* Paper prepared for the Education for All Forum, New Delhi, India.

Myers, R. (1992). *The twelve who survive.* London: Routledge.

UNICEF. (1990). *The state of the world's children.* New York: Oxford University Press.

World Conference on Education for All. (1990, April). *World declaration on education for all and framework for action to meet basic learning needs,* New York: Inter-Agency Commission for the World Conference on Education for All.

The Next Baby Boom

┌─ SUMMARY ─────────────────────────────────

The 72 million children of baby boomers form a huge
generation that will come of age in the next five years.
They will be the first generation to accept mixed races,
"nontraditional" families, and gender-bending sex roles
as mainstream. Unlike the original baby boomers, most
will think their parents are cool. They will also cope
with stark economic divisions based on high-tech skills.

Susan Mitchell

Susan Mitchell is the author of The Official Guide to the Generations *(New Strategist, 1995) and a contributing editor of* American Demographics.

Two-year-old Julie couldn't wait for Halloween.

"What are you going to be, Julie?"

"Geen powie anja! Geen powie anja!"

If you need a translator, you aren't a parent. Julie, like millions of her playmates, went trick-or-treating as the green Power Ranger.

The youngest Americans are opinionated consumers before they even learn to speak. Teenage Mutant Ninja Turtles, Barney the purple dinosaur, and now a multiracial fivesome of teenage boys and girls—the Mighty Morphin' Power Rangers—capture the imagination of young children and a huge quantity of their parents' dollars. Their teenage brothers and sisters already exert a heavy influence on music, sports, computers, video games, and dozens of other consumer markets. Yet the consumer power of today's children is just the first ripple of a huge wave.

Americans aged 18 and younger will form a generation as big as the original baby boom. Like the baby boom before them, their huge numbers will profoundly influence markets, attitudes, and society. Their true power will become apparent in the next five years as the oldest members come of age. Their habits will shape America for most of the 21st century.

A HUGE GENERATION

Our country wasn't always on a demographic roller coaster. In the first half of the 20th century, the annual number of births in the U.S. remained fairly steady, at 2.7 million to 3 million a year. Then, about nine months after the end of World War II, the number of births began a quick, steep climb. It rose from 2.9 million in 1945 to 3.4 million in 1946 to 3.8 million in 1947. The boom continued for 19 years, with 4.3 million babies born in the peak year of 1957. Births remained above 4 million until 1965, when they dropped to 3.8 million. When it was all over, a grand total of nearly 76 million baby boomers had arrived.

Through the late 1960s and early 1970s, births remained well below 4 million a year, dipping to only 3.1 million in 1973. But in 1977, the beginning of the next baby boom, annual births began climbing again. Births topped 4 million in 1989 and continued at that high level through 1993. In 1994, however, the next baby boom finally came to a close. Last year's births dipped just below 4 million, to 3,979,000.

The next baby boom is 72 million Americans, and their proportion of the total U.S. population rivals that of the original boom. Children and teens aged 18 or younger are 28 percent of the total population; the original baby boom, now aged 31 to 49, is 30 percent.

This new generation differs from the baby boom in significant ways. While the boomer generation was a relatively uniform group, the children of the next boom

---

In 1994, fewer than two-thirds of newborns were non-Hispanic white.

---

differ radically from each other in race, living arrangements, and socioeconomic class. The children of this generation also face much more serious problems than the boomers did when they were children. AIDS, crime, violence, and divorce cast long shadows over their world. As the children of working parents, they often have to assume adult responsibilities at an early age.

Members of the next baby boom may be more competent, confident, and wary

---

THE NEXT BOOMERS ARE

Self-Confident Leaders

Today's entering college students are the leading edge of the next baby boom. They are more confident and ambitious than baby boomers were as freshmen.

(attitudes of college freshmen, 1971 and 1993)

REASONS NOTED AS VERY IMPORTANT IN DECIDING TO GO TO COLLEGE:	1993	1971
parents wanted me to go	34.6%	22.9%
get a better job	82.1	73.8
gain general education	65.3	59.5
make more money	75.1	49.9
learn more about things	75.2	68.8
prepare for graduate/professional school	61.1	34.5
OBJECTIVES CONSIDERED TO BE ESSENTIAL OR VERY IMPORTANT:		
raise a family	70.6	60.2
be very well off financially	74.5	40.1
help others in difficulty	63.3	62.7
be successful in own business	42.6	41.9
participate in community action	25.6	25.9
STUDENT RATED SELF ABOVE AVERAGE OR TOP 10 PERCENT IN:		
academic ability	56.2	50.6
leadership ability	55.9	34.9
mathematical ability	43.0	32.0
popularity	45.6	29.2
self-confidence (intellectual)	59.6	34.8
self-confidence (social)	51.3	27.4

Source: The American Freshman, Higher Education Research Institute University of California-Los Angeles

---

than the original baby boom. If you could sum them up in one word, the word would be diverse.

ACCEPT MIXED RACES

In the 20th century, international migration and differing fertility rates have made each generation of Americans more racially and ethnically diverse than its predecessor. The original baby boomers are 75 percent non-Hispanic white, according to Census Bureau estimates. Eleven percent are black, 9 percent are Hispanic, and 4 percent are Asian or American Indian, Eskimo, or Aleut. The next baby boomers are only 67 percent non-Hispanic white; 15 percent are black, 14 percent are Hispanic, and 5 percent are Asian or American Indian, Eskimo or

Aleut. Within this generation, younger cohorts are even more racially diverse. Only 64 percent of infants born in 1994 are non-Hispanic white. Sixteen percent of infants are Hispanic, 15 percent are black, and 5 percent are Asian or American Indian, Eskimo, or Aleut.

The Census Bureau's broad racial and ethnic categories tell only part of the diversity story. The next baby boom will be the first generation to seriously question all traditional racial categories. The reason is that many of today's children and teens are of mixed races. In 1990, there were nearly 2 million children under age 18 who were reported as being "of a different race than one or both of their parents," according to the Census Bureau. The largest group is children of black and

How Times Have Changed

Compared with their parents, the next baby boomers are growing up in a more dangerous and complex world.

(10 cultural attributes of the original baby boom and the next baby boom)

original baby boom	next baby boom
cold war	regional wars
nuclear threat	terrorist threats
mother's care	day care
"Father Knows Best"	father isn't home
TV dinners	low-fat fast food
network TV	cable TV
45s and "American Bandstand"	CDs and MTV
Ma Bell	Internet
VW buses	minivans
free love	condoms

Source: American Demographics

12 to 17 believe members of minority racial and ethnic groups receive too little respect. And reflecting their greater tol-

One in 35 members of the next baby boom is multiracial.

erance for diversity in all forms, 57 percent believe gays are also too little respected, according to the Gallup Institute.

While increased diversity might lead to greater racial tolerance, other signs point to further polarization among the races. Schools were successfully integrated decades ago, but many neighborhoods are as firmly segregated as ever. Race-related violence and organized racial "hate groups" are increasingly visible, and schools around the country report increased racial tensions among students.

For the original baby boom, racial issues were explosive and defining. Race will be just as important to the next baby boom, but in a different way. More of today's kids have first-hand experiences with integration, prejudice, and other race issues.

"NONTRADITIONAL" FAMILIES

When the original boomers were children, new friends would often ask each other, "What does your father do for a living?" But for the children of the next baby boom, the question is more likely to be, "Does your dad live with you?" The next boomers' family arrangements are widely varied, and increasingly, they do not include a father.

In 1970, 85 percent of children under age 18 lived with two parents and 12 percent lived with one parent. By 1993, this had changed significantly. Only 71 percent of children have two parents present, and 27 percent live with a single parent, according to the Census Bureau.

Striking racial differences in family composition are driving the diversity of this new generation. In 1993, 77 percent of white children and 65 percent of Hispanic children live in two-parent families.

white parents, but close behind are children of white and Asian parents. That translates into about 1 mixed-race child for every 35 members of the next baby boom, or about one in every school classroom.

The larger share of minorities in the next baby boom means that there is far more interaction between people of different races than there was for most of the baby-boom generation. The oldest half of the original boomers was born into a fully segregated society, with separate schools, neighborhoods, and public facilities for whites and blacks. The next baby boom is the product of a more integrated society.

Today, white kids have nonwhite playmates, a casual appreciation for "ethnic foods," and heroes of every race. Teens of all races listen to rap, hip hop, and Tejano music. "Minority teen culture has an incredible influence on white teens," according to Peter Zollo of Teenage Research Unlimited. "Everything from music to fashion to language seems to be adopted by a large number of suburban white teens."

One reflection of racial and ethnic diversity among children can be seen in the

toy market. Mattel, Tyco Toys, and Playskool are just some of the big players that are responding to ethnic and racial diversity. "We have Dream Doll House families that are African American, Hispanic, Asian, and Caucasian," says Laurie Strong of Fisher-Price, a subsidiary of Mattel.

Zollo says the key is inclusion. "Advertisements, even those for large mainstream brands should be very inclusive," he says. That's why some marketers now shoot different versions of the same ad using rap, alternative rock, and even country music to reach all the different groups of teens and children.

Teens know their world is multicultural, even if grownups don't. Almost three-fourths of 12-to-17-year-olds say they receive too little information at school about Muslims, according to a 1991 poll by the George H. Gallup International Institute. About two-thirds say they receive too little information about "Africans before they came to this country" and about nonwhite women. Well over half feel that Asian Americans and Hispanics are given short shrift in school.

In addition, the majority of people aged

1. PERSPECTIVES

Yet only 36 percent of black children have two parents present.

Since the 1970s, more children (and their families) have had to move into grandparents' homes for economic reasons. In 1991, 5 percent of all children lived in grandparents' homes, including 12 percent of black children, 6 percent of Hispanic children, and 4 percent of white children, according to the Population Reference Bureau. In about half of these cases, the mother also lives there. Both parents live with grandparents in 17 percent of these cases. In 28 percent of these households, neither parent is present and grandparents are solely responsible for their grandchildren. Even children in "intact" families may have an absent parent. Among children of the next baby boom who live with two parents, 16 percent live with a stepparent, according to the Census Bureau.

Children today are also far more likely to live with a never-married mother than boomers were. Among children living with one parent, 7 percent in 1970 and 31 percent in 1990 were living with a parent who had never married. Among single-mother families in 1993, 21 percent of white mothers, 35 percent of Hispanic mothers, and 55 percent of black mothers have never been married.

As the children of divorce, the next baby boomers will grow up determined to have strong marriages for themselves. Three-fourths of children aged 13 to 17 believe it's too easy to get divorced, and 71 percent believe people who have divorced did not try hard enough to save their marriages, according to a 1992 survey by the Gallup Institute. This could mean divorce rates will plunge in the next decade, as the next boomers work harder to save their new marriages. Or it could bring further delays in marriage, as the next boomers wait longer to take their vows.

PARENTS ARE COOL

When the original baby boom came of age, America was rocked by a huge clash of values between young adults and their parents. Much of that generation gap

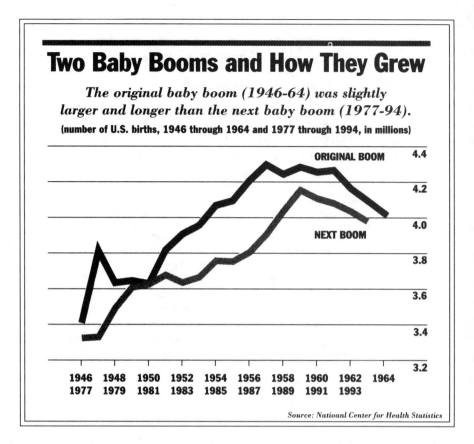

Two Baby Booms and How They Grew

The original baby boom (1946-64) was slightly larger and longer than the next baby boom (1977-94).

(number of U.S. births, 1946 through 1964 and 1977 through 1994, in millions)

Source: Natioanl Center for Health Statistics

persists today, as attitude surveys show a solid demarcation between people under and over the age of 50. The major reason for the gap is higher educational attainment, which pits the boomer generation against their less-educated parents.

Today, there is little evidence of a comparable gap between the original boomers and their next-generation children. While many of the boomers' parents never finished high school, nearly nine in ten boomers did. This achievement should be realized again with the new generation. One-fourth of boomers completed college, and about the same percentage of their children are also expected to obtain college degrees, according to the Census Bureau.

Nearly half of children think their parents are "up to date" on the music they like, according to a 1993 study by *Good Housekeeping* and Roper Starch Worldwide. Few boomers could make the same claim of their parents when they were teenagers. The children surveyed also say their parents' opinions matter most to them when it comes to drinking, spending money, and questions about sex and

AIDS. They even listen more to their parents than their friends about which snack foods to eat.

The next baby boom will not attach a stigma to young men and women who still live with their parents. On the contrary, they will seek close bonds with parents and other relatives as a way to find security in an uncertain world.

GENDER-BENDING

The next baby boom may also reject advertising that sells a product or service specifically to men or women. Calvin Klein

> **The next baby boom may reject advertising that sells a product or service specifically to men or women.**

has seen the future in "cK one," a unisex fragrance. Tomorrow's young men will be more likely to try hair color and jewelry, while women will be more likely to visit the hardware store.

The next baby boom is growing up in

an era when the shifting sex roles of the 1970s and 1980s have become the new social norms of the 1990s. Young women already outnumber men at college, and they are making substantial headway in professions traditionally dominated by men, such as law and medicine. The women of the next baby boom will take these gains even further. Fifty-eight percent of young women and 44 percent of young men believe the women's movement has done a good job. Twenty-five percent of young men, but only 5 percent of young women, believe it has "gone too far," according to a 1991 Gallup Institute poll.

In fact, the young women of the next baby boom are taking the women's movement into new arenas such as sports and entertainment. Title 9, a federal law prohibiting sex discrimination at colleges, including college athletics, "has done a lot to make girls more prepared to take their place in new areas," says Irma Zandl, president of the Zandl Group in New York City. While they are gaining as athletes, young women are also gaining greater attention and status as musicians and entertainers.

But the battle between the sexes is still far from over. Young women are more likely than young men to believe that men do not understand the issues that concern women the most—62 percent of teenage girls believe this, compared with 56 percent of teenage boys. Yet 67 percent of teenage boys and girls believe that the gains women have made have not come at the expense of men, according to the Gallup Institute.

Most social scientists expect the daughters of employed women to have a positive view of having a career. But Peter Zollo of Teenage Research Unlimited found that teenage girls with stay-at-home moms expect to work for a slightly different reason. "What's driving young women to want to have their own careers is that divorce rates are so high they don't want to rely on any man," he says. Even their fathers are pushing them to make sure they can be self-reliant and not dependent on a husband.

STARK ECONOMIC DIVISIONS

In 1959, at the peak of the first baby boom,

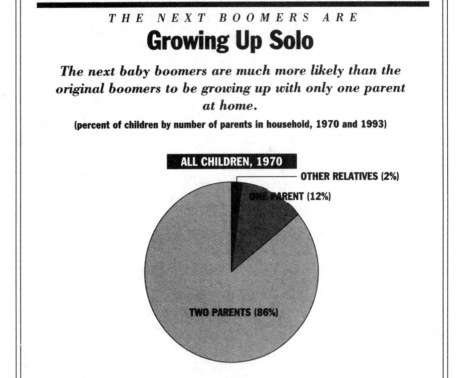

THE NEXT BOOMERS ARE

Growing Up Solo

The next baby boomers are much more likely than the original boomers to be growing up with only one parent at home.

(percent of children by number of parents in household, 1970 and 1993)

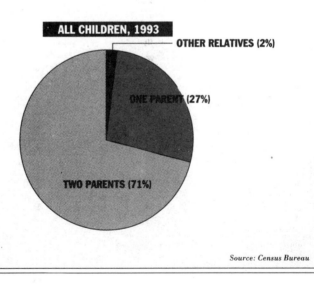

ALL CHILDREN, 1970

OTHER RELATIVES (2%)
ONE PARENT (12%)
TWO PARENTS (86%)

ALL CHILDREN, 1993

OTHER RELATIVES (2%)
ONE PARENT (27%)
TWO PARENTS (71%)

Source: Census Bureau

27 percent of children lived in poverty. In 1993, a smaller percentage—23 percent—of children under age 18 were poor. But the finances of the next baby boom are far from secure. In fact, their situation is getting worse.

From 1950 until 1969 the average family's economic situation was improving. The poverty rate for children dropped from 27 percent to 14 percent. During the 1970s, the proportion of children in poverty fluctuated between 14 and 17 percent. For the next baby boom, however, the years of their birth have coincided with steadily increasing poverty among children, with rates rising from 16 percent in 1977 to 23 percent in 1993.

Even more significant for this generation is the racial difference in poverty rates. While 18 percent of white children are poor, 46 percent of black children live in poverty. For black children, the proportion of poor children has not been

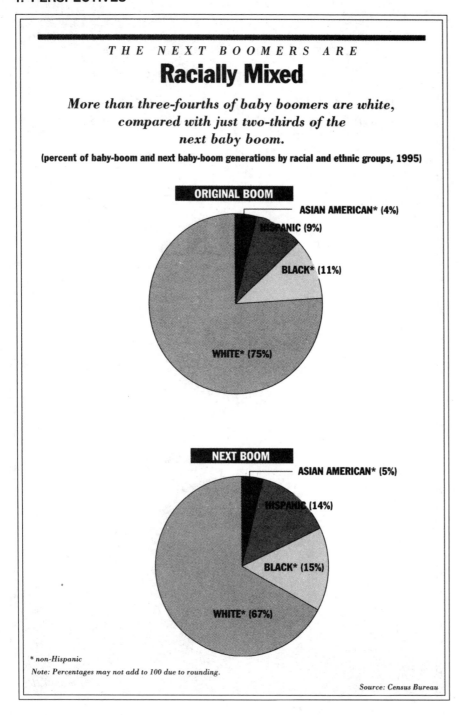

THE NEXT BOOMERS ARE

Racially Mixed

*More than three-fourths of baby boomers are white,
compared with just two-thirds of the
next baby boom.*

(percent of baby-boom and next baby-boom generations by racial and ethnic groups, 1995)

ORIGINAL BOOM

ASIAN AMERICAN* (4%)

HISPANIC (9%)

BLACK* (11%)

WHITE* (75%)

NEXT BOOM

ASIAN AMERICAN* (5%)

HISPANIC (14%)

BLACK* (15%)

WHITE* (67%)

* non-Hispanic

Note: Percentages may not add to 100 due to rounding.

Source: Census Bureau

lege graduates earning over $50,000, according to a 1994 survey by The Times Mirror Center for The People & The Press. But computers are present in only 15 percent of homes where the householder did not graduate from college and has earnings of less than $30,000. Half of college-educated parents say their children use PCs at home, compared with only 17 percent of parents with a high school diploma or less.

Changes in the computer market may eventually narrow this gap. "A lot of kids say they only have an old computer or access through a friend or someone else," says Zollo. "The gap in access may decrease as technology becomes more affordable and kids have more opportunities to use up-to-date technology at school."

Regardless of access, the next baby boom is convinced that computers are cool. Sixty-two percent of those aged 12 to

> **The next boomers are divided into haves and have-nots according to their access to technology.**

19 say online computing is 'in,' but only about 13 percent have been online in the past month," says Zollo. "That gap represents a huge opportunity."

Education is still the ticket out of poverty, and members of the next baby boom value education even more than their parents did. In 1971, 60 percent of college-bound boomers were motivated by a desire to gain a general education and 69 percent wanted to "learn more about things that interest me." In 1993, 65 percent were interested in education in general and 75 percent wanted to learn more about things of interest, according to the Higher Education Research Institute at the University of California, Los Angeles.

The freshman class of 1993 sees a dual role for education: it is a worthy goal in itself, and also the key to financial success. In 1971, 74 percent of boomers indicated they decided to go to college to get a better job and 50 percent cited the de-

lower than 40 percent since 1959, when the Census Bureau first measured childhood poverty rates.

The rapidly changing nature of the workplace makes it more difficult for some people to escape poverty. Even the lowest-paid jobs are increasingly dependent on high-tech equipment, such as computerized cash registers and inventory systems. Children who have little or no experience with technology early in life may have little comfort or facility with

it as adults. Unfortunately, the next boomers are divided into haves and have-nots according to their access to technology and the ability to build important skills early in life.

This technology gap worsens the existing socioeconomic divisions among children and teens. The poorest members of the next baby boom are the least likely to have access to up-to-date technology. Two-thirds of households with personal computers in the home are headed by col-

sire to make more money. Among 1993 freshmen, 82 percent said they were go-

> **The next baby boom may become the largest and most influential generation in U.S. history.**

ing to college to get a better job and 75 percent wanted to increase their earning power.

Twenty-four years ago, baby boomers were noted for their self-confidence. Yet the freshmen of 1993 are even more confident of their abilities than were the freshmen of 1971. One-third of baby-boomer freshmen rated themselves above average in leadership, mathematics, popularity, and intellectual and social self-confidence. In 1993, 43 percent of entering students rated themselves above average in these areas.

The next baby boom will need all the confidence it can get. Their parents, the original boomers, experienced social tur-

moil during their childhood and young adulthood. But many of the issues facing today's young adults are far more frightening. They live in a world where violence and infectious diseases compete for attention with savage economic competition and rapid technological change.

As a new century begins, the next baby boom will enter the adult world and begin struggling with these problems. But their place in the record books is already secure. They may one day surpass their parents to become the largest and most influential generation in U.S. history.

THE WORLD'S 5 BEST IDEAS

Other countries are doing a better job of caring for their infants, educating their children and tending to their sick than we are. Here are the lessons we can learn. In some cases, we could save money by adapting their ideas for use here.

Denise M. Topolnicki

1 LEAVES AND AFFORDABLE DAY CARE THAT HELP PARENTS IN SWEDEN

Imagine an America where: ■ *All parents could take time off from their jobs with pay until their children were beyond infancy and enrolled in high-quality day care.* ■ *All children could attend free preschools.* ■ *All grade schoolers would have to master a rigorous core curriculum.* ■ *All young people entering the labor force would have a chance to be groomed*

2 FREE PRESCHOOLS THAT ACCOMMODATE NEARLY ALL OF THE YOUNG IN FRANCE

for highly paid, skilled jobs. ■ *All people would have equal access to first-rate health care. Each of these programs is a reality somewhere else in the world. And each could be adapted to work here, assuming there was a national consensus to improve*

3 GRADE SCHOOLS THAT HOLD KIDS TO HIGH STANDARDS IN JAPAN

child care, education, job training and health care. Now that Congress and the nation are debating President Clinton's ambitious domestic agenda, the time is right to identify the best ideas from other countries that America might borrow and modify. To that end, MONEY reporters spent three months and traveled 22,500 miles to scrutinize social and educational pro-

4 TRAINING THAT READIES TEENS FOR WORK IN DENMARK

grams that experts identified as the world's most effective. We cast critical eyes on parental leave, day care and welfare in Sweden, preschools in France, grade schools in Japan, job apprenticeships in Denmark, and health care in Canada—and found much worth imitating. We also learned that these programs aren't necessarily expensive; some actually cost less than the deeply flawed patchwork plans we now have in place.

5 HEALTH INSURANCE THAT COVERS EVERYONE FOR LESS IN CANADA

 From *Money*, June 1993, pp. 74-83, 87, 89. © 1993 by Time Inc. Magazine Company. Reprinted by special permission.

SWEDEN
How to care for our young ones

MINIMUM AMOUNT OF LEAVE TIME THAT EMPLOYERS MUST GIVE NEW PARENTS:

SWEDEN	15 MONTHS, PAID
U.S.	3 MONTHS, UNPAID

Compared with other wealthy democracies, our country does little to help parents cope with new babies or pay for child care. Granted, the Family and Medical Leave Act that President Clinton signed last February lets parents of newborns and newly adopted children take as much as 12 weeks off from their jobs. However, the law excludes the 61% of workers whose companies employ fewer than 50. The leave also is unpaid, making it a luxury few low-income families can afford. In addition, the dearth of inexpensive day care swells our welfare rolls because many single mothers can't find work that pays enough to support child care, so they go on the dole.

Contrast our miserly system with the more generous benefits in Sweden, where parents get 15 months of government-paid leave to divide between them as they wish during the first eight years of a child's life. For the first 360 days, a parent on leave receives a munificent 90% of salary, up to a maximum of 258,000 Swedish kronor (about $35,300 per year; all subsequent figures are in U.S. dollars using the exchange rates prevailing in late April). The last 90 days are paid at a flat $8 a day. Eighty-five percent of the $2.4 billion annual cost comes from Sweden's social insurance fund, which also pays for universal health insurance and other benefits and is financed by an employer-paid payroll tax of 31% (ours is 7.65%); the other 15% comes out of general tax revenues.

Then when Swedish mothers like Ulla Nord, who is profiled at left, return to work, they can enroll their preschoolers in city-run day-care centers that are 89% funded by local and national tax dollars. The rest comes from parents, who pay only $135 to $250 a month, depending on their incomes. By contrast, the aver-age monthly cost of day care in the U.S. is $277, and only 3.3% of all families get direct government aid to cover fees.

Sweden's social policies are not without drawbacks, of course. Its day-care centers cost more to run ($10,730 a year per child, on average) than similar facilities in other countries (in the U.S., the cost is about $3,330 per child). Apparently, there's little incentive for the government to increase the efficiency of its day-care monopoly. And Sweden's parental leave policy fosters rampant discrimination against women in the private sector. Says Hansi Danroth, a male 27-year-old real estate broker in Stockholm: "Prospective employers have asked my sister if she plans to have kids. If I'm competing for a job with an equally qualified girl my age, it's an unwritten rule that I'll get it." Result: More than half of the working women are employed in the public sector, vs. only 22% of men.

But though no budget-minded American politician would advocate adopting the Swedish system wholesale, child development experts argue persuasively that some aspects of it are worth borrowing. First, we would not reduce our global competitiveness by making parental leave a universal, paid benefit, as it is in nearly every industrialized nation. Susanne A. Stoiber, director of social and economic studies at the National Research Council, argues that the burden needn't be overwhelming even for small companies if the leave is relatively short—say, six months. "That's about as far as you can push it without hurting employers and damaging women's chances of getting hired," concludes Stoiber, who has studied parental leave in three European countries. She also advocates paying parents on leave 50% to 60% of their after-tax incomes. Estimated annual cost: $8.3 billion to $10 billion, based on the U.S. General Accounting Office's assumption that 908,000 Americans would qualify for such leave under the Family and Medical Leave Act.

As for child care, studies show that we would be wasting tax dollars if we gave subsidies to the affluent, as Sweden does. According to a 1990 Urban Institute survey, the 32% of families who earn more than $50,000 a year devote a manageable 6.2% of their income to child care. In sharp contrast, the 17% of families making less than $15,000 pay a debilitating 25%. Though families can claim a tax credit of as much as $1,440 for these expenses, the poor are less likely than others to do

so, often because they are ignorant of the law. The best way to provide affordable high-quality child care, say many child-care experts, is to subsidize the enrollment of poor children in day-care centers operated by religious or non-profit groups, which figure to run them more efficiently than the government would. To qualify, centers would have to meet higher staffing and safety standards than they do now. Interestingly, the Swedes themselves, who replaced a socialist government with a right-center coalition in 1991, are leaning toward privatization. Says vice prime minister and minister of social affairs Bengt Westerberg: "In the next decade, I would like to see parents have more freedom to choose between state-run and private day-care centers."

Guaranteeing decent child care to low-income parents would do much to fulfill President Clinton's campaign promise to end welfare as we know it. And rather than encouraging single mothers to go on the dole, our welfare system could do as Sweden's does—provide incentives to postpone child-bearing (teenagers account for only 6% of all unmarried mothers there, vs. 33% here) and keep working. Consider that a 25-year-old Swedish woman earning $20,000 a year who bears a child out of wedlock can collect a total of $21,200 in

Reporter associate: Baie Netzer

government benefits for the first 12 months she's on leave, while an unmarried teenage mother who doesn't work gets only $3,200. Says Martin Rein, professor of social policy in the Department of Urban Studies and Planning at the Massachusetts Institute of Technology: "Single mothers in Sweden can't afford not to work."

FRANCE

How to prime kids for school

PERCENTAGE OF THREE- TO FIVE-YEAR-OLDS ENROLLED IN PRESCHOOL:

FRANCE	98%
U.S.	43%

While Americans proclaim the social and academic benefits of early-childhood education, the French deliver it: Virtually all children attend preschool, and eight of 10 go to free, government-run institutions. By contrast, fewer than half of American kids attend preschool. Even the federally funded $2.8 billion-a-year Head Start program, which aims to offer children from families below the poverty line solid pre-elementary training, reaches only 34% of the 2.1 million preschoolers whom the federal government aims to serve.

President Clinton has proposed to spend $10 billion over the next four years to expand and improve the 1,370 Head Start projects, but before he does so, he might ask First Lady Hillary Rodham Clinton about the French preschools she visited on a French-American Foundation study tour in 1989. Unlike Head Start, French preschools are demonstrably effective: A 1983 study by the French National Ministry of Education found that children from families of all socioeconomic levels greatly increased their chances of passing first grade if they attended preschool for the maximum three years. Even boosters of the Head Start program, on the other hand, admit that its effectiveness varies widely from project to project. Yale psychologist Edward Zigler, one of Head Start's founders, estimates that 25% of the projects are "poor in quality."

Disturbingly, it costs more than twice as much to enroll a child in Head Start

($3,720 a year) than in a French preschool (about $1,600), according to economist Barbara Bergmann of American University in Washington, D.C., who is writing a book on French child welfare programs. Yet French preschools are open 4½ days a week vs. only 2½ days (actually, five half-days) for Head Start. A typical eight-hour day for a French preschooler like the one profiled opposite includes stories and songs, art, reading- and math-readiness exercises, gymnastics, two to three recesses and a four-course hot lunch (cost: about $4 a day, depending on family income). Only the food isn't top quality; a typical lunch of beef patties, glutinous vegetables and supermarket cheese stops just short of sullying France's reputation as the culinary capital of the world.

The key reason why the French schools accomplish more than Head Start, yet spend less, is that the national government hires highly trained teachers who are capable of handling large classes. Says Colette Durand, a preschool inspector in Paris: "We are running pre-elementary schools, not nursery schools. Our teachers are not glorified babysitters; they are educators, like primary and secondary school teachers, and so they are paid on the same scale." Preschool instructors, who are required by the national Ministry of Education to have the equivalent of a master's degree, earn $19,500 to $37,300 a year, whereas Head Start teachers, 85% of whom never graduated from college, earn as little as $9,000. On average, there are 28 kids in a French preschool class, compared with 18 in Head Start.

Despite the class size, French teachers, who create lessons within a curriculum established by the Ministry of Education, seem able to command their students' attention. Says Françoise Rollet, director of a preschool in Paris' Montparnasse district: "It would be ideal to have only 20 to 25 students in a class and to employ a teacher's aide as well as a teacher for each group. But educators here are not convinced that such changes are required for academic success." American critics who argue that the French system of larger classes wouldn't work in the U.S. because of the greater ethnic diversity of American schools aren't paying attention to their own country's research. When the U.S. Department of Education studied elementary schools in 1988, it found no clear relationship between class size and student achievement.

The cost of Head Start is also driven up by the fact that, like many antipoverty programs that date from the 1960s, it is run to benefit the poor financially and psychologically by giving them jobs in the agencies that aid them. As a result, many Head Start payrolls are padded with positions for students' parents, most of whom have no expertise in early-childhood education.

If Congress expanded the Head Start program to cover all 11.2 million three- to five-year-olds in the U.S., it would cost a whopping $41.6 billion a year. But the same number of kids could be educated in French-style preschools for $17.9 billion—only $8 billion more than President Clinton proposes to spend to educate just the underprivileged.

JAPAN

How to fix our grade schools

AVERAGE NUMBER OF DAYS IN THE SCHOOL YEAR:

JAPAN	240
U.S.	180

If you live in a suburban U.S. school district that isn't plagued by violence or a high dropout rate, you may think that only our inner-city schools need improvement. Test statistics say you're wrong. The results of exams given in 1991 to kids around the world by the Educational Testing Service show that our top 10% of students compare favorably with other countries' brightest boys and girls. However, the other 90% don't even reach the *average* score attained by their foreign counterparts. When compared with their peers in 14 other countries, American 13-year-olds rank next to last in math and just one notch better than that in science.

How can we ensure that all students, not just the gifted, learn the skills necessary to compete in the global economy? One idea is to get kids off to a better start by revamping our grade schools along the lines of Japan's. (We should not look to Japanese high schools for inspiration, however, since they overemphasize rote learning to prepare students for multiple-choice college entrance exams.) Japanese grade schools don't owe their success to lavish funding (per-pupil expenditures average just $2,243 a year, compared with $4,083 here), technological gimcrackery or trendy theories about empowering teachers, parents or students. Instead, Japanese elementary schools work for three simple reasons:

■ **They are open more days a year.** By the time Japanese kids leave high school, they have spent the equivalent of two more years in school than American students have. Yet their daily schedules are actually less grueling than those of our kids. Japan's elementary school students get four or five 10- to 30-minute recesses and a 40-minute lunch period daily. Ours rarely get more than one recess and usually have half an hour or less to eat lunch.

■ **They follow a national curriculum.** By setting uniform, minimum standards for learning during each grade, Japan's national Ministry of Education ensures that all students—rich or poor, urban or rural—are exposed to the basics. By contrast, the education plan President Clinton proposed in April would set only *voluntary* national goals, not mandatory ones, and even that modest proposal faces stiff opposition from state and local school officials intent on preserving their fiefdoms.

■ **They don't segregate students by ability.** All Japanese grade schoolers are encouraged to master the same curriculum, even though some don't perform as well as others. Says Hiroko Oohisa, a

fourth-grade teacher in Sendai, Japan: "About a third of my students seem slower than the rest, so I work with them after school because I want all of them to understand." In the U.S., on the other hand, gifted kids take advanced classes—often taught by the most imaginative teachers—while other students

---

THESE KIDS CRAM BUT STILL HAVE TIME TO RELAX

If you've ever wondered why Japanese kids beat Americans on achievement tests, consider the schedules of Yoko Asano, 11, and her brother Haruhiko, 8, of Sendai. They are in class 240 days a year, vs. 180 for the average U.S. grade schooler. Yoko attends a juko, or cram school, five afternoons a week; Haruhiko goes on Saturdays (cost: $275 a month). Their father, Toshihiko, 46, a high school chemistry teacher, worries about the strain: "Nowadays children are expected to learn too much too soon," he says. Student life isn't all bad: Kids get plenty of recesses, and the jukos teach many non-academic subjects like piano, swimming and volleyball. Haruhiko even manages four hours of TV a day, about an hour more than American kids watch.

—Baie Netzer

---

are relegated to "dumbed down" lessons that are less demanding. "The Japanese don't undermine their educational system by holding some kids to a lower standard," concludes James W. Stigler, co-author of *The Learning Gap: Why Our Schools Are Failing and What We Can Learn From Japanese and Chinese Education* (Summit Books, $20). Stigler found no evidence that the brightest Japanese suffer as a result; 88 of the 100 fifth-graders who scored highest on tests he administered were Japanese. Only one was an American. One caveat: Whether we dismantle our tracking system or not, we should continue to provide extra help to students with serious learning disabilities. Indeed, the Japanese are studying our schools to determine how they might better serve children with special needs.

Since Japan now spends 45% less on grade schools than we do, it shouldn't be expensive to adopt their ideas. Lengthening the school year will require more money, but those costs could be offset by increasing our class sizes. The number of students per class averages 40 in Japan

vs. 24 in the U.S. Like the French, the Japanese don't think large classes impede learning.

A final word to the unconverted: Despite extensive publicity about pervasive and sometimes fatal bullying in Japanese schools, student violence is far less common there than here, where one student in 20 claims to carry a gun. And contrary to popular belief, Japan's rigorous educational system isn't driving students to suicide. In fact, the suicide rate for 10- to 14-year-olds is more than twice as high in the U.S. as in Japan.

DENMARK
How to train teenagers for real jobs

PERCENTAGE OF HIGH SCHOOL GRADUATES WHO SERVE APPRENTICESHIPS:

DENMARK	**50%**
U.S.	**3%**

Six in 10 U.S. high school students prepare to attend college, while the rest lay the foundations for nothing in particular and too often wind up in low-pay, low-status jobs. Many European nations avoid this waste of human potential by channeling students who aren't headed to college into apprenticeships after the ninth grade. In Denmark, for example, about a third of students attend college-prep high schools called gymnasiums starting in the 10th grade, but the others (including the teen profiled at right) enter commercial or technical schools that train them to become bank tellers, bookkeepers, clerical workers, toolmakers and the like. In the U.S., critics complain that training programs slot kids into lower-paying careers without giving them the opportunity to make more of themselves. However, that's simply not true in Denmark, where vocational students continue to take liberal arts courses and can get back on the college track if they wish.

President Clinton, who created a European-style youth apprenticeship program as governor back in Arkansas, now proposes to spend $1.2 billion over four years on high school apprenticeships nationwide. If Congress approves, the plan could initiate a sea change in U.S. job training. Our training now focuses on older, laid-off workers and welfare recipients rather than on teenagers; as a result, only 3% of high school graduates serve apprenticeships and a minuscule 0.08% of students do so while still in school.

Under the Danish model, a typical technical course lasts four years—80 weeks of classwork and 128 weeks of on-the-job training at private companies. Employers pay apprentices only 30% to 50% of what skilled workers make and are partially reimbursed from funds contributed to by all companies. Net cost to employers: an average of $8,900 per apprentice a year. At that price, it would cost about $26.6 billion a year to create apprenticeships for our 3 million 10th-, 11th- and 12th-graders who aren't college-bound.

At its best, the Danish system pushes such students to work hard so that they can step into skilled jobs. At worst, it provides cheap labor to employers. Of course, apprenticeships aren't a cure-all for the blue-collar blues. Denmark's unemployment rate is 12%, compared with Europe's 9.8%, and employers are creating only 35,000 full apprenticeships a year—forcing some 10,000 kids either to accept shorter training programs or to get their vocational training in the classroom. Still, enlightened educators and employers note that some kind of program inspired by the Danes would be a

---

WITH SCHOOL LIKE THIS, WHO NEEDS A SHEEPSKIN?

Unlike most young Americans who aren't college-bound, 19-year-old Hanne Madsen of Nordborg, Denmark, is on her way to a lucrative career. A third-year computer science student at technical school, Madsen earns $7.42 an hour as an apprentice at Danfoss, a heating and refrigeration manufacturer that is Denmark's largest employer. She landed one of 75 apprenticeships last year after daylong tests that eliminated 80% of the applicants. Since then, she's spent six months in on-the-job training. Even if Madsen isn't among the 40% Danfoss ultimately hires, she has a fallback plan: "I wouldn't mind becoming a computer technician," she says. Indeed, 20% of Danfoss' apprentices attend college or continue education in technical schools after the apprenticeships end.

—D.M.T.

---

vast improvement over our current system, which leaves so many high school graduates floundering.

CANADA
How to get medical care for all

PERCENTAGE OF GROSS DOMESTIC PRODUCT SPENT ON HEALTH CARE:

CANADA	**9%**
U.S.	**12.4%**

Although President Clinton appears to be ignoring Canada's universal health insurance system as he pushes for medical reform, Congress need not make the same mistake. After all, our neighbors to the north spend less on health care than we do and yet get better results than we and most other countries do.

When Canada first implemented government-sponsored coverage for all residents 21 years ago, it devoted about as much of its GDP—7%—to medical care as we did. Today, we spend the most in the world (12.4%, or $2,566 per person per year), yet 17% of Americans under age 65 lack insurance. By contrast, Canada expends only 9% of its GDP on medicine and spends just $1,730 per person a year.

Canadians enjoy better health for their money too. They boast the eighth highest life expectancy in the world, 77.03 years, while Americans, at 75.22 years, rank 33rd, behind even Jamaicans and Dominicans. Canada's infant mortality rate of 7.9 per 1,000 live births is the 10th lowest in the world; our rate of 10 per 1,000 births ranks 21st.

The Canadian system, which is regionally, not nationally, controlled, also seems particularly adaptable to our nation of 50 states. Canada's 10 provinces and two territories make their own rules within a broad, national framework. Most cover mental health services and prescription drugs for hospital patients, welfare recipients and anyone over age 65. Private insurance, which most Canadians have through their jobs, covers only items that government plans exclude, such as private hospital rooms, outpatient drugs, and dental and vision care.

Under this so-called single-payer system, the government—not hundreds of private insurance companies—pays for health care with dollars raised by federal and local taxes. The provinces, which actually send checks to doctors and hospitals, also negotiate fee schedules with provincial medical associations to hold down costs. Although physicians are Canada's highest-paid professionals, they earn an average of only $87,000 a year, vs. $170,000 for American doctors. And hospitals must obtain provincial approval to buy expensive, high-tech equipment. One result is that such gear is scarcer: The U.S. has nearly eight times more magnet-

---

WHY CANADIANS SAY THEIR HEALTH PLAN IS TO DIE FOR

Although the Warners of Hamilton, Ontario, have enough maladies to fill a medical text, they have been well served by Canada's tax-supported universal health-care system. Gary, 52, a French teacher at McMaster University, sees physicians twice a year for his glaucoma and as often as once a week for his high blood pressure. Wife Joy, 48, has had operations for colon polyps and hearing loss. Daughter Clare, 21, suffers from asthma; son Kassim, 13, has Osgood-Schlatter disease, a joint ailment; and daughter Jody, 23, gave birth to a son last year and had all but prescription drug costs covered. (Only son Remi, 19, hasn't needed much doctoring—yet.) Comments Joy: "The one thing Canadians would die defending is their health-care system."

—D.M.T.

---

ic resonance imaging (MRI) and radiation therapy units per capita than Canada, for example. Medical researchers have yet to show, however, that lots of high-tech wizardry improves our health. Canadians admit that they sometimes have to wait for nonemergency heart surgery, organ transplants, radiation therapy and the like. But they rarely queue up for run-of-the-mill services. In fact, a 1991 survey of 11,924 people by Statistics Canada, the government's statistical branch, found that 95% get the care they need within 24 hours (see the profile).

When there is a waiting list, a patient's spot on it is determined by doctors' ongoing evaluation of his condition. Delays vary by province and procedure, but to cite one example, there are usually 100 to 120 patients awaiting heart surgery in Ontario's central-west region (which includes Hamilton), where one cardiac surgery unit serves 1.8 million people. Waits average eight to 10 weeks, and some patients have to travel as far as 90 miles to the hospital. Americans with health insurance, by contrast, can shop for a doctor who will schedule them for tests or surgery immediately. But Americans who lack insurance often delay treatment until their deteriorating condition finally lands them in either the emergency room or the morgue.

Clearly, Canadians who have to wait for treatment are inconvenienced. But are they harmed? Research is scanty, but a 1992 study by doctors at the University of Manitoba and Dartmouth Medical School in New Hampshire reported mixed results. When the researchers compared postsurgical mortality rates in Manitoba and New England, they found that the immediate outcomes varied little for low- and moderate-risk procedures but that the survival rate after three years was better in Manitoba. For high-risk procedures, short-term results were better in New England, but the survival rate three years after surgery was similar.

Contrary to what many Americans believe, few Canadians cross the border to get care they would have to line up for at home. Of 7,654 Ontario residents having heart surgery in 1990 and 1991, for example, only 533—or 7%—went to the U.S. or other nations. And most (59%) of those who did were emergency patients who were stricken abroad and wouldn't have had to wait in Canada anyway.

Would Americans trade our system, which rations care based on ability to pay, for a Canadian-style plan where medical necessity is what counts? They might, but only if they understood that they wouldn't have to fill out another insurance claim form nor have limits placed on their choice of doctors, as happens under the increasingly popular managed-care plans in the U.S. Replacing our 1,300-company health insurance industry with a Canadian-style, single-payer system could even save as much as $3 billion a year, according to a 1991 report by the U.S. General Accounting Office. Up till now, fervent opposition by doctors and health insurers—who stand to earn less under a Canadian-style system—seems to have quashed public discussion of that option. But some health-care experts believe it's time to reopen the debate.

It's Hard to Do Day Care Right—and Survive

Sue Shellenbarger

Staff Reporter of The Wall Street Journal

Donna Krause is in a cutthroat business. When she raises prices just 3%, she loses customers to cheaper competitors. While she tries to provide high-quality service, she can't pay enough to keep trained workers. To cut costs, she has professional employees scrub toilets and mop floors, and she spends her evenings shopping for cheap supplies. Still, twice in the past month she has had to dip into her personal savings just to meet the payroll.

Ms. Krause's business: She cares for children. "There just aren't enough resources to go around," says the owner and director of Creative Learning and Child Care Center in Dundalk, Md. "We drive ourselves crazy and we drive our parents crazy" trying to make ends meet.

U.S. child care is increasingly under attack by researchers as mediocre or even harmful to children. A new generation of studies concludes that only a small minority of the estimated nine million children in child care outside their homes get the nurturing attention they need. "Compared with what we used to see in the 1970s, I would have to say that the quality of child care is declining," says Carollee Howes, a professor at the University of California, Los Angeles, and a leading child-care researcher.

A close look at the economics of child care suggests that quantum leaps in quality won't come soon. A vast underground market for cheap, unregulated care acts as a ball-and-chain on centers' prices. Most experts believe that low teacher turnover, staff training, ample materials and a planned curriculum help to achieve quality day care. But despite their good intentions, directors of child-care centers must make excruciating tradeoffs to attain even one or two of these goals.

Ms. Krause, who has a master's degree in education, pours all the resources she can into teacher pay and training. She spent $2,000 last year to expand an in-house teacher resource center and runs training courses. She ekes out 25- to 50-cent-an-hour annual raises for her teachers, who start at a minimum of $4.50 an hour, partly by spending her evenings shopping for cheap cleaning fluids and sink strainers. Last year, when the center finished the year with a small profit, she split it among the teachers.

But giving raises is getting harder each year. When Ms. Krause raised tuition just 50 cents a day a few years ago to $70 a week, she lost six families from her 90-child center. So she badgers her parents to help fix gate latches and donate toys, and she runs constant fund-raisers, blanketing the neighborhood with kids selling candy bars. To make ends meet, she had to fire the cleaning service and ask teachers to wash cots and scrub toys. "That's a dirty job for someone who has a degree," she says. Asked where the next budget cut will come from, she says, "There is no other" that can be made.

Increasingly, her teachers are quitting for higher-paying jobs. When one teacher left abruptly earlier this year to take a temporary job at General Motors for $13 an hour, painful ripples spread through the center. "Her partner cried all day" out of a sense of betrayal and frustration that she would have to train a new co-worker in the thousands of details of running a classroom, Ms. Krause says. Worse yet, "boom, she's out of the lives of the kids."

Mary Wortman's three-year-old, one of the children in the room, "just doesn't understand where [his teacher] went. He wants to see her," his mother says. Ms. Wortman, a first-grade teacher and former child-care worker herself, worries that if too many important people depart from a preschooler's life, "it becomes very hard for a child to trust anybody."

Some centers, particularly nonprofit centers that receive donated space, manage to hold teacher turnover down by using as much as 80% of their budgets for salaries. Still, they often have to sacrifice basic equipment. Bob French, director of three nonprofit centers in New Bedford, Mass., holds turnover to 10% a year partly by starting staff at $8.32 an hour. He has put together a "tattered patchwork" of subsidies and grants by working seven days a week. But he can't afford to put in a playground at one center even though he has the space; children have to walk to a neighborhood park instead.

Sue Britson, director of the nonprofit Step One School in Berkeley, Calif., pays well enough to attract experienced teachers with college degrees. But she spent a week recently trying to shave $1,000 off the center's insurance costs. She also had to make painful cuts in materials, using recycled toys and cheap art supplies. "Kids get less interested in painting" with poor paints, she says. "They have to work so much harder to get a lousy watercolor to perform for them."

Among the 35% of child-care centers that operate for profit, many don't make any money. Others eke out slim margins by paying teachers less, while a few target the small proportion of more affluent parents who will pay higher tuition.

Despite the improving economy, center directors say parental resistance to higher prices is intensifying. For many years, Ms. Britson, whose school is in an affluent area, raised tuition 4.5% annually to finance 6% teacher-pay raises. But this year, the formula no longer works. Parents "squeezed their time down to fewer hours so they didn't need full-time care" anymore, she says.

The Economics Of Child Care

Where the Revenue Comes From ...

Tuition	93%
In-kind donations*	5
Fund-raisers	1
Parent fees for extra services	1

*Services, supplies and equipment donated by parents and director

... And Where It Goes

Staff pay and benefits	70%
Rent	15
Supplies	5
Staff training and materials	3
Loans and bank fees	3
Utilities	2
Insurance	1
Miscellaneous	1

Source: Creative Learning and Child Care Center, Dundalk, Md.

Nancy Doniger

Inflation-adjusted pay for the lowest-paid assistant teachers has actually fallen 1.5% since 1988 to an average of $5.08 an hour, or $8,890 a year, a 1992 study by the Child Care Employee Project shows, leaving many child-care workers below the poverty line. Renee Sutton, a Raleigh, N.C., child-care worker, had to support herself and her two daughters on food stamps while working full-time at $5.40 an hour for a child-care chain.

And annual teacher turnover, already about 25% to 40% industrywide, threatens to get worse as service industries generate more jobs paying $5 to $8 an hour. Ms. Krause has lost two of her 10 teachers in the past month. When she advertises, she fights a losing battle for applicants with a new Home Depot store nearby.

Consuelo Marie Sullivan, one of the teachers leaving Ms. Krausë's center, loves the work and moonlighted 16 hours a week selling shoes to pay for night classes in child development. "When parents say, 'Christopher talked about this today,' I can say to myself, 'I taught him that,' " she says. But she is getting married next year and wants to save money, so she has taken a higher-paying job in retailing. "I gotta do what I gotta do," she says.

The best teachers often leave first. Kevin Becketti, a bearded six-footer who works at Step One School, has a talent for working with aggressive kids. He plays basketball with them and tells stories that help them develop self-control. At parties, he delights them by donning a pirate suit. "He is a fabulous teacher," says his boss, Ms. Britson.

But come fall, Mr. Becketti will leave Step One. The only car he can afford, an aged Volkswagen van, can't even make it to the top of the hill where the school is located. "I can't maintain this [salary] and do any of the things I might want to do later on, like have a better car and maybe a house one day," he says.

Though advocacy groups have campaigned to get parents to pay more for child care, parents resist. They are already paying 6% to 30% of their income for day care and either can't or won't pay more. Child care is seen as a low-paying service, "and changing it is not just a matter of changing people's moral sensibility," says James Greenman, a vice president of Resources for Child Care Management, Morristown, N.J.

And unlike France, Belgium, Sweden and Finland, where child care is part of public education, the U.S. leaves child care mostly to the private sector. Day-care costs for some poor families are subsidized, but few people expect government to start financing universal child care.

Improved management alone isn't the answer either. A three-year study at 20 Minneapolis-area child-care programs found that improving management increased resources about 10%. "You're going to need a lot more than a 10% increase in the budget to get those teachers up to $9 or $10 an hour," says Nancy Johnson, director of center-management services for the nonprofit Greater Minneapolis Day Care Association.

"The problem is much bigger," Ms. Johnson says. "This is a failure in the marketplace."

Helping Crack-Affected Children Succeed

Mary Bellis Waller

Mary Bellis Waller is the Clinical Program Coordinator at the University of Wisconsin-Parkside. Her address is Wood Rd., Box 2000, Kenosha, WI 53141-2000.

A classroom for young children affected by crack does not look like other early childhood settings with their mobiles, bright bulletin boards, and a constant stimulation of the senses. The classroom for crack-affected students is austere. There are no bulletin boards and no examples of children's art until, perhaps, late in the year, when the children can handle such stimulation. Only a few toys and books are in view, and other materials are hidden on shelves behind a simple fabric curtain. The lights are low, and there is little to distract the child. Learning and teaching areas are set up so that each child can be alone while learning. Play equipment usually used outdoors, like basketballs and climbing bars, is available inside the classroom so children can learn how to handle it appropriately and hone their gross motor skills with simple exercise. Tumbling mats are also available for the same purpose.

The classroom I'm describing isn't necessarily lacking in funds, nor is it a place where the teacher has failed to provide the kind of rich environment students need. On the contrary, this teacher has made the important modi-

> **Children impaired by this cheap form of cocaine are as intelligent as other children; their affect and social skills are damaged. Adaptations in teaching methods and the classroom environment can help them achieve academic success.**

fications needed to meet the special needs of children exposed to crack and cocaine. As former Wisconsin governor Lee Sherman Dreyfus observed, "There are only two kinds of school districts: those that have crack-affected children, and those that will have."

Who Are Crack-Affected Children?

Chasnoff and associates (1990) report that about 14 percent of pregnant women use drugs or alcohol that can cause permanent physical damage to a child during pregnancy. Approximately 400,000 children are born

annually to mothers who used crack or cocaine during pregnancy. These drugs are chemically similar and have the same effects on fetuses.

A recent study by Yazigi and associates (1991) shows that cocaine molecules bond to human sperm in lab tests. The ramifications of this are not clear, but it is possible that some children are affected by paternal use of these drugs immediately prior to conception. Extensive medical research documents actual changes in the fetal central nervous system in response to crack and cocaine (Chasnoff et al. 1985, 1986, 1989, 1991; Lewis et al. 1989; MacGregor 1987; Rodning 1989; Ryan 1987). This has enormous implications for early care providers and schools.

How They're Different

Children affected by crack and cocaine look like other children: they show the full range of size, vigor, and intelligence. However, many of them also show a number of problems that do not simply resolve themselves. Unless those crack-affected children receive specially designed interventions, they will continue to experience the problems during each developmental stage.

Infancy. Crack-affected infants are susceptible to Sudden Infant Death Syndrome (SIDS), apnea, and other sleeping disorders. Many have tremors and convulsions. They are easily overwhelmed by stimuli, responding with a hyper-startle or, in the extreme, by losing consciousness. These infants have difficulty paying attention, and they cannot track visually (Ryan 1987; Schneider 1990; Weston et al. 1989; Van Baar et al. 1989a, 1989b).

More important, crack-affected infants are often averse to being touched and to being looked at, as these strong stimuli threaten to over-load them. Consequently, they do not cuddle and often fail to bond with a caregiver. This failure to bond is an important indicator that the child may have great difficulty forming relation-ships in the future.

In a series of interviews with teachers who had worked with crack- and cocaine-affected children, I found that the problems identified in infants by medical researchers continue in different form through elementary school and into the teens (Waller, unpublished). As a teacher educator working with hundreds of these chil-dren and their instructors, I also found that teachers have discovered effective methods for working with such children.

Preschool. As toddlers, crack-affected children are often hyperac-tive, late in developing language, and late in walking. They are self-absorbed, impulsive, unaware of others, and unable to focus attention for any length of time. By age 3, they are often isolated because other chil-dren do not trust their unpredictable mood swings and sometimes violent outbursts.

These toddlers do not understand cause and effect relationships, either in classroom discipline that prescribes a timeout for certain behaviors or in play where jumping off a table causes pain. They do not feel remorse for hurting others, and they do not seem to develop conscience.

Crack-affected toddlers can do what they are told and shown, but they cannot plan their own time or activities. In general, they seem to have trouble organizing their experiences and making sense out of them. Their play is random, disorganized, and pointless. They often do not understand games, and they are unable to focus attention long enough to learn them.

School age. The oldest crack-

Crack-affected children are overwhelmed by ordinary experiences, and they need stability, routine, and sameness in the classroom to feel secure enough to learn.

affected children today are only 8 years old, but older children whose mothers took cocaine during preg-nancy offer us a window on how crack-affected children will act when they reach high school. Teachers report that cocaine-affected school-age children are still impulsive and some-times violent. Also, they are distractible, hyperactive, and disrup-tive, and school discipline does not seem effective. These children show learning and memory problems, and they are slow to develop friendships. They often remain isolated, even into high school, and their social skills are hampered by their inability to set limits or recognize appropriate limits for speech and behavior. As they grow older, they embarrass peers because of their inappropriate social behaviors and blurted comments. Cocaine-affected children are unable to catch nonverbal cues. Their efforts to make friends are hampered by this, because they do not understand what another's smile or frown means in terms of their own behaviors. This makes classroom motivation and discipline especially difficult because a teacher's expres-sions have no meaning.

Their learning is affected by a

continuing problem with cause and effect. Middle school teachers report that the cumulative and sequential nature of mathematics has posed a substantial problem to cocaine-affected teens, while language-based subjects are more accessible for them. They are still unable to structure or plan their own activities, and they are easily influenced by others because they are lonely and lack friends.

How Can Schools Respond?

Teachers report that crack-affected children who experience early inter-vention tailored to their problems can be mainstreamed successfully into regular classes. They estimate that if children are identified by age 2, a two-year intervention will teach a child enough to be mainstreamed. If the schools do not see a student until age 5, as often happens, a longer interven-tion may be necessary. Few believe that the crack-affected child will need to be in special education classes all through school, unless no appropriate intervention is ever provided.

Schools must acknowledge that cocaine and crack are easily available in any area of the country and that affluence does not protect against recreational drug use. Schools must also acknowledge that many exposed children will never officially be identi-fied. There is tremendous denial on the part of drug-using parents, and only a fraction of them will admit to behav-iors which harmed their children.

On the basis of identification of a cluster of behaviors often associated with crack use, children need to be placed into an intervention environ-ment where special teaching tech-niques will be used. Placement must be understood as only temporary, for a period of 1 to 3 years. The child will return to regular classes as soon as basic academic and social skills have been mastered.

Inside the Intervention Classroom

Teachers in intervention classrooms need to emphasize long-term expecta-tions for their students. It can be frus-trating to teach and reteach the same thing daily for weeks and find that students still don't understand it, but this is what often happens with crack-affected children. Their intellect works, and can be reached, but a longer timeline may be necessary.

Teachers need to forget all they know about their repertoire of exciting teaching styles. Crack-affected children can be overwhelmed by ordinary experiences, and they need stability, routine, and sameness in the intervention classroom to feel secure enough to learn.

Since their affect appears to be flawed, teachers must work with the intellect, which is undamaged. Words are the way to the intellect, so early therapy with speech is vital to reach the crack-affected child at all. Facial expressions have no meaning (or inappropriate meaning) to crack-affected children, so they must be taught *in words* in home and school. Encouragement and praise must be done verbally, not simply with a smile or a friendly look.

It's important to use one teaching modality. Because of their inability to order their experiences, crack-affected children cannot recognize one lesson taught five different ways. Crack-affected children will believe they're learning five different things! Teachers must teach, tell, reteach, retell, model, demonstrate, and have the child demonstrate the lesson.

Teachers of crack-affected children report idiosyncratic learning and memory problems. Students are taking in all the information, but the "filing system" required to recall information is flawed. Teacher after teacher tell stories like this: A 5-year-old child learns to tie her shoelaces one morning and demonstrates she knows how to do it. That afternoon, she again demonstrates her skill. But day after day, the child cannot remember how to tie her shoes, and must be retaught.

The parents finally buy her shoes that are fastened with Velcro. Two weeks later, the teacher sees the child tying another child's shoes. This same disrupted rhythm is exhibited in academic areas. All the 6- and 7-year-olds I have seen so far have been able

Crack-affected children who experience early intervention can be mainstreamed into regular classes.

to read, but their comprehension lags far behind decoding. Teachers may respond to such memory problems by allowing more wait time for students to respond, but they also must be prepared to reteach and reteach.

Teaching Social Skills
Social skills also must be taught in words and modeling. Since the children are unable to pick up on nonverbal cues on their own, words are again the vehicle. Hints and facial expressions are meaningless to a crack-affected child; direct instruction in sharing, greeting, and thanking is necessary. Role playing is appropriate for school-age children, because it allows actual practice in face-to-face interactions with other children, providing a structured social occasion with specific tasks to achieve.

Play must also be taught in words and modeling. Play has no intrinsic value to crack-affected children; they are disorganized and make no sense out of their experience. Their physical activities are random and without point. Play and games must be taught by direct instruction, then by guided play, then by play under supervision. The instruction must be specific so children do not see play and games as a time they need to arrange for themselves.

Routine and familiarity are vital in maintaining attention and facilitating learning. Transitions are particularly hard for crack-affected children, and the teacher must prepare students for transitions from active to quiet activi-

ties, from class to lunch or dismissal, from school to field trips, and from one subject to another. Preparation is done by talking about and reviewing all the things that will happen with the change, perhaps by questioning the children about the transition or sometimes by role playing (as in preparing for a field trip).

Effective Restraint
Teachers of crack-affected children must also know how to safely restrain children when they become hyperactive or threaten to hurt others. This restraint serves as a safety mechanism for the child, who cannot regain self-control when hyperactive. Teachers report that children who have been restrained become conditioned to eventually calm themselves when merely hugged for a moment by the teacher. The child struggles momentarily, then sighs and relaxes, achieving balance again.

Teachers cannot assign blame for disruptive behaviors. The most successful teachers with crack- and cocaine-affected children are those who recognize that the child has no self-control and the behavior needs to be changed. Time-outs are often effective, but physical restraint may be necessary. For children with good language skills, it can be effective to take away privileges and give a full explanation of why and under what circumstances privileges are lost. This needs to be explained over and over.

Avoiding Overload
Small groups are effective for presenting one idea or set of materials at a time and ensuring that children have achieved mastery. Teachers need to check on task completion frequently, because lack of perseverance is often a problem.

Teachers should focus students' attention on the paper, book, or toy in the lesson. For example, the teacher may place the child's hand on the page and move it down to focus attention. A good teacher knows that touching a child, speaking to her, and looking into her eyes at the same time can be overwhelming. There is a better chance of success if the teacher touches the child's hand while speaking in a low voice and avoiding eye contact.

Art and music must be carefully introduced in a highly structured manner. Without structure, these subjects are too stimulating because they reach several senses simultaneously. Teachers suggest working with one color crayon at a time, or teaching simple songs without accompaniment. Several teachers have reported success with humming or singing without words, so students aren't overloaded.

The Future

Interviews with teachers, parents, and foster parents of older cocaine-affected children, some of them teenagers, indicate that the behaviors seen in younger children can persist until adulthood. Without intervention, the impulsivity and inability to internalize rules of appropriate behavior will result in early sexual activity and drug and alcohol use. This probably means drug-impaired children born to drug-impaired children who are unable to care for them.

Without intervention, we are looking at millions of healthy, vigorous, intelligent sociopaths in the schools and in society. A long-term research study on the moral development of crack-affected children is now under way in Wisconsin (Waller, in press), and it will provide information on whether interventions can help in the development of conscience and internalization of social rules.

With intervention, children can learn and complete school. With intervention, children can learn appropriate social behaviors and interactions.

Schools have a choice.

Without intervention, we are looking at millions of healthy, vigorous, intelligent sociopaths in the schools and in society.

References

Chasnoff, I.J., K. A. Burns, W. J. Burns, and S. H. Schnoll. (1986). "Prenatal Drug Exposure: Effects on Neonatal and Infant Growth and Development." *Neurobehavioral Toxicology and Teratology* 8: 357-362.

Chasnoff, I. J. (1991). ""Cocaine Use in Pregnancy: Mother and Child." Keynote address to the Illinois Special Education Leadership Institute Third Annual Initiative Conference.

Chasnoff, I.J., D. R. Griffith, S. MacGregor, K. Dirkes, and K. A. Burns. (1989). "Temporal Patterns of Cocaine Use in Pregnancy: Perinatal Outcome." *Journal of the American Medical Association* 261, 12: 1741-1744.

Chasnoff, I.J., H. J. Landress, and M. E. Barrett. (1990). "The Prevalence of Illicit-Drug or Alcohol Use During Pregnancy and Discrepancies in Mandatory Reporting in Pinellas County, Florida." *The New England Journal of Medicine* 322, 17: 1202-1206.

Chasnoff, I.J., W. J. Burns, S. H. Schnoll, and K. A. Burns. (1985). "Cocaine Use in Pregnancy." *The New England Journal of Medicine* 313, 11: 666-669.

Lewis, K.D., B. Bennett, and N. H. Schmeder. (1989). "The Care of Infants Menaced by Cocaine Abuse." *American Journal of Maternal Child Nursing* 14: 324-329.

MacGregor, S.N., L. G. Keith, I. J. Chasnoff, M. A. Rosner, G. M. Chisum, P. Shaw, and J. P. Minogue. (1987). "Cocaine Use During Pregnancy: Adverse Perinatal Outcome." *American Journal of Obstetrics and Gynecology* 157: 686-690.

Rodning, C., L. Beckwith, and J. Howard. (1989). "Prenatal Exposure to Drugs: Behavioral Distortions Reflecting CNS Impairment?" *NeuroToxicology* 10: 629-634.

Ryan, L., S. Ehrlich, and L. Finnegan. (1987). "Cocaine Abuse in Pregnancy: Effects on the Fetus and Newborn." *Neurotoxicology and Teratology* 9: 296-299.

Schneider, J.W. (1990). "Infants Exposed to Cocaine In Utero: Role of the Pediatric Physical Therapist." *Topics in Pediatrics*. Lesson 6.

Van Baar, A.L., P. Fleury, and C. A. Ultee. (1989a). "Behavior in First Year After Drug Dependent Pregnancy." *Archives of Disease in Childhood* 64: 241-245.

Van Baar, A. L., P. Fleury, S. Soepatmi, C. A. Ultee, and P. J. M. Wesselman. (1989b). "Neonatal Behaviours after Drug Dependent Pregnancy." *Archives of Disease in Childhood* 64: 235-240.

Waller, M. B. (In press). *Crack-Affected Children: A Teacher's Guide*. Newbury Park, Calif.: Corwin Press.

Waller, M. B. (Unpublished). Survey of Teachers of Crack-Affected Children.

Weston, D.R., B. Ivins, B. Zuckerman, C. Jones, and R. Lopez. (June 1989). "Drug Exposed Babies: Research and Clinical Issues." *Bulletin of National Center for Clinical Infant Programs* IX.

Yazigi, R. A., R. R. Odem, and K. L. Polakoski. (1991). "Demonstration of Specific Binding of Cocaine to Human Spermatozoa." *Journal of the American Medical Association* 266, 14: 1956-1959.

Companies Help Solve Day-Care Problems

Sue Shellenbarger

Staff Reporter of The Wall Street Journal

Innovative solutions for some of the nation's child-care problems are coming from an unexpected source: employers.

A growing number of companies, convinced that bad child care hurts productivity, are introducing programs that would have been called radical a few years ago. Some of them are joining other companies to offer quality day care to low-paid workers. Others are financing improvements in community-run day care or taking child-care help directly to the factory floor.

In the past few years, federal grants and tax credits have helped fuel growth in child care. But the quality of the care varies widely, and lower-middle-class and working-poor parents are deeply vulnerable to bad care. They make too much to qualify for much government help, and corporate child-care assistance has typically benefited higher-income employees.

With 136,000 hourly employees in service jobs, **Marriott International** Inc., Bethesda, Md., depends heavily on low-paid workers. Yet child-care and other family and personal problems fuel entry-level turnover of as much as 300% a year at some of its hotels, as well as high absenteeism on the job.

Recently, two Marriott hotels in Atlanta signed on another employer with similar problems—a competing Omni hotel—to build a subsidized round-the-clock child-care and family-services center, set to open by early 1995, with 80% of its 250 slots reserved for low-income families. Hyatt and Hilton hotels are considering joining the venture, Marriott says, and it hopes to replicate the partnership in other cities.

As a kind of 1990s-style "company town," the center will offer family-support services from public and private agencies, immunizations, parenting workshops and links with social workers. "We may be defining a new role for the corporation," says J. W. Marriott Jr., chairman and president of Marriott.

For Ethel Turner, a housekeeper at the Marriott Marquis Hotel in Atlanta and a single mother, the center will mean fewer missed days at work. The center's sick-child program will be particularly helpful—she was out three days last month because her four-month-old was ill. She looks forward to spending lunch hours at the center and expects its trained teachers to give her daughter developmental advantages over the neighbor she relies on for child care now. Marriott will also help Ms. Turner apply for subsidies that will put her costs below the $55 a week, or 30% of take-home pay, that she now pays the neighbor.

Other companies are taking child-care assistance programs to the plant floor. Good child care is scarce in the towns where many of **Levi Strauss** & Co.'s 22,000 hourly workers live. And most of the employees, primarily women with children, can't afford good care anyway.

So in a pilot program that has drawn widespread attention from other employers, Levi is offering three kinds of help at plants in El Paso and San Antonio, Texas, and Fayetteville, Ark. Resource and referral counselors help employees find and choose care, visiting the plant to talk to those without telephones. The company also pays up to half the cost for low-income employees. Then it provides grants to improve the quality of child-care programs in the community.

One program that has received Levi funding, a YWCA child-care center in El Paso, moved its opening time back an hour to 5:30 a.m. to accommodate plant workers and is building a new playground. Levi money also enabled a federally funded Head Start program for low-income children to move into the YWCA building, enriching both programs.

Other companies are subtly pressuring parents to demand better quality. **NationsBank** Corp. ties its child-care subsidies for lower-income employees to a requirement that care givers be licensed by the state or—if no license is required—operating legally. One-third of the enrollees have used the money to upgrade their day-care arrangements, says a study by Work/Family Directions Inc., a Boston-based consultant.

No one expects employers to solve all the nation's child-care problems. But company efforts are helping spark the broader initiatives that many child-care researchers and advocates believe are needed. In the most promising trend, about 40 state and community-planning groups nationwide are bringing early-childhood education and child-care professionals together, getting parents more involved and studying ways to finance broad improvements in child-care quality, says Ellen Galinsky, co-president of the Families and Work Institute, a New York research group.

Members of the American Business Collaboration, a 144-employer consortium formed in 1992, have backed child-care improvement efforts at the state and local level. Collaboration members are helping to fund a nonprofit program in Chapel Hill, N.C., the TEACH Early Childhood Project, that helps finance tuition, books, time off and pay raises for child-care workers who want to get college degrees while working full-time.

There are also incentives for child-care centers to improve. The Collaboration and **AT&T** Corp. have given grants to more than 500 child-care centers to help them win accreditation from the National Association for the Education of Young Children, a Washington, D.C., professional educators' group. The association sets higher child-care standards than many states and forces center directors and teachers to focus on improving the classroom interaction between teacher and child, an important indicator of quality.

Employers are also using the power of example to raise community standards. High-quality child-care facilities financed by the Collaboration in several cities serve the public as well as member companies' employees, and have helped raise parents' awareness of quality. In Charlotte, N.C., "many parents were shocked" at tuition rates when a Collaboration-sponsored center opened in 1991, says Cheryl Partida, director of the center, which is operated by Bright Horizons Children's Centers Inc., Cambridge, Mass.

But Ms. Partida seldom hears that complaint now. Many parents have seen the impact on their children of top-flight materials and staffing and are rushing to sign up their kids' siblings. The center has a long waiting list, and Ms. Partida believes its example helped persuade North Carolina regulators to raise standards. When even a few center in a community focus on quality, "it has a great impact," she says. "It has helped make people aware of what quality care is."

Child Development and Families

- Child Development (Articles 8–11)
- Families (Articles 12–16)

We cannot separate the child from his or her family or home environment. Therefore, for professionals in early childhood education, much of what is done involves the child's family. Teachers and caregivers know that families come in many different arrangements, and the more familiar teachers and caregivers are with the people the child sees on a regular basis, the easier communication with those individuals will be. Professionals who are aware of the enormously varied life circumstances that children and parents experience today are mindful not to offer a magic formula, quick remedies, or simplistic solutions to complicated, long-standing problems. Instead, parents appreciate a sense that they are respected and given up-to-date, objective information about their child. "Creativity and the Child's Social Development" by Martha Nabors and Linda Edwards answers questions teachers have about the best strategies for supporting the young child's creative and social development. These strategies can be shared with families. Parents, when they understand that the education process involves a partnership between them, the teachers and school staff, and community groups, will be more willing to share relevant information.

Families and their childrearing beliefs and strategies have changed greatly in the last few decades, and so must parent education. More than one-half of all American children can be expected to spend part of their childhood in some type of nontraditional family. By the year 2000, it is estimated that 60 percent of children will spend some time before the age of 18 in a single-parent family. In Michele Ingrassia and John McCormick's article, "Why Leave Children with Bad Parents?" some hard questions are asked. Is the policy that is prevalent in most courts and social service agencies, that families are to be preserved at all costs, really working? Should families be preserved at the cost of young lives murdered or severely scarred physically and emotionally for life? A long list of recent cases with tragic endings has drawn attention to the practice of reuniting children with their abusive parents, often over the strong objections of people close to the family. Can all families be saved? Should everyone have the right to be a parent? Under which circumstances should children be permanently removed from the parents' custody?

"Life without Father" and "Homeless Families: Stark Reality of the '90s" address growing social concerns related to major changes in children's lives, both economical and social.

The news on families is not all negative. *Working Mother* researched how families are changing and, in an article included here, reports how the changes are bringing about positive benefits for all involved. Children raised in single-parent and dual-income families are learning to contribute to the day-to-day operation of the family by being responsible for chores that are appropriate for their age and development. The days when a stay-at-home mom did all the laundry and all the cooking and cleaning are long gone for many families.

When asked about major changes that occur in children between the ages of 5 and 7, one might immedi-

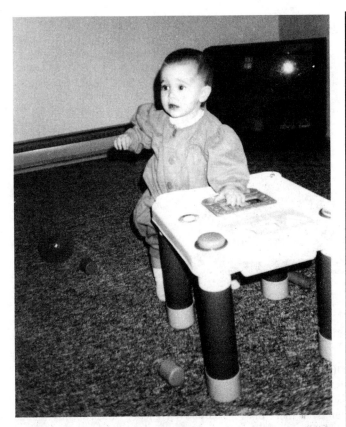

ately think of the large, toothless grins that are visible across these childrens' faces. But a much more subtle

change occurs in the cognitive skills of these children. Psychologists have termed this change in thinking "the 5- to 7-year shift." Husband-and-wife researchers Arnold Sameroff and Susan McDonough, in their article, explore the mind and thinking of kindergartners and first graders. If teachers are to provide an environment where discovery and learning can occur, it is imperative to understand how a child of that age range thinks. The child's capacity for thinking in the abstract and the excitement of learning for the pure joy of learning are two special characteristics of the 5- to 7-year shift.

Looking Ahead: Challenge Questions

Why is it important for teachers and caregivers to know about major changes affecting young children and their families?

What can educators do to assist children in the 5- to 7-year shift to make the transition to the primary grades?

What steps should be practiced to keep children healthy in child care?

Why are children returned to homes where they were abused? Under what circumstances should a child be removed from a home?

How does the absence of a father affect a child's development academically, socially, and emotionally?

What steps should teachers follow when recommending a family for a referral? Where should a teacher turn first for assistance?

Educational Implications of Developmental Transitions
Revisiting the 5- to 7-Year Shift

Understanding the nature of the 5- to 7-year shift is a major prerequisite if educators are to help children make a successful transition into elementary school, the authors maintain.

By Arnold Sameroff and Susan C. McDonough

ARNOLD SAMEROFF is a professor of psychology and a research scientist in the Center for Human Growth and Development at the University of Michigan, Ann Arbor, where SUSAN C. McDONOUGH is an assistant professor in the School of Social Work.

Illustration by Kay Salem

WHEN OUR child was 7 years old and experiencing the enlightenment provided by the local school system, she came home tearfully one day to question us about something we had protected her from since birth. Her classmates had informed her that there was no Santa Claus. When we admitted that what she had heard was true, she stared at us dolefully as she came to an even more disheartening conclusion. "This probably means that there is no Easter Bunny or Tooth Fairy either!" she charged.

Many of us have witnessed a child's sad discovery that a favorite belief is not true. But what is especially interesting in the above vignette is that a normative, but often unnoticed, intellectual extension — one that should frame educational theory — has taken place. The child revealed a belief in the existence of a conceptual category that included unseen figures who bring gifts. When it was discovered that one of these figures did not really exist, she made the logical extension that other members of this cognitive category did not exist.

These kinds of observations provide evidence of what developmental psychologists have called the 5- to 7-year shift. Children's thinking after age 7 seems to be quite different from their thinking before age 5.

What we will present here is a discussion of a different shift: a shift in the way the 5- to 7-year transition is understood by developmentalists. Current developmentally appropriate practices are based on Piagetian theory, in which the education of the child depends on a match between the curriculum and the child's emerging mental abilities.[1]

Piaget resolved the classic nature/nurture debate by arguing that every educational achievement was a developmental achievement. In Piaget's view, learning was the result neither of some intellectual trait native to the child, as believed in the United States and in some European countries, nor of the excellence of the education system, as believed in most Asian countries.[2] Instead, learning was a co-construction of the child and the teacher. New knowledge was the result of a creative activity in which the child built on prior mental constructions and the teacher provided the appropriate building material. Successful learning required a match between the curricular material and the state of the child's understanding. Revisions of Piagetian theories are changing the way we understand this match and are leading to new versions of nativism and environmentalism. Neo-Piagetian reformulations are changing our understanding of what capacities the child brings to the school on the nature side and of what makes a successful educator on the nurture side. These theoretical developments may have major implications for future educational theory, practice, and training.

Understanding developmental changes in the child during the 5- to 7-year period is especially important for educators because these are the years during which institutionalized schooling generally begins. Although the 5- to 7-year shift was not officially christened until 1965, when Sheldon White gave it that label, this developmental change, which is the basis for most formal educational systems, has long been recognized.[3] In his historical analysis of childhood, Philippe Ariés quotes a 14th-century poem that sets the limits of childhood, after which the child was immediately absorbed into the world of adults.

> The first six years of life on earth
> We to January would compare
> For in that month strength is as rare
> As in a child six years from birth.[4]

From ancient times there was a widespread cultural awareness that differences in children's behavior around 6 years of age permitted them to take on adult-like roles. These included care of other children, hunting and gathering, and, in industrial societies, child labor. Anthropological studies have found that most cultures begin formal training around age 6. Barbara Rogoff and her colleagues examined ethnographies from 50 communities around the world to determine at what age the expectations for children's roles and responsibilities underwent major changes.[5] They found a modal pattern of such changes when children were between 5 and 7 years of age, after which children were given increased responsibility for taking care of younger children, tending animals, and doing household chores. Most important, from an educational perspective, children were also expected to be teachable. In general, children after the age of 7 were thought to have common sense or rationality.

The 5- to 7-Year Shift

White provided a wealth of evidence to support the positing of this transition. He analyzed 21 kinds of developmental studies in a variety of cognitive, linguistic, and perceptual domains, showing that children younger than 5 behaved in one way while those older than 7 behaved in another. Among the architects of those studies, White noted Piaget, who in 1965 was just beginning to make an impression on mainstream American psychological studies and educational practice.[6] It was Piaget, of course, who placed at the center of his theory of cognitive development the 5- to 7-year shift — a period during which children move from dependence on appearance to an understanding of reality, from centering on single aspects of a situation to the ability to coordinate multiple perspectives, and from an egocentric focus on their own points of view to an appreciation that other minds have alternative outlooks on the world.

The water-glass problem is perhaps the best known of Piaget's examples of how children's logic changes during this age period. The younger child believes that, if water is poured from a short, fat glass into a tall, thin one, there is more water because the level is higher. The older child recognizes a relationship between multiple dimensions, in which the increase in height is compensated for by a decrease in width, and will frequently state a logical principle: "Because nothing was added or taken away, there must be the same amount of water." In classification tasks the older child is able to consider more than one level at a time in a conceptual hierarchy and knows the difference between *all* and *some*. When younger children are shown a bouquet of roses and daffodils and asked whether there are more roses or more flowers, they frequently reply that there are more roses. A 7-year-old will say that all of them are flowers but that only some of them are roses, so there cannot be more roses than flowers.

Piaget did not believe that the advanced intellectual performance of the older child was the result of learning. He viewed it as the result of developmental processes. Children younger than 5 used a different system of logic than children older than 7, and they needed to develop in order to move ahead. Learning taught a child the names of flowers, and more learning meant more names. But it was *development* that led a child to know that there were more flowers than roses. Moreover, according to Piaget, these changes in the logic of thinking were not restricted to school topics. Developmental advances in the understanding of the physical world were matched by advances in the logic children applied to social situations, especially in the area of rules and moral judgments. Whereas younger children believed that what was right and wrong depended on the consequences — whether or not they were punished — older children recognized the existence of a system of morality based on social agreement.

The implications of Piaget's work were not lost on educators, who soon began to create Piagetian curricula and assessments in which the details of children's knowledge were regarded as secondary to the logical processes by which children arrived at these details. Through the Sixties and Seventies and up to his death in 1980, Piaget's theories dominated the environment of those interested in the cognitive development of children.

maturation

However, at about the same time as his physical demise, Piaget's work was undergoing a major theoretical demise in scientific circles. The post-Piagetian critique came from two directions: a nativist position arguing that Piaget was wrong in believing that younger children could not engage in logical thinking and an environmental position arguing that Piaget had ignored major environmental influences that produced developmental changes in thought.

Nature: Performance Versus Competence

The heart of the Piagetian position is that children's intelligence develops over time, moving through successive stages, each one building on the achievements of the previous one. Furthermore, Piaget believed that, when children moved from one stage of development to another — for example, from preoperational to operational intelligence — behavior in every cognitive domain changed as they consolidated their new intellectual capacities. The first group of neo-Piagetians argued that there was no general change in children's logic from one stage to the next. There may be stage-like transitions in individual domains of behavior — such as classification problems or the understanding of number concepts or even moral judgment — but these changes were seen to be content-specific and not evidence for a universal shift based on a single central process of cognitive reorganization.[7] Children did not change their thinking across all areas at once; they might be quite advanced in some areas but somewhat delayed in others.

Then an even more serious set of criticisms argued that what Piaget believed to be changes in the cognitive competence of the child, even within individual domains, were only changes in performance. What Piaget had seen as new intellectual breakthroughs by the 5- to 7-year-old child were already within the capacity of much younger children and were perhaps even innate.[8] Complex understanding of number concepts, spatial transformations, and causality could be found in preschoolers and even in infants. These critics argued that Piaget confused performance with competence — that children had more cognitive abilities than Piaget could detect in his research because his experiments restricted their ability to show their competence. Experiments designed especially to reveal the logical capacities of young children revealed a surprising precocity, even in moral judgment.

Does this mean that there is no 5- to 7-year shift? Not exactly. If the question is whether younger children demonstrate these precocious capacities in their general behavior, then the answer is no. Early indicators of intellectual competence appeared only when the situation was right, when the environmental stimuli and required responses were highly simplified, and when the child's emotional and attentional conditions were optimized. When the task was to educate groups of children in a school setting with socially relevant and useful lessons, starting after age 6 still seemed to work best.

A good example of this situation is the child's ability to consider multiple dimensions at the same time in a conceptual task, such as whether a balance scale will go up or down. To answer correctly, the child must consider both the dimension of weight and the distance from the fulcrum. Robert Siegler found that 5-year-olds showed this talent when conditions were simplified. However, they did not when a task was unfamiliar, required a quantitative comparison between alternatives, and included a dominant dimension that led them to the wrong answer. In other words, when asked to solve the problem in a typical classroom situation, 5-year-olds could not do so. For children to demonstrate this talent regularly, they had to be older than 7.[9]

Nurture: Narration and Activities

The second revision of Piagetian theory stems from the environmentalist view that Piaget did not pay enough attention to the effects of children's experiences on the course of their cognitive development. These experiences might arise in the family, in the community, or in the classroom. For example, the shift in thinking between 5 and 7 may be a consequence of schooling rather than a prerequisite for schooling. This hypothesis is very difficult to test in a society in which all children begin school at about the same age.

However, some ingenious researchers found a way to overcome this problem. In a unique set of studies Fred Morrison and Elizabeth Griffith compared two groups of children of nearly the same age: one group whose birthdays were just before the cutoff for entry into kindergarten and another group whose birthdays were just after the cutoff.[10] As most educators would predict, after two years the researchers found that schooling accounted for a number of differences in behavior between the two groups. Those who had been in classrooms for two years, kindergarten and first grade, had a number of memory, language, and quantitative skills that exceeded those of children who had been kept out of school for the first year and had completed only kindergarten. But another set of memory, language, and number skills were no worse in the group of children who were held out of school for another year. The latter findings provide evidence for a developmental effect independent of classroom experience. What such research is revealing is that there is no simple formula for distinguishing in advance the intellectual skills that the child brings to school from those that are produced by the school.

However, the experience of schooling is only one element in the learning environment of the child. Early experiences in the home may be another determinant of the child's developmental progress. Recent research on the development of memory is a good example of an unexpected environmental effect. Changes in the ability to remember may be related to the extent to which memories are shared with others.

A general finding in research on memory is that there is an infantile amnesia; people cannot remember anything about their lives before about age 3. The original explanation was that young children did not have good memories, but more recent research has found that infants can remember events for up to two years. That is, they will show recognition when placed in similar situations. What they lack is the ability to recall such early events when they have grown older, a capacity that appears to be intimately connected to their experience with narration.[11]

Parents play an active role in framing and guiding their children's descriptions of what happened. Through conversations with their parents, children learn simultaneously how to talk about memories and how to formulate their own memories as narratives for themselves. Parents who are more elaborative — who ask their children what happened when, where, and with whom — have children who have more extensive memories. Preschool children do not remember specific events for long periods of time unless they have the opportunity to talk about them with their teacher or parent. The beginning of autobiographical memory in early childhood, which has been viewed as the result of brain maturation processes, can also be viewed as the result of specific experiences in a social context. The educational implication is that memory skills in children can be enhanced by fostering narrative exchanges between children and others.

The changes in memory during the 5- to 7-year shift are a further elaboration of the use of language as a tool for thinking. Prior to this time of life, children use language primarily for communication and secondarily for cognitive organization. During this period, however, language becomes a tool for reflecting on thought and action, enabling the child to call to mind and reexperience events from the past. Membership in a linguistic community provides a tool for further advances in cognition and memory. However, because such advances are a consequence of the experience of narrating memories to others, the age range when these new capacities emerge is wide and depends on the opportunities provided for such experiences. For example, the average age for the beginning of autobiographical memory is around 3, but the range is from 2 to 8, and there is also wide variation in the number of early memories. To the extent that parents and educators encourage narration, children's memory capacities may be precocious. To the extent that children are placed in passive roles in educational settings, memory and cognitive development may be delayed.

Cultural factors add another level of environmental influence on children's cognitive abilities. From a contextualist perspective, the abilities of children cannot be understood apart from their participation in the ongoing activities of their family and cultural group. The age at which a shift will occur depends on the social activities of the child.

Barbara Rogoff, a strong proponent of this position, argues that changes in children's abilities can be understood only in terms of their sociocultural activities.[12] In her cross-cultural comparisons she had found that some societies began formal education with 2-year-olds and some with 15-year-olds. To understand this wide range in age of onset of schooling requires attention to the beliefs, practices, needs, and resources of each culture. She argues for a shift in focus from what children *can* think to what they *do* think. Changes in what children do think between 5 and 7 vary widely across different cultures that engage children in different kinds of social activities.

Rogoff argues that the age when a child moves from one stage to another depends on the meaning and support given that transition in the life of that culture. One example is the age at which children begin to take care of other children. The major cognitive requirement for such a role is that the caregiver be able to assume the perspective of the younger child in order to understand the child's signals and ensure its well-being. In industrial societies, such perspective taking is not found until after the 5- to 7-year shift, and children usually do not become babysitters until they are at least 10 years old. Among the Mayan villagers of Guatemala, 3- to 5-year-olds are able to be babysitters because of the social organization of family roles and the cultural expectations of that community. Rogoff suggests that this difference is to be found in the Mayan training of children to become interdependent members of the community, while children in the U.S. are encouraged to assert individuality and be competitive.

The consequences of these differing social values were observed during home visits. Preschool Mayan caregivers were seen to give over whatever their younger siblings wanted, whereas middle-class U.S. preschoolers negotiated or tussled with babies over toys until parents intervened. Similarly, children as young as age 3 in other cultures are found to have the cognitive abilities to engage in skilled gardening and household work and the social abilities to engage in complex social interactions both within and outside of the family. What is significant in the sociocultural perspective is that developmental transitions are seen to be neither solely within the child nor solely within the education system. Rather, developmental transitions result from shifts in the roles and responsibilities associated with participation in a social group.

Shifts in Social and Emotional Behavior

White's proposal of a 5- to 7-year shift in behavior was originally restricted to cognitive functioning, but it has been extended by a new generation of developmental scientists into social and emotional domains, especially with regard to self-concept. Similarly, educators are aware that the social and emotional condition of the child is a major determinant of whether schooling will be effective. Therefore, awareness of changes in these capacities in the child is an important at-

tribute of the successful teacher of young children. Although there is still considerable debate about the relative contributions of social and school experience to cognitive development, there is far more agreement that, in the social/emotional domain, a child's experiences of relationships are major determinants of a child's behavior.

If child development is a function of a child's engagement in cultural activities, then schooling must be reframed as a social activity whose significance goes beyond the training of children in reading, writing, and arithmetic. The characteristics of school activities will have an impact not only on what children learn, but also on how children evaluate themselves as learners — that is, on their self-concepts.

The most detailed descriptions of shifts in self-understanding between ages 5 and 7 have been provided in the studies of Susan Harter.[13] Shifts occur in the nature of self-attributes, in the structure and organization of the self, in the understanding of combined and conflicting emotions, in the balance between positive and negative attributes, in the emergence of self-affects, and in the ability to be self-critical. The self-attributes used by preschoolers refer to their behavior: "I can jump high. I like pizza. I have a dog." School-age children use more higher-order generalizations that are more trait-like to describe themselves: "I am smart. I am popular." Preschoolers do not believe that you can have two emotions at the same time, whereas school-age children know that they can both like and dislike the same person and can describe themselves as both smart and dumb, depending on the subject. In addition, whereas preschoolers are generally positive in their self-descriptions, school-age children are more balanced, offering both positive and negative descriptions. Finally, it is not until about age 8 that children can verbalize their sense of self-esteem — whether or not they like themselves and how much.

In this shift in self-understanding, what is especially salient for educators is the emergence of the self-affects, pride and shame. Although these are experienced as young as infancy, it is not until after the 5- to 7-year shift that children express these emotions verbally. Moreover, the degree to which a child feels and expresses pride or shame is strongly determined by the action of others — parents, teachers, and friends. Changes in the behavior of important adults are among the environmental experiences of children entering school. In the elementary school classroom increasing attention is paid to social comparisons rather than to individual accomplishments. No matter how high the quality of a child's school activities, they are judged relative to the activities of other children in the class. How these comparisons are handled by the teacher has consequences for the child's sense of self-worth.

Although the quality and importance of social relationships does not change during the 5- to 7-year shift, the child's social network goes through a major expansion, including new settings, new classmates, and new teachers. Given responsive and friendly interactions, the child's self-concept can follow a positive course, whereas teasing and criticism will produce the opposite. The major developmental difference is that, as children grow older, it becomes more and more difficult to change their self-concepts. For the younger child, where the self-system and the social setting are less structured, it is easier to feel bad in one situation but good in another. For the older child, where the self-system is gaining in coherence and consistency, negative experiences and negative reputations can become far more pervasive and even overwhelming in their effects on self-esteem.

Shifts in School Experience

The 5- to 7-year shift for most children in this country involves a transition from the experiences of the preschool to those of the elementary school. Children do not enter kindergarten with a clean slate. Based on their previous time spent in school-like settings, they have many expectations about the experiences they will encounter. Just as teachers need to be aware of the quality and range of intellectual capacities children bring to the classroom, they also need to be aware of the quality and range of children's social experiences. The child's prior experience with social interactions, social comparisons, and self-esteem experiences in the home, in day care, and in the preschool are especially important. There are general differences in these settings that produce problems for children who expect the elementary school experience to be a continuation of the preschool experience.

Social interactions in the home and in the preschool tend to have been collaborative, whereas in the elementary school pressure for individual behavior and self-control increases. When children talk with

one another and share activities with other children, it may be less a sign of disrespect for the elementary teacher than the consequence of previous classroom experience. In the elementary school new enrollees may be confused about the new conditions they face. In preschool, the focus is not on comparisons with other children in the class. Children new to elementary school may perceive that their teacher believes that doing things faster and getting higher scores than other children are more important than doing a good job. All these changes have an impact on the self-esteem of children. Parents of children new to elementary school are often asked, "Why wasn't I a bad girl in preschool?" The only meaningful answer educators can provide is through teaching without producing such self-concepts in children.

Reframing the 5- to 7-Year Shift

Current thinking about behavioral shifts between the ages of 5 and 7 has moved away from a belief in a cognitive reorganization that permits the child to be educated. When the logical structure of any particular skill is analyzed, precursors and analogs can be found in much younger children if task conditions are simplified and motivation is maximized. Preschoolers can be taught to speak in complex sentences, to read, and even to solve mathematical puzzles. But these achievements require individual attention, sensitivity, and devotion on the part of the educator. What appears to be unique about the period between 5 and 7 is that for most children task conditions do not need to be simplified, and motivation does not have to be maximized.

Preschoolers can be taught the skills needed to engage in useful work in the home and in the field. But these achievements require a culture that integrates the child into meaningful social activities. After the 5- to 7-year shift, most children can learn things that have no obvious social connection. In the typical classroom situation, academic skills are learned apart from a meaningful cultural context. The primary achievement of this age period may be the attainment of this capacity for abstraction, the capacity to learn for learning's sake.

Understanding the nature of the 5- to 7-year shift is a major prerequisite if educators are to help children make a successful transition into the elementary school. The timing and quality of this shift

is influenced by characteristics of the child, the home environment, the cultural context, and previous experiences with group learning. When the resulting heterogeneity of children's characteristics and capacities is met by a uniformity of teacher expectations and behavior, many children become cognitive and social casualties. If we wish to change these outcomes, then the elementary school must become much more attuned to the individuality that each child brings to the classroom. The existence of the 5- to 7-year shift is evidence for what *is* rather than what *could be*.

1. David Elkind, "Developmentally Appropriate Practice: Philosophical and Practical Implications," *Phi Delta Kappan*, October 1989, pp. 113-17.

2. Harold W. Stevenson, Chuansheng Chen, and Shin-Ying Lee, "Mathematics Achievement of Chinese, Japanese, and American Children: Ten Years Later," *Science*, vol. 259, 1993, pp. 53-58.

3. Sheldon H. White, "Evidence for a Hierarchical Arrangement of Learning Processes," in Lewis P. Lipsitt and Charles C. Spiker, eds., *Advances in Child Development and Behavior* (New York: Academic Press, 1965), pp. 187-220.

4. Philippe Ariés, *Centuries of Childhood: A Social History of the Family* (New York: Vintage, 1962).

5. Barbara Rogoff et al., "Age of Assignment of Roles and Responsibilities to Children," *Human Development*, vol. 18, 1975, pp. 353-69.

6. Jean Piaget, *The Psychology of Intelligence* (London: Routledge and Kegan Paul, 1950).

7. Charles Brainerd, "The Stage Question in Cognitive Developmental Theory," *Behavioral and Brain Sciences*, vol. 1, 1978, pp. 173-82.

8. Rochel Gelman and Renée Baillargeon, "A Review of Some Piagetian Concepts," in Paul H. Mussen, ed., *Handbook of Child Psychology*, vol. 3 (New York: Wiley, 1983), pp. 167-230.

9. Robert Siegler, "Five Generalizations About Cognitive Development," *American Psychologist*, vol. 38, 1983, pp. 263-77.

10. Fred Morrison and Elizabeth M. Griffith, "Nature-Nurture in the Classroom: Entrance Age, School Readiness, and Learning in Children," *Developmental Psychology*, in press.

11. Katherine Nelson, "Towards a Theory of the Development of Autobiographical Memory," in Andrew Collins et al., eds., *Theoretical Advances in the Psychology of Memory* (Hillsdale, N.J.: Erlbaum, 1993), pp. 116-65.

12. Barbara Rogoff, *Apprenticeship in Thinking: Cognitive Development in Social Context* (New York: Oxford University Press, 1993).

13. Susan Harter, "Causes, Correlates, and the Functional Role of Global Self-Worth: A Life-Span Perspective," in John Kolligan and Robert Sternberg, eds., *Perceptions of Competence and Incompetence Across the Life Span* (New Haven, Conn.: Yale University Press, 1990).

The Amazing Minds of Infants

Looking here, looking there, babies are like little scientists, constantly exploring the world around them, with innate abilities we're just beginning to understand.

Text by **Lisa Grunwald**
Reporting by **Jeff Goldberg**

Additional reporting: **Stacey Bernstein, Anne Hollister**

A light comes on. Shapes and colors appear. Some of the colors and shapes start moving. Some of the colors and shapes make noise. Some of the noises are voices. One is a mother's. Sometimes she sings. Sometimes she says things. Sometimes she leaves. What can an infant make of the world? In the blur of perception and chaos of feeling, what does a baby know?

Most parents, observing infancy, are like travelers searching for famous sites: first tooth, first step, first word, first illness, first shoes, first full night of sleep. Most subtle, and most profound of all, is the first time the clouds of infancy part to reveal the little light of a human intelligence.

For many parents, that revelation may be the moment when they see their baby's first smile. For others, it may be the moment when they watch their child show an actual

---

At three months, babies can learn—and remember for weeks—visual sequences and simple mechanical tasks.

---

preference—for a lullaby, perhaps, or a stuffed animal. But new evidence is emerging to show that even before those moments, babies already have wonderfully active minds.

Of course, they're not exactly chatty in their first year of life, so what—and how—babies truly think may always remain a mystery. But using a variety of ingenious techniques that interpret how infants watch and move, students of child development are discovering a host of unsuspected skills. From a rudimentary understanding of math to a

sense of the past and the future, from precocious language ability to an innate understanding of physical laws, children one year and younger know a lot more than they're saying.

MEMORY

Does an infant remember anything? Penelope Leach, that slightly scolding doyenne of the child development field, warns in *Babyhood* that a six- to eight-month-old "cannot hold in his mind a picture of his mother, nor of where she is." And traditionally psychologists have assumed that infants cannot store memories until, like adults, they have the language skills needed to form and retrieve them. But new research suggests that babies as young as three months may be taking quite accurate mental notes.

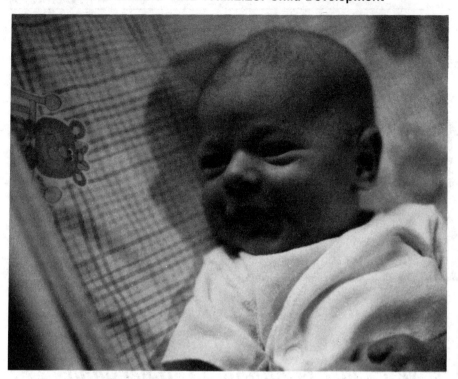

Babies show an unexpected ability to remember surprisingly intricate details.

In his lab at the University of Denver, psychologist Marshall Haith has spent much of the past four years putting infants into large black boxes where they lie and look up at TV screens. The program they see is a Haith invention: a sequence of colorful objects appearing on different sides of the monitor. Using an infrared camera linked to a computer, Haith follows the babies' eye movements and has found that after only five tries the babies can anticipate where the next object will appear. With a little more practice, they can foresee a four-step sequence. And up to two weeks later, most can still predict it. Says Haith: "The babies are not just looking. They're analyzing, creating little hypotheses."

Similar findings by Carolyn Rovee-Collier, a psychologist at Rutgers University, suggest that infants can remember surprisingly intricate details. In a typical experiment, she places a baby in a crib beneath an elaborate mobile, ties one of the baby's ankles to it with a satin ribbon, then observes as the baby kicks and—often gleefully—makes it move. When, weeks later, the baby's feet are left untied and the mobile is returned to the crib, the baby will try to kick again, presumably recalling the palmy days of kicking the last time. But if the mobile's elements are changed even slightly, the baby will remain unmoved—and unmoving. "When we change things," explains Rovee-Collier, "it wipes out the memory. But as soon as we bring back what had become familiar and expected, the memory comes right back. What we've learned from this is that even at two and a half months, an infant's memory is very developed, very specific and incredibly detailed."

Rachel Clifton, a psychologist at the University of Massachusetts, says that an infant's experience at six months can be remembered a full two years later. Clifton stumbled upon her findings while researching motor and hearing skills. Three years ago she placed 16 six-month-olds in a pitch-dark room with objects that made different sounds. Using infrared cameras like Haith's, she observed how and when the infants reached for the objects. Later, realizing she had created a unique situation that couldn't have been duplicated in real life, she wondered if the babies would remember their experience. Two years after the original experiment, collaborating with psychologist Nancy Myers, she brought the same 16 children back to the lab, along with a control group of 16 other two-and-a-half-year-olds. Amazingly, the experimental group showed the behavior they had at six months, reaching for objects and showing no fear. Fewer control-group toddlers reached for the objects, and many of them cried.

Says Myers: "For so long, we didn't think that infants could rep-

At five months, babies have the raw ability to add.

resent in their memories the events that were going on around them, but put them back in a similar situation, as we did, and you can make the memory accessible."

MATH

At least a few parental eyebrows—and undoubtedly some expectations—were raised by this recent headline in *The New York Times:* "Study Finds Babies at 5 Months Grasp Simple Mathematics." The story, which reported on the findings of Karen Wynn, a psychologist at the University of Arizona, explained that infants as young as five months had been found to exhibit "a rudimentary ability to add and subtract."

Wynn, who published her research in the renowned scientific journal *Nature,* had based her experiments on a widely observed phenomenon: Infants look longer at things that are unexpected to them, thereby revealing what they do expect, or know. Wynn enacted addition and subtraction equations for babies using Mickey Mouse dolls. In a typical example, she had the babies watch as she placed a doll on a puppet stage, hid it behind a screen, then placed a second doll behind the screen (to represent one plus one). When she removed the screen to reveal three, not two, Mickey Mouse dolls, the infants stared longer at such incorrect outcomes than they had at correct ones. Wynn believes that babies' numerical understanding is "an innate mechanism, somehow built into the biological structure."

Her findings have been met with enthusiasm in the field—not least from Mark Strauss at the University of Pittsburgh, who a decade ago found that somewhat older babies could distinguish at a glance the difference between one, two, three and four balls—nearly as many objects as adults can decipher without counting. Says Strauss: "Five-month-olds are clearly thinking about quantities and applying numerical concepts to their world."

Wynn's conclusions have also inspired skepticism among some researchers who believe her results may reflect infants' ability to perceive things but not necessarily an ability to know what they're perceiving. Wynn herself warns parents not to leap to any conclu-

sions, and certainly not to start tossing algebra texts into their children's cribs. Still, she insists: "A lot more is happening in infants' minds than we've tended to give them credit for."

LANGUAGE

In an old stand-up routine, Robin Williams used to describe his son's dawning ability as a mimic of words—particularly those of the deeply embarrassing four-letter variety. Most parents decide they can no longer speak with complete freedom when their children start talking. Yet current research on language might prompt some to start censoring themselves even earlier.

At six months, babies recognize their native tongue.

At Seattle's University of Washington, psychologist Patricia Kuhl has shown that long before infants actually begin to learn words, they can sort through a jumble of spoken sounds in search of the ones that have meaning. From birth to four months, according to Kuhl, babies are "universal linguists" capable of distinguishing each of the 150 sounds that make up all human speech. But by just six months, they have begun the metamorphosis into specialists who recognize the speech sounds of their native tongue.

In Kuhl's experiment babies listened as a tape-recorded voice repeated vowel and consonant combinations. Each time the sounds changed—from "ah" to "oooh," for example—a toy bear in a box

was lit up and danced. The babies quickly learned to look at the bear when they heard sounds that were new to them. Studying Swedish and American six-month-olds, Kuhl found they ignored subtle variations in pronunciation of their own language's sounds—for instance, the different ways two people might pronounce "ee"—but they heard similar variations in a foreign language as separate sounds. The implication? Six-month-olds can already discern the sounds they will later need for speech. Says Kuhl: "There's nothing external in these six-month-olds that would provide you with a clue that something like this is going on."

By eight to nine months, comprehension is more visible, with babies looking at a ball when their mothers say "ball," for example. According to psychologist Donna Thal at the University of California, San Diego, it is still impossible to gauge just how many words babies understand at this point, but her recent studies of slightly older children indicate that comprehension may exceed expression by a factor as high as a hundred to one. Thal's studies show that although some babies are slow in starting to talk, comprehension appears to be equal between the late talkers and early ones.

PHYSICS

No, no one is claiming that an eight-month-old can compute the trajectory of a moon around a planet. But at Cornell University, psychologist Elizabeth Spelke is finding that babies as young as four months have a rudimentary knowledge of the way the world works—or should work.

James M. Ward/photo

Babies learn how physical objects behave by moving their body parts.

*Babies have a built-in
sense of how objects
behave.*

Spelke sets her young subjects up before a puppet stage, where she shows them a series of unexpected actions: a ball seems to roll through a solid barrier, another seems to leap between two platforms, a third seems to hang in midair. Like Karen Wynn with her math experiments, Spelke measures the babies' looking time and has recorded longer intervals for unexpected actions than for expected ones. Again like Wynn, Spelke be-

lieves that babies must have some "core" knowledge—in this case, about the way physical objects behave. Says Spelke: "At an age when infants are not able to talk about objects, move around objects, reach for and manipulate objects, or even see objects with high resolution, they appear to recognize where a moving object is when it has left their view and make inferences about where it should be when it comes into sight again."

The notion of an infant's possessing any innate mechanism—other than reflexes like sucking that fade with time—would have shocked the shoes off the pioneers of child development research, who believed, as some still do, that

what we know can be learned only through experience. But the belief in biologically programmed core knowledge lies at the heart of the current research—not only with math and physics but with other cognitive skills as well. Indeed, Carnegie Mellon's Mark Johnson believes that the ability of infants to recognize the human face is not learned, as previously thought, but is present at birth. Studying infants, some only 10 minutes old, Johnson has observed a marked preference for pictures of faces to pictures of blank ovals or faces with scrambled features. He believes that we are born with a "template" of the human face that aids our survival by helping us recognize our meal ticket.

EMOTIONS: THE SHY AND THE LIVELY

*A growing number of researchers believe early temperament
may indicate later troubles.*

One thing that infants are *not* good at is hiding what they feel. Fear, glee, rage, affection: Long before babies start talking, emotions tumble out of them in gestures, tears and belly laughs. But measuring infant temperament—finding a way to quantify its traits—has always been harder than measuring skills.

Around the country, researchers are now combining questionnaires filled in by parents, home visits by trained observers, and newly devised lab tests to explore the mystery of temperamenat. Concentrating on babies older than eight months (the age at which the full range of infant emotions has emerged), investigators have designed more than 50 experimental situations to provoke emotions from fear to sadness, from interest to pleasure. Most children's reactions fall within an average range on such tests. But there are babies on either extreme, and psychologist Nathan Fox at the University of Maryland has begun to explore their responses. Putting his babies in electroencephalogram (EEG) helmets, he has found that particularly inhibited babies show a distinctive brain-wave pattern, which others believe may predict later emotional problems, including depression. Although some scientists agree that early behavior can predict later temperament, other researchers argue that enduring character traits are the exception, not the rule. For psychiatrist Stanley Greenspan of Bethesda, Md., the ability of infants to change is an article of faith. Specializing in babies as young as three months, Greenspan says he can treat what he calls the garden-variety problems of sleep disorders, tan-

Long before babies begin talking, emotions are graphically expressed in their gestures and facial expressions.

trums and anger in a few sessions. (Don't imagine tiny couches for infant patients; although the babies are closely observed, it's the parents who often get treatment.) For more severe problems, such as suspected learning disorders, he recommends more intensive early intervention—often involving a team of therapists—and has found that this can make a huge difference: "Babies who were very scared, shy and inhibited can completely change and become very assertive, outgoing and confident over a number of months."

The University of Washington's Mary Rothbart has compared infants in Japan, the Netherlands and the U.S. and notes that northern European mothers are most prone to ignore their babies' fussiness with a stiff-upper-lip approach. When tested at one year by having their mothers leave a room, the Dutch babies are the most distressed and ignore their mothers upon their return. Psychologists call this response an "insecure attachment relationship," and some regard it as an early warning of later anxiety disorders. Says Rothbart: "In the process of soothing a baby, you're helping to teach it to shift its attention away from negative sensations. Adults with anxiety disorders may never have learned to do this." Tellingly, when Dutch mothers were instructed to soothe and play with their fussy babies, the follow-up sessions showed positive results. "With intervention," concludes Rothbart, "you can turn things around."

TAKING INFANTS SERIOUSLY

The ultimate question becomes, should education begin at three months?

One question that might leap to the minds of parents newly informed of their infants' skills is a simple one: So what? What does it mean if children really have these unexpected abilities?

Pointing to the findings on memory that she has published with partner Rachel Clifton, Nancy Myers suggests that if memories of the babies' experience allowed them to be unafraid in the pitch-black room, then exposing children to a wide variety of events and places may make them more accepting of similar situations later on. "I don't want to say that mothers should make an extreme effort to stimulate their babies," Myers says, "but taking a baby to different places, allowing him to see and smell different things, is an important means of establishing familiarity. It will allow the baby to feel freer in the future."

But what about other kinds of skills: Should infants' innate abilities with language or math be consciously nurtured and pushed along?

In Philadelphia, instructors at the Institutes for the Achievement of Human Potential have been coaching parents since 1963 to teach their babies to read from birth. Touting "genetic potential," their program recommends that parents write out on cards everything from "nose" to "kiss" to "Mommy." The new findings about infants' skills have hardly gone unnoticed at the Institutes, where director Janet Doman says: "For the past thirty years, we've been saying that children can learn at very early ages. It's nice to know that science is finally validating what we've known all along."

Yet many of the scientists performing the experiments question the value of such intensive efforts. Says Rutgers's Carolyn Rovee-Collier: "Most of us agree that an infant could be taught to recognize letters and numbers. But the problem is that parents who do these kinds of programs start investing a lot in their infants and become very bound up in their success. It puts great strain on the infants and the parents."

University of Denver psychologist Marshall Haith agrees: "Babies are born prepared to take on the world. We've got to get away from the feeling that we've got this wonderful brain sitting there and we've got to keep pumping information into it. Nature wouldn't have done anything so stupid."

To most researchers, the moral of the story seems to be: Respect your baby, but don't go nuts. "Don't waste your child's fun months," says Karen Wynn, who says her findings about math "should be viewed as no more than a new insight for parents who have young children." Says the University of Pittsburgh's Mark Strauss: "Ideally, we can tell parents a lot more about subtle things they can watch happening in their infants, and that will make watching and getting involved more fun."

Creativity and the child's social development

MARTHA L. NABORS
LINDA C. EDWARDS

Martha L. Nabors, Ph.D., and *Linda C. Edwards*, Ed.D., are associate professors of early childhood education at the College of Charleston in South Carolina.

Two-year-old Alex is playing alone at the block center, exploring the various shapes and sizes of colorful blocks. He picks up a shiny red block and turns it over and over in his hands. After a minute or two he looks over in the housekeeping center where he sees his friend Joe. Suddenly, Alex stands up and toddles over to the housekeeping center, carrying the red block. He approaches the miniature ironing board and uses the block to carefully iron his laundry. Noticing that Alex has removed a block from the block center, Mrs. Whisdale immediately reprimands him for taking a block from its proper center and tells him, in front of the other children: "Blocks belong in the block center! I want you to put it back on the shelf now."

Psychosocial development

Let us consider how Mrs. Whisdale's behavior may affect Alex's social development, in light of Erikson's *psychosocial theory*, which categorizes social development into eight conflicts or crises (Erikson, 1963, 1968, 1975). (See figure 1.) Alex was playing alone and exploring the world of blocks. Asserting his will, he made the choice to take a block into the dramatic play, or "housekeeping," center. Once there, his imagination transformed the block into an iron and he explored the new function of the block. According to Erikson (1963), Alex was developing some degree of independence and autonomy. Mrs. Whisdale gave Alex the clear message that he could not make choices. When caregivers consistently restrict children's environment by exerting external control over their play, they can plant the seeds of shame and doubt. The negative outcome of this crisis is loss of self-esteem. Mrs. Whisdale discouraged independence that could have led to Alex having feelings of pride and good will. Alex learned to doubt his own judgment.

Lakesha is a bright, energetic five-year-old who loves to wear polka dots. She also loves her kindergarten teacher. The children have been learning about herbs and spices and how to grow herb gardens. The class was given a large section of the outdoor play area for use as a garden. Mr. Thomas, Lakesha's teacher, announced that each child would have her own section in the class garden. He asked children to think about how they would plant their sections and the herbs they would like to grow. Lakesha decided to plant her seeds in circles.

Planting day arrived. Mr. Thomas reviewed all they had learned about planting herb gardens. Each child was given a packet of seeds, a trowel for digging, and a cup of water. Using her finger, Lakesha began to make little circles in the dirt in preparation for planting her seeds. She made three little circles: one for basil, one for rosemary, and one for mint. Then she planted her seeds, each variety in its own special circle. As Lakesha was covering the last of her seeds, Mr. Thomas approached and said: "Lakesha, where are your straight rows?" Lakesha began to explain how her seeds were planted in circles like the polka-dots on her blouse. Mr. Thomas told her that herb gardens are always planted in straight rows and that she must replant her seeds. Lakesha's chin dropped to her chest and she started to cry.

Lakesha had taken initiative while using her motor and intellectual abilities to create a unique herb plot. She was exploring her environment and assuming responsibility for carrying out her own plans. She was pleased with the pattern of her garden. By not accepting Lakesha's initiative, Mr. Thomas instilled feelings of failure and guilt in a once excited little girl. Erikson's psychosocial theory (1963) asserts that if a task is not mastered, and the conflict of initiative versus guilt is not satisfactorily resolved, the ego is damaged in the process.

Jane is a seven-year-old second-grader with a wonderful sense of humor. One Wednesday afternoon, during a lesson in a unit about animals, the teacher gave each child a lump of clay and told them to make animals. For what seemed like a long time, Jane just looked at the clay. Finally, she

From *Dimensions of Early Childhood*, Fall 1994, pp. 14-16, 48. © 1994 by the Southern Early Childhood Association. Reprinted by permission.

began to pull and poke at it and eventually she started to model it into a form. Her teacher, Mrs. Barto, was pleased to see that Jane was finally working with her clay. Jane laughed out loud as an idea for her animal came to mind. She would make a "bird-dog," a creature with a beak, wings, and a long tail. When all the children had finished making their animals, Mrs. Barto asked them to tell the class about their animals. Timmy made a huge elephant with a long trunk. Peter made a cat. The twins, Marty and Linda, made monkeys. When Jane's turn came to share, she giggled as she proudly held up her "bird-dog." It had a long beak like a hummingbird, wings like an eagle, a big, massive body and a long, skinny tail.

This fun-loving girl glanced over at Mrs. Barto for approval and her eyes were met with a cold stare. Mrs. Barto admonished the children for giggling with Jane and told Jane to go back to her desk and make a real animal.

It was clear that Jane had not met the demands or expectations of her teacher. Any feelings of self-worth Jane may have felt because of her creation were wiped out by the teacher's comment, which could have made Jane feel inferior to her classmates. Erikson (1963) stresses that repeated frustration and failure may lead to feelings of inadequacy and inferiority, thereby negatively affecting one's view of self.

The classroom experiences of Alex, Lakesha, and Jane illustrate that Eriksons' crises (1963) can occur during everyday interactions with others. The outcomes of these crises can be positive or negative in their effects on self-esteem. Such typical psychosocial conflicts also can affect young children's creative development.

Creative development

Research literature essentially agrees that there are four basic phases in the creative process (Wallas, 1926; Patrick, 1937; Kneller, 1965; Boles, 1990; Sapp, 1992) and four basic characteristics of creativity (Barron, 1969, 1978; MacKinnon, 1976, 1978; Torrance, 1962, 1979, 1981a, 1981b, 1984). (See Figures 2 and 3.) In the experiences of Alex, Lakesha, and Jane, creative development is contingent upon the positive solution of each child's psychosocial conflict. The negative reso-

Psychosocial Conflict (Crisis)	Age
Trust versus mistrust	Birth to 18 months
Autonomy versus shame or doubt	18 months to three years
Initiative versus guilt	Three to six years
Industry versus inferiority	Six to 12 years
Identity versus role confusion	Adolescence
Intimacy versus isolation	Young adulthood
Generativity versus stagnation	Mature adulthood
Integrity versus despair	Old age

Figure 1: The eight stages of development in Erikson's Theory of Psychosocial Development. Adapted from Erikson, 1963.

lution of their psychosocial conflicts resulted in the stifling of the creative development of each child. Alex's play with the block demonstrated several characteristics of creativity (Figure 3). Alex was *fluent* in his approach to the possibilities the block held for him. He was *flexible* as he experimented with different ways of using the block. While his idea may not have been completely *original*, he did transform the block into an iron. For Alex, this was a novel idea! When Mrs. Whisdale interrupted his ironing, she also denied him the opportunity to build on his idea. No *elaboration* occurred.

The first three phases in the creative process (Figure 2), also pertain to Alex's situation. He *prepared* by exploring with blocks of different shapes, sizes, and colors. Alex's ideas for using the block could have been *incubating* as he turned the block over and over in his hand before wandering into the housekeeping center. His "'a-ha' moment" (*illumination*) occurred as he changed an ordinary wooden block into an iron. But excitement (*verification*) was short-lived. Mrs. Whisdale made sure her blocks remained in the block center where she thought they belonged. Alex was denied verification of his creative idea.

Lakesha also experienced fluency as she thought about the possibility of a circular garden. She was flexible as she explored different ways of making her circles. Her idea was so original, it conflicted with Mr. Thomas' understanding of garden design. He interrupted her at-

tempt at elaboration.

Like Alex, Lakesha was successful in her preparation phase. She thought about making a circular garden to match the polka-dots on her dress. The polka-dots gave her the information she needed to get started. For Lakesha, incubation occurred as she made circles in the dirt with her fingers in preparation for planting the herbs. Lakesha might have thought: "How perfect. Three circles for three herbs." Illumination had happened; her garden came together. Unfortunately, verification never occurred for Lakesha. Mr. Thomas' insistence upon straight rows prevented Lakesha from any verification of her exciting idea.

Jane was successful in three of the four basic characteristics of creativity. Fluency and flexibility were evident as she poked and pulled at her clay. She was thinking of ways to create her animal. "A bird-dog. What a clever idea!" Jane clearly expressed originality; she put a new stamp on an existing animal. One cold stare from an inflexible Mrs. Barto blocked all chances of Jane being allowed to elaborate on her creation. During the preparation phase of the creative process, Jane drew on her sense of humor and her knowledge of hunting dogs. Staring at the clay and poking it with her fingers provided an incubation period. Jane's ideas jelled. Her "Eureka!" came when she invented her own pun: a "bird-dog." As with elaboration, Mrs. Barto's stare and comment prevented verification form occurring.

The connection between psychosocial development and creative development

A careful examination of Erikson's theory of psychosocial development (1963), the characteristics of creativity (Torrance, 1984), and the phases in the creative process (Sapp, 1992), strongly suggest that the positive resolution of the psychosocial conflict is central to successful creative development. Likewise, experiences in creative development can lead to the positive resolution of the central psychosocial conflicts. In Alex's, Lakesha's, and Jane's stories, a positive psychosocial-creative connection almost occurred. The inability of each child to progress through elaboration and verification had a negative impact on the resolution of their psychosocial conflict. At the same time, the negative resolution of the psychosocial conflict interrupted completion of their creative development. Mrs. Whisdale could have facilitated the connection between Alex's psychosocial and creative development simply by allowing Alex to use the block as an iron in the housekeeping center. Had she let him use the block for his own idea, Mrs. Whisdale would have encouraged autonomy. She could have encouraged his creativity by letting him elaborate on his idea and by giving him time for verification—as eas-

---

Preparation
Gathering materials and ideas to begin

Incubation
Letting ideas "cook" and develop

Illumination
The "a-ha" moment when ideas and materials jell; the "light bulb" phenomenon

Verification
When the exhilaration of the moment has passed and only time will confirm the efforts

---

Figure 2: Phases in the creative process. Adapted from Wallas, 1926; Patrick, 1937; Kneller, 1965; Boles, 1990; Sapp, 1992.

ily as she stopped Alex from using the block as an iron.

Mr. Thomas should have recognized and respected Lakesha's layout of her herb plot. He was in a perfect position to praise her initiative. He could have said: "I like your circular garden. What a great idea!" Simple words like these could have

---

Fluency
To allow ideas and thoughts to flow freely

Flexibility
To explore various ways of using ideas and materials

Originality
To have a new or novel idea or to put a new stamp on something that already exists

Elaboration
Adding finishing touches or decoration

Figure 3: Characteristics of creativity. Adapted from Barron, 1969, 1978; MacKinnon, 1976, 1978; Torrance, 1962, 1979, 1981a, 1981b, 1984.

also been instrumental in Lakesha's development of elaboration and verification.

Jane was also unable to complete the process through elaboration and verification. Mrs. Barto should have recognized that Jane's sense of humor guided her in making such a creative animal. Clearly, when Mrs. Barto told Jane to go back to her table and make a "real" animal, Jane must have felt inferior to her peers. Instead of a cold stare, Mrs. Barto could have joined in the fun with a wink and a smile. This same response could have led Jane to feelings of industry. It also would have opened a door for Jane to elaborate and, finally, to verify her "bird-dog" animal.

Each child could have made a positive connection between psychosocial development and creative development. Teachers and caregivers can encourage children and foster learning environments so that these connections can occur. These suggestions can guide adults in supporting the marriage of psychosocial and creative development:

- Be flexible.
- Consider children's feelings.
- Encourage time for preparation and incubation.
- Foster independence.
- Give children adquate time to complete their projects.
- Recognize children's novel ideas.
- Embrace the "'a-ha' moments."
- Value autonomy.
- Praise industry.
- Acknowledge competence.

References

Barron, F. (1969). *Creative person and creative process.* New York: Holt, Rinehart and Winston.

Barron, F. (1978). An eye more fantastical. In G.A. Davis and J.A. Scott (Eds.), *Training creative thinking.* Melbourne, FL: Krieger.

Boles, S. (1990). A model of routine and creative problem-solving. *Journal of Creative Behavior, 24*(3), 171-189.

Erikson, Erik H. (1963). *Childhood and society.* (2nd ed.). New York: Norton.

Erikson, Erik H. (1968). *Identify, youth, and crisis.* New York: Norton.

Erikson, Erik H. (1975). *Life history and the historical moment.* New York: Norton.

Kneller, G.F. (1965). *The art of science and creativity.* New York: Holt, Rinehart and Winston.

MacKinnon, D.W. (1976). Architects, personality types, and creativity. In A. Rothenberg and C.R. Hausman (Eds.), *The creativity question.* NC: Duke University Press.

MacKinnon, D.W. (1978). Educating for creativity: a modern myth? In G.A. Davis and J.A. Scott (Eds.), *Training creativity thinking.* Melbourne, FL: Krieger.

Patrick, C. (1937). Creative thought in artists. *Journal of Psychology, 4,* 35-67.

Sapp, David D. (1992). The point of creative frustration and the creative process: a new look at an old model. *The Journal of Creative Behavior, 26*(1), 21-28.

Torrance, E.P. (1962). *Guiding creative talent.* New Jersey: Prentice Hall.

Torrance, E.P. (1979). *The search for satori and creativity.* New York: Creative Education Foundation.

Torrance, E.P. (1981a). Non-test ways of identifying the creatively gifted. In J.C. Gowan, J. Khatena, and E.P. Torrance (Eds.), *Creativity: Its educational implications.* Iowa: Kendall/Hunt.

Torrance, E.P. (1981b). *Thinking creativity in action and movement.* Illinois: Scholastic Testing Service.

Torrance, E.P. (1984). Teaching gifted and creative learners. In M. Wittrock (Ed.), *Handbook of research on teaching.* Chicago: Rand-McNally.

Wallas, G. (1926). *The art of thought.* New York: Harcourt, Brace.

Keeping Kids Healthy in Child Care

Best ways to guard against colds, flu and other infections

Mark Deitch

Mark Deitch, the father of two, writes frequently on medicine and health.

Your child is about to start group care. She has so many experiences to look forward to: new caregivers, friends, opportunities for learning and sharing and—not to be overlooked—new germs. Indeed, one of the inescapable facts of child care is that putting a bunch of infants or toddlers together for a large part of the day tends to expand the pool of microorganisms each child is exposed to. For many youngsters, the result is an increased number of colds, tummyaches and other routine infectious illnesses.

"Children under the age of three who have not previously been in child care and who do not have older siblings don't have much in the way of immunity to common germs and viruses," says George Sterne, MD, a New Orleans pediatrician and a leader in the effort to set national guidelines for child care health and safety. "These youngsters also have no sense of hygiene, so their bodily secretions get shared quite liberally."

Eliminating all risk of infectious disease in group care is clearly an impossible task. But with simple preventive measures, child care personnel can significantly reduce the spread of germs. Parents also need to understand these basics—to know what to look for in selecting, monitoring and improving child care.

RESPIRATORY INFECTIONS TOP THE LIST

By far the most common cause of illness among youngsters in child care is respiratory infection—colds, flu and their complications, such as middle-ear infections. Nevertheless, says Dr. Sterne, respiratory infections, which are usually short-lived and easy to manage, rarely constitute a major health problem.

Whether children in group care get more frequent—and more serious—respiratory infections than children who stay home has been the subject of long-standing debate. Recent research offers some interesting new answers to this question.

The parents of more than 2,000 U.S. children ages six weeks to 59 months were interviewed by Eugene S. Hurwitz, MD, and co-investigators at the Centers for Disease Control in Atlanta. About half of the children were in some kind of group care for at least 40 hours a week. The parents were asked to determine how many of these children had caught a cold or other illness during the two weeks preceding the interview. In analyzing the results, the researchers subdivided the study population into three age ranges (under 18 months, 18–35 months and 36–59 months) and also looked at whether the children had older siblings, which would presumably increase their exposure to infection.

Among youngsters in child care, only two groups—those under 18 months and those 18–35 months without older siblings—had significantly more respiratory infections than children who spent their days at home. In each age-group, the more months a child spent in child care, the less likely he was to get sick. Furthermore, the children who had spent the most time in child care (more than 27 months) had approximately half the risk of respiratory infection of those of the same age who had stayed home.

The bottom line: Children under three years old who enter groups get more colds and other respiratory infections *at first* than kids who stay home. But in the long run, the group care children may actually be healthier when they get older. The most likely explanation is that greater exposure to infection early on stimulates the immune system and confers greater resistance down the road.

On the downside, however, is the fact that the initial increase in respiratory infections probably contributes to an increased risk of complications—primarily middle-ear infections—among youngsters in child care under three years old. A report published in the *Journal of Family Practice* in March 1991 tends to bear this out. The study looked at 1,335 children in nine countries (including the U.S.) and found that youngsters in child care had more frequent and severe ear infections than those cared for at home.

GROUP DYNAMICS

The size and stability of a child care group can influence the risk of respiratory infections. The more children in a group, the larger the germ pool. Similarly, a group with high turnover of children and caregivers will be more vulnerable to new infections than a more stable group.

It's best to avoid intermixing of child care groups as much as possible, according to Susan Aronson, MD, clinical professor of pediatrics at the University of Pennsylvania School of Medicine in Philadelphia. "You have to look at how many opportunities there are to transmit infection," she says. "To the extent that you can minimize the size of the group and the number of different interactions, you will decrease the risk of exposure."

From *Working Mother,* February 1994, pp. 67-69. © 1994 by Mark Deitch. Reprinted by permission.

What to Look For

Licensing: Many—but not all—states regulate child care facilities. What this means is that at least a minimal standard of safety and health is mandated. The stringency of these regulations, and how carefully they are enforced varies widely. According to Susan Aronson, MD, professor of pediatrics at the University of Pennsylvania School of Medicine, "Parents should find out not only if a program is regulated but what is required for licensing, what kind of inspection had taken place, by whom, and how recently. Keep in mind that sanitation inspection may not be required in some states."

Accreditation: In addition to state licensing, accreditation from the National Association for the Education of Young Children (for child care centers) or the National Association for Family Care (for family care homes) provides additional evidence of competency, safety and health. Both accrediting programs were begun recently, however, and so relatively few centers or homes have been accredited to date.

Doctor or nurse on call: The program should have access to a consulting pediatrician, family doctor or pediatric nurse in the community.

Hand-washing: Child care workers should have ready access to soap and water for hand-washing, especially after diapering and before food handling. Supervised hand-washing should also be encouraged for children.

Hot water: To ensure cleanliness and sanitation, the water used to wash dishes in the dishwasher should be at least 140F. However, to prevent scalds, the hot water children use to wash their hands should be no more than 120F coming out of the tap. A booster heater in the dishwasher is usually necessary.

Immunizations: Does the program require proof of immunization for *all* children? Are the records checked and updated to ensure that subsequent immunizations are given on schedule?

Diapering and toileting: Diaper-changing and/or toilet areas should be set off from the main activity room and should not be immediately adjacent to eating or food preparation areas. Hand-washing after diapering or wiping is a must for staff and should be encouraged for children. (In some programs, caregivers use disposable gloves for diapering.) Chang-

ing surfaces should have a disposable cover that is replaced after *each use.* Proper diaper disposal is important, too. Potty chairs, fine for individual use at home, require too much handling—with the attendant risk of spillage and contamination—for a child care setting.

Meals and snacks: To prevent spoilage and contamination, appropriate storage and refrigeration should be provided for packed lunches or snacks that are brought from home.

Pesticides: Children are highly susceptible to toxic chemicals like pesticides. Exterminators tend to spray along the baseboards and at floor level—exactly where small children crawl and play. Find out if, when and how pest control is carried out at the center you are investigating.

Ventilation: Access to fresh air is better for diluting potential contaminants (germs and pollutants) than central mechanical circulation. If at all possible, the room should be aired out thoroughly every day.

—M.D.

DIARRHEA AND OTHER COMMON INFECTIONS

The next most prevalent health problem in child care is diarrhea, especially among children not yet toilet trained. The problem occasionally results from something a child ate, but the most likely cause is a virus, bacterium or parasite passed on by another child.

Diarrhea is usually not a serious health threat to children (at least not in the U.S.). However, certain viruses that may be spread via contact with a child's urine and feces can produce severe illness among adults. In particular, hepatitis A, which has no major symptoms in infected children, can be punishing to adults. And cytomegalovirus infection, which rarely causes symptoms in children or healthy adults, can result in birth defects if contracted by a pregnant woman.

A host of other common infections and infestations may crop up in the child care setting. These include conjunctivitis, pin-worms, head lice, scabies and impetigo—"more hysteria items than real health problems," says Dr. Sterne. "People get all upset when they hear about them," he says, "but all you have to do is start the child on treatment, and in a day or so he's no longer infectious."

Strep throat has been thought to be unusual among children under four, although outbreaks have occurred in child care. According to Dr. Sterne, "strep is usually more of a problem once kids start grade school." Chicken pox, on the other a hand, can have quite an impact, because it is so contagious.

Outbreaks of more serious infections, such as bacterial meningitis, have also occurred in child care centers. This disease, most prevalent among youngsters under two years old, can be largely pre-

vented with the *Hemophilus influenzae* type b (Hib) vaccine, which is now required for all children starting at age two months.

IMMUNIZATIONS ARE ESSENTIAL

Many of the most severe childhood infections—from diphtheria, meningitis, pertussis and polio to measles, mumps and rubella—are easily and routinely prevented by making sure your child has all the standard immunizations. A properly health-minded child care center, says Dr. Sterne, not only should require documentation of a child's immunizations on entry, but also should make sure that the record is updated and that subsequent immunizations are given on schedule.

HAND-WASHING: THE KEY TO EVERYDAY PREVENTION

Infection is spread in three ways: child to child, caregiver to child, and child to caregiver. As Dr. Sterne points out, the spread of germs from one child directly to another is hard to prevent, considering that "small children tend to fall all over each other and put things in their mouths and share toys."

Many infections, however, are spread by caregivers, who handle one child after another and thereby serve as unwitting vehicles of transmission. *These* infections are preventable—by washing hands.

"Hand-washing is the number one line of defense against spreading infection," emphasizes Dr. Sterne. "The single most important thing that all caregivers need to understand is that after they change one baby, after they wipe one child's nose, before they do anything else, they must wash their hands."

Of course, this advice is easier given than followed when a caregiver is faced with five toddlers howling for juice and a sixth who needs her diaper changed. Even so, the availability of sinks for hand-washing and the use of disposable disinfectant towelettes in the changing area is something that parents can look for when checking out a child care facility. By quietly and unobtrusively observing a routine diaper-changing, you can get a pretty good idea of how closely the caregiver—and by extension, the program—observes basic rules of hygiene.

It's also important to ask about a program's sick-child policy. Is a child sent home if he is noticeably under the weather? Is there a quiet area where a sick child can rest, apart from the others, while waiting to be picked up? Are there rules specifying when and for how long an infectious child must stay home?

According to Dr. Sterne, a child with a mild cough, runny nose or low-grade fever (under 101F) with no other outstanding symptoms does not necessarily pose a risk to others. In fact, children with respiratory infections are most likely to spread their germs *before* symptoms appear. However, youngsters with diarrhea—especially infants and toddlers not yet toilet trained—should stay out until their bowel movements stabilize.

MORE HYGIENE HINTS

Nose-wiping presents disease transmission problems akin to those of diapering, and just because it may be required more frequently, especially in the winter months, doesn't make preventive precautions any less important. Nasal secretions carry germs, which can be passed to hands and wiping materials. Caregivers should therefore use disposable tissues for nose-wiping, and should never reuse them with another child.

Conjunctivitis, or "pink eye," can spread in a similar way. Youngsters with this infection tend to have crusty, runny eyes, which they rub with their hands. Caregivers should use disposable materials, such as cotton balls, to clean the child's eyes. But unless the child's and the caregiver's hands are immediately washed and the wiping materials thrown away, other children will be exposed to the infection.

As a general precaution, toys and other objects and surfaces that are handled frequently (like doorknobs) should be cleaned and disinfected on a regular basis—preferably at the end of each day.

IN FAVOR OF FRESH AIR

Good ventilation can also help cut down the spread of respiratory infections, according to Dr. Aronson. "Some child care programs are housed in what are called 'sick buildings,' or facilities with inadequate ventilation," she says. The children spend the day filling the air with their germs; without sufficient air exchange, the opportunity for infection goes way up. Moreover, poor ventilation also increases the toxic risk of chemical pollutants or pesticides that may be in a building's air.

Parents should look for windows that open (from the top, of course, or with safety screens) or central mechanical circulation that has been approved by a certified contractor, advises Dr. Aronson. At least once a day, the windows should be opened for a sufficient time to allow a full exchange of air in the room.

Outdoor play is also very important, for it provides a less germ-dense environment than the indoors. Many parents fear that exposure to cold air will cause illness, when, in fact, it is too much time indoors, regardless of the weather, that promotes the spread of infection.

PARENTAL INVOLVEMENT: A MUST

Most states now require some kind of licensing for child care centers, but licensing by itself does not guarantee a safe and healthy environment. Much of the responsibility falls on the parents to assess how well health issues are incorporated into a program's daily activities.

You'll need to observe carefully and ask the right questions. The more you know about the health risks in child care in general, the better off you'll be. The box "What to Look For" offers basic tips to guide your observations and questions.

Meanwhile, if you need assistance finding child care in your area, call the Child Care Aware National Information Line at 1-800-424-2246. You'll be directed to a local resource and referral agency that can give you the help you need.

Why Leave Children With Bad Parents?

Family: Last year, 1,300 abused kids died—though authorities knew that almost half were in danger. Is it time to stop patching up dead-end families?

MICHELE INGRASSIA AND JOHN McCORMICK

THE REPORT OF DRUG PEDdling was already stale, but the four Chicago police officers decided to follow up anyway. As they knocked on the door at 219 North Keystone Avenue near midnight on Feb. 1, it was snowing, and they held out little hope of finding the pusher they were after. They didn't. What they discovered, instead, were 19 children living in horrifying squalor. Overnight, the Dickensian images of life inside the apartment filled front pages and clogged network airwaves.

For the cops that night, it seemed like a scavenger hunt gone mad, each discovery yielding a new, more stunning, find. In the dining room, police said, a half-dozen children lay asleep on a bed, their tiny bodies intertwined like kittens. On the floor beside them, two toddlers tussled with a mutt over a bone they had grabbed from the dog's dish. In the living room, four others huddled on a hardwood floor, crowded beneath a single blanket. "We've got eight or nine kids here," Officer John Labiak announced.

Officer Patricia Warner corrected him: "I count 12." The cops found the last of 19 asleep under a mound of dirty clothes; one 4-year-old, gnarled by cerebral palsy, bore welts and bruises.

As the police awaited reinforcements, they could take full measure of the filth that engulfed this brigade of 1- to 14-year-olds. Above, ceiling plaster crumbled. Beneath their feet, roaches scurried around clumps of rat droppings. But nothing was more emblematic than the kitchen. The stove was inoperable, its oven door yawning wide. The sink held fetid dishes that one cop said "were not from that day, not from that week, maybe not from this year." And though the six mothers living there collected a total of $4,500 a month in welfare and food stamps, there was barely any food in the house. Twice last year, a caseworker from the Illinois Department of Children and Family Services (DCFS) had come to the apartment to follow up reports of serious child neglect, but when no one would let her in, the worker left. Now, it took hours to sort through the mess. Finally, the

police scooped up the children and set out for a state-run shelter. As they left, one little girl looked up at Warner and pleaded, "Will you be my mommy?"

Don't bet on it. Next month the children's mothers—Diane Melton, 31; Maxine Melton, 27; May Fay Melton, 25; Denise Melton, 24; Casandra Melton, 21; and Denise Turner, 20—will appear in Cook County juvenile court for a hearing to determine if temporary custody of the children should remain with the state or be returned to the parents. Yet, for all the public furor, confidential files show that the DCFS is privately viewing the 19 children in the same way it does most others—"Goal: Return Home."

Why won't we take kids from bad parents? For more than a decade, the idea that parents should lose neglected or abused kids has been blindsided by a national policy to keep families together at almost any cost. As a result, even in the worst cases, states regularly opt for reunification. Even in last year's budget-cutting frenzy, Congress earmarked nearly $1 billion for family-preservation programs over the next five years. Yet there is mounting evidence that such efforts make little difference—and may make things worse. "We've oversold the fact that all families can be saved," says Marcia Robinson Lowry, head of the Children's Rights Project of the American Civil Liberties Union. "All families *can't* be saved."

Last year there were 1 million confirmed

cases of abuse and neglect. And, according to the American Public Welfare Association, an estimated 462,000 children were in substitute care, nearly twice as many as a decade ago. The majority of families can be repaired if parents clean up their acts, but experts are troubled by what happens when they don't: 42 percent of the 1,300 kids who died as a result of abuse last year had previously been reported to child-protection agencies. "The child-welfare system stands over the bodies, shows you pictures of the caskets and still does things to keep kids at risk," says Richard Gelles, director of the University of Rhode Island's Family Violence Research Program.

Nowhere has the debate over when to break up families been more sharply focused than in Illinois, which, in the last two years, has had some of the most horrific cases in the nation. Of course, it's not alone. But unlike many states, Illinois hasn't been able to hide its failures behind the cloak of confidentiality laws, largely because of Patrick Murphy, Cook County's outspoken public guardian, who regularly butts heads with the state over its aggressive reunification plans. The cases have turned Illinois into a sounding board for what to do about troubled families.

The Chicago 19 lived in what most people would consider a troubled home. But to veterans of the city's juvenile courts, it's just another "dirty house" case. In fact, Martin Shapiro, the court-appointed attorney for Diane Melton, plans to say that conditions could have been worse. He can argue that Melton's children weren't malnourished, weren't physically or sexually abused and weren't left without adult supervision. He's blunt: "Returning children to a parent who used cocaine—as horrific as that might seem—isn't all that unusual in this building." If only all the cases were so benign.

What Went Wrong?

ON THE LAST NIGHT OF JOSEPH Wallace's life, no one could calm his mother's demons. Police say that Amanda Wallace was visiting relatives on April 18, 1993, with 3-year-old Joseph and his 1-year-old brother, Joshua, when she began raving that Joseph was nothing but trouble. "I'm gonna kill this bitch with a knife tonight," Bonnie Wallace later told police her daughter threatened. Bonnie offered to keep the boy overnight, but Amanda refused, so Bonnie drove them to their apartment on Chicago's impoverished West Side. It's unclear what forced Amanda's hand, but authorities tell a harrowing tale: at about 1:30 a.m., she stuffed a sock into Joseph's mouth and secured it with medical tape. Then she went to the kitchen, retrieved a brown extension cord and wrapped it around Joseph's neck several times. She carried her

son to the living room, stood him on a chair, then looped the cord around the metal crank arm over the door. In the last act of his life, Joseph waved goodbye.

Amanda Wallace, 28, has pleaded not guilty to charges of first-degree murder. No one ever doubted that Amanda was deeply troubled. When Joseph was born, she was a resident at the Elgin Mental Health Center in suburban Chicago, and a psychiatrist there warned that Amanda "should never have custody of this or any other baby." Three times, the DCFS removed Joseph from his mother. Yet three times, judges returned him to Amanda's dark world. Six months after the murder—which led to the firing of three DCFS employees—a blue-ribbon report blasted the Illinois child-welfare system, concluding that it had "surely consigned Joseph to his death."

Even in the most egregious instances of abuse, children go back to their parents time and again. In Cook County, the public guardian now represents 31,000 children. Only 963 kids were freed for adoption last year. But William Maddux, the new supervising judge of the county's abuse and neglect section, believes the number should have been as high as 6,000. Nationwide, experts say, perhaps a quarter of the children in substitute care should be taken permanently from their parents. U S Stats.

But it's not simply social custom that keeps families together, it's the law. The Adoption Assistance and Child Welfare Act of 1980 is a federal law with a simple goal—to keep families intact. The leverage: parents who don't make a "reasonable effort" to get their lives on track within 18 months risk losing their kids forever. The law itself was a reaction to the excesses of the '60s and '70s, when children were often taken away simply because their parents were poor or black. But the act was also one of those rare measures that conservatives and liberals embraced with equal passion—conservatives because it was cheap, liberals because it took blame away from the poor.

By the mid-'80s, though, the system began to collapse. A system built for a simpler time couldn't handle an exploding underclass populated by crack addicts, the homeless and the chronically unemployed. At the same time, orphanages began shutting their doors and foster families began quitting in droves. The system begged to know where to put so many kids. It opted for what was then a radical solution: keeping them in their own homes while offering their parents intensive, short-term support—child rearing, housekeeping and budgeting. But as family-preservation programs took off, the threat of severing the rights of abusive parents all but disappeared. What emerged, Gelles argues, was the naive philosophy that a mother who'd hurt her child is not much different from one who can't keep house—and that with enough supervi-

sion, both can be turned into good parents.

In hindsight, everyone in Chicago agrees that Joseph Wallace's death was preventable, that he died because the system placed a parent's rights above a child's. Amanda could never have been a "normal" parent. She had been a ward of the state since the age of 8, the victim of physical and sexual abuse. Between 1976 and Joseph's birth in 1989, her psychiatrist told the DCFS, she swallowed broken glass and batteries; she disemboweled herself, and when she was pregnant with Joseph, she repeatedly stuck soda bottles into her vagina, denying the baby was hers. Yet 11 months after Joseph was born, a DCFS caseworker and an assistant public defender persuaded a Cook County juvenile-court judge to give him back to Amanda, returning him from the one of the six foster homes he would live in. The judge dispatched Amanda with a blessing: "Good luck to you, Mother."

Over the next two years, caseworkers twice removed Joseph after Amanda attempted suicide. But a DCFS report, dated Oct. 31, 1992, said she had gotten an apartment in Chicago, entered counseling and worked as a volunteer for a community organization. And though the report noted her turbulent history, it recommended she and Joseph be reunited. Joseph Wallace was sent home for the last time 62 days before his death, by a judge who had no measure of Amanda's past. "Would somebody simply summarize what this case is about for me and give me an idea why you're all agreeing?" the judge asked. Amanda's lawyer sidestepped her mental history. Nevertheless, the DCFS and the public guardian's office signed on. When Amanda thanked the judge, he said, "It sounds like you're doing OK. Good luck."

Murphy says that deciding when to sever parents' rights should be obvious: "You remove kids if they're in a dangerous situation. No one should be taken from a cold house. But it's another thing when there are drugs to the ceiling and someone's screwing the kids." Ambiguous cases? "There haven't been gray cases in years."

No one knows that better than Faye and Michael Callahan, one of the foster families who cared for Joseph. When Joseph first came to them he was a happy, husky baby. When he returned after his first stretch with Amanda, "he had bald spots because he was pulling his hair out," Faye says. By the third time, she says, Joseph was "a zombie. He rocked for hours, groaning, 'Uh, uh, uh, uh'." The fact that he was repeatedly sent home still infuriates them. Says Michael: "I'd scream at those caseworkers, 'You're making a martyr of this little boy!' "

See No Evil, Hear No Evil

EARLY LAST THANKSGIVING, ARETHA McKinney brought her young son to the emergency room. Clifford Triplett was semiconscious, and his body was pocked with burns, bruises and other signs of abuse, police say. The severely malnourished boy weighed 17 pounds—15 percent less than the average 1-year-old. Except Clifford was 5.

This wasn't a secret. In a confidential DCFS file obtained by NEWSWEEK, a state caseworker who visited the family last June gave a graphic account of Clifford's life: "Child's room (porch) clothing piled in corner, slanted floor. Child appears isolated from family—every one else has a well furnished room. Child very small for age appears to be 2 years old. Many old scars on back and buttocks have many recent scratches." In April, another caseworker had confronted McKinney's live-in boyfriend, Eddie Robinson Sr., who claimed that Cliff was a "dwarf" and was suicidal—neither of which doctors later found to be true. Robinson added that Cliff got "whipped" because he got into mischief. "I told him that he shouldn't be beat on his back," the caseworker wrote. "Robinson promised to go easy on the discipline."

It's one thing to blame an anonymous "system" for ignoring abuse and neglect. But the real question is a human one: how can caseworkers walk into homes like Clifford's, document physical injury or psychological harm and still walk away? A Cook County juvenile-court judge ruled last month that both McKinney and Robinson had tortured Clifford (all but erasing the possibility that he'll ever be returned to his mother). But caseworkers are rarely so bold. In Clifford's case, the April worker concluded that abuse apparently had occurred, but nine days later another found the home "satisfactory." Says Gelles: "Caseworkers are programmed by everything around them to be deaf, dumb and blind because the system tells them, 'Your job is to work to reunification'."

Murphy charges that for the past two

SAONNIA BOLDEN

"The amount of stress and frustration has been reduced. Sadie appears to have a lot more patience with her children and she continues to improve her disciplinary techniques." The same day the worker wrote this, Sadie's daughter Saonnia died after boiling water was poured on her. An autopsy uncovered 62 injuries, many recent.

FROM CASEWORKER REPORT ON SAONNIA BOLDEN

years, Illinois has made it policy to keep new kids out of an already-clogged system. "The message went out that you don't aggressively investigate," he says. "Nobody said, 'Keep the ----ing cases out of the system'." But that, he says, is the net effect. "That's just not true," says Sterling Mac Ryder, who took over the DCFS late in 1992. But he doesn't dispute that the state and its caseworkers may have put too much emphasis on reunification—in part because of strong messages from Washington.

The problems may be even more basic. By all accounts, caseworkers and supervisors are less prepared today than they were 20 years ago, and only a fraction are actually social workers. Few on the front lines are willing, or able, to make tough calls or buck the party line. In the end, says Deborah Daro, research director of the National Committee to Prevent Child Abuse, "the worker may say, 'Yeah, it's bad, but what's the alternative? I'll let this one go and pray to God they don't kill him'."

In most cases, they don't. Nevertheless, children who grow up in violent homes beyond the age of 8 or 10 risk becoming so emotionally and psychologically damaged that they can never be repaired. "The danger," says Robert Halpern, a professor of child development at the Erikson Institute in Chicago, "is not just the enormous dam-

age to the kid himself, but producing the next generation of monsters."

Clifford Triplett is an all-too-pointed reminder of how severe the injuries can be. He has gained eight pounds, and his physical prognosis is good. But there are many other concerns. "When he came, he didn't know the difference between a car and a truck, the difference between pizza and a hot dog," says his hospital social worker, Kathleen Egan. "People were not introducing these things to him." Robinson and McKinney are awaiting trial on charges of aggravated battery and felony cruelty. McKinney's attorney blames Robinson for the alleged abuse; Robinson's attorney declined to comment. Clifford is waiting for a foster home. A few weeks ago he had his first conversation with his mother in months. His first words: "Are you sorry for whipping me?"

Band-Aids Don't Work

ACCORDING TO THE CASEWORKER'S report, 2½-year-old Saonnia Bolden's family was the model of success. Over 100 days, a homemaker from an Illinois family-preservation program called Family First worked with Sadie Williams and her boyfriend Clifford Baker. A second helper—a caseworker—shopped with Sadie for shoes and some furniture for her apartment; she evaluated Sadie's cooking, housekeeping and budgeting. She even took her to dinner to celebrate her progress. On March 17, 1992, the caseworker wrote a report recommending that Sadie's case be closed: "Due to the presence of homemaker, the amount of stress and frustration has been reduced. Sadie appears to have a lot more patience with her children and she continues to improve her disciplinary techniques."

What the Family First caseworker evidently didn't know was that, just hours before she filed her report, Saonnia had been beaten and scalded to death. Prosecutors claim that Williams, angered because her young daughter had wet herself, laid the child in the bathtub and poured scalding water over her genitals and her buttocks. Williams and Baker were charged with first-degree murder; lawyers for Baker and Williams blame each other's client. Regardless of who was responsible, this wasn't

Race of Foster Children

Contrary to public opinion, foster care is not dominated by minorites. Nearly half the kids there are white.

white	47.2%
hispanic	13.7%
black	30.8%
others	4.6%
unknown	3.7%

SOURCE: AMERICAN PUBLIC WELFARE ASSOCIATION

Where Do Children Go?

Two thirds of children who leave foster care are reunited with their parents; only a fraction are adopted.

reunited	66.6%
adopted	7.7%
adulthood	6.5%
other	15.7%
unknown	3.5%

SOURCE: AMERICAN PUBLIC WELFARE ASSOCIATION

A One-Man Children's Crusade

Twenty years ago, an angry young lawyer named Patrick Murphy wrote a book that exposed an injustice: state social workers too often seized children from parents whose worst crime was poverty. Today Murphy is the scourge of a child-welfare system that too often leaves kids with their abusive, drugged-out parents. He has not made the about-face quietly. In many cities, confidentiality laws protect caseworkers and judges from public outcries when their bad decisions lead to a parent's murder of a child. In Chicago, Murphy calls blistering press conferences to parcel out the blame. To those who say he picks on parents who are poor, black and victimized, he hotly retorts: "So are their kids."

Murphy is the Cook County (Ill.) public guardian, the court-appointed lawyer for 31,000 abused and neglected children. He's also a self-righteous crusader. last year, campaigning to rein in one "family preservation" program, Murphy sent every Illinois legislator color autopsy photos of a little girl scalded and beaten to death after caseworkers taught her family new disciplinary skills. It's a loner's life, poring over murder files and railing at fellow liberals who think the poor can do no wrong. "A lot of people hate my guts," Murphy shrugs. "I can't blame them."

His views on family reunification changed because child abuse changed. Drugs now suffuse 80 percent of the caseload; sexual and physical assaults that once taxed the imagination are now common. Murphy believes that most families should be reunited—but the child-welfare agencies waste years trying to patch up dead-end families when they should be hurrying to free children for early adoption. Murphy, 55, blames such folly on bleeding hearts like himself, who once lobbied for generous social programs without working to curb welfare dependency and other ills.

Now children of troubled families must pay the price—sometimes with their lives. "We inadvertently pushed a theory of irresponsibility," he says. "And we created a monster—kids having kids."

To Murphy's critics, that smacks of scorn for the less fortunate. "He's a classic bully," says Diane Redleaf of the Legal Assistance Foundation of Chicago, who represents parents trying to win back their kids. "Thousands of poor families are *not* torturing their children." Redleaf has drafted legislation that would force Murphy to get a judge's order each time he wants to speak about a case. That would protect children's privacy—and give the system a convenient hiding place. Murphy will fight to keep things as they are. His is the only job, he says, in which a lawyer knows that his clients are truly innocents.

J.M.

the first assault. The autopsy on Saonnia's visibly malnourished body found 62 cuts, bruises, burns, abrasions and wrist scars, among other injuries. Eleven were still healing—meaning they probably happened during the time the homemaker was working with the family.

Since Illinois's Family First program began in 1988, at least six children have died violently during or after their families received help. In many other instances, children were injured, or simply kept in questionable conditions. Such numbers may look small compared with the 17,000 children in Illinois who've been in the program. But to critics, the deaths and injuries underscore the danger of using reunification efforts for deeply troubled families. Gelles, once an ardent supporter of family preservation, is adamant about its failures. "We've learned in health psychology that you don't waste intervention on those with no intention of changing," he argues.

A University of Chicago report card issued last year gave the Illinois Family First program barely passing grades. Among the findings: Family First led to a slight *increase* in the overall number of children later placed outside their homes; it had no effect on subsequent reports of maltreatment; it had only mixed results in such areas as improving housing, economics and parenting, and it had no effect on getting families out of the DCFS system. John R. Schuerman, who helped write the report, says it's too simplistic to call Family First a

failure. Still, he concedes that the assumption that large numbers of households can be saved with intensive services "just may not be the case."

Nevertheless, in the last decade, family-preservation programs have become so entrenched there's little chance they'll be junked. Health and Human Services Secretary Donna Shalala carefully sidesteps the question of whether it's possible to carry the reunification philosophy too far. Asked where she would draw the line in defining families beyond repair, she diplomatically suggests that the answers be left to child-welfare experts. "Nobody wants to leave children in dangerous situations," says Shalala. "The goal is to shrewdly pick cases in which the right efforts might help keep a

family together." So far, not even the experts have come up with a sure way to do that.

Where Do We Go From Here?

POLICYMAKERS BELIEVE THAT IF THEY could just remove the stresses from a family, they wouldn't have to remove the child. But critics argue that the entire child-welfare network must approach the idea of severing parents' rights as aggressively as it now approaches family reunification. That means moving kids through the system and into permanent homes quickly—before they're so damaged that they won't fit in anywhere. In theory, the Adoption Assistance Act already requires that, but no state enforces that part of

CLIFFORD TRIPLETT

"I talked to him [Eddie Robinson, Cliff's mother's boyfriend] about Cliff and the old scars on his back. Robinson said . . . Cliff had a tendency to get into a lot of mischief," the caseworker noted. "This is why Cliff was whipped—however I told him that he shouldn't be beat on his back. Robinson promised to go easy on the discipline. (Said he wasn't doing the whipping.)"

FROM CASEWORKER REPORT ON CLIFFORD TRIPLETT

CHICAGO TRIBUNE

the law. Illinois is typical: even in the most straightforward cases, a petition to terminate parental rights is usually the start of a two-year judicial process—*after* the 18-month clean-up-your-act phase.

Why does it take so long? Once a child is in foster care, the system breathes a sigh of relief and effectively forgets about him. If the child is removed from an abusive home, the assumption is that he's safe. "There's always another reason to give the parent the benefit of the doubt," says Daro. "They lose their job, the house burns down, the aunt is murdered. Then they get another six-month extension, and it happens all over again. Meanwhile, you can't put a child in a Deepfreeze and suspend his life until the parent gets her life together."

In the most blatant abuse and neglect cases, parents' rights should be terminated immediately, reformers say. In less-severe cases, parents should be given no more than six to 12 months to shape up. "You have social workers saying, 'She doesn't visit her child because she has no money for carfare'," says Murphy. "But what parent wouldn't walk over mountains of glass to see their kids? You know it's a crock. You have to tell people we *demand* responsibility."

And if parents can't take care of them, where are all these children supposed to go? With just 100,000 foster parents in the system, finding even temporary homes is difficult. For starters, reformers suggest professionalizing foster care, paying parents decent salaries to stay home and care for several children at a time. Long range, many believe that society will have to confront its ambivalence toward interracial adoptions. Perhaps the most controversial alternative is the move to revive orphan-

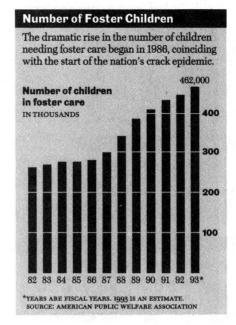

Number of Foster Children

The dramatic rise in the number of children needing foster care began in 1986, coinciding with the start of the nation's crack epidemic.

Number of children in foster care
IN THOUSANDS

462,000

400

300

200

100

82 83 84 85 86 87 88 89 90 91 92 93*

*YEARS ARE FISCAL YEARS. 1993 IS AN ESTIMATE.
SOURCE: AMERICAN PUBLIC WELFARE ASSOCIATION

ages, at least for teenagers, who are the least likely to be adopted. One of the fiercest supporters is Maddux, the new supervising judge of Cook County's abuse section. Maddux, 59, says that his own family was so desperately poor they once lived in a shanty with two rooms—one of which was an old car. When the family broke up, he and his younger brother went to live at Boys Town, Neb. He believes that many foster children today could benefit from the nurturing-yet-demanding atmosphere of group living. "I wasn't raised in a family after the age of 12," Maddux says. "I didn't miss it. Thousands of kids at Boys Town knew that being in a destitute, nonfunctioning family was a lot worse than not

being in a family." In Illinois, some are taking the idea seriously—among the proposals is turning closed military bases into campuses for kids.

Ironically, Illinois could wind up with one of the best child-welfare systems in the nation. Pressed by public outrage over Joseph Wallace's death, state legislators last year passed a law that puts the best interest of children ahead of their parents'. Foster parents will be given a voice in abuse and neglect cases. And the DCFS is beefing up caseworker training, so that those in the field will learn how to spot dangerous situations more quickly.

Some of the toughest changes are already underway in Cook County. The much-criticized Family First program has been replaced with a smaller, more intensely scrutinized family-preservation project known as Homebuilders. And the county's juvenile-court system has been expanded so that there are now 14 judges, not eight, hearing abuse and neglect cases; that cuts each judge's caseload from about 3,500 to about 2,000 children per year. But reform doesn't come cheap. The DCFS budget has tripled since 1988, to $900 million, and it could top $1 billion in the next fiscal year.

Whether any of this can save lives, it's too soon to tell. In its report on Joseph Wallace's death, the blue-ribbon committee was pessimistic. "It would be comforting to believe that the facts of this case are so exceptional that such cases are not likely to happen again," the panel wrote with a dose of bitterness. "That hope is unfounded." The temptation, of course, is to blame some faceless system. But the fate of children really lies with everyone—caseworkers, supervisors, prosecutors, judges—doing their jobs.

LIFE WITHOUT FATHER

In exclusive excerpts from 'Fatherless America,' to be published Tuesday, the author argues that fathers are an endangered species — and offers a plan to save them

DAVID BLANKENHORN

The author of these excerpts is chairman of the National Fatherhood Initiative, one of several groups attempting to call attention to the importance of fathers in solving today's most pressing social problems. Board members range from former U.S. Education Secretary William Bennett to actor James Earl Jones. Blankenhorn lives in New York with his wife, Raina, and their 4-year-old son, Raymond.

The United States is becoming an increasingly fatherless society. A generation ago, a child could reasonably expect to grow up with his or her father. Today, a child can reasonably expect not to. Fatherlessness is approaching a rough parity with fatherhood as a defining feature of childhood.

This astonishing fact is reflected in many statistics, but here are the two most important: Tonight, about 40 percent of U.S. children will go to sleep in homes in which their fathers do not live *(see chart, opposite page)*. More than half of our children are likely to spend a significant portion of childhood living apart from their fathers. Never before in this country have so many children been voluntarily abandoned by their fathers. Never before have so many children grown up without knowing what it means to have a father.

Fatherlessness is the most harmful demographic trend of this generation. It is the leading cause of the decline in the well-being of children. It is also the engine driving our most urgent social problems, from crime to adolescent pregnancy to domestic violence. Yet, despite its scale and social consequences, fatherlessness is frequently ignored or denied. Especially within our elite discourse, it remains a problem with no name.

Surely a crisis of this scale merits a name — and a response. At a minimum, it requires a serious debate: Why is fatherhood declining? What can be done about it? Can our society find ways to invigorate effective fatherhood as a norm of male behavior? Yet, to date, our public discussion has been remarkably weak and defeatist. There is a prevailing belief that not much can or even should be done to reverse the trend.

As a society, we are changing our minds about men's role in family life. Our inherited understanding of fatherhood is under siege. Men are increasingly viewed as superfluous to family life: either expendable or part of the problem. Masculinity itself often is treated with suspicion, and even hostility, in our cultural discourse. Consequently, our society is unable to sustain fatherhood as a distinctive domain of male activity.

'Fatherlessness is the engine driving our most urgent social problems, from crime to adolescent pregnancy to domestic violence'

The core question is simple: Does every child need a father? Increasingly, our society's answer is "no." Few idea shifts in this century are as consequential as this one. At stake is nothing less than what it means to be a man, who our children will be and what kind of society we will become.

My book is a criticism not simply of fatherlessness but of a *culture* of fatherlessness. For, in addition to fathers, we are losing something larger: our idea of fatherhood. Unlike earlier periods of father absence in our history, such as wartime, we now face more than a physical loss affecting some homes. The 1940s child could say: My father had to leave for a while to do something important. The '90s child must say: My father left me permanently because he wanted to.

This is a cultural criticism because fatherhood, much more than motherhood, is a cultural invention. Its meaning is shaped less by biology than by a cultural script, a societal code that guides — and at times pressures — a man into certain ways of acting and understanding himself.

Like motherhood, fatherhood is made up of both a biological and a social dimension. Yet, across the world, mothers are far more successful than fathers at fusing these dimensions into a coherent identity. Is the nursing mother playing a biological or a social role? Feeding or bonding? We can hardly separate the two, so seamlessly are they woven together. But fatherhood is a different matter. A father makes his sole biological contribution at the moment of conception, nine months before the infant enters the world. Because social paternity is linked only indirectly to biological paternity, a connection cannot be assumed. The phrase "to father a child" usually refers only to the act of insemination, not the responsibility for raising the child. What fathers contribute after conception is largely a matter of cultural devising.

Moreover, despite their other virtues, men are not ideally suited to responsible fatherhood. Men are inclined to sexual promiscuity and paternal waywardness. Anthropologically, fatherhood constitutes what might be termed a necessary problem. It is necessary because child well-being and societal success hinge largely on a high level of paternal investment: men's willingness to devote energy and resources to the care of their offspring. It is a problem because men frequently are unwilling or unable to make that vital investment.

Because fatherhood is universally problematic, cultures must mobilize to enforce the father role, guiding men with legal and extralegal pressures that require them to maintain a close alliance with

DISAPPEARING DADS

U.S. KIDS LIVING WITH ...	1960	1980	1990
Father and mother	80.6%	62.3%	57.7%
Mother only	7.7	18	21.6
Father only	1	1.7	3.1
Father and stepmother	0.8	1.1	0.9
Mother and stepfather	5.9	8.4	10.4
Neither parent	3.9	5.8	4.3

Sources: *America's Children* by Donald Hernandez; U.S. Census Bureau. Because the statistics are from separate sources, they don't total 100%.

their children's mother and invest in their children. Because men don't volunteer for fatherhood as much as they are conscripted into it by the surrounding culture, only an authoritative cultural commitment to fatherhood can fuse biological and social paternity into a coherent male identity. For exactly this reason, anthropologist Margaret Mead and others have observed that the supreme test of any civilization is whether it can socialize men by teaching them to nurture their offspring.

The stakes could hardly be higher. Our society's conspicuous failure to sustain norms of fatherhood reveals a failure of collective memory and a collapse of moral imagination. It undermines families, neglects children, causes or aggravates our worst social problems and makes individual adult happiness, both female and male, harder to achieve.

Ultimately, this failure reflects nothing less than a culture gone awry, unable to establish the boundaries and erect the signposts that can harmonize individual happiness with collective well-being. In short, it reflects a culture that fails to "enculture" individual men and women, mothers and fathers.

In personal terms, the main result of this failure is the spread of a me-first egotism hostile to all except the most puerile understandings of personal happiness. In social terms, the results are a decline in children's well-being and a rise in male violence, especially against women. The most significant result is our society's steady fragmentation into atomized individuals, isolated from one

12 WAYS TO PUT FATHERS BACK IN THE PICTURE

25 PERCENT OF U.S. BABIES born in 1993 were to unmarried mothers who ran their households alone, Blankenhorn estimates. To create a stronger national focus on the value of fatherhood, he recommends:

■ A coalition of civic groups should ask every man to pledge that "every child deserves a father, marriage is the pathway to effective fatherhood, part of being a good man is being a good father, and America needs more good men."

■ The president, acting through the White House Domestic Policy Council, should issue a brief annual report to the nation on the state of fatherhood.

■ A few good men should create Fathers' Clubs in their communities.

■ Congress should assist community organizers, clergy members and other local leaders who are serious about creating higher standards of male responsibility.

■ Community organizers and veterans of the poor people's and civil rights movements should help build the infrastructure for a new grass-roots movement to empower families and strengthen community life.

■ Policies should be changed to encourage a higher percentage of married couples in public housing.

■ An interfaith council of religius leaders should speak up and act up on behalf of marriage.

■ Congress should pass, and the president should support, a resolution stating that policymakers' first question about domestic legislation should be whether it will strengthen the institution of marriage.

■ Local officials across the nation should follow the example of the Hennepin County (Minn.) Board of Commissioners by issuing a "vision statement" that urges citizens to move toward a community in which a "healthy family structure is nurtured."

■ States should regulate sperm banks, prohibiting the sale of sperm to unmarried women and limiting artificial insemination to infertile married couples.

■ Well-known pro athletes should organize a public service campaign on the importance of fatherhood.

■ Prominent family scholars should write better high school textbooks about marriage and parenthood.

another and estranged from the aspirations and realities of common membership in a family, a community, a nation, bound by mutual commitment and shared memory.

Many voices today, including many expert voices, urge us to accept the decline of fatherhood with equanimity. Be realistic, they tell us. Divorce and out-of-wedlock childbearing are here to stay. Growing numbers of children will not have fathers. Nothing can be done to reverse the trend itself. The only solution is to remedy some of its consequences: More help for poor children. More sympathy for single mothers. Better divorce. More child-support payments. More prisons. More programs aimed at substituting for fathers.

Yet what Abraham Lincoln called the better angels of our nature always have guided us in the opposite direction. Passivity in the face of crisis is inconsistent with the American tradition. Managing decline never has been the hallmark of American expertise. In the inevitable and valuable tension between conditions and aspirations — between the social "is" and the moral "ought" — our birthright as Americans always has been our confidence that we can change for the better.

Does every child need a father? Our current answer hovers between "not necessarily" and "no." But we need not make permanent the lowering of our standards. We can change our minds. We can change our minds without passing new laws, spending more tax dollars or empaneling more expert commissions. Once we change our philosophy, we might well decide to pass laws, create programs or commission research. But the first and most important thing to change is not policies, but ideas.

Our essential goal must be the rediscovery of the fatherhood idea: For every child, a legally and morally responsible man.

If my goal could be distilled into one sentence, it would be this: A good society celebrates the ideal of the man who puts his family first. Because our society is lurching in the opposite direction, I see the Good Family Man as the principal casualty of today's weakening focus on fatherhood. Yet I cannot imagine a good society without him.

AIDING FAMILIES WITH REFERRALS

Karen Stephens

With the exception of family relatives, early childhood teachers and caregivers are often the first persons to become closely involved in the lives of young children. Parents and teachers often form close bonds as they marvel at development's unfolding sequence. The "bird's eye view" teachers have of children's development and family life can also prove to be a challenging "occupational hazard." Parents often turn to teachers hoping they can provide quick (free) advice on how to handle a wide variety of parenting concerns. These may include, but are not limited to: coping with developmental delays, adjusting to single parenthood or new family members, living with eating disorders, or even coping with domestic violence between mother and father.

Obviously, no one early childhood professional is qualified to provide advice on all of these issues. Although it is tempting to listen and be compassionate with parents, the temptation to become a personal therapist or family counselor needs to be avoided. But how DO you help parents without burning yourself out trying to be all things to all people? Following are some basic guidelines that may help you.

❑ **Know your area of expertise.** Give opinions and advice only when you are well informed through experience and have suitable qualifications through specialized training. Learn to say, *"I'm not the best person to answer that question or solve that problem for you. I'll be glad to help you find someone who is more suitable."*

❑ **Be approachable,** but resist the urge to solve all problems for all parents. Tell parents you are glad they felt they could approach you with their problem. THEN refer them to appropriate agencies (or personnel) who are better equipped to help them. (Suggestions will follow at the end of this article.)

❑ **Draw boundaries.** It is a very delicate line between being a family-support professional and a personal friend. Parents sometime step over the line unintentionally, especially if they are emotionally upset and feel that you are someone who is warm and caring. If you feel you have fallen into the trap of listening to family gossip rather than discussing children's well-being, respectfully communicate a limit to the parent.

❑ **Be credible and true to your calling.** This part takes some soul-searching. If you spend lots of time listening to parents' personal problems (be they parenting, marital, or work-related), then you are in the wrong profession. Consider additional training to become a social worker, family therapist, or child psychologist, if that is most rewarding for you.

Up until now I have talked about cases where parents approach you with a problem or concern. As you well know, there are times when parents don't perceive a problem, but teachers do. This usually relates to children's social behavior or learning abilities. Often teachers hesitate to confront a problem during a parent conference because they are afraid parents will become angry, disagree, or deny there is any problem. However, it is better for the child if you bring up the issue with the parents. Even if the parents deny the problem, you will have been the first to draw their attention to it. Once the child goes to another program or to elementary school, they might hear the same comment from another teacher. Usually after three professionals (from different programs or agencies) point out the same issue, parents are motivated to look further into the issue. The sooner children's problems are identified the greater the chance of preventing larger problems in later childhood.

When deciding whether to confer with a parent and provide referrals, ask yourself if any of the following conditions exist.

❏ Is the child's behavior harmful to himself or others?

❏ Is the child's ability to learn or that of his classmates' impaired by the problem?

❏ Is the classroom's social environment frequently disrupted and tense due to the problem?

❏ Have co-teachers or other professionals also noted the same concerns/behaviors?

❏ Does the problem situation persist regardless of multiple strategies and/or attempts to cope with the problem without outside help?

❏ Is the child's behavior or problem significantly unusual compared to typical child development?

If you answer, "Yes," to more than a few of these questions, it is time to consider helping parents find professional help within the community.

It takes some searching, but communities often have more family support resources than you might expect. To be proactive, programs should have a written sheet of referrals for typical child and family-related problems. Some communities have a Chamber of Commerce, United Way, Child Care Resource and Referral Agency, Health Department, Special Education Office, or University which maintain a referral list already. Before you spend time compiling an exhaustive list yourself, contact agencies in your area. In addition to a referral list, have on file or display brochures from a wide variety of family support agen-

cies. These brochures should describe services, location, hours of operation, phone number, and cost. Parents in need require information fast. Giving parents something to hold in their hand right away motivates them to begin the problem-solving process.

Whenever developing a referral list or brochure display, be sure to include services that are provided on a sliding fee basis. (When referring families for family therapy this takes away one excuse they may use to avoid dealing with the problem.) The list above will give you sample referrals that you may need to make in the course of your early childhood career. I'm sure you will add more to the list!

PROBLEMS AND APPROPRIATE REFERRAL AGENCY/PERSON

❏ *Child Behavior Problems* —child psychologist

❏ *Child Nutrition Problems*—Nutritionist; Women, Infant, Children Feeding Program; Health department; Welfare Office Food Stamp program

❏ *Child Abuse*— Department of Social Services, family therapist, child sexual abuse counselor

❏ *Speech and Language Problems*—speech therapist, University Speech and Language Clinic, Health Department Hearing Screening

❏ *Vision Problems*—Health Department Vision Screening, local opthamologist

❏ *Family Member Drug Dependence*—Health Department, Hospital Chemical Dependence Unit

❏ *Domestic Violence*—Domestic Violence Shelter, Legal Assistance Hot-line, Family Counseling, local police

❏ *Bill Payment Problems*—Credit card counseling agency, emergency loan options

❏ *Home Utility Payment Problems*—Community Action Agencies, United Way

❏ *Childhood Illness*—Health Department, Support groups for specific illnesses, i.e. cancer, AIDS

❏ *Developmental Delays*—Special Education Office, Local School Superintendent's Office, State Board of Education, United Way Funded Agencies list

❏ *Childhood Poisonings*—Health Department Lead Screening Clinic, Poison Control Center

❏ *Death in Family*—family counselor, funeral home director

Homeless families: stark reality of the '90s

Researchers look into one of America's most disturbing problems: homeless families.

Tori DeAngelis

Monitor staff

The landscape of homelessness has changed since the early 1980s, when nearly all homeless people were men. Today, families—typically women with two children under age 5—make up about 30 percent of the homeless population.

Psychologists are starting to look more closely at the basic characteristics of homeless families: how they become homeless, how homeless mothers' mental health and substance abuse compares to that of other groups and how homeless children compare in behavioral and mental health problems, school functioning and other characteristics to poor youngsters who have housing.

Several factors have conspired to increase the numbers of homeless families since the mid-1980s, said John C. Buckner, PhD, associate director of research at the Better Homes Foundation and lecturer in the department of psychiatry at Harvard Medical School. Demographically, the "baby boom" led to larger numbers of people competing for the same number of affordable living spaces, he noted. On top of that, for the poor, children "are a vulnerability factor" who "make your living expenses higher and make it harder for you to hold down a full-time job," he said. "Plus, if you're doubled up" with other families, "children may become a liability" who can "strain the good will" of those poor families [they] are living with, he said.

The rise in the number of homeless people has led to a growing amount of research in the area, Buckner said. While researchers have looked at the "skid row" homeless for some 100 years, only since the late 1970s have they started examining the general homeless population in earnest, he said. Their work on homeless families is even more recent, beginning in the mid-1980s.

"Basically, researchers see families as another at-risk group for homelessness," he said.

HOMELESS WOMEN

In the last several years, some research consensus has emerged on homeless families: In general, "homeless families look very different from homeless individuals," said Marybeth Shinn, PhD, psychology professor in the Community Psychology Project at New York University. A range of studies has shown, for instance, that these families "have much lower levels of substance-abuse and mental health problems" than homeless individuals, she said. Homeless families are also younger on average than poor-housed families, studies have found.

And compared to other kinds of homeless women—those without children and those who have children but whose children live elsewhere—homeless women with children fare better in several ways, studies show. In a study she conducted last year and is now analyzing, for instance, Marjorie Robertson, PhD, senior scientist at the California Pacific Medical Center's Institute of Epidemiology and Behavioral Medicine in Berkeley, and colleagues are finding that homeless women whose children are with them are the most likely to have finished high school and to have the lowest average number of adult arrests of the three groups. In addition, homeless women with children are homeless for the lowest average total days, and are more likely to receive welfare payments and food supplies, the team is finding.

Homeless women with children also attempt suicide less often than single homeless women, other studies have found. And while homeless women with children have lower rates of mental illness than homeless single women, they show greater psychological distress, studies show.

About half of all homeless women are ethnic minorities, and many of those are mothers, according to a policy paper being prepared by a task force of the American Psychological Association's Div. 27 (Community). Robertson's study shows that approximately 28 percent of homeless women have some of their children on the street with them, while another 43 percent have children who aren't with them.

Research has also found "a higher level of recent and past domestic violence in the lives of homeless women," than among the housed poor, Robertson said. "These women are already vulnerable economically." Domestic violence "is just one more element in a living situation they have little control over."

The Div. 27 task force report—and many researchers in the field—conclude that poverty is the root of the increase in homeless families, not individual factors like mental illness or domestic violence.

According to the report, the poorest 20 percent of families became even poorer during the 1980s. That decline was greatest among the poorest single mothers and the poorest young families with children, it states.

Although psychological researchers have accumulated some basic knowledge on homeless families, "we are just now beginning to study them in a way that gives us some insight into their lives," Robertson said.

RECENT STUDIES

In New York, Shinn and colleagues at New York University have been trying to determine what differentiates poor homeless families from other poor families in an attempt to find the precursors to homelessness. Hers is one of the major ongoing studies to date on homeless families.

The team interviewed mostly women in the study, which has two phases. In the first, conducted in 1988, Shinn and James Knickman, PhD, and Beth Weitzman, PhD, of the university's Wagner School of Public Service, collected data on 700 families that requested shelter and 524 housed families on public assistance to detect "early warning signs for homelessness among people on a public-assistance caseload," Shinn said.

Interviewing women directly before they entered shelters let the team examine causes versus consequences of homelessness—something researchers have not previously done because they usually begin their studies after people have been homeless for a while, Shinn noted.

In the second phase, which Shinn and Weitzman are now completing, the two are reinterviewing and examining public records of 915 people from the original group. The purpose is to look at "predictors of mental health and the long-term consequences of homelessness for mothers and children, and to determine what helps people establish stable residences in the community," Shinn said.

SOME PREDICTORS

In analyzing the first set of data, the team found that 44 percent of shelter requesters had never been primary tenants in a residence, compared to 12 percent of the housed poor. More than 80 percent of shelter requesters had dou-

bled up with another family, compared to 38 percent of the housed poor. About 45 percent of shelter requesters had lived with three or more people per bedroom, compared to 26 percent of the housed poor. And 47 percent of shelter requesters experienced two or more serious building problems, such as rats or lack of heat in the winter, compared to 38 percent of the housed poor.

Shelter requesters were also pregnant in greater numbers than their housed counterparts: 34 percent compared to 6 percent. However, family sizes were smaller among shelter requesters, probably a reflection of the fact they were younger on average, Shinn said.

In keeping with other studies, the team found that family factors such as childhood victimization and early separation from the family of origin occurred more often for those requesting shelter than for the public-assistance group, Shinn said.

So far, the study suggests that "our most vulnerable folks are the ones who are becoming homeless," Shinn said.

HOMELESS CHILDREN

Researchers at the Better Homes Foundation—a nonprofit organization established by *Better Homes* magazine in 1988 to study and help the homeless—are comparing homeless women and children to poor housed women and their children, Buckner said. The team plans to collect data on 250 people in each group. Results should be out this fall, he said.

Only a quarter of homeless children were with their mothers. About 10 percent were in foster care; the rest were living with other family members.

As in Shinn's study, the team will try to isolate risk factors for homelessness by looking at differences between the two groups, and will also examine "the immediate consequences of homelessness on women and children," he said.

Like the New York team, the Better Homes researchers hope to untangle which factors cause and which are a

result of homelessness, Buckner said. For instance, past research has "identified group differences between homeless and housed children in developmental delays and behavioral and disciplinary problems," with homeless children exhibiting higher levels of those difficulties than their poor housed peers, he said. "But it's not clear how much those differences are attributable to the experience of homelessness or to coexisting factors such as parental substance abuse, mental health problems and family violence."

As part of a larger study on homeless adults, Robertson, Alex Westerfelt, PhD, and Cheryl Zlotnick, DrPH, interviewed 179 homeless families in Alameda County, Calif. Zlotnik is with the Center for the Vulnerable Child at Children's Hospital in Oakland, Calif.; Westerfelt is with the University of Kansas School of Social Welfare.

To the researchers' surprise, only a quarter of the children of homeless mothers were with their mothers, Robertson said. About 10 percent were in foster care; the rest were living with other family members, she said.

The findings suggest "that [homeless] women with children are having a very hard time keeping their families together," Robertson said. Although she doesn't have hard data on why, "I'm imagining it as a choice the mom is making for her children," she said.

Interviews with some of the women partly confirmed that hypothesis. One woman, for instance, told Robertson that three of her five children were living with the woman's mother, because she thought they would be better off.

In a study of stress levels in homeless and poor housed children, Pamela Reid, PhD, and doctoral students at the City University of New York confirmed other psychologists' findings that there are more similarities than differences between very poor and homeless children, including their feelings about their top stressors.

The team conducted in-depth interviews from 1990 to 1992 with 45 homeless and poor housed second- and fifth-graders. The two groups reported having the same two major concerns that were constant realities in their lives, Reid said: violence and the death and loss of parents, relatives and friends. "A lot of kids were handling death on their own," and reported a high rate of it in their circles, Reid said.

One difference Reid found is that the homeless youngsters reported less peer support than the housed poor children, as one might expect given their living conditions, she said.

Besides their research program, the team set up an after-school program where older homeless and poor housed children tutored the younger ones and the doctoral students tutored the older children, Reid said.

While the programs weren't formally evaluated, the teachers said they "could see changes in the kids who attended," Reid said. The school kept the programs for two years, but cut them this year because of budget problems, she said. Their success underscores the need for "simple, direct interventions that can make a difference," Reid believes.

The Div. 27 report notes that homeless children share a number of common physical and emotional problems, including malnutrition, poor physical development, severe stomach disorders, delayed social and emotional development, ag-gressive and demanding behaviors, sleep disorders, abnormal social fears and speech difficulties. For children older than age 5, more than half need psychiatric help, and their "school performance is consistently below average," the report states.

THE FATHER'S ROLE

While many questions remain about homeless families, homeless fathers remain a research black hole, Shinn commented. "I don't think we have a handle on the men who are involved" with homeless mothers, she said.

One reason so little is known about homeless fathers is that the fathers often are not part of homeless families. For another, "many shelters are not eager to have men around," because of concerns about privacy and heightened levels of aggression and violence, and researchers tend to gather a lot of their data from shelters, she said.

A third reason is methodological, Shinn said. In her New York study, 22 percent of shelter requesters and 6.5 percent of the housed group reported having male partners, she said. "If you believe our data, it says having men around is a big risk factor for homelessness—but I don't believe our data," she said.

Shinn explained that homeless and housed women may not respond truthfully to surveys because those on public assistance stand to lose their benefits if they report they have husbands. Homeless men can't enter some shelters with families unless they can prove they are a woman's legal spouse or a child's biological father, she said.

Shinn hopes to get around those problems by "asking a more sensitive set of questions about women's relationship status" in the second round of her study, she said.

HOW FAMILIES ARE CHANGING . . . FOR THE BETTER!

*Men are better fathers, kids are learning more, moms' enjoy a new respect.
Here, a report that celebrates what's right about our lives*

Betty Holcomb

Betty Holcomb is the Deputy Editor of
WORKING MOTHER.

When Amanda Allison started her first day of kindergarten in Ortonville, Michigan, last September, it was her father, Tim, who held her hand through those first anxious moments.

Later that morning, when the teacher asked Amanda for a statement about her family life to put on display in the classroom, she volunteered, "My daddy plays Barbie with me."

"That quote stayed up on the wall for months," laughs Amanda's mother, Louanne. "For me, it was a sign of how times are changing."

Indeed, Tim Allison is far more involved with his children than the fathers of earlier generations were with theirs. Most days, he drops Amanda at her before-school program and takes her younger sister, Amy, to child care. He often picks Amanda up from Girl Scouts and other after-school activities.

Tim also does the laundry and half of the housecleaning. "He likes everything so neat," says Louanne. "My sisters-in-law are always riding their husbands, saying 'Why can't you be more like him?'"

Tim is so involved with the kids mostly because his job is more flexible than Louanne's. He sells computer software and other communications systems out of their home, so he can adjust his hours to meet the girls' needs. Louanne is a General Motors service engineer, and her schedule doesn't have much give. "Tim has more freedom to set his hours and he's very supportive," says Louanne. "My own parents lived a lot differently. My dad saw his job as bringing home the money, and my mom saw hers as taking care of the kids and the house. Tim and I do both and we find each role very rewarding."

NEW KIND OF FAMILY

The Allisons show just how much family life in America has changed in the last generation—all in response to the growing number of mothers who now work outside the home. Between 1975 and 1993, the number of dual-earner families rose from 42 percent to 64 percent, making them the solid majority today.

"That changes everything. We now have a new family form," says Rosalind Barnett, PhD, a visiting scholar at the Murray Research Center at Radcliffe College and a leading expert on two-career couples. Indeed, Americans have literally reinvented the family, redefining what it means to be a wife or husband, mother or father, daughter or son.

"One of the biggest changes is the idea that men should be active participants in raising children," says Lois Hoffman, professor of psychology at the University of Michigan and one of the top experts on how maternal employment affects families.

"The public dialogue about families today has shifted ground, especially about men," agrees Faye Crosby, professor of psychology at Smith College, who has studied women's changing roles. "Just look at the football player last winter [Houston Oiler David Williams] who missed a game to be at the birth of his child. People were very positive about his decision. Fifteen years ago, they would have asked 'Does this man wear pantyhose?' or 'Is he henpecked?'"

The fact that two thirds of all moms now work outside the home has transformed family life in other ways as well:
- Women's new economic clout has made marriages more egalitarian, offering both men and women more flexibility in the way they pursue careers and family life.
- Many parents are consciously raising their children to have new values about men's and women's roles.
- Day care creates a new social life for both children and parents and sometimes even serves as an extended family.
- Institutions outside the family—the workplace and the schools, in particular—are creating some of the biggest stresses for today's dual-earner couples.

Just as important, many of the dire predictions about mothers entering the workplace have simply not come to pass. Researchers have not found any evidence that the mere fact a mother is employed has negative consequences for her children or her marriage.

Rather, the researchers now say, the effects of Mom's job are complex and vary from family to family. "We are starting to ask far better questions about the strains and gains of men's and women's changing roles," says Nancy Marshall, senior research associate at Wellesley College's Center for Research on Women. "We have begun to look more closely at the *quality* of their various roles.

"When a woman enjoys her work, she's a lot more likely to be happy in life—and so is her family—than if she's at a boring job," says Marshall. "It sounds so simple when you think about it, but it's taken researchers a long time to sort through all our cultural biases and reach some sophisticated answers about family life today."

MEN: ON THE CUSP OF CHANGE

Drop by the Downey household in Bryan, Texas, and you may find Mike Downey cleaning the bathroom. "I hate cleaning bathrooms," Mike confesses. "But I'd rather do that than unload the dishwasher. I get it done quickly and have a sense of accomplishment."

There's no question about it, the experts say, men's behavior has definitely begun to change. "The domestic labor gap between men and women is finally beginning to shrink," says Kathleen Gerson, author of *No Man's Land: Men's Changing Commitments to Family and Work* (Basic Books). And, she adds, that trend is most pronounced in dual-earner households.

The most authoritative studies of how Americans use their time, by John Robinson at the University of Maryland, show that men now do about a third of the domestic work, compared to just 15 percent in 1965. Over the same period, women spent 7.5 fewer hours a week on housework. Most interesting of all, men have begun to do more of the chores traditionally defined as "women's work," such as cooking and cleaning.

A growing number of men are also getting more involved with their children. Many do the daily drop-off or pickup at the day care center, as well as feeding, dressing and bathing the kids.

Just last year, researchers at the U.S. Census Bureau were startled to discover that men are now the *primary* caregiver in one out of every five dual-earner households with preschool children. That indicates "a much higher proportion of fathers have significant child care responsibility than is usually

thought," asserts psychologist Joseph Pleck in an essay in the book *Men, Work, and Family* (Sage Publications).

A number of pressures have prompted this change. First and foremost, women have demanded it, and women's growing economic power has forced men to comply. On average, married women who work full time now earn about 40 percent of the family income; one out of every three makes *more* than her husband. Studies consistently show men with working wives do more around the house. In other words, the fact that so many mothers now bring home the bacon gives them more say about who cleans up after eating it.

"I would never come home after work and do all the child care, laundry and cooking. That just wouldn't be fair and I wouldn't allow it," says Judy Watts, the tax director of General Nutrition Corporation in Pittsburgh, Pennsylvania.

Many younger men have become accustomed to women working outside the home. They are no longer surprised to see women in professional and managerial positions. They have come to respect women's accomplishments and competence in the workplace. They choose wives they see as their equals and concede, if somewhat reluctantly, that it's only fair that men share domestic duties.

Men are also responding to new economic realities in the workplace; their earning power has eroded and so has their job security. "Many men today feel very vulnerable, even rather powerless," says Gerson. "They can no longer lay claim to the breadwinner role."

In response, a significant and growing number of men are looking for a new lifestyle, one that allows them more time for their families. They talk about wanting to be close to their children—closer than they were with their own fathers. (See "Three Kinds of Men.")

Some are finding, just as women have, that it's not easy to strike a balance between job and family duties. "There's new stress for men today," agrees James Levine, head of the Fatherhood Project at the Families and Work Institute in New York City. "They are still as concerned about providing for their families. But now they're also concerned about having a close bond with their kids."

As a consultant to corporations on work and family conflict, Levine runs seminars for workers on how to balance job and household duties. Until recently, he said, few fathers showed up. "Then

Three Kinds of Men

Men today tend to fit roughly into one of three profiles, according to Kathleen Gerson, sociologist and author of *No Man's Land: Men's Changing Commitments to Family and Work* (Basic Books): the new egalitarians who are in the vanguard of change; old-fashioned breadwinners; and those she calls "autonomous" men who flee from family life altogether.

The most interesting group of men—about a third of the 138 men Gerson studied—are more involved with their families. The vast majority of these new egalitarians are married to women who are "work-committed"—that is, who work full time and share household financial decisions.

Some of these men take on child care and housework out of choice; others only at the insistence of their wives. Only a few say they had envisioned such a role for themselves when they were growing up, but most say they find it rewarding because it brings them closer to their children. Gerson found that many of the egalitarian men say it took longer to advance in the workplace or that they had to scale back their careers to make time for their families.

The second group of men, also about a third of her sample, hold fiercely to the role of family provider. "Some even take on a second job just to make sure they are the family's only breadwinner," Gerson says. Nearly half have wives who do not work outside the home at all; only 16 percent are married to women with full-time jobs.

These traditionalists find that life in the 1990s is quite different from life just a few decades ago, however. "They say their wives often get questioned about staying home, and the women's morale is not always so great," says Gerson. "These men know the world around them is changing. Some even express a twinge of guilt over not doing more around the house."

The last group, labeled "autonomous," ran from family commitments. Fewer than half are married and almost all have had troubled relationships with women. Most have no children, and a few are divorced. Many of these men fear being trapped in the role of breadwinner and resent women who would become dependent on them.

What does all this add up to? Gerson believes that egalitarian men are the trendsetters: "Men's patterns are definitely beginning to change, and the most progressive changes are in households where women work."

around 1990, something clicked," he says. "I began to see a lot more men."

Most recently, he has even been invited to run seminars for working fathers by some major corporations, including Bausch & Lomb, Merrill Lynch and American Express, to help men cope with their changing roles.

"Listening to these men talk is like listening to women," Levine adds. "If you changed the pitch of the voices, you couldn't tell the difference. Men open up about how hard it is to be a good parent and advance in the workplace, how stressed they are when a child has a school event and they can't get there."

Other researchers have also noted the distinct change in men's voices and concerns today, especially men who are most involved with their children. In one landmark study, Kyle Pruett, MD, a psychiatrist at Yale University, followed the progress of 17 families in which the fathers were primary caregivers for their children. A few of the men were unemployed; the rest had a wide range of jobs, and their incomes ranged from $7,000 to $125,000. Some stayed home full time; others returned to work after a paternity leave. Virtually all reported feelings identical to those of new mothers, including a reluctance to leave their new baby in anyone else's care—even that of their wives!

Both men and their babies benefit from this sort of attachment, studies show. Dads feel more competent and satisfied in their parental role, and the children thrive. Mike Downey, who took a six-week paternity leave after his daughter, Chelsea, was born three years ago, is typical. "I wouldn't trade being Chelsea's dad for anything," he says. "It's easily the most important role in my life." He has remained closely involved with his child, sharing her daily care. "I know her friends at day care, her toys, her books, her movies. I know the way she likes to have the socks on her feet. I know what she means when she's pointing at something," Mike says proudly.

Of course, most women know that men like Mike are far from the norm. He is especially noteworthy because he shares not only child care, but also the housework. "Mike is the kind of man other men hate," his wife, Rebecca, laughs. Indeed, if the studies show that most men are now doing a third of the household chores, women are still doing twice as much. Women still retain the title of domestic manager, and often feel they are doing even more than that. (See "The Chores That Men Do.")

"I go around with lists in my head all the time. I usually think of things way in

advance. It doesn't occur to John that it's time for our daughter to get a haircut or have her fingernails trimmed," says Caroline Thomson, a secretary at the University of Northern Iowa in Cedar Falls. "When a notice comes home from school, he doesn't always read it. It's as if it's written only for me," she says. "Sometimes that baffles me."

Still, Caroline adds, things are changing at her house. She can vividly recall the day, about three years ago, when John volunteered to pitch in more around the house. "I was working full time, and I had responsibility for Ellen and for all the housework and errands," she says. "I was exhausted, so we sat down and had a big talk.

"John finally said, 'Just tell me the job you hate the most and I'll do it.' I told him the grocery shopping," she says. "Since then, she adds triumphantly, she has rarely set foot in a grocery store.

About two years ago, John quit his job as a recording engineer in a local music studio. "He was putting in fifty or sixty hours a week and felt he was missing out on his family," she says. Now he runs a home-based business repairing amplifiers and watches Ellen all day. "There's a major improvement in men today," Caroline says, "although I sometimes think it will be another two generations before everything is fifty-fifty."

Sociologists and psychologists who study the family concede that progress is slow. "This is an evolution, not a revolution," says James Levine. "We're talking about changing basic values. This change is happening gradually over a number of years, as it has for women."

MODERN MARRIAGE: I'M HAPPY WHEN YOU'RE HAPPY

Change comes so slowly because it takes so much work. Marriage has become one long negotiation, as couples hammer out new roles and responsibilities. Couples find themselves stumbling over the minutiae of daily life, haggling over who will do the dishes or pick up the kids.

"Neither of us does anything without talking to the other about how it's going to impact the family," says Kristen Storey, a training coordinator in the human resources department at the University of Michigan in Ann Arbor. Her husband, David, works as a chef in a local restaurant during the week and a tow-truck driver one or two nights on the weekend. "We have to talk all the time to see how our schedules are going to work

and to make sure we can all reconnect and have family time," she says. "We have to work like a team."

Of course, it's not always that easy to work like a team, especially when a man's and a woman's expectations about the division of domestic labor do not match. "We had to go into marriage counseling over these issues," says Laura Koenig, an occupational therapist in Appleton, Wisconsin. "My husband never used to take responsibility for the kids. He saw it as my job, and only helped if I asked him to. If he gave them a bath, he'd say he did it for me. If he put on their pajamas, he'd say he did it for me."

He'd also arrive home from work and feel free to read a newspaper or watch television, even if the kids needed something or dinner was yet to be prepared.

Finally, she says, "I blew up. I asked him, 'Why is it always my job? Don't you

---

The Chores That Men Do

Experts say men are beginning to do more around the house, even though they still lag far behind women. Here's a rundown from a recent survey of men's behavior.

The Part Men Say They Play

Domestic Chores

Grocery shopping	28%
Doing the dishes	24%
Vacuuming the house	24%
Cooking meals	19%
Washing floors	17%
Doing the laundry	13%

Caring For Children

Disciplining the children	46%
Helping the children with their homework	33%
Dealing with the children's schools	32%
Planning the meals children eat	16%

Miscellaneous

Doing household repairs	79%
Paying bills	40%
Making social plans	39%
Caring for elderly parents	35%

SOURCE: "GREAT SEXPECTATIONS," D'ARCY MASIUS BENTON & BOWLES

enjoy these children? Aren't they your children, too?'" When she threatened separation, she says, "he realized I was serious about these issues, and we went into counseling."

Many discussions in therapy helped the Koenigs work out more equity at home. "We're happier than ever now. He began to understand my frustration and to see that he had to be more involved at home," she says. "He will now take the initiative to have dinner on the table or put on the children's pajamas."

Clinical therapists say it's not surprising that many two-career couples have rocky moments. "They struggle with issues of competition with each other in their careers, and with questions about gender roles at home," says Lisa Silberstein, author of *Dual-Career Marriage: A System in Transition* (Lawrence Erlbaum) and a clinical psychologist in New Haven, Connecticut. "Women's foray into the world of work has dramatically changed the terms of marriage."

As a result, Silberstein and other experts say, success in marriage depends largely on two things: The extent to which couples share expectations and their ability to talk about these issues. "They need to keep the issues between them on the table," Silberstein says, "or the marriage will be in jeopardy."

Yet if marriage today is a demanding proposition, it also provides ample rewards. Studies show that dual-career couples who share family responsibilities have the most successful marriages. Such a relationship makes both husband and wife feel valued and supported, and allows a new kind of intimacy, according to sociologist Pepper Schwartz, who has conducted broad surveys of marriage in America. "Their mutual friendship is the most satisfying part of their lives," says Schwartz in her new book, *Peer Marriage* (The Free Press).

A marriage of equals also allows couples to tailor their marriage to their own strengths. Men no longer have to be the family's sole breadwinner, with everyone depending on them for financial security. And women no longer need to look to men for financial security. Couples can create the arrangements that best suit their individual abilities and interests.

"I've always been the primary breadwinner, and now I'm the only one," says Melissa Stevens, a marketing executive at Borland International in Scotts Valley, California. She has supported the family for several years, while her husband, Russell, studies to be a nurse.

"I like my job and I've always been more aggressive than my husband," says Melissa. Russell, who was working as a salesman in a sporting-equipment store, quit his job to stay home with their first child, Jeanne. The decision made perfect sense for both of them. "He wasn't really happy with his job and he was earning less than I was," Melissa recalls. "And Jeanne was a preemie, very vulnerable. We both wanted someone home with her until she was at least a year old. We decided Russell would stay home for a year, then either find another job or go back to school to get a new career."

When Jeanne was a year old, the couple entrusted her to a family day care provider and Russell began school. He has three more years until he gets his degree. "It's worth it to me that he'll be able to do something he likes when he gets out of school," Melissa says.

When asked if married life had turned out the way she had planned it, she laughs. "I suppose I thought I would have a husband who supported me. My work would be just for fun and extra income." Then she adds, "But I can see now that I never would have been happy with a more traditional marriage. Neither would Russell. We are very happy this way because he is so involved with our kids and I enjoy what I do."

NEW WAYS TO RAISE KIDS

Perhaps it is because men and women have had to wrestle with their own roles so much that they hope to change things for the next generation. Many are working hard, in fact, to raise kids who don't pigeonhole people by sex.

"Our boys see both of us working outside the home and sharing things at home. They see Dad doing the wash. I think that's very important nowadays. I don't want my boys to be raised to think women do all the cooking and cleaning," says Barbara Brazil, a human resources assistant for the Kent, Washington, school district.

Jill Richardson, a product manager for a division of AT&T in Dayton, Ohio, and the mother of two young boys, finds herself constantly evaluating her behavior to make sure she doesn't send the wrong messages. "I remember once when the vacuum broke the first thing I did was say 'Oh, we'll wait until Daddy gets home to take a look at it.' But then I thought, I know as much about vacuum cleaners as he does. I can fix this. And I did," she says. "I want to show the boys how capable women can be."

Working moms with daughters hope to instill aspirations and pride. "I'm glad my daughter sees me enjoying a job," says Caroline Thomson, the secretary at the University of Northern Iowa. "It may not be the loftiest career, but I get great satisfaction from it. It makes me a very happy person. I hope it shows Ellen that she can have something she loves to do when she grows up."

Many parents also encourage their children to break sex barriers in school. The number of high-school girls playing in organized sports has mushroomed from 4 percent in 1971 to over 30 percent in 1991, according to the Women's Sports Foundation. The number of boys signing up for home economics classes has increased from 4.2 percent in 1968 to better than 40 percent today.

Research does show that kids raised with such values turn out differently. Girls of employed mothers, for example, are more likely to do well in school and pursue careers. Girls and boys with involved fathers turn out to be more flexible about gender roles in adulthood.

THE DAY CARE DIFFERENCE

Melissa Stevens, the marketing executive from Scotts Valley, California, spends a lot of time talking with her good friend Audrey Atkins. "We're very close, and we talk about our children and our husbands," Melissa says. The Christmas before last, the two families spent the day together. "My son was born on December twenty-second, and I was in no shape to do anything for the holidays, so Audrey had us over."

Audrey is not just a good friend, however; she is also the day care provider for the Stevens family. They met shortly after Melissa had her first child four years ago. Now both of the Stevens children spend their days at the Atkins house, a family day care home.

"Our children are like brothers and sisters," says Melissa, "and they have a wonderful time here. They get lots of attention, just as they would at home."

With women flooding the workplace, child care has become an integral part of today's family life. The number of children in child care quadrupled between 1976 and 1990, according to a report from the Committee for Economic Development. For many moms, the day care center or family day care home now serves as the new community, providing the sorts of relationships that used to be forged over the backyard fence.

"In the last year, we've gotten really, really close to families of other toddlers at the center," says Kristen Storey, the University of Michigan training coordinator. "Our children play together, and we even call each other in a pinch to drop off or pick up each other's kids. Some mothers even regard this situation as extended family."

Families also turn to child care centers for new kinds of services. "I have to get out of the house at seven-thirty, which would be a nightmare without our day care center," says Jill Richardson, the AT&T manager from Dayton. Both her sons, four-year-old Matthew and six-year-old Andy, attend a local KinderCare center. They both get breakfast, and Kinder-Care then buses the older one to kindergarten. Many chains and independent centers now serve breakfast and offer before- and after-school programs. Just last year, KinderCare added amenities such as UPS pickups and frozen-dinner orders at many of its centers around the country. Children's World Learning Centers tailors its services to requests made by parents.

And many moms believe that high-quality care offers significant benefits to their children. The overwhelming majority of 1,700 working mothers polled last year by WORKING MOTHER and the Child Care Action Campaign say their children have valuable educational experiences in child care.

"Chelsea learns a lot just by being around other kids. She has great social skills and has learned how to get along with other kids," says Rebecca Downey, whose daughter goes to a private day care center. Rebecca, a communications specialist in human resources at Texas A&M University, says the stimulating environment has also spurred Chelsea's cognitive and emotional growth: "Even my parents, who questioned my decision to return to work, say that day care is good for Chelsea."

Many also believe early-childhood programs help prepare their kids for school. "My older son knew how to write his name. He knew his numbers, letters, shapes. He had been on field trips and done lots of artsy-craftsy projects," says Jill Richardson. "He was real outgoing and ready for kindergarten. I think that's because of his day care experiences."

FAMILY TIME COMES FIRST

But today's working moms also say that child care acts as an enriching supplement to and not a substitute for their own attention. "Even though we work full time, we make sure that the kids don't miss out on much," says Barbara Brazil of Kent, Washington. "I use a lot of my time off for school activities, and my husband gets off work early so he can usually take our older son to soccer and T-ball practices."

In fact, she adds, "I guess I'm much more involved than my mother was. In extracurricular activities, I'm there for the kids no matter what." How does she do it? "When I have extra time, I spend it with the kids, not cleaning the house. My husband and I don't do much besides work and be with the kids."

Barbara's family is typical of today's dual-earner household. Women spend less time on housework and give up their own leisure to be with their kids, according to several studies. One, by Steven Nock and P.W. Kingston at the University of Virginia, looked at 226 couples and concluded that the biggest difference between families who had two earners and those with only one was that the dual-earner parents had less free time and cut corners on homemaking.

A recent study by W. Keith Bryant, PhD, of Cornell University and Cathleen Zick, PhD, of the University of Utah showed that married working moms spent as much time as stay-at-home moms in direct child care such as bathing, dressing and supervising homework—an average of 10,500 hours when raising two kids to the age of 18.

Many moms also say they work hard to retain the rituals that strengthen family bonds. "The family dinner is one thing we're not willing to give up, no matter how busy we are," says Judy Watts, the tax director of General Nutrition in Pittsburgh. Luckily for Judy, her husband is usually home in time to have supper waiting on the table. "We really enjoy our time together, and our three-year-old daughter, Emma, just revels in our attention at the end of the day."

It takes creative strategies and inventions like the microwave to make that possible, of course. "There are so many healthy choices at the store now that make it possible to get dinner on the table fast. You can stop at a salad bar or pick up lettuce in a bag, already prepared. A baked potato can cook quickly

Single Moms: A Closer Look

By now, we are all too familiar with this statistic: Eight million American families are now headed by single moms. Most have also heard the litany of ills associated with such families: poverty, drug abuse and crime. Politicians from Dan Quayle to Daniel Patrick Moynihan have linked single-parent households with the breakdown of society.

"We are stereotyped as unique, unpleasant and unfortunate," says Andrea Engber, editor of SingleMOTHER, the newsletter of the National Organization of Single Mothers.

Yet a close look at the data tells a more complicated story. "Single-parent families are as diverse—and as similar—as any other kind of family. We're large and small, demonstrative and reserved, neat and sloppy, even rich and maybe (sometimes!) broke," write Marge Kennedy and Janet Spencer King in The Single-Parent Family: Living Happily in a Changing World (Crown Publishers).

Indeed, census figures show that nearly 400,000 families headed by women now have incomes of $50,000 or more. Another 1.5 million are living on $30,000 or more.

It's certainly true that women's earnings typically lag behind men's, so that most women raising kids alone have a much tougher time making ends meet. The latest figures show that the median income of a female-headed household with kids under 18 was just $13,000, compared to $24,000 for male-headed households and $43,000 for dual-earner families.

But when all things are equal—when a single mom has a decent job and is basically happy with her life, her children fare just as well as those from other families, according to authorities on single-parent families.

Researchers at Temple University have found no behavioral differences between kids raised by single mothers or by two parents, as long as the single mom was not overly stressed. (Studies show that kids raised by two parents are also negatively affected when one parent is depressed.)

In the end, then, each family must be looked at individually. "I know lots of single moms are very creative and resourceful," says Engber. "We come to depend on ourselves more and that can be a very positive experience. We learn some skills that we might not have had to." She mentions women who have learned to do plumbing, car repair and home maintenance. "That sort of thing makes you feel good about yourself," she says.

in the microwave," says Jill Richardson. "That makes it possible for us to eat together five times a week at home."

A study conducted by the Massachusetts Mutual Life Insurance Company of 702 parents with kids between the ages of three and 12 revealed that "working parents will brave rush hours and pack themselves on commuter trains to make it home by dinnertime an average of six nights a week."

Moms also say that they find time just to have fun. "We go for walks together. We go paddle-boating and fishing. We like to rent videos, and we have a family ritual of watching *America's Funniest Home Videos* every week together," says Louanne Allison, the working mother from Michigan who shares child care with her husband, Tim.

And today's parents report that their biggest satisfaction is the same one enjoyed by previous generations. "My biggest pleasure is just watching my kids grow. At every stage—the first smile, the first steps—I say to my husband, 'This is so great,'" says Jill Richardson. "But then they go to the next stage and I say 'Oh, this is so great too!'"

That's a good sign about the health of today's families, according to Nancy Marshall of the Center for Research on Women at Wellesley College. One of the biggest predictors for parental happiness is simply taking pleasure in watching your child develop.

New Sources of Family Stress

Of course, it would be naive and unrealistic to say that today's families aren't facing some extraordinary stresses—caused in large part by the fact that society hasn't caught up to their lifestyle yet. The majority of today's workplaces, for example, still do not offer flexible schedules to employees. Most schools are run as if Mom is still at home.

This means parents are sometimes expected to be two places at once. Leshbia Morones, mother of five, couldn't drop her children off at school before eight a.m., which often meant she was five minutes late to work. In response, her employer, the California Department of Motor Vehicles, docked her pay. Morones challenged the pay cut, and a state administrative judge ruled that "inadequate child care and inadequate public transportation" had caused her tardiness. Nonetheless, the state personnel board overruled the judge and cut her pay.

Work schedules can wreak even more serious havoc on family life. Hundreds of thousands of postal workers, for example, many of them single mothers, start night shifts at 11 p.m. Others work a swing shift, from 10 p.m. to six a.m.

"I hear stories about mothers faced with waking their kids up at night to take them to a day care center to sleep," says Phil Tabbita of the American Postal Workers Union. "Then they may have to wake them up at five a.m., take them home to go back to sleep and then wake them up again to go to school."

The children of school bus drivers, grocery clerks and nurses are subjected to equally disruptive schedules. "I have a dispatcher who works for the city transportation center who must drop off his eight-year-old at three-thirty a.m. every day so he can get to work on time," says Careth Reid, director of the Whitney Young Child Development Center in San Francisco, one of the few centers that stay open round the clock in that city. Of the 250 children in her center, about 20 must be there during the evening or night shift. Many parents, such as the grocery clerks, also have their schedules changed from week to week, or even from day to day, which makes it hard to find child care at all.

Inflexible schedules are one of the top sources of stress for working parents today, according to a major study of the work force conducted by the Families and Work Institute last year. Having to put in overtime on hourly jobs or being required to work more than 40 hours a week in a managerial position also ranked high on the stress charts for parents with children under the age of 18.

Other research has also found that rigid job schedules are a key source of parental stress. "Families have adjusted about as far as they can to fit the needs of the workplace. In the future, the workplace will have to adapt to changing families for employees to be productive. This will mean providing lots more flexibility to get work done," says Fran Rodgers, president of Work/Family Directions, one of the nation's leading experts on work/family issues.

The shortage of high-quality, affordable child care also affects the day-to-day lives of today's families. No one has exact figures, but there are plenty of indications that the problem is serious: The Families and Work Institute reports that it takes parents an average of five weeks to find child care. Parents in focus groups conducted for the Child Care Action Campaign said they tried two or three different arrangements before they found one they were comfortable with. A recent study on the status of children in Florida revealed that 200,000 kids under the age of nine spend at least two hours alone each day.

Infant care is particularly hard to find. Many centers do not take children less than six months old even though employers often require that a woman be back on the job much sooner. A study of day care centers around the country for the U.S. Department of Education found that only 10 percent had openings for children under the age of one.

Many parents also say that they cannot afford to pay for the best care, even when it is available. Infant care in some of the nation's best centers runs to $1,100 a month—an amount that for most families is well out of reach.

Child care costs most parents about $3,100 a year, or about 10 percent of their income. Those earning under $15,000 a year lay out 23 percent.

When families are forced to compromise the safety of their children, they are, not surprisingly, quite distressed. Mothers are more likely to be anxious or depressed if they are worried about their children's care, according to a study of 300 dual-earner couples conducted by Wellesley's Center for Research on Women. Men were likely to have the same feelings, if they were involved in the daily care of their children.

"If people really wanted to improve family life today," says Nancy Marshall, one of the researchers, "they would give serious attention to seeing how our society can improve child care."

They've Seen the Future and They Like It

Some institutions are beginning to change, of course. The number of schools with before- and after-care programs is growing. New federal money for child care has spurred many states to improve both the quality and quantity of child care since 1990. And by some accounts, about a third of the nation's largest employers now offer flextime.

With the proper kind of support, working moms say that family life is definitely changing for the better. "Mike and I have a great relationship," says Rebecca Downey. "And we share everything about Chelsea. He knows just as much about her as I do. We think she's better off for having two involved parents instead of just one. And I enjoy my career. What could be better?"

Educational Practices

- **Preschool and Primary Programs (Articles 17–22)**
- **Assessment and Evaluation (Articles 23–25)**

Educational practices with young children seem to be always changing, yet always the same. For any educational practice to be considered good practice, it must stem from a corresponding philosophy. The search for exactly what is good practice has resulted today in two extremes in early childhood education. One approach is traditional, with skill and drill methods, apparent structure, and time on task. Its underlying philosophy is psychometric. The other approach is developmentally appropriate, with the curriculum matched to children's abilities and freedom of choice. Supporting this practice is progressive philosophy.

How does a person recognize good practice? Basically, look for action in the center or classroom. *Appropriate practice is children in action.* Children are busy constructing with blocks, working puzzles, and creating with paintbrushes. They invent, cook, and compose throughout the day. *Appropriate practice is teachers in action.* Teachers are busy holding conversations, guiding activities, and questioning children. They observe, draw conclusions, plan, and vary the activities throughout the day. Appropriate practice goes beyond a list of do's and don'ts, because the learning environment of busy people is constantly in flux. Practice should be based on broad developmental principles, but designed within the context of a particular program. This is the emphasis of Marjorie Kostelnik's article, "Recognizing the Essentials of Developmentally Appropriate Practice."

Appropriate practice means teaching children, not curriculum. Sandra Stone's article, "Strategies for Teaching

Children in Multiage Classrooms," tackles ways to individualize teaching for groups of children who stay with the same teacher for several years. A vital element of making multiage classrooms work is to use a process approach to learning, with plenty of opportunities for open-ended projects based on integrated curriculum. To accomplish this approach, the teacher takes on the role of learning facilitator. Such a flexible role allows children to engage in planning and carrying out their learning activities. Several articles in this unit provide strategies for adapting learning to all children.

An essential of appropriate practice is authentic assessment of children's progress. The articles in the second part of this unit address better assessment practices. As Lorrie Shepard points out in "The Challenges of Assessing Young Children Appropriately," testing should occur only when it is used for beneficial results. So, more inclusive techniques that are integrated with the curriculum become necessary. Teachers find it useful to develop skills in a variety of observational formats that can be carried out within the context of the program. One technique currently being used by teachers is the assessment portfolio, which is a way to archive the work done by children. Keeping periodic records of children's development along with their work aligns well with appropriate practice. This variety of assessment methods provides a much broader picture of children's performance than is available in programs that are test-driven. The unit concludes with John O'Neil's investigation of the controversial process of assessing learning out-

comes. Schools moving to outcome-based education (OBE) are grappling with ways to define learner outcomes and align programs with standards of performance. "Aiming for New Outcomes: The Promise and the Reality" gives details of different interpretations that keep OBE from being implemented.

Authentic appropriate practice, based on children's development, has no shortcuts and cannot be trivialized. Putting thought and planning and process behind the words involves using knowledge of child development to inform caregiving decisions and curriculum choices. By working out specifics of routines and procedures, curriculum, and assessment suitable for young children, the early childhood professional strengthens skills in decision making. This is a crucial task for a teacher interested in developmentally appropriate practice.

Looking Ahead: Challenge Questions

What does "learning by doing" mean? Give a specific example of something you learned by doing.

Before reading the article "Fourth-Grade Slump: The Cause and Cure," consider reasons why many bright, achieving primary-grade children have difficulty making the transition to upper grades.

Comment on the idea that there are multiple ways of being intelligent.

Other than by testing, how can teachers of young children assess progress?

Bringing the DAP Message to Kindergarten and Primary Teachers

Gaye Gronlund

Gaye Gronlund, M.A., is an early child-hood education consultant in Indianapolis and works with school and district agencies around the country. She is a national faculty member for the Work Sampling System developed by the Assessment Project at the University of Michigan.

> **Children learn by doing, through active engagement. Many adults can identify with this because they see that they also learn in this way.**

M y work as an early childhood education consultant gives me the opportunity to interact with kindergarten and primary teachers around the country. In those interactions I am often introducing NAEYC's *Developmentally Appropriate Practice* (DAP) (Bredekamp 1987) and explaining how those practices are effective with 5- through 8-year-olds.

I have learned that teachers really appreciate pictures of practice in action, whether those pictures be video, slides, or demonstrations that they can observe and then participate in themselves. But, along with those pictures must be some philosophical foundation, some structure that provides the reasons and justifications for the recommended choices to make with children. Highlighting three key elements in DAP has helped me build this foundation for kindergarten and primary teachers. These key elements have been the lightbulbs of understanding for many—the "Ahas" as they integrate their own extensive knowledge of children's learning with the newer ideas in *Developmentally Appropriate Practice.*

The first key element

The first key element has been the notion that *children learn by doing, through active engagement.* Many adults can identify with this element because they see that they also learn this way. I use the example of someone trying to show you how to use the copy machine. You stand off to the side and listen, but finally, in frustration say, "Let *me* do it!" And, then, you exclaim, "Oh . . . now I get it!" This story is greeted with warm laughter as teachers recognize themselves in familiar situations.

When we make the connection to children and think of *all* or at least most of their learning occurring through active participation, folks really stop and pause. How much time in their classrooms is spent on sitting and listening or on paper-and-pencil skill and drill, as opposed to exploring and discovering, organizing and discussing, building and creating, questioning and thinking, reading and writing, measuring and computing, and so on? I often introduce teachers to several classroom schedules that illustrate using blocks of time for active learning (David Birchfield's from the video by NCREL [1992], Selma Wassermann [1990], the Indiana Department of Education [1989]) for them to consider and compare to their own daily routines.

Engagement is also a critical part of an active learning environment. Asking teachers if they know when their children are engaged brings forth interesting responses. Many describe the children's eyes—when they're engaged, their eyes "sparkle," "there's a fire for learning." When not engaged, those same eyes "glaze over" or "stare into space." Measuring again the time they estimate children are excited about learning in their classrooms often does cause folks to think seriously about the teaching approaches they are using.

Some "Yes . . . buts" often are raised at this point in discussions:

"But I have so much curriculum to cover."

"But I'm accountable to the state-mandated standardized tests given for one week in March."

"But it's not my job to entertain kids."

"Kids have to learn this is the *real* world where work is hard, not fun."

These are some very serious concerns on the part of teachers. As a facilitator, I have found no perfect response to any of them. However, when I see a group begin to ask these difficult questions, I get excited. Their anxiety indicates to me that they are seriously considering these new ideas. I see the rightness of DAP as its match to children. And, I believe that most kindergarten and primary teachers are folks who care deeply about children. However, in my opinion, teachers have concluded that they are

From *Young Children*, July 1995, pp. 4-13. © 1995 by the National Association for the Education of Young Children. Reprinted by permission.

only accountable to parents, the school district administration, and the community. They receive messages constantly that reinforce that idea. But the most important people in the whole process have been left out of the accountability picture—*the children!*

When we discuss active learning and engagement, both such easily measurable and observable factors in a classroom, we bring the children back into the picture. Teachers who care deeply about young children want to do right by them as well as be accountable to the other elements of public education. My job as a consultant is to help them combine new ideas with their anxiety-provoking concerns, blending the very-real demands that are placed upon them day in and day out with the understanding of how children learn best.

I propose that kindergarten and primary teachers' vision is to help children learn, grow, and develop to their full potential. In all of the groups with whom I have worked, this vision has been agreed upon. But asking teachers to help children in active learning environments in which children are engaged in exploration and discovery is frightening.

"Where do I start?"

"What do my lesson plans look like?"

"How do I know they're learning anything?"

"Won't it be chaos?"

"What will others (colleagues, parents, administrators) think?"

These questions evidence a cry for the skills needed to set up and manage a DAP classroom.

My excitement, then, as a facilitator, when I see this anxiety, is that I have a clear directive from the group: "Give me the skills I need to use these teaching practices, so I can be accountable to the children I care about as well." I know we've got a good beginning and a clear direction from here.

The second key element

The second key element that I have found successful with kindergarten and primary teachers is introducing the idea of *play with intent and purpose.* Those of us who have been in the field of early childhood education for awhile have heard the criticisms, "Oh, all they do in *that* classroom is play; they don't learn anything" or "That's a play-based curriculum, not an academic one." We have had to become excellent communicators to explain the value of learning through play to others who did not evaluate children's active involvement with the same understandings we did. Elizabeth Jones and Gretchen Reynolds give the following explanation of the value of play:

Young children ... play in order to find their way around in what is for them the foreign country of adults, to master its daily scripts .... Pretending enables children to represent problems and practice solving them, to ask questions and learn about the world in terms they can understand. Play is self-motivated practice in meaning-making; its themes are repeated over and over until the child is satisfied that she's got *this* figured out. In the process, she is acquiring learning strategies, knowledge, and skills. Issues of right and wrong arise as children negotiate with each other and as adults mediate. Shapes, colors, and numbers are embedded in the properties of dishes and blocks, puzzles and paints .... (1992, 10)

Teachers who are considering DAP in their classrooms are anxious about those criticisms. They say, "At least when I'm teaching the whole group from the teacher's manual, I know I've *covered* the material I'm supposed to for *all* the children" [emphasis theirs]. I often ask if I may change the emphasis on that statement and note *who* did the covering—"I know *I've* covered the material"—and also point out the meaning of *cover* as opposed to *uncover* or *discover.* The final question I pose is, "How do you know *all* of the children understand or grasp the material?"

Folks often admit they don't know for sure. Observing a group of passive learners as one gives new information does not yield total assurance that all grasped the concepts. When teachers think in these terms, the "letting go" involved in running an active learning environment does not seem quite so frightening. In ad-

dition, when children are engaged in learning by doing, they can demonstrate their new understanding in so many different ways: sorting, organizing, grouping, naming, identifying, questioning, measuring, computing, reading, recording, creating, applying, and so on.

Selma Wassermann's book *Serious Players in the Primary Classroom* has been an invaluable tool to me in moving teachers beyond the notion of DAP as "just play." She states, "It is one thing to believe in the importance of play but another to consider how play may help stimulate intellectual development in the classroom" (1990, xi). She describes play as purposeful engagement in inquiries that children have invented. The defining aspect of such play is that it's open-ended. There are many potential ways to use the materials that teacher and/or child have chosen. Wassermann

designs "Inquiry Studies" to focus children's investigative play in certain ways. But the teacher-designed focus still allows for a variety of uses of the materials, as well as conclusions. The play activity, says Wassermann, "should not set narrow parameters that

Introduce teachers to the idea of play with intent and purpose.

limit the play, nor should it lead pupils to 'correct answers'. . . . A good indicator of the effectiveness of the play activity is the extent to which it stimulates children's investigations" (1990, 100). Through careful planning and questioning techniques before, during, and after the child's involvement, she defines the intent and purpose for the child, allows him to add to that intent and purpose with his own

interests and creative ideas, and assesses the child's learning through observing his interaction with the materials and answers to debriefing questions.

A very simple example of a language arts inquiry study suggested by Wassermann (1990) contrasts beautifully with a common approach to teaching children to recognize rhyming words. Many of us, myself included, have spent hours creating "word-family wheels" with cute animals or figures as the base for the wheel ("Dog" for the "og" family; "Cat" for the "at" family, and so on). Children sit with the wheel, turning it, changing the initial consonant to form a new word in the family, and reading the words as they go.

Wassermann's Inquiry Study allows children to move to higher levels of learning. She suggests that the teacher write individual words of many rhyming families on index cards and give them to the children with the question, "How can you organize these word cards?" Children then demonstrate their understanding of a

© The Growth Program

© The Growth Program

variety of concepts. One child may group by initial consonants, another by rhyming words. Further questioning by the teacher, such as "Are there other ways?" or even directive questioning, "Can you group them by rhyming word families?" can help define the intent and purpose and assist the teacher in the assessment of children's understanding.

But the beauty of the Inquiry Study, as opposed to the rhyming-word wheels, is the active involvement of the child in setting up the actual learning for herself. The child with the wheel is playing a far more passive role

© BmPorter/Don Franklin

Figure 1. Framework-Based Problems for Nurturing and Assessing Place Value Understanding

	Pre-place value Level 1-1	Initial place value Level 1-2	Extended place value 1 Level 2-1	Extended place value 2 Level 2-2
Counting	We found 9 meatballs on the grass and 2 on the sidewalk. How many meatballs did we find?	After a big storm, meatballs were packed in bags of 10. There were 6 bags, 2 extra. How many? Add 1 more bag. How many now?	On Monday it rained 33 meatballs in Henry's yard. On Tuesday it rained 30 more. How many then?	By the end of the week we had 172 meatballs. Over the weekend we found 210 more. How many then?
Partitioning	There are 10 biscuits hidden in these 2 bags. How many could be in each bag?	You can buy loose biscuits or bags of 10. We need 68 for a party. How could they be bought?	I need 87 biscuits for a party. I have 64. How many more are needed?	The 4-H group made 134 biscuits. They need 260. How many still need to be made?
Grouping	Here are 5 brussels sprouts (cubes in the open hand). Take a handful of your own. About how many? Count them. How could you place them to make it quick and easy for me to count?	Enter the festival contest. Pick up 2 handfuls of brussels sprouts (cubes). About how many? Count them. How could you place them to make it quick and easy for me to count?	Grandma wants to buy some of the brussels sprouts that rained last night. This bag is 25¢; the bigger one is 38¢. Grandma only has 70¢. Does she have enough for both? How do you know?	The General Store of Chewandswallow has 2 baskets for brussels sprouts. One holds 175, the other 150. Henry wants to buy 330 for a party. Will the 2 baskets be enough? How do you know?
Number relationships	Spin the wheel for the number of pancakes you'll take from the roof. Tell how many more or less than 5(10) that number is.	At the pancake breakfast, Henry wrote the numbers between 60 and 69. Help him reverse the digits and tell which of the numbers becomes bigger, gets smaller.	At the Maple Syrup Festival, Grandpa picked 2 numbers from a 100s Chart and added them. Help him reverse the digits of the 2 numbers and add again. Which sum is greater?	The pancake cook posed a riddle. Write a number so that when you • reverse the digits and • add to the first number, • the sum is between 25 and 50.

Note: All problems are based on the story Cloudy with a Chance of Meatballs *(Barrett 1978), which is read prior to the problem solving.*

than the one involved in the Inquiry Study. Defining as many open-ended, higher-learning-level activities in a variety of curricular areas is really helpful to kindergarten and primary teachers in allaying their concerns about setting up an active learning environment and planning accordingly.

The third key element

The third key element that has really helped many teachers embrace DAP more enthusiastically has been the idea of *moving from the simple to the complex* in planning for learning in active and engaging ways. The idea of play with intent and purpose instead of "just play" leads itself to the idea that children's learning through play will move along a continuum from simpler understanding to ever-increasing complexity. Therefore, teachers must plan activities that will help children move along this continuum, realizing that each child will do so at his own pace. In *Dimensions of Teaching–Learning Environments*, Jones and Prescott define different ways of complicating learning through the environment and teacher behaviors: "A simple environment contributes to children's focus on completion of closed tasks . . . . A complex environment contributes to innovation and the development of imagination" (1984, 33). Wassermann says the same thing in a different way: "The richer the play, the more potential it has for concept development, creative and investigative opportunities, and the examination of issues of substance" (1990, 27).

Instead of textbook writers and publishers determining scope and sequence, developmentally appropriate kindergarten and primary teachers do so themselves to truly meet the individual as well as the age-appropriate needs of the children from year to year. Jones and Pres-

cott's continuum idea helps folks see that within a classroom one can plan for children's learning to occur at different points on a continuum from simple to complex. A teacher must constantly think of varying learning behaviors that build toward understanding a concept. He must find ways to develop behaviors that demonstrate understanding and ways a child can apply that knowledge with ever-increasing complexity and sophistication.

An example of this movement from simple to complex in planning for primary students can be found in the teaching of place value in first, second, and third grades. Constance Kamii (1985) and others have cited numerous research studies that indicate that primary children are *not* grasping the concept of place value; only 42% of third graders studied demonstrated understanding of numeral placement (Jones & Thornton 1993). Kamii advocates not teaching place value at all but posing situations in which children will discover it for themselves. She emphasizes the simpler concept of number sense as being essential before moving on to understanding place value. Jones and Thornton (1993) even break down the development of number sense into

© The Growth Program

four levels that build toward understanding of place value (Figure 1). Both Kamii and Jones and Thornton suggest active learning opportunities, such as games with playing cards and manipulatives and integrated units related to children's literature and classroom problem solving (e.g., planning for a party).

One second-grade teacher told me that she realized she had been moving much too fast on place value in her class. She had been concentrating her efforts on numerical representation of addition and subtraction problems that required trading to and

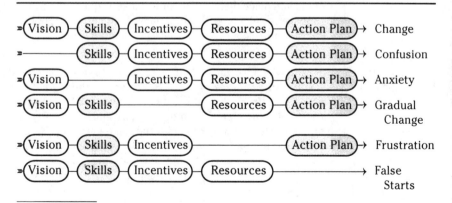

Figure 2. **Managing Complex Change**

Vision	Skills	Incentives	Resources	Action Plan	→ Change
	Skills	Incentives	Resources	Action Plan	→ Confusion
Vision		Incentives	Resources	Action Plan	→ Anxiety
Vision	Skills		Resources	Action Plan	→ Gradual Change
Vision	Skills	Incentives		Action Plan	→ Frustration
Vision	Skills	Incentives	Resources		→ False Starts

Reprinted with permission of the Houston-based American Productivity & Quality Center Consulting Group.

from the 10s column. She reported that many children were confused by the concepts involved and did not seem to understand place value at this abstract, complex level. After learning a variety of simple to increasingly complex games and activities, she decided to offer several of these activities in her classroom to meet the needs of all of the children at all levels in her class. She included grouping actual objects (buttons, paper clips) by 4s, 5s, and 6s (for those who were not ready to group by 10s), as well as grouping objects by 10s. She added games with place-value mats and cups for placing groups of 10 objects, addition and subtraction with real objects, followed by numerical recording. In this case, the continuum from simple to complex moved from manipulating real objects to manipulating abstract numerals. This teacher wisely identified her children's needs and backed up on that continuum to offer more hands-on activities to build the number sense needed to grasp place value at more abstract levels.

All curricular areas can be viewed on this simple to complex continuum. Textbook scope-and-sequence charts can be used as resources, as well as child development information (see *The Primary Program: Growing and Learning in the Heartland* [Nebraska Department of Education et al. 1993] for the Appendix "Widely Held Expectations, Ages Birth through 13"), and other information about each specific group of children. These resources can assist teachers in planning the following:

1. Activities that build skills and understandings necessary to grasp concepts.
2. Ways to practice those new understandings.
3. Ways to challenge the children to apply their new knowledge in

similar and different situations. Kindergarten and primary teachers have a professional responsibility to look at their particular group of children and determine the range of activities that will best meet their needs. But, also, they have a responsibilty to be always complicating the learning, moving the children along in their development toward competency in a variety of areas.

This idea of challenging children has been a surprise to many of the teachers with whom I work. When they first consider play and exploration in active learning environments, they assume these approaches are the opposite of traditional academic teaching methods. With the ideas of play with intent and purpose that continually move toward the complex and challenging, teachers see the academic side of DAP. Content of the curriculum is not necessarily changed by changing teaching approaches nor are expectations for children's learn-

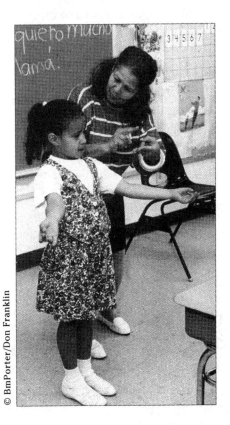

© BmPorter/Don Franklin

ing and performance. Instead, the environment, daily schedules, use of materials, teacher planning, and children's and teachers' behaviors in classrooms are changed. For many folks, this realization has been a major piece of the puzzle for them to fit into their notion of developmentally appropriate practice, and it is not a comfortable piece. When people are asked to change themselves, disequilibrium, if not total rejection, occurs. But identifying the three key elements cited above provides a beginning for teachers to consider for themselves.

The change process

A model for managing complex change in organizations from the American Productivity and Quality Center is very helpful (see Figure 2). In this model, effective change will occur when each piece of the process is in place. The necessary pieces for change are the following: Vision, Skills, Incentives, Resources, and Action Plan. When a piece is missing, other problems will arise and effective change will not result. The problems include these: Confusion, Anxiety, Gradual Change, Frustration, and False Starts. According to this model, when anxiety appears, people are evidencing the need for skills. Their vision or goals are intact, but the second piece of the change process is missing. If confusion arises, the vision is not clear. If there is only gradual change, perhaps incentives are not great enough. If there is frustration, the problem lies with resources being available. And finally, if there are false starts, a clear action plan is needed.

I have used this model in analyzing teacher reactions to the message I have been bringing about developmentally appropriate practices. The most common reaction from teachers is anxiety, so I conclude that I need to focus on the development of skills. Thus, some of my inservice workshops now focus on very specific topics, such as "Managing an Active Learning K–3 Classroom by Giving Children Choices," with all sorts of real teacher stories to document ways of sharing power with children, paying attention to individual learning styles, and not having total chaos in a classroom. In this way I can answer teachers' cries for help by focusing on their growing classroom management skills. I have also found this model very useful in analyzing the change process with administrators. Perhaps there has not been a clear statement of vision on the part of a district or program, and therefore people are confused. Or perhaps incentives have not been high enough, and the pace of change is very slow. Principals and curriculum directors have responded very favorably to this way of analyzing their situations and helping the change process along.

Time is an imperative part of the process of change so that new ideas can be incorporated with teachers' extensive experience base with children, and new approaches can be tried out in ways that are not confusing or anxiety provoking. Just as children learn by doing, so do adults. Giving teachers opportunities to explore and play with DAP in their own classrooms is essential to building the skills they need to use these approaches successfully.

I have been fortunate to work with school districts that have been committed to supporting teachers in their change efforts *over time*. As teachers are introduced to these new ideas, they are given time to experiment in their own classrooms, whether that experimentation involves just thinking about changes as they become more aware of their own practices or involves moving toward more active learning through play and exploration, inquiry studies, and so on. Teachers, then, return for further inservice and discussion, comparing notes on their new thoughts and practices, sharing frustrations and solutions. In this way each person can grow individually with her own unique style of DAP for her particular group of children.

One group of teachers reached some interesting conclusions after considering these approaches over a semester. I asked them to list what they saw as the advantages and disadvantages of DAP (Figure 3). I served as scribe for their ideas. When they finished giving their suggestions, I stepped back and asked them to look for any commonalities or themes in their ideas. All of us were amazed at how the list of advantages showed the overwhelming benefits *for children* and the list of disadvantages focused on problems *for the adults involved*. This group of teachers found this list humorous and profound. They believed deeply that the focus of their work was the children. To see that their list of disadvantages did not include a single one that primarily affected children but, rather, included items that mainly affected teachers really seemed a powerful conclusion to all of their learning about developmentally appropriate practice. One teacher said it for us all, "I think we should call it Developmentally Cool!"

Many teachers struggle with these ideas, however. Change is a difficult process for human beings and often takes place slowly. Teachers who have embraced DAP at the kindergarten and primary levels have reported that their adaptation of their own teaching approaches has taken two to three years, and their development of a comfort level with DAP has taken five years. Empathizing with folks as they consider

---

Figure 3. Developmentally Appropriate Practice

What are the advantages?
- children learning to manage themselves
- children taking risks, feeling more competent
- children gaining self-confidence, self-esteem going up.
- children happier, feeling more valued and in control
- no failure resulting
- being individualized

What are the disadvantages?
- evaluating
- managing behavior
- dealing with change
- needing extra time for planning and making materials

---

educating children in active, playful, and challenging ways and assuring them that time is a necessary part of their own growth and development can be helpful.

Encouraging teachers to take small steps rather than to change dramatically has been successful. One third-grade teacher announced that he would try to offer choices to the children in his classroom for one hour a

---

Instead of textbook writers and publishers determining scope and sequence, developmentally appropriate kindergarten and primary teachers do so themselves to truly meet the individual as well as the age-appropriate needs of the children from year to year.

week. A kindergarten teacher started a Journal Writing Time for one-half hour a day. Children could choose their own topics and explore writing through inventive spelling, scribble writing, and pictorial representation. In a second-grade classroom, children chose a variety of thematically related learning centers for one or two weeks each month. The other two weeks, the teacher used more whole-group, skill-based instruction. For some teachers, moving desks together to form learning groups might be a major step. Placing materials on shelves and allowing children to get what they need can be the first

move in the process of "letting go" and employing developmentally appropriate practices.

In *The Primary Program* (Nebraska Department of Education et al. 1993), the authors have developed a "Continuum of Change" (Figure 4). I have used this continuum to help people see how the change process occurs and identify the many steps involved. Some teachers react negatively to the idea of "appropriate practices" versus "inappropriate practices." They see themselves using many teaching strategies that are labeled "inappropriate," and they reject the

© The Growth Program

whole idea of DAP out of self-defense. As an alternative approach, I have asked teachers to identify their thinking on the

---

Figure 4. A Continuum of Change for Kindergarten and Primary Classrooms

From less-appropriate practices:	To more-appropriate practices:
Child adapts	Schools adapt
Child as passive and dependent	Child as active partner in learning
Whole-group instruction	Whole-group, small-group, and individual instruction
Individual tasks	Balanced small groups, cooperative and individual tasks
Preset material covered	Children's capacity to learn extended
3Rs instructional focus	Focus on concepts, skills, processes, and attitudes
Separate subjects	Integrated subjects
Workbooks	Concrete materials, quality literature, and a variety of resource materials
Verbal information emphasis	Constructivist, problem-solving, thinking emphasis
Single correct answers	Alternative solutions generated
Work and play divided	Play as one condition of learning
Holiday rituals marked	Multicultural content based on the study of social experience
Teacher as the sole arbitrator of what is correct	Children as theory builders and negotiators
Grouping by ability or age	Group developed by interest, motivation, and learning needs
Assessment of what a child already knows	Assessment focusing on how a child learns and what a child "can do"
Assessment for classification and reporting	Assessment ongoing for purposes of instructional decisionmaking
Child as the recipient of the teacher's teaching	Child as collaborator in own learning
Answers valued	Questions valued
Paper-and-pencil representations	Multiple ways of representing knowledge

Adapted by permission of the Nebraska Department of Education from *The Primary Program: Growing and Learning in the Heartland.* First published in D.P. Fromberg, "Kindergarten: Current Circumstances Affecting Curriculum," *Teachers College Record* 90 (1989): 392–403.

"Continuum of Change" chart by marking where they see themselves in the shift from left side to the right (from inappropriate to more developmentally appropriate teaching practices). They analyze each left-to-right item as having a range of possibilities for its particular aspect of DAP, and they rank themselves by making a mark on the dotted line to represent where they see their own practice. For example, one group of kindergarten teachers saw children as active partners in learning; therefore, they marked themselves far to the right on the dotted line. However, they still saw work and play as divided, and they grouped children by ability. On these two items, they marked themselves to the far left. This exercise gave them the option to say, "Well, I haven't changed very much on this item. However, I am moving toward this one. Oh, and I am way over here on this one! I guess I am in the process of change." Not feeling quite so defensive then about their present approaches, teachers are more open to consider new ideas.

But, most importantly, reminding them of the vision or purpose of their work can provide a strong foundation upon which they can stand. Referring back to our model for Managing Complex Change (Figure 2), without vision people become confused. In my work I am continually impressed with the clarity of purpose and dedication demonstrated by kindergarten and primary teachers. They care deeply about reaching children and helping them reach their potential as learners. With such a strong foundation, developmentally appropriate practice is recognized as a tool to help make that vision a reality.

Finding the commonality of purpose, providing pictures of practice in action to help teachers see DAP more clearly, giving them key philosophical elements to guide the choices they make with and for children, and building skills for them to implement these practices in their own classrooms over time can be helpful strategies in reaching out to teachers who have not heard the DAP message before.

Learning is finding out what you already know.

Doing is demonstrating that you know it.

Teaching is reminding others that they know just as well as you.

You are all learners, doers, teachers. (Bach 1977)

References

Bach, R. 1977. *Illusions*. New York.
Barrett, J. 1978. *Cloudy with a chance of meatballs*. New York: Macmillan Children's Group.
Bredekamp, S., ed. 1987. *Developmentally appropriate practice in early childhood programs serving children from birth through age 8.* Exp. ed. Washington, DC: NAEYC.
Indiana Department of Education. 1989. *Kindergarten guide*. Indianapolis: Center for School Improvement & Performance, PRIME TIME Unit.
Jones, E., & E. Prescott. 1984. *Dimensions of teaching–learning environments: A handbook for teachers in elementary schools and day care centers*. Pasadena, CA: Pacific Oaks College.
Jones, E., & G. Reynolds. 1992. *The play's the thing: Teachers' roles in children's play*. New York: Teachers College Press.
Jones, G.A., & C.A. Thornton. 1993. Research in review. Children's understanding of place value: A framework for curriculum development and assessment. *Young Children* 48 (5): 12–18.
Kamii, C. 1985. *Young children re-invent arithmetic: Implications of Piaget's theory.* New York: Teachers College Press.
Nebraska Department of Education, Iowa Department of Education, Iowa Area Education Agencies, & Head Start–State Collaboration Project. 1993. *The primary program: Growing and learning in the heartland.* Lincoln: Nebraska Department of Education.
NCREL (North Central Regional Educational Laboratory). 1992. *Meeting children's needs: Conference # 5.* Video. Chicago: Author.
Wassermann, S. 1990. *Serious players in the primary classroom: Empowering children through active learning experiences.* New York: Teachers College Press.

For further reading

Bredekamp, S., & T. Rosegrant, eds. 1992. *Reaching potentials: Appropriate curriculum for assessment for young children.* Vol. 1. Washington, DC: NAEYC.

Teaching Young Children

Educators Seek 'Developmental Appropriateness'

A kindergarten student having observed the classroom aquarium carefully over several days, notices that the water level is slightly lower each day. He says to his teacher: "We have to put more water in the tank because the fish are drinking it."
How should the teacher respond to best support the child's learning? Should she leave him to continue his observations unaided? Should she try to teach him about evaporation and molecules, simplifying the concepts as far as possible? Or should she do something else?

Scott Willis

How best to teach young children—pupils in preschool, kindergarten, and the early grades—has long been a subject of lively debate. Over the past decade, however, a consensus has arisen among experts in early childhood education, most of whom endorse the idea of "developmentally appropriate practice." The National Association for the Education of Young Children (NAEYC), in particular, has championed this idea through its position statements and publications.

What do experts mean by this unwieldy phrase?

Simply put, developmentally appropriate practice "takes into account those aspects of teaching and learning that change with the age and experience of the learner," says Lilian Katz, director of the ERIC Clearinghouse on Elementary and Early Childhood Education at the University of Illinois, Urbana-Champaign. Today "we have better research than ever on how children learn at different ages," she notes—and that knowledge has many implications for schooling.

We know, for example, that children aged 4–6 learn better through direct, interactive experiences than through traditional teaching, where the learner is passive and receptive. (The latter might be "okay" for children aged 8 or older, Katz says.) Further, the younger children are, the more what they learn needs to be meaningful on the day they learn it, not just in the context of some future learning.

Developmentally appropriate practice has two dimensions, says Sue Bredekamp, director of professional development for the NAEYC. First, it is age-appropriate: it reflects what we know about how children develop and learn. Second, it is appropriate to the individual child: it takes into account each child's own development, interests, and cultural background. Teachers need to consider both dimensions, she says.

In choosing a learning experience for a child, knowing what's age-appropriate "gets you in the ballpark," Bredekamp says, but the teacher must also consider the individual. She offers an analogy to choosing a toy for a 3-year-old. Knowing the child's age gives one a general idea of what kind of toy would be suitable, but without knowing the individual child—her interests, whether she's "young" or advanced for her age—one can't choose with confidence.

Given the diversity seen in any group of young children, attention to individual appropriateness is crucial—yet too often neglected, Bredekamp says. "There's a wide range of individual variation that everyone recognizes, but it's rarely paid the attention it deserves," she asserts. This neglect occurs because the curriculum imposes a norm, and because teachers find it easier to plan to some predicted norm. But teachers whose instruction is developmentally appropriate "don't expect all the children to learn the same things in the same way on the same day," she emphasizes.

Teachers must also consider all aspects of the child, experts advise. Developmentally appropriate practices "challenge individual children to learn and reach their potential in all areas of development," says consultant David Burchfield, who teaches at Brownsville Elementary School in Albemarle County, Va. Teachers must attend not only to the cognitive domain but to children's social, emotional, and physical needs as well. "Typically in schools, we pay too much attention to the cognitive," he says. "We shouldn't ignore the complexity of children."

Developmentally appropriate practice is not a recipe but a *philosophy* for teaching young children, experts explain. "It's not a curriculum or an exact prescription," says Burchfield, "It offers guidelines." Some teachers may find this unsettling. "Teachers are so used to being told, 'Do it this way,' " he notes. By contrast, the developmentally appropriate philosophy says, " 'Keep these things in mind' when considering your kids, the classroom environment, what you teach and how."

Developmentally appropriate practice is "a set of principles, not a methodology," agrees Barbara Bowman, vice president of programs at Loyola University of Chicago's Erikson Institute. Beyond advising teachers to honor the sequence of child development and their pupils' individual differences, "you can't make hard and fast rules," she says. Instead, teachers must exercise their professional judgment, based on training and reflection. "That's the piece that's gotten lost" in the past, she believes.

Pushed-Down Curriculum

In large measure, early childhood experts are promoting developmentally appropriate practice in response to a phenomenon dubbed the "escalated" or "pushed-down" curriculum. Over the past few decades, observers say, preschool classes and kindergartens have begun to look more like traditional 1st grade classes: young children are expected to sit quietly while they listen to whole-class instruction or fill in worksheets. Concurrently, teachers have been expecting their pupils to know more and more when they first enter their classrooms.

Experts cite many reasons for this trend. The urge to catch up with the Russians after the launching of Sputnik led to "young children doing oodles of sit-still, pencil-and-paper work"—a type of schoolwork inappropriate for 5- to 7-year-olds, says Jim Uphoff, a professor of education at Wright State University in Dayton, Ohio. (Today, the urge to compete with Japan yields the same result, experts say.) Another cause of the pushed-down curriculum is the widespread—yet incorrect—notion that one can teach children anything, at any age, if the content is presented in the right way, says David Elkind, a professor of child study at Tufts University.

In addition, more children today attend preschool, and preschools market themselves as academic, says Marilyn Hughes, an education consultant and veteran elementary teacher from Aspen, Colo. Some parents, too, favor the pushed-down curriculum in their zeal to give their children a head start in life. And, in general, Americans believe that faster is better. "We worship speed," Uphoff says. "That's an integral part of our beliefs."

Jacqueline Flare, principal of Todd Hall School in Lincolnwood, Ill., says that a pushed-down curriculum used to prevail in her district. Under pressure from parents and the central office, kindergartners were expected to use workbooks—despite their teachers' concerns. "Now we're saying, 'Less is more'; then, it was just the opposite,"

she recalls. "We were saying, 'Let's see how much we can cram into their heads.' "

While the intentions of those pushing down the curriculum may be good, the effects on children are bad, experts say.

For one thing, giving children material far beyond what they can do is simply inefficient, says Elkind. While 4-year-olds need "eons" of time to learn subtraction, 6-year-olds can grasp the concept in a few hours, he says. Similarly, 4th graders typically need months to learn decimal fractions, whereas 6th graders can master them with far less effort. Although educators *can* push down the curriculum, "what's the point?" Elkind asks. "Certainly there should be challenge, but it should be intelligent challenge."

Requiring young children to do overly advanced work has another harmful effect: it causes them to miss something else they *should* be doing, says Hughes. If children are only responding to teacher cues. "They are missing natural learning experiences"—direct, sensory experiences of their world—which form the foundation for later, more abstract learning.

Yet another drawback of the pushed-down curriculum is its effect on children's attitude toward learning. When young children are introduced to formal instruction too early, in a form that is too abstract, they *may* learn the knowledge and skills presented, but at the expense of the disposition to use

---

Assess Your Curriculum

The National Association for the Education of Young Children (NAEYC) recommends that educators reviewing a curriculum for young children consider these questions, among others:

Does the curriculum
- promote interactive learning and encourage the child's construction of knowledge?
- encourage active learning and allow children to make meaningful choices?
- foster children's exploration and inquiry, rather than focusing on "right"

answers or "right" ways to complete a task?
- lead to conceptual understanding by helping children construct their own understanding in meaningful contexts?
- embody expectations that are realistic and attainable at this time, or could the children more easily and efficiently acquire the knowledge or skills later on?
- encourage development of positive feelings and dispositions toward learn-

ing while leading to acquisition of knowledge and skills?
- help achieve social, emotional, physical, and cognitive goals and promote democratic values?
- promote and encourage social interaction among children and adults?

Condensed from NAEYC's Reaching Potentials: Appropriate Curriculum and Assessment for Young Children, Vol. I *(see Resources).*

Staff Development Key to Success

As assistant superintendent for curriculum and instruction in Lincolnwood, Ill., Mark Friedman was asked to plan an early childhood program for the district. Staff development was a major focus, says Friedman, who is now superintendent of the Libertyville, Ill., public schools.

When changes in instruction were proposed, some teachers felt an "invalidation" of what they had been doing in the classroom, Friedman says. To counter this inevitable feeling, he tried to convey the message that "we've learned that there are other ways to do things."

The district provided a lot of "awareness training" about developmental appropriateness, Friedman says, using videotapes and "fireside chats" (informal discussions with teachers about their concerns). They also put together "article banks"—phonebook-sized volumes of articles on the topic. Teachers were also given training in a variety of instructional strategies. Consultants showed them how to teach reading without reading groups, for example, and how to integrate reading with other disciplines. Teachers were also trained in the "Math Their Way" program, which makes extensive use of manipulatives.

A "big issue" for teachers, Friedman says, was the definition of developmentally appropriate practice: teachers wanted to know just what was expected of them. Some teachers wanted almost a checklist, he recalls—but this was precisely what the central office did not want to give them. They did not want teachers merely to adopt the "surface aspects" but to grasp the underlying philosophy.

Classroom visits were an especially powerful staff development tool, Friedman says. Through networking with other districts, teams of teachers (of the same grade level) were able to visit classrooms in other districts—including private schools and the laboratory school at the University of Chicago—to "get a flavor of good teaching practices at various sites." The teacher teams "culled some good stuff out of every visit," he says.

---

them, Katz says. Obviously, destroying students enthusiasm for learning in exchange for some short-term gains is a poor bargain.

Further, when young children are repeatedly coerced into behaving as though they understand something—such as the calendar or arithmetic—when they really do not, their confidence in their own abilities is undermined, Katz says. "If you can't relate to what's going on, you believe you're stupid," she says. And over time, children bring their behavior into line with this belief.

Active Learning

If traditional, lecture-driven teaching is not appropriate for young children, then how *should* they be taught?

According to Katz, what children learn generally proceeds from "behavioral" knowledge to "representational" knowledge—from the concrete and tangible to the abstract. Therefore, the younger the learners, the more opportunities they need to interact with real objects and real environments.

In a developmentally appropriate classroom, Bredekamp says, the teacher provides lots of organized activity. Children are actively involved in learning: writing, reading, building with blocks, doing project work, many choices. Young children need hands-on experiences and social interaction around content, she says. In math, for example, students grasp concepts better when they grapple with real-life problems and work with manipulatives.

Teachers must respect how young children learn best: through social interaction, Bredekamp says. "It shouldn't be chaos," but children should be discussing their pursuits with peers. Research shows that children learn to solve problems better when they work in groups, she says. So while some whole-group instruction may be useful teacher lecture should *not* be the rule of the day.

For the most part, teachers should avoid whole-group instruction, Katz agrees. When a teacher tries to teach something to the entire class at the same time, "chances are, one-third of the kids already know it: one-third will get it: and the remaining third won't. So two-thirds of the children are wasting their time." To learn a particular concept, "some children need days: some, ten minutes," says Hughes—but the typical lockstep school schedule ignores this fundamental fact.

Because children learn idiosyncratically, teachers need to provide a range of learning opportunities, says Judy Zimmerman, principal of Indian Fields Elementary School in Dayton, N.J. If a teacher wants to teach that every sentence begins with a capital letter, for example, she could introduce that idea to the whole group, perhaps by pointing it out in a "big book." Some children will immediately grasp the concept: others might recognize an individual capital letter: still others might miss the point entirely, Zimmerman says. Therefore, the teacher must continue to provide opportunities for pupils to learn the concept. "The teacher should constantly expose them to this [idea], and push them along."

Teachers can help individualize instruction through small-group work and opportunities for children to do their own investigating, Katz says. "Children are born with a powerful natural impulse to investigate their environment. *That's* what we should be capitalizing on in the curriculum," she asserts. For young children, investigation is a natural way of learning; they make hypotheses all the time. To capitalize on this inclination, educators should consider how to provide contexts for worthwhile investigations.

How, for example, could the teacher in the anecdote at the beginning of this article best help her pupil investigate whether the fish in the aquarium were actually drinking the water? According to NAEYC's *Reaching Potentials: Appropriate Curriculum and Assessment for Young Children* (the source of this example), the teacher should enable the child to test his hypothesis. She could say, "Oh, do you think that if we had another tank of water with no fish in it, the water level would stay the same? Let's try it and find out." By responding in this way, the teacher engages the child's participation and challenges his thinking, the NAEYC document says.

One excellent way to encourage student investigations is through the project approach, Katz says. Children should study real phenomena in their environment through in-depth projects that combine all the disciplines, she advises.

Children in a small Vermont town, for example, investigated the question: "Who measures what in our town?" They studied the daily measurements of length, time, cost, distance, and so on, made by people throughout their community. The project lasted for weeks, and parents and businesses were involved. The children collected measurement devices and created an exhibit. "The kids got into it," Katz reports.

Long-term projects help teachers nurture students' interest—which is not to be confused with excitement, Katz says. One mistake teachers make, she believes, is to confuse getting kids excited—"a short-term turn-on"—with engaging their interest: inducing them to "wrap their minds around" a topic for an extended period. Projects help children develop this ability, she says.

Using Themes

The traditional curriculum is fragmented, many experts complain. In too many classrooms, children study South America in the morning and Colonial America in the afternoon, making school studies a "giant Trivial Pursuit," says Teresa Rosegrant, an associate professor of early childhood education at George Mason University and a former kindergarten teacher. The pieces don't fit together, especially for young children.

Teachers can avoid this pitfall by using a thematic approach, Rosegrant says. For example, a 1st grade class could study the five senses in language arts, science, math, and art. A thematic approach makes learning more coherent, Rosegrant says: it also makes the curriculum accessible to parents, who can reinforce learning at home. A young child is incapable of summarizing "what happened at school today" if learning is a confusing array of unrelated facts, she notes. But with a thematic approach, a young child could say, "We learned about the tongue, and we tasted salt, sugar, and spices."

Kindergarten teacher Lynn Michelotti uses a thematic approach in her classroom at Todd Hall School. "We do a lot with pumpkins and apples in the fall," she says, citing one example. Her pupils take a field trip to a pumpkin farm; then they observe pumpkins in science, weigh and measure pumpkins in math, read about how pumpkins grow, and learn to cook pumpkin pie.

Without a thematic approach, the curriculum may ask teachers to do some illogical things, Rosegrant says. As a kindergarten teacher, she was expected to teach about the moon, although teaching about the sun was reserved for 1st grade! (The district has since moved to a thematic approach, she says.)

Learning Centers

Many teachers of young children use learning centers to individualize instruction and to allow pupils some choice and control over their learning, experts say. "Learning centers are designed to give an experiential approach and to provide for student differences," says early childhood expert Barbara Day of the University of North Carolina–Chapel Hill, who is a Past President of ASCD.

In his rural Virginia classroom, Burchfield provides many learning centers, including areas devoted to art, math and science, a library, a computer, blocks, and a stage. Allowing his students some choice yields several benefits. "I see them being able to persist in their work much longer," he says. His pupils also strive for quality, feel a sense of ownership, and have a tremendous sense of pride. "They see value and meaning in their school experience," Burchfield says.

Learning centers "allow for the broadest range of interactions," says Hughes. Her own classroom featured 20 hands-on learning centers, which were run on student contracts. Some of the centers were set up for independent work; others, for pairs or small groups. Students could respond to the centers in a variety of ways: linguistic, visual, kinesthetic. Hughes taught her pupils how to move independently through the centers, giving them a chance to pace themselves. The centers placed "hundreds of materials within the reach of the children," she says.

The Role of Academics

A common myth about developmentally appropriate practice, experts say, is that it is not academically rigorous—that it allows pupils to "do whatever they want." Advocates are quick to refute this charge.

Developmentally appropriate practice is not unacademic, Elkind says; it's simply academic in a more appropriate way than traditional instruction. It encourages curiosity, not rote learning, and it creates a sounder base of knowledge that is more retainable.

The belief that developmentally appropriate practice lacks rigor is a misunderstanding, says Bredekamp. "The opposite is true. It can be *more* rigorous than a basic skills approach" because it is not limited to skills alone. Skills are infused and taught in context—through project work, for example.

Others, however, would prefer more emphasis on the direct teaching of skills.

A Look Inside a K–2 Literacy Portfolio

What kinds of student work and other information should be collected in a literacy portfolio? In the South Brunswick (N.J.) School District, a pupil's K–2 literacy portfolio contains the following:

- Self-portraits drawn by the child at both the beginning and end of the school year.
- Notes from an interview, conducted in September, during which the child is asked about his or her favorite pastimes and reading activities at home.
- A questionnaire sent to parents at the beginning of the school year that solicits their input and helps build a working relationship between parents and the teacher.
- A test of the child's understanding of the conventions of books and print that is administered at both the beginning and end of kindergarten.
- A "word awareness writing activity, administered at the end of kindergarten and at the beginning and end of 1st grade.
- Unedited samples of the child's free writing, which may include translations by the teacher if invented spelling or sketchy syntax make them difficult to read.
- A "remodeling" sample, collected three times a year, that allows teachers to appraise the strategies each child is using to deal with print Two techniques are used: a running record for emergent readers and a miscue analysis for independent readers.
- A record of the child's ability to retell a story, recorded three times over the course of the school year.
- A class record that profiles the accumulated knowledge about the class on a one-page matrix.

Adapted from The Education and Care of Young Children: Report of the ASCD Early Childhood Consortium (*see Resources*).

Donna Siegel, an associate professor of education at the University of Science and Arts of Oklahoma, is a stout supporter of teaching basic skills to young children, especially the disadvantaged. Children who aren't exposed to literacy at home need to be taught basic decoding, she believes. (Children from middle-class backgrounds fare better with less direct teaching because their parents teach them basics such as the alphabet, she says.) Siegel is concerned that an emphasis on allowing children to explore and discover may leave them unprepared academically. "It's hard to *discover* how to do math or how to read," she says. "Some things you have to sit down and learn."

Young children learn basic skills much faster through direct instruction or modeling than through exploration, Siegel says. Further, adults can teach academics to young children without harming their disposition to learn, she believes. The teacher should explain in a step-by-step fashion, help pupils along, and keep them trying. "I'm not talking about drill all the time," she emphasizes. "You don't want to stress children out."

If a child can read on entering 1st grade, he or she is more likely to have success all through school, Siegel says. "Reading is so critical to later school success; a little head start can only be beneficial."

Bredekamp believes formal reading instruction, such as phonics drill, is not appropriate until 1st grade, and then only when needed. She too is concerned about disadvantaged children, but she diagnoses their needs differently. "The key is to have a program in which kids are getting numerous experiences with print, starting at age 3 probably," she says. In particular, they should be read to constantly.

Too often, children who have not been exposed to literacy at home get only the alphabet and phonics at school, Bredekamp says. They are "drilled and killed on basic skills in isolation," despite their lack of experiences on which to "hang" this learning. (Children who are exposed to literacy in many ways outside of school can better weather a decontextualized skills approach, she says.)

"In the past we taught language as though it was a jigsaw puzzle: hopefully, by magic, sometime the pieces would fit together," Uphoff says. By taking this fractured approach, "we've taught a lot of kids to read but to not *want* to read."

Challenge to the Teacher

Experts in early childhood education agree that teaching in a developmentally appropriate way is more demanding than traditional, lecture-driven teaching. It "requires more input, time, and energy," says Elkind, because it demands more individualized instruction "geared to where kids are."

"It's more challenging," agrees Bredekamp, because it requires teachers to use their judgment. The traditional notion that "the curriculum rules" is being overturned. "There's no such thing as a teacher-proof developmentally appropriate curriculum, she points out—a fact some teachers find hard to accept.

Rather than following a skill-based, lock-step approach, teachers must guide and support children through a broad range of strategies, so each child has "more than one pathway," says Rosegrant. Teachers must be experimenters, willing to try different means to reach a child, sensitive to the fact that children respond differently to materials and strategies. "You can't think that there's *a* way" to teach a concept, but "many, many alternative ways," she says.

Teaching in a developmentally appropriate way is "much more difficult," says Feare. "Ego is part of it," The teacher used to be the center of attention, the know-it-all, she says; now the teacher must act as a facilitator. Making this shift is difficult for some veteran teachers who are used to being the focal point. "You must have the disposition not to need to be the center of your own universe," adds Hughes.

Elkind, however, cautions that we must allow a wide range of teaching styles, because some teachers are more at home with direct instruction. Often, this preference is a matter of temperament, he believes—not a reflection of training and habit. Some younger teachers prefer teaching in the traditional way, he notes.

"I don't think we've taken sufficient account of these personality factors," Elkind says. "Some teachers just feel more comfortable with a traditional, structured classroom organization," as opposed to giving children more choice. And some children need more structure. "It's wrong to say the traditional approach is wrong for everybody," he asserts.

Given the challenging nature of developmentally appropriate teaching, it's not surprising that experts underscore the need for better teacher training.

"Generally, teachers are not well-prepared to do this," Bredekamp says. "A lot of states don't even have an early childhood certificate." Training is especially important, she says, in light of the fact that more knowledge is being generated all the time—about how children learn in small-group settings, for example.

Teachers "absolutely need training" in developmental appropriateness, says Hughes. "It just isn't happening at the college level." Schools of education should spotlight the finest teachers of young children as master models, she proposes.

Child development needs to be seen as an integral part of education courses, says Shirle Moone Childs, director of curriculum and instruction for the Windham Public Schools in Willimantic, Conn., who heads ASCD's Early Childhood Education Network. "It's important that we make the connection" between child development courses and education courses, she says, noting that when she was in college, child development courses were considered part of Home Economics.

Better Assessment

Like curriculum and instruction, assessment practices should be developmentally appropriate, experts agree. Most recommend a move to "authentic" forms of assessment.

Compared to paper-and-pencil tests, portfolios and performance assessments give teachers "a much better read on what children really know," says Feare. "You can see how the child is progressing—and not progressing." These forms of assessment are "far more diagnostic."

For many reasons, paper-and-pencil assessments of young children tend to be inaccurate, Elkind says. Children are not very good with symbols; they tend not to understand—or follow—instructions well; and their mood can greatly affect their performance. Fortunately, there are many observational ways to assess children, Elkind says. Their use of language is very revealing, for example. If they use the words "shorter" and "longer," they have mastered the unit concept. Similarly, if they play games with rules, they have grasped syllogistic reasoning.

Teachers need to be close observers of young children, experts agree. With less direct instruction, "keeping track of what kids know becomes terribly important," Bowman says. "The teacher must spend a good part of the day *not* talking," but "watching and listening a lot," adds Rosegrant.

Kindergarten teacher Michelotti says she devotes much of her time to observing and evaluating her pupils.

"The teacher's a facilitator: the process is more important than the product," she explains. "I'm trying to spend more time really watching kids and making more anecdotal records."

Good ways to assess young pupils include observation, portfolios, and interviews, says Bredekamp. "We do far too much testing," she says, to the degree that our teaching looks like testing: children sitting quietly, filling in blanks. Instead, she believes, the influence ought to flow in the opposite direction: assessment should resemble good instruction.

Portfolios and journals are more appropriate for young children, Uphoff says, because they "allow children to do more at their own rate of development." Moreover, "the child is part of his own assessment; he can see his own progress." Thus, the child gains the ability to self-evaluate: "It's not just 'the great expert' evaluating you."

Literacy portfolios are central to the program offered at Indian Fields Elementary School, says Principal Judy Zimmerman. Over the course of each child's K–2 school career, pieces of student work and other indicators are collected in the portfolio (see "A Look Inside a K-2 Literacy Portfolio"). Teachers do not collect exactly the same information on every child (more is collected on children who appear to be having difficulties), but what is the same is standardized through a six-point scale.

The portfolios provide "a failsafe method for explaining to parents what we're doing," Zimmerman says. The school's program is validated when parents see the progress their children are making in writing and spelling. As a public relations tool, the portfolios have been "a savior for us."

But use of portfolios alone to assess what children know is not adequate, cautions Rosegrant. "You need more than the work itself," she says. "You need the critical adult," probing what understandings the child's work represents. "The issue here is to get closer to the process," she asserts.

Teachers must avoid the "trap" of providing developmentally appropriate instruction yet asking children to show their learning on a written test,

Hughes says. Instead, teachers must allow children to demonstrate their learning in a variety of modes. For example, after a science exploration on weather, children could show what they learned through writing, creating charts, or building a model. "It's the children's responsibility to choose a way to show the *most* they know," she says—with the proviso that children also need to expand their repertoires.

"Assessment is the key to a developmentally appropriate program," Hughes says. "It tells you how sophisticated (students') connections are." And, she adds, given the power of testing to drive other aspects of schooling, "if your assessment is not developmentally appropriate, nothing else you do will be."

Relations with Parents

Developmentally appropriate teaching can sometimes be a hard sell with parents, many of whom find the break with tradition disturbing. "Most parents want workbooks and papers to put on the fridge; they understand these things," says Uphoff of Wright State University. "Parents are anxious to help students at home," Zimmerman adds, and they feel "insecure and frightened if they don't have worksheets to help them with."

To give parents confidence in a developmentally appropriate program, educators need to spend time with them, helping them understand what they see in their children's work, Zimmerman says. "We have to help our parents put on a new set of eyes. It's very hard to do." Teachers at her school communicate with parents frequently, Zimmerman says, explaining what children are learning about and describing what they'll bring home. They use Voice-mail and leave messages almost daily. For example, they tell parents, "Ask your child how we measured the perimeter of the classroom" or "Ask how they dug their garden and what they planted." Indi-

vidual conferencing with parents also helps allay concerns as does inviting parents to observe or volunteer in the classroom.

"The communication is absolutely key," Zimmerman emphasizes. Teachers need to be "clear, consistent, frequent communicators—and partners—with parents," she says. And they must show parents, all along, that their children are learning more than they would in a more traditional program.

Teachers do a disservice by not communicating with parents at least weekly, Feare says. (Teachers at her school send home a newsletter.) If parents are kept informed, and their children are happy in school, parents are satisfied, she says.

"We've been highly successful in changing our model," Feare says. "We've made changes in my school that people said couldn't be done"—including the elimination of workbooks, worksheets, and the spelling book. They won public support for the changes because "parents could see that kids were learning."

Looming Obstacles

Despite the consensus among early childhood educators that developmentally appropriate practice is best for young children, obstacles loom between theory and practice.

To spread developmentally appropriate practice will be "an uphill fight," says Bowman, primarily because it is expensive. "The cost factor has not been faced up to," she says "To get wonderful results, you have to invest in the program," including improving teacher-to-pupil ratios and providing training for teachers.

Bredekamp also sees "a real challenge in terms of school financing" to provide smaller class sizes, more materials, and richer experiences—in a time of tighter budgets. "The challenge is to use budgets more wisely," she believes. For example, rather than buying

30 desks, a school might purchase several tables and some hands-on materials.

For Rosegrant, the main obstacle lies in the lockstep curriculums from publishers, which meet the needs of so few children, yet are so expensive. Developmentally appropriate practice will never become widespread "as long as the curriculum comes in boxes," she asserts. When teachers must meet the requirements of the curriculum, "there's so much to juggle, they drop concerns for individuals to plow through stuff." To overcome this obstacle, teachers need time, far in advance of the school year, to plan, she believes.

Yet another obstacle, says Feare, is the tyranny of the expectations of the teacher at the next level, who might complain that incoming children were not well prepared. "The bashing has just got to stop," she declares. At her school, 1st grade teachers have a new faith that the kindergarten teachers are "giving it their best shot," she says. "Our philosophy is that we're not getting kids ready for the next grade: we're getting them ready for life."

"It takes nerve and money" to move to developmentally appropriate practice, Feare adds. "You need to acquire all kinds of hands-on things." But, she notes, these purchases are actually cost-effective in the long run: manipulatives last a long time, whereas workbooks are consumables.

Burchfield sees an obstacle in the mismatch between instruction and assessment. Teachers are being asked to change their instruction (to literature-based reading, for example) while assessment remains unchanged (most often, standardized tests). The lack of congruence has spawned a great fear among teachers that he finds justified. "We're running into some dangerous territory."

People in power positions—administrators, school boards, superintendents—are still appealing to "the numbers" for accountability purposes, Burchfield says. *Qualitative* evidence of children's learning needs to be made understandable, he believes—although he wonders, "How do you take a portfolio and make it understandable to a school board, when you can't present it in an aggregate way?"

Looking to the Future

What do experts foresee for the movement toward developmentally appropriate practice?

Most are cautiously optimistic that the trend will continue, primarily because of the great number of complementary trends, such as the new process orientation in mathematics and the widespread interest in integrated curriculum and whole language. Bredekamp is heartened by the congruence she sees among these trends, but she also fears that the impetus toward national standards could mow down any progress if it perverts

the curriculum to a reductive skills-based approach.

"I am optimistic," says Burchfield of the prospects for developmentally appropriate practice. But he emphasizes that those in leadership positions, including principals and central office staff, need to be involved in training and discussions about the concept. Like teachers, "they must be given a lens to see what good practice can look like."

Resources

- To join ASCD's network on Early Childhood Education, contact Shirle Moone Childs, Windham Public Schools, 322 Prospect St., Willimantic, CT 06226; Tel.: (203) 423-8401; Fax: (203) 456-O859.

- *Early Childhood Education,* a video-based staff development program produced by ASCD in 1991, features a developmentally appropriate K–1 classroom at Seawell Elementary School in Chapel Hill, N.C. The consultant for the program was Barbara Day. For more information, contact ASCD's

Order Processing Dept., 1250 N. Pitt St, Alexandria, VA 22314-1453; (703) 549-9110. Stock no. V91128.

- *In Education and Care of Young Children: Report of the ASCD Early Childhood Consortium* was published in April 1992 by ASCD. It contains summaries of the experiences of the 12 school districts that belonged to the Consortium. Among the authors are Judy Zimmerman and Mark Friedman. To order ($10 each), contact ASCD's Order Processing Dept.,

1250 N. Pitt St, Alexandria, VA 22314-1453; (703) 549-9110. Stock no. 611-92109.

- *Reaching Potentials: Appropriate Curriculum and Assessment for Young Children,* Vol. I, edited by Sue Bredekamp and Teresa Rosegrant, was published in 1992 by the National Association for the Education of Young Children (NAEYC). For more information, contact NAEYC, 150916th St, N.W., Washington, DC 20036-1426; (202) 232-8777 or (800) 424-2460.

A look at DAP in the real world

Recognizing the Essentials of Developmentally Appropriate Practice

A group of four year olds have been in circle time for 40 minutes.
— not DAP

Aiysha wants the easel all to herself. LaToya wants a turn. The provider helps the girls develop a time table for sharing over the next several minutes. — DAP

Carlos, a kindergartner in an after school program, laboriously copies a series of words onto lined paper. — not DAP

Marjorie J. Kostelnik, PhD

Marjorie J. Kostelnik, PhD, is a professor in the Department of Family and Child Ecology at Michigan State University and is the program supervisor of the Child Development Laboratories on campus. A former child care, Head Start, and nursery school teacher, she has been actively involved in helping a variety of early childhood programs explore the implications of developmentally appropriate practice and translate their understandings into action.

Taken at face value, it seems easy to determine whether or not the preceding child care situations reflect developmentally appropriate practices. Closer scrutiny, however, may prompt us to reassess our original judgments.

For instance, we might revise our opinion about the circle time upon learning that the children are enthralled by a storyteller who actively involves them in the storytelling process and who has prolonged the group in response to the children's requests to "tell us another one." Likewise, helping children to share is usually a worthy endeavor. But, in this case, Aiysha only recently became a big sister and is having to share many things for the first time — attention at home, her room, and most of her things. Knowing this, we might determine that making her share the easel on this occasion is unnecessarily stressful. Helping LaToya find an alternate activity that will satisfy her desire to paint could be a better course of action for now. A second look at Carlos reveals that he is working hard to copy the words "happy birthday" for a present he is making for his mom. He is using a model created by another child and is writing on paper he selected himself. Within this context, it no longer seems so questionable for Carlos to be engaged in copy work.

Scenarios such as these illustrate that figuring out what does or does not constitute developmentally appropriate practice requires more than simply memorizing a particular set of do's and don'ts. It involves looking at every practice in context and making judgments about each child and the environment in which he or she is functioning.

Judgments Related to DAP

The guidelines for developmentally appropriate practice put forward by the National Association for the Education of Young Children (NAEYC) and later corroborated and embellished by organizations such as the National Association of State Boards of Education (NASBE) and the National Association of Elementary School Principals (NAESP) provide an excellent resource for thinking about, planning, and implementing high quality programs for young children. They serve to inform our decision making and to give us a basis for continually scrutinizing our professional practices.

Yet, regardless of how well they are developed, no one set of guidelines can tell us everything there is to know about early childhood education. Neither can they be applied unthinkingly. Every day practitioners find themselves in situations in which they must make judgments about what to value and what to do. Some of these situations demand on-the-spot decision making; others allow time for longer deliberation.

Some involve relatively minor incidents; others are much more serious. Some require making major changes in the environment or in one's teaching behavior; others necessitate only minimal changes or none at all. Yet, hurried or meticulously planned, small or large, involving more or less action, practitioners continually have to decide whether or not their actions and programs enhance or detract from the quality of children's lives.

Confusion Over DAP

Spokespersons for NAEYC, NASB, and NAESP have tried to underscore the evolving nature of developmentally appropriate practice and the contextual nature of its application. Unfortunately, some people eager for quick answers or a finite set of rules for working with young children have overgeneralized the guidelines. Suggested alternatives have become ironclad rules — issues of "more and less" have become "all or none." A number of erroneous assumptions have also arisen about DAP. Some of these include:

• There is only one right way to carry out a developmentally appropriate program.

• Developmentally appropriate programs are unstructured ones in which practitioners offer minimal guidance, if any at all, to the children in their care.

• In developmentally appropriate programs the expectations for children's behavior and learning are low.

• Developmentally appropriate practices cannot be adapted to meet the needs of particular culture groups or children of varying socio-economic backgrounds.

• Developmentally appropriate practice can be achieved simply by acquiring certain kinds of toys.

Assertions such as these have fueled a growing debate about the meaning, usefulness, and unitary nature of DAP. The resulting examination and exchange of views is healthy for the field, but it has also led some child care administrators to feel confused about what developmentally appropriate practice really is and how to achieve it. In addition, some directors are unsure which elements of developmentally appropriate practice are the most critical or where to begin in operationalizing the concept in their programs.

All of this uncertainty is compounded by the fact that every child care staff is comprised of people whose familiarity and experience with developmentally appropriate practices vary. Furthermore, some staff members may question whether certain of the practices espoused in written documents are sensitive to the unique needs of the population with whom they work. Others may feel overwhelmed at the thought of memorizing a long list of guidelines. Still others may not see an item on the list that addresses a particular situation with which they must cope. Many of these concerns arise from a preoccupation with the details of developmentally appropriate practice rather than with its essence. That essence lies in three principles common to every major interpretation of DAP suggested thus far.

The Essence of DAP

1. Developmentally appropriate means taking into account everything we know about how children develop and learn and matching that to the content and strategies planned for them in early childhood programs.

2. Developmentally appropriate means treating children as individuals, not as a cohort group.

3. Developmentally appropriate means treating children with respect — recognizing children's changing capabilities and having faith in their capacity to develop and learn.

In other words, we must first think about what children are like and then create activities, routines, and expectations that accommodate and complement those characteristics. In addition, we must know more than a few descriptive facts about a child, such as age and gender, to design appropriate programs. We have to look at children within the context of their family, culture, community, past experience, and current circumstances to create age-appropriate, as well as individually-appropriate, living and learning environments. Finally, we must recognize the unique ways in which children are children, not simply miniature adults. Experiences and expectations planned for children should reflect the notion that early childhood is a time of life qualitatively different from the later school years and adulthood.

Although each of us may interpret these basic tenets in slightly different ways, they provide a common foundation for defining high quality early childhood programs. Such programs are ones in which children of all abilities, ages, races, cultures, creeds, socio-economic, and family lifestyle backgrounds feel lovable, valuable, and competent.

The Need for Knowledge

Having specialized knowledge about child development and learning is the cornerstone of professionalism in early childhood education. Such knowledge encompasses recognizing common developmental threads among all children as well as understanding significant variations across cultures. Interviews with child care providers and observations of their work with children consistently find that those who have such knowledge are better equipped and more likely to engage in developmentally appropriate practices. Instead of treating their interactions with children as wholly intuitive, they bring factual information to bear on how they think about children and how they respond to them.

Understanding child development provides practitioners with insights into children's behavior and helps adults better grasp the context within which those actions occur. This expands providers' notions of what constitutes normal child behavior. As a result, they are more likely to accept typical variations among children as well as accurately recognize potential problems that may require specialized intervention. Familiarity with child development also offers clues to child care workers about the sequence in which activities might be presented to children and the degree of developmental readiness necessary for children to achieve particular goals.

Understanding how young children think and expand their concepts and skills is the key to creating appropriate physical environments for children, to determining appropriate adult/child interactions, and to developing activities and routines that support rather than undermine children's natural ways of learning.

Children As Individuals

Practitioners are called on daily to make decisions that require them to see each child as distinct from all others. The adult must weigh such variables as the child's age, what the child's current level of comprehension might be, and what experiences the child has had. Although *age* is not an absolute measure of a youngster's capabilities and understanding, it does serve as a guide for establishing appropriate expectations. For instance, knowing that

preschoolers do not yet have a mature grasp of games with rules, child care workers would not consider a four year old who spins twice or peeks at the cards in a memory game as cheating. Nor would they require preschoolers to adhere to the rules of the game in the same way they might expect grade-schoolers to do.

The kinds of *previous knowledge and skills* a child brings to a situation should also be taken into account. Obviously, children with little or no exposure to a particular situation or skill would not be expected to perform at the same level of competence as children whose backlog of experience is greater. For instance, standards for dressing independently would be different for a three year old than those for a six year old, not only because of differences in maturity, but because the older child has had more practice.

Contextual factors also contribute to determining the developmental appropriateness of certain decisions. For example, under normal circumstances, Ms. Sanchez's goal is to foster independence among the children in her family child care home. Ordinarily, children are given the time to make their own decisions, to repeat a task in order to gain competence, and to do as much as possible for themselves. However, these goals and strategies have to be modified during a tornado drill. Under such circumstances, children have no choice about taking shelter, nor can they take their time dressing themselves. As a result, slow dressers get more direct assistance than is customarily provided.

Physical resources and available time affect judgments as well. This explains why a huge mud puddle on the playground could be viewed as a

place to avoid or an area for exploration. Which judgment is made depends in part on what kind of clothing the children are wearing, whether soap and water is available for clean up, whether it is warm enough to go barefoot, and whether there is enough time for children to both play in the mud and get cleaned up before moving into the next part of the day.

The Function of Respect

Respect involves having faith in children's ability to eventually learn the information, behavior, and skills they will need to constructively function on their own. Thus, having respect for children implies believing that they are capable of changing their behavior and of making self-judgments. Caregivers manifest respect when they allow children to think for themselves, make decisions, work toward their own solutions, and communicate their ideas.

For instance, it is out of respect for children that child care workers allow them to make choices ranging from which activity to pursue to where to sit at the lunch table. For this reason, too, practitioners encourage toddlers to pour their own juice, preschoolers to become actively involved in clean up, and school-age children to help determine the activities for the day. Although any of these activities could be more efficiently and skillfully accomplished by adults, respect for children's increasing competence involves allowing them to experience the exhilaration of accomplishment. Similarly, adults who respect children know that self-control is an emerging skill that children achieve over time given adequate support and guidance. With this in mind, children's transgressions are handled as gaps in knowledge and skills, not as character flaws.

Applications

Each time child care workers are faced with having to determine to what extent their actions are congruent with developmentally appropriate practice, it is useful to ask the following questions:

• Is this practice in keeping with what I know about child development and learning?

• Does this practice take into account the children's individual needs?

• Does this practice demonstrate respect for children?

These queries can be used to address immediate concerns or to serve as the basis for long-term deliberations. They can stimulate individual thinking or consideration of program practices by an entire staff. Newcomers to the field use the preceding questions to hone their understanding of the fundamental nature of children. Seasoned veterans often go beyond the basics to consider the extent to which their practices take into account gender and cultural differences among children as well as differences related to socioeconomic status. In every circumstance, the answer to all three questions should be yes. If any answer is no, it is a strong sign that the practice should be reconsidered, revamped, or discarded. If there is uncertainty about a question in relation to a certain practice, that practice is worth examining further.

To illustrate the power of these essential principles as tools for meaningful reflection, take a moment to consider the first question above. In my own experience, I have started the reflective process by asking child care workers to describe the children with whom they work (focusing on how they believe those youngsters develop and learn). Often practitioners use adjectives such as active, curious, talkative, or playful. The procedure of generating descriptive words often leads to thought-provoking discussions to which both experienced and less experienced members contribute. If people decide they aren't sure about some items (e.g., What do children really learn from play? Do children from varied backgrounds develop and learn in the same way?), their questions serve as the impetus for staff research or the basis for additional in-service training. Next, we create a chart to examine what implications such characteristics have for program practice. This is accomplished by listing child development and learning traits in one column and corresponding practices that support or match those traits in a second column. A typical example is offered below.

A chart such as the one illustrated here serves two major functions. First, the people who create it become increasingly invested in the practices they identify. These are likely to be ones they take care to address in the future because they can see the logic of such strategies in

Child Traits	Child Care Practices
Children are active learners.	**The child care teacher:** gives children opportunities for gross motor activities each day. includes a daily free-choice period during which children can move freely. creates a schedule in which quiet, inactive times are followed by longer, more active periods. keeps inactive segments of the day short.
Children are curious.	**The child care teacher:** builds activities around children's interests. provides many chances for children to explore materials and concepts. encourages children to pose problems and investigate solutions.
Children are playful.	**The child care teacher:** integrates play throughout the day. provides children with a variety of props and other manipulative objects. encourages children to create and use their own ideas within their play. creates a classroom design and schedule that allows children to move about freely. monitors and enhances children's play as an observer or as a participant. evaluates the sound and activity level within the program in terms of the quality of children's play — recognizes that high quality play is often noisy and active.

relation to children they know and care about. Second, their ideas can be compared to those in published documents. As practitioners make such comparisons, they find many similarities between their ideas and those of experts in the field. This contributes to greater staff confidence and helps to make the NAEYC guidelines for developmentally appropriate practice more personally meaningful.

Summary

Ultimately, for DAP to have a major impact on the early childhood profession, people must see the principles which undergird it as extensions of their own values. These shared values will be what make DAP an integral part of our thoughts and actions rather than just a fad soon to be replaced by another.

In addition, fundamental values such as these are likely to remain constant, even as the strategies we use to address them differ from one circumstance to another or change over time. Supporting child care workers as they examine the essentials of developmentally appropriate practice is not only an important administrative responsibility, it is one that promises to yield lasting rewards for staff and for children.

Infants and Toddlers with Special Needs and Their Families

A Position Paper of the Association for Childhood Education International by David Sexton, Patricia Snyder, William R. Sharpton and Sarintha Stricklin

David Sexton is Professor and Chair and William R. Sharpton is Associate Professor, Department of Special Education and Habilitative Services, University of New Orleans, Louisiana. Patricia Snyder is Assistant Professor, Department of Occupational Therapy, Louisiana State University Medical Center, New Orleans. Sarintha Stricklin is Instructor, Human Development Center, LSU Medical Center.

Several recent trends reflect increased interest in developing and providing services for infants and toddlers with special needs and their families. First, evidence is mounting that indicates early intervention is valuable for diverse groups of very young children who exhibit a variety of special needs and for their families (Guralnick, 1991). Second, legal safeguards were established for the rights of individuals with disabilities, which have important implications for service-providing agencies and individuals. Third, there is much discussion about lowering the age for entering public schools (Gallagher, 1989). Fourth, more people are becoming aware of the need to provide greater support for child and family care (Kelley & Surbeck, 1990; Shuster, Finn-Stevenson & Ward, 1992).

Finally, a consensus is emerging that the functions of early intervention, child care and early childhood education (birth through age 8) are inextricably bound together; that "quality" or "best practices" cannot be achieved without systematically addressing the interrelationships among all three fields (Kagan, 1988, 1989; Mitchell, 1989; Salisbury, 1991; Sexton, 1990). In fact, Burton, Hains, Hanline, McLean and McCormick (1992) suggest that if quality early intervention, child care and early childhood education services are ever to become a reality, then it will be necessary to formally unify the three historically distinct fields.

Recognizing the widespread concern for infants and toddlers, including those with special needs and their families, the Association for Childhood Education International (ACEI) addresses three related issues in this position paper: 1) access to services, 2) quality assurance and 3) preparation of personnel. The final section offers some major conclusions and recommendations related to infants and toddlers with special needs and their families.

ACCESS TO SERVICES

ACEI reaffirms its belief that all young children and their families have a fundamental right to quality care, education and special intervention.

ACEI leads the way in advocating for the right of all children and their families to quality care and education. For example, ACEI/Gotts issued a position paper on this fundamental right in 1988. Although children with special needs and their families are not explicitly addressed, the paper clearly argues for complete, open access to care and education as one of the most fundamental rights of all young children, including infants and toddlers.

Many other professional organizations support ACEI in its position on open access to services. In its guidelines for developmentally appropriate practices, the National Association for the Education of Young Children (NAEYC) unequivocally takes the position that all young children deserve access to a quality program (Bredekamp, 1987). The Division for Early Childhood (DEC) of the Council for Exceptional Children (CEC) issued a position paper supporting the right of young children with disabilities to education and care in settings with typically developing children (McLean & Odom, 1988). The Association for Persons with Severe Handicaps (TASH) adopted the position in 1988 that people with disabilities must have opportunities to achieve full integration into society (Meyer, Peck & Brown, 1991).

ACEI also recognizes the need for comprehensive and ongoing screening, monitoring and assessment services for all infants and toddlers and their families. The goal of such services must be to facilitate early identification of children's special needs and ensure provision of appropriate interventions. Early identification activities should be an integral part of a comprehensive early childhood system, birth through age 8, and needed interventions should be embedded within typical child care, education, home and health routines.

Further, ACEI recognizes and supports the legal right of children with special needs and their families to regular child care and education services. The 1991 amendments (P.L. 102-119) to Part H of the Individuals with Disabilities Education Act (IDEA) (P.L. 101-476) require early intervention services to be provided in regular settings with typically developing children, as appropriate for each child. The term "natural environments" is used to refer to regular settings for typically developing age peers.

In 1990, the Americans with Disabilities Act (ADA) was signed into law. The ADA rules went into effect January 26, 1992. All public accommodations are now prohibited from discriminating against individuals because of a disability. Under Title III of the Act, the law specifically includes nursery schools, child care centers and family child care homes in the definition of "public accommodation" (Rab, Wood & Stanga, 1992; Surr, 1992).

ACEI recognizes that increasingly diverse populations of infants and toddlers represent great challenges to child care and education systems and affirms the need for immediate action to support these systems.

The population of infants and toddlers entering or seeking entry into child care and education systems is changing to include special needs and at-risk children. Service providers and decision-makers must respond to these changes if children and families are to reach their full learning and developmental potential (Stevens & Price, 1992). "Special needs" and "at-risk" are popular terms used to describe an extremely heterogeneous population (Hrncir & Eisenhart, 1991). Care must be taken to consider the extreme diversity within a particular special needs or at-risk subgroup. For example, the popular media image of "crack babies," as Griffith (1992) notes, is that they are all severely affected and little can be done for them. In fact, the effects vary dramatically from infant to infant and are moderated or exacerbated considerably by other factors.

The special needs population requires particular attention not only because of its diversity, but also because of the large numbers needing services. As the following statistics illustrate, we clearly need to take immediate action.

■ Each year, some 425,000 infants are born who will manifest a disability within the first four years of life (Garwood, Fewell & Neisworth, 1988). At the end of 1990, only approximately 600,000 children with special needs, birth through 5, were receiving intervention services (Hebbeler, Smith & Black, 1991).

■ Some 350,000 to 375,000 newborns each year have been exposed prenatally to drugs, including alcohol (Pinkerton, 1991; Stevens & Price, 1992). Fetal alcohol syndrome (FAS) is now recognized as the leading known cause of mental retardation in the Western world. Conservative estimates indicate that approximately one in 500 to 600 children in the U.S. are born with FAS and one in 300 to 350 are born with fetal alcohol effects (FAE) (Burgess & Streissguth, 1992; see also, Cohen and Taharally, 1992).

■ Each year, 412,000 infants are born prematurely (Bartel & Thurman, 1992).

■ An estimated 16 percent of all American children (3 to 4 million children) have blood lead levels in the neurotoxic range (Neddleman, 1992).

■ Human immunodeficiency virus (HIV) has become the greatest infectious cause of pediatric mental retardation in the U. S. In October of 1992, the Centers for Disease Control (CDC) reported 3,426 cases of acquired immunodeficiency syndrome (AIDS) among children under the age of 13 and estimated that several times as many children are infected with HIV (Seidel, 1992).

■ An estimated 3,000,000 to 4,000,000 Americans are homeless (Eddowes & Hranitz, 1989; Heflin, 1991). The number of children in the U. S. who are homeless on any given night range from 68,000 to 500,000 (Linehan, 1992).

Much recent rhetoric by politicians and policymakers centers on ensuring that all children are ready to enter school (e.g., *America 2000*). In a recent survey of U.S. state expenditures, however, half of the states spend less than $25 per child on the care and education of young children and one-third of the states spend less than $17 per child (Adams & Sandfort, 1992). Feeg (1990) reminds us that the U. S. is ranked 18th among industrialized nations in infant mortality and compares poorly in protecting and immunizing well children.

These facts clearly indicate the need for immediate action at national, state and local levels to ensure that additional dollars are made available to support child care, education and health systems in providing high quality, comprehensive services for all children. Such support is critical as these systems begin to upgrade early care and education services for more traditional populations, while simultaneously providing quality services for less familiar, special needs populations.

ACEI affirms the position that child care and education reform movements must be inclusive, addressing the needs of infants and toddlers with special needs and their families within the broader context of society.

Recently, movements to "restructure" or "reform" the education and child care systems have gained much momentum. One such movement is *America 2000* (U. S. Department of Education, 1991), a set of six national education goals developed by President Bush and the nation's governors. The first goal is of particular relevance to infants and toddlers with special needs and their families: "By the year 2000, all children in America will start school ready to learn." While this goal, widely touted as the cornerstone of *America 2000*, clearly focuses attention on the importance of learning during the early years, significant inherent problems remain.

First, children with special needs or disabilities are not specifically mentioned in this or any of the other goals. It is imperative that national programs value

and include the needs of *all* children. The second problem is defining "readiness" according to an expected level of skills and abilities children should possess prior to school entry. Such an approach serves a gatekeeping function of keeping some children out and ignores the central question of how "ready" the education system is for the child (Kelley & Surbeck, 1991; Willer & Bredekamp, 1990). Gatekeeping to exclude children with special needs and their families from the mainstream, whether implemented consciously or unconsciously, is nothing new and is certainly not even remotely related to "restructuring" or "reform." As Bowman (1992) notes:

What is a special-needs child? The usual answer is a child with a disability that prevents him or her from functioning effectively. But is the disability always in the child? I suggest that in most instances, the disability is not in the child, but in the misfit between the child and the environment. (p. 106)

ACEI receives support for this position from DEC, which issued a position statement on the first goal of *America 2000*, and from NAEYC, which endorsed the DEC statement (Holder-Brown & Parette, 1992).

ACEI strongly supports refocusing the reform and restructuring movements to recognize that school success is dependent upon families receiving the comprehensive health, education and social services they need in order to support children's development and learning, beginning with prenatal care. Willer and Bredekamp (1990) and Kelley and Surbeck (1991) argue for a restructured early childhood care and education system that extends well before and beyond the school and classroom to encompass health and human services.

An important step in this direction is the new Family Leave Law, which combines parental leave with disability insurance so that all families at all economic levels can afford to take time off to care for their children (Bond, Galinsky, Lord, Staines & Brown, 1991). New resources must be invested and current ones redirected to ensure that restructuring and reform efforts focus on making the system "ready" to respond to the needs of all children and their families.

QUALITY ASSURANCE

Quality assurance must not be overlooked when attending to the crisis in child care, health care and early childhood education (Daniel, 1990; Kagan, 1988; Willer, 1987). Quality assurance issues for infants and toddlers with special needs and their families must be addressed within the context of ensuring that *all* young children benefit from developmentally appropriate practices. An integrated service system should be designed to support, and not supplant, the role of families.

All young children and their families have a right to expect that child care, health care, and education and intervention systems are designed to enhance and promote their well-being. To ensure that quality services are delivered, some definable, measurable quality indices must be established, validated and adopted by health, child care, education and intervention systems. Such an outcome requires the collaboration of individuals representing multiple agencies and programs, both private and public, as well as consumers. These stakeholders must undertake systematic efforts toward evaluating and developing the context for collaboration, including:

- setting clear and manageable goals
- developing an operational structure that matches the goals
- developing mandates that are facilitative
- arranging for joint leadership
- pooling existing resources and identifying new ones
- establishing processes and policies that are clearly understood. (Kagan, 1991)

ACEI affirms that standards for quality infant and toddler programs must be validated and adopted for all young children, benefiting children, their families and all of society.

Several professional groups support ACEI (ACEI/Gotts, 1988) in advocating for quality assurance standards for child care and early childhood education programs, including NAEYC (Bredekamp, 1987) and the Alliance for Better Child Care (National Association for the Education of Young Children [NAEYC], 1987). Also, the Division for Early Childhood of the Council for Exceptional Children (DEC/CEC) recently published quality indicators for early intervention programs (Division for Early Childhood/CEC, 1993).

The care and education standards promulgated by the early childhood and early intervention communities are similar in philosophy and content. The similarities most likely result from the growing recognition that all children benefit from care environments that are safe, responsive, developmentally appropriate and competency-enhancing. Care environments that meet these and other identified standards should promote children's well-being and, from a transactional/ecological perspective, that of families and society (Bronfenbrenner, 1986; Hamburg, 1991).

A large consensus group comprised of parents, practitioners, policymakers, researchers and advocacy groups from all early childhood communities must collaborate to ensure that appropriate standards for all children are validated and adopted. The accreditation process developed by NAEYC (1986) is certainly a welcome step in this direction.

ACEI recognizes that government regulation through child care licensing is one of the primary policy mechanisms for establishing and overseeing quality care (Kagan, 1988; Phillips, Lande & Goldberg, 1990). The battle continues on a state-by-state basis to establish licensing standards, with many states seeing an erosion in established standards due to nonenforcement or exemption (Lindner, 1986; Willer, 1987). There is no denying that quality early childhood programs require time and money, as well as commitment and broad-based support. Resources must be available to develop and maintain high quality programs that meet the needs of children, parents and staff.

ACEI affirms the position that quality child care and education systems must promote full inclusion.

The most important indicators that must be present in early childhood quality assurance standards include those that address program policies, structures and practices supporting full inclusion of special needs children in settings designed for their age peers without disabilities (Demchak & Drinkwater, 1992; Hanline & Hanson, 1989; Salisbury, 1991). As Campbell (1991) notes, "More than any area of special education, the benefits of noncategorical programming where young children with disabilities are educated with those with typical development have been empirically supported"(p. 473).

Inclusion benefits both children and families. For example, children with and without disabilities benefit developmentally and socially from interaction in a child care environment that individualizes care and promotes ongoing regular contact among children (Demchak & Drinkwater, 1992; Odom & McEvoy, 1988). Families whose children experience inclusion frequently cite the development of empathy, respect for differences and respect for individuals as important outcomes for both themselves and their children.

Campbell (1991) makes the compelling argument that, beyond the cited benefits of inclusion, the real issue is whether we can justify removing children from the normal life experiences to which they are entitled by virtue of being young children. ACEI shares this view, affirming that infants and toddlers with special needs and their families should not be excluded from such experiences or from systems designed to serve all children and families. Developing one quality inclusive system of care, education and intervention can result in improved services for all children and families.

ACEI affirms the position that quality child care, health care and education systems must be integrated and that individualized, or personalized, care and education must be provided all infants and toddlers and their families.

The unique characteristics of all infants and toddlers must be considered in developing quality care, education and intervention programs. As a group, infants and toddlers with special needs are extremely heterogeneous. Individualized care, education and intervention must be provided to capitalize on the unique characteristics of each child and family. In fact, provisions of Part H of IDEA require that intervention for infants and toddlers having known or suspected disabilities include an Individualized Family Service Plan (IFSP) that systematically focuses on the individual family's priorities, resources and concerns (Sexton, 1990).

Kelley and Surbeck (1990) note that individualization, or "personalization," of care is also essential for typically developing infants, toddlers and their families. No accepted, single standard exists regarding the nature of services provided young children prior to school entry. ACEI endorses the principle that services for infants and toddlers with special needs should be designed according to the same standards as those for all other infants and toddlers. Programs adhering to such standards will provide care and education that are individualized, family-directed and culturally normative.

ACEI affirms the position that quality child care and education systems must embed needed interventions for infants and toddlers with special needs within the natural routines, schedules and activities of child care and home settings.

Quality child care and education systems must develop and utilize environments that promote active engagement of children with peers, adults and materials (McWilliam & Bailey, 1992). The learning environment should not be structured by strict schedules or insistence that children remain seated and quiet. Space, equipment, people and materials should be arranged instead to free children to move, choose and busy themselves. As Olds (1979) notes, "For all its manifestations, the environment is the curriculum" (p. 91). The true curriculum for infants and toddlers is everything they experience during the day (Bredekamp, 1987; Hignett, 1988).

Programs serving infants and toddlers with special needs should embed needed interventions within the natural routine or schedule of the child's day (Sexton, 1990). Needed special therapies (e.g., occupational, physical, speech, etc.) should be integrated within caregiving routines. Busenbark and Ward (1992) argue for integrated therapy that:

- lends itself to the inclusion and active involvement of nondisabled peers

---

Table 1: Core Competencies for Personnel Preparation

- Organize learning environments that are safe, healthy and stimulating.
- Promote all children's physical, intellectual, social, adaptive and communicative competence.
- Select curriculum and teaching/intervention strategies that: a) are developmentally appropriate, b) address all areas of development, c) are responsive to a wide variety of individual needs and d) are based on normal routines.
- Facilitate the success of children in all learning situations.

- Collaborate with families in all aspects of care, education and intervention.
- Ensure that all practices are respectful of and sensitive to cultural diversity.
- Integrate academic and practical experience via field experiences such as practicum, student teaching/internship and technical assistance/support at the job site.
- Maintain a commitment to professionalism via interdisciplinary and interagency teaming, continuing education, and systems change through individual and group advocacy.

- is delivered in the child's natural environment
- affords opportunities for modeling intervention strategies for staff and families during caregiving routines
- promotes focusing on child and family goals that are realistic, appropriate, functional and meaningful
- improves the child's social interaction skills
- builds a strong collaborative partnership among therapist, program staff and parents.

PREPARATION OF PERSONNEL

All disciplines concerned with infants and toddlers and their families agree that overall program quality or developmental appropriateness is determined directly by the knowledge and skills of the individuals caring for and serving this population (Bredekamp, 1987, 1992; Granger, 1989; Klein & Campbell, 1990; Kontos, 1992; Sexton, 1990). Available data indicate, however, enormous personnel problems that demand immediate attention. Granger (1989) reports that the annual personnel turnover rate in child care and early childhood programs not located in public schools is as high as 40 percent. Kontos (1992) also estimates that the annual turnover rate among child care providers is approximately 40 percent. The results of several national surveys (Bailey, Simeonsson, Yoder & Huntington, 1990; Meisels, Harbin, Modigliani & Olson, 1988; U. S. Department of Education, 1990) and state surveys (Hanson & Lovett, 1992; McCollum & Bailey, 1991; Sexton & Snyder, 1991) clearly note that:

- there are critical shortages of early intervention personnel across disciplines
- these critical shortages are predicted to continue, or even worsen, in the future
- there is a dearth of training content at both undergraduate and graduate levels related to working with infants and toddlers who have special needs and their families.

How adequately these and related personnel preparation issues are addressed will determine the future of our youngest children and the education profession (Bredekamp, 1992). A personnel system must be developed that addresses both preservice and inservice education needs.

ACEI promotes collaboration among the fields of early childhood education, child care, early intervention and supporting disciplines in the design and delivery of personnel training.

One key issue in personnel preparation is whether preservice and inservice training programs for early interventionists should be developed and delivered in isolation or in collaboration with general early childhood and care programs. Miller (1992) argues convincingly against educating personnel to work with *either* "regular" *or* "special needs" young children. Concerns over segregated personnel preparation programs have resulted in collaborative efforts among numerous professional groups, such as NAEYC, Association for Teacher Educators (ATE) and DEC, to achieve consensus on personnel preparation issues (Bredekamp, 1992).

ACEI endorses such efforts as absolutely necessary and, in addition, advocates inclusion of related professional groups (e.g., American Occupational Therapy Association and American Speech and Hearing Association) in future efforts. Joint collaboration has the potential to help ensure that full inclusion of infants and toddlers with special needs and their families becomes a reality.

An integrated personnel preparation system is imperative for numerous reasons. First, Part H of IDEA mandates that infants and toddlers with special needs be cared for and served in natural environments available to their typically developing age peers. Therefore, personnel in education and care settings will increasingly educate and care for infants and toddlers with special needs within these more natural and normalized environments. Early interventionists will spend much more of their time providing technical assistance to education and care personnel, collaborating with them on transition and inclusion issues.

IDEA, Part H, also requires that specific early intervention services must be delivered by interdisciplinary teams. Collaboration and joint training must occur across related disciplines such as occupational and physical therapy, audiology, speech and language therapy, social work and psychology. An integrated and collaborative preservice and inservice training system is an efficient, effective mechanism to address shared and related competencies.

Second, a consensus is growing among historically distinct fields that, if quality child care, education and intervention are to be provided all infants, toddlers and their families, an interdisciplinary approach to personnel preparation must build on "core" competencies identified by different professional groups (Burton et al., 1992; Demchak & Drinkwater, 1992; Miller, 1992; NAEYC, 1988). These core competencies should serve as a basis for developing an integrated personnel system. For example, personnel competency domains (Table 1) have been identified by the Council for Early Childhood Professional Recognition in its Child Development Associate (CDA) requirements for infant and toddler caregivers (Council for Early Childhood Professional Recognition, 1992); NAEYC, in its developmentally appropriate practice guidelines (Bredekamp, 1987); and DEC, in its recommendations for certification of early childhood special educators (McCollum, McLean, McCartan & Kaiser, 1989).

There is also growing recognition across fields that inservice or outreach training must receive priority within any personnel preparation system (Bruder & Nikitas, 1992; Granger, 1989; Kontos, 1992; Miller, 1992). Bailey (1989) defines inservice education as the process by which practicing professionals participate in experiences designed to improve or change professional practice. Given the high turnover rates in all areas of child care, education and intervention and the paucity of preservice training programs, inservice or outreach training opportunities must be coordinated, interdisciplinary and immediate. Kontos (1992) presents convincing data that indicate inservice training and technical assistance result in improved child care, as well as a dramatically lower turnover rate for family care workers.

ACEI also recognizes the importance of including administrators in any personnel preparation system. Specific competencies related to integrated early care, education and intervention must be included in preservice and inservice leadership training programs. The extent to which education, care and intervention personnel employ integrated and collaborative practices is directly related to an administrator's ability to identify, nurture and reward such behaviors.

ACEI affirms the right of all infants, toddlers and family members to child care, education and intervention delivered by trained personnel who have appropriate certification and/or licenses and who are adequately and equitably compensated.

One important step in establishing any field as a profession is some means to assess each individual's work performance and to license or credential those deemed competent according to criteria developed by the profession (Radomski, 1986). National surveys across fields, however, clearly indicate the lack of a credentialing or certification system that recognizes and monitors an individual's competency in the education, intervention or care of very young children.

After completing a survey of child care regulations in the U.S., Phillips et al. (1990) concluded:

Among the most disturbing findings in the state-by-state analysis is the lack of attention given to specialized training for child care providers. It is the rare state that requires both pre- and in-service training of center- or home-based staff; many more states fail to require either form of training. (p. 175)

Data reported by NAEYC (1988) indicate that only 24 states and the District of Columbia certify early childhood teachers as distinct from elementary teachers. Only three states define early childhood to be birth through age 8, as does ACEI. Furthermore, in a national survey of personnel standards for Part H of IDEA, Bruder, Klosowski and Daguio (1991) found that few regulatory standards were specific to personnel providing services to infants and toddlers.

ACEI recognizes the importance of formal licensing or credentialing of early childhood educators, care providers and early interventionists for at least two reasons. First, and most important, studies have consistently found developmentally appropriate practices are best predicted by the combination of an individual's formal education and training in child development/early childhood education and his/her exposure to supervised practical experiences (Fischer & Eheart, 1991; Snider & Fu, 1990). Evidence indicates that these same factors also affect the quality of services provided by early interventionists (Kontos & File, 1992).

Second, a credentialing or certification system based on national standards of care, education and intervention for all infants and toddlers, but flexible enough to accommodate the unique needs of different states, could focus the efforts of historically distinct fields to join forces and empower personnel. As Bredekamp (1992) observes:

The most overwhelming barrier to all our work on behalf of children is always financial; we know that we must improve compensation to ensure that we attract and keep the best and brightest in our profession, but we have not figured out how to get the money. (p. 37)

Bellm, Breuning, Lombardi and Whitebook (1992) report that real earnings by child care teachers and family child care providers have actually decreased by nearly one-quarter since the mid-1970s. Historically, professionals have not organized around the issue of compensation, perhaps perpetuating the general perception that child care, education and intervention are basically unskilled labor and that anybody can "watch" children (Modigliani, 1988; Morin, 1989; Phillips et al., 1990). ACEI solicits the support and collaboration of other professional groups to help ensure an integrated system that recognizes and monitors the competencies of personnel via formal credentialing or certification and that equitably rewards individuals accordingly.

CONCLUSIONS

Recent efforts to develop a comprehensive system of intervention for infants and toddlers with special needs and their families have provided opportunities to examine service access and quality issues. The key question in formulating public policy, particularly under Part H of IDEA, is: Should we create or continue a segregated system for early intervention or should we focus on collaborative efforts to support and improve general child care and education systems? It is becoming clear that one inclusive child care and education system is needed. Moreover, a collaborative approach is required if needed special interventions are to be embedded within the system.

The building of such a system entails constructive attention to:

- ensuring access to services for all children
- developing and enforcing quality control assurance standards
- training personnel and administrators to meet the needs of an extremely diverse population in developmentally appropriate ways.

Such a system also requires public policies that provide resources to achieve the collaboration necessary to improve child care and education. Such policies benefit all infants and toddlers and their families, as well as society in general. Now is the time for individuals and groups representing historically distinct areas to join forces with families and decision-makers in creating the best possible system of services and care for our youngest children—our most vulnerable, yet most valuable, resources.

References

Adams, G., & Sandfort, J. R. (1992). State investments in child care and early childhood education. *Young Children, 47*(6), 33-35.

Association for Childhood Education International/E. E. Gotts. (1988). The right to quality child care. Position paper. *Childhood Education, 64,* 268-275.

Bailey, D. B. (1989). Issues and directions in preparing professionals to work with young handicapped children and their faimilies. In J. Gallagher, P. Trohanis, & R. Clifford (Eds.), *Policy implementation and P.L. 99-457: Planning for children with special needs* (pp. 97-132). Baltimore, MD: Paul H. Brookes.

Bailey, D. B., Simeonsson, R. J., Yoder, E. E., & Huntington, G. S. (1990). Preparing professionals to serve infants and toddlers with handicaps and their families: An integrative analysis across eight disciplines. *Exceptional Children, 57*(1), 26-35.

Bartel, N. R., & Thurman, S. K. (1992). Medical treatment and educational problems in children. *Phi Delta Kappan, 74,* 57-61.

Bellm, D., Breuning, G. S., Lombardi, J., & Whitebook, M. (1992). On the horizon: New policy initiatives to enhance child care staff compensation. *Young Children, 47*(5), 39-42.

Bond, J. T., Galinsky, E., Lord, M., Staines, G. L., & Brown, K. R. (1991). Beyond the parental leave debate: The impact of laws in four states. *Young Children, 47*(1), 39-42.

Bowman, B. T. (1992). Who is at risk and why. *Journal of Early Intervention, 16,* 101-108.

Bredekamp, S. (1987). *Developmentally appropriate practice in early childhood programs serving children from birth through age 8.* Washington, DC: National Association for the Education of Young Children.

Bredekamp, S. (1992). The early childhood profession coming together. *Young Children, 47*(6), 36-39.

Bronfenbrenner, U. (1986). Ecology of the family as a context for human development research perspectives. *Developmental Psychology, 22,* 723-742.

Bruder, M. B., Klosowski, S., & Daguio, C. (1991). A review of personnel standards for Part H of P.L. 99-457. *Journal of Early Intervention, 16,* 173-180.

Bruder, M. D., & Nikitas, T. (1992). Changing the professional practice of early interventionists: An inservice model to meet the service needs of Public Law 99-457. *Journal of Early Intervention, 16,* 173-180.

Burgess, D. M., & Streissguth, A. P. (1992). Fetal alcohol syndrome and fetal alcohol effects: Principles for educators. *Phi Delta Kappan, 74,* 24-30.

Burton, C. B., Hains, A. H., Hanline, M. F., McLean, M., & McCormick, K. (1992). Early childhood intervention and education: The urgency of professional unification. *Topics in Early Childhood Special Education, 11*(4), 53-69.

Busenbark, L., & Ward, G. (1992). Service delivery for preschool children with disabilities. *Early Childhood Report, 3*(9), 67.

Campbell, P. H. (1991). An essay on preschool integration. In L. H. Meyer, C. A. Peck, & L. Brown (Eds.), *Critical issues in the lives of people with severe disabilities* (pp. 473-477). Baltimore, MD: Paul H. Brookes.

Cohen, S., & Taharally, C. (1992). Getting Ready for Young Children with Prenatal Drug Exposure. *Childhood Education, 69,* 5-9.

Council for Early Childhood Professional Recognition. (1992). *The child development associate assessment system and competency standards: Infant/toddler caregivers in center-based programs.* Washington, DC: Author.

Daniel, J. (1990). Child care: An endangered industry. *Young Children, 43*(2), 27-32.

Demchak, M. A., & Drinkwater, S. (1992). Preschoolers with disabilities: The case against segregation. *Topics in Early Childhood Special Education, 11*(4), 70-83.

Division for Early Childhood/CEC. (1993). *DEC recommended practices: Indicators of quality in programs for infants and young children with special needs and their families.* Reston, VA: Author.

Eddowes, E. A., & Hranitz, J. R. (1989). Educating children of the homeless. *Childhood Education, 65,* 197-200.

Feeg, V. D. (1990). Health issues in a changing society. In E. Surbeck & M. F. Kelley (Eds.), *Personalizing care with infants, toddlers and families* (pp. 52-61). Wheaton, MD: Association for Childhood Education International.

Fischer, J. L., & Eheart, B. K. (1991). Family day care: A theoretical basis for improving quality. *Early Childhood Research Quarterly, 6,* 549-563.

Gallagher, J. J. (1989). The impact of policies for handicapped children on future early education policy. *Phi Delta Kappan, 71,* p. 121-124.

Garwood, S. G., Fewell, R. R., & Neisworth, J. T. (1988). Public Law 94-142: You can get there from here! *Topics in Early Childhood Special Education, 8*(1), 1-11.

Granger, R. C. (1989). The staffing crisis in early childhood education. *Phi Delta Kappan, 71,* 130-134.

Griffith, D. R. (1992). Prenatal exposure to cocaine and other drugs: Developmental and educational prognoses. *Phi Delta Kappan, 74,* 30-34.

Guralnick, M. J. (1991). The next decade of research on the effectiveness of early intervention. *Exceptional Children, 58,* 174-183.

3. EDUCATIONAL PRACTICES: Preschool and Primary Programs

Hamburg, S. K. (1991). The unfinished agenda must be met. *Young Children, 46*(4), 29-32.

Hanline, M. F., & Hanson, M. J. (1989). Integration considerations for infants and toddlers with multiple disabilities. *Journal of the Association for Persons with Severe Handicaps, 14,* 178-183.

Hanson, M. J., & Lovett, D. (1992). Personnel preparation for early interventionists: A cross-disciplinary survey. *Journal of Early Intervention, 16,* 123-135.

Hebbeler, K. M., Smith, B. J., & Black, T. L. (1991). Federal early childhood special education policy: A model for the improvement of services for children with disabilities. *Exceptional Children, 58,* 104-112.

Heflin, L. J. (1991). *Developing effective programs for special education students who are homeless.* Reston, VA: Clearinghouse on Handicapped and Gifted Children, Council for Exceptional Children.

Hignett, W. F. (1988). Infant/toddler care, yes: But we'd better make it good. *Young Children, 47*(6), 73-77.

Holder-Brown, L., & Parette, H. P., Jr. (1992). Children with disabilities who use assistive technology: Ethical considerations. *Young Children, 47*(6), 73-77.

Hrncir, E. J., & Eisenhart, C. (1991). Use with caution: The "at-risk" label. *Young Children, 46*(2), 23-27.

Kagan, S. L. (1988). Current reforms in early childhood education: Are we addressing the issues? *Young Children, 43*(2), 27-32.

Kagan, S. L. (1989). Early care and education: Beyond the schoolhouse doors. *Phi Delta Kappan, 71,* 107-112.

Kagan, S. L. (1991). *United we stand: Collaboration for child care and early education services.* New York: Teachers College Press.

Kelley, M. F., & Surbeck, E. (1990). Infant day care. In E. Surbeck & M. F. Kelley (Eds.), *Personalizing care with infants, toddlers and families* (pp. 62-70). Wheaton, MD: Association for Childhood Education International.

Kelley, M. F., & Surbeck, E. (1991). *Restructuring early childhood education.* Bloomington, IN: Phi Delta Kappa Educational Foundation.

Klein, H. K., & Campbell, P. (1990). Preparing personnel to serve at-risk and disabled infants, toddlers, and preschoolers. In S. J. Meisels & J. P. Shonkoff (Eds.), *Handbook of early childhood intervention* (pp. 679-699). New York: Cambridge.

Kontos, S. (1992). *Family day care: Out of the shadows and into the limelight.* Washington, DC: National Association for the Education of Young Children.

Kontos, S., & File, N. (1992). Conditions of employment, job satisfaction and job commitment among early intervention personnel. *Journal of Early Intervention, 16,* 155-165.

Lindner, E. W. (1986). Danger: Our national policy of child carelessness. *Young Children, 41*(3), 3-9.

Linehan, M. F. (1992). Children who are homeless: Educational strategies for school personnel. *Phi Delta Kappan, 74,* 61-66.

McCollum, J. A., & Bailey, D. B. (1991). Developing comprehensive personnel systems: Issues and alternatives. *Journal of Early Intervention, 15,* 57-65.

McCollum, J. A., McLean, M., McCartan, K., & Kaiser, C. (1989). Recommendations for certification of early childhood special educators. *Journal of Early Intervention, 13,* 195-211.

McLean, M., & Odom S. (1988). *Least restrictive environment and social interaction.* Reston, VA: Division for Early Childhood, Council for Exceptional Children.

McWilliam, R. A., & Bailey, D. B. (1992). Promoting engagement and mastery. In D. B. Bailey & M. Wolery (Eds.), *Teaching infants and preschoolers with disabilities* (2nd ed.) (pp. 229-255). New York: Macmillan.

Meisels, S. J., Harbin, G., Modigliani, K., & Olson, K. (1988). Formulating optimal state early childhood intervention policies. *Exceptional Children, 55*(2), 159-165.

Meyer, L. H., Peck, C. A., & Brown, L. (1991). *Critical issues in the lives of people with severe disabilities.* Baltimore, MD: Paul H. Brookes.

Miller, P. (1992). Segregated programs of teacher education in early childhood: Immoral and inefficient practice. *Topics in Early Childhood Special Education, 11,* 39-52.

Mitchell, A. (1989). Old baggage, new visions: Shaping policy for early childhood programs. *Phi Delta Kappan, 70,* 665-6723.

Modigliani, K. (1988). Twelve reasons for the low wages in child care. *Young Children, 43*(3), 14-15.

Morin, J. (1989). We can force a solution to the staffing crisis. *Young Children, 44*(6), 18-19.

National Association for the Education of Young Children. (1986). Accreditation: A new tool for early childhood programs. *Young Children, 41*(4), 31-32.

National Association for the Education of Young Children. (1987). Alliance for Better Child Care (ABC). *Young Children, 42*(4), 31-33.

National Association for the Education of Young Children. (1988). Early childhood teacher education. Traditions and trends: An executive summary of colloquium proceedings. *Young Children, 44*(1), 53-57.

Neddleman, H. L. (1992). Childhood exposure to lead: A common cause of school failure. *Phi Delta Kappan, 74,* 35-37.

Odom, S. L., & McEvoy, M. A. (1988). Integration of young children with handicaps and normally developing children. In S. L. Odom & M. B. Karnes (Eds.), *Early intervention for infants and children with handicaps: An empirical base* (pp. 241-268). Baltimore, MD: Paul H. Brookes.

Olds, A. R. (1979). Designing developmentally optimal classrooms for children with special needs. In S. J. Meisels (Ed.), *Special education and development: Perspectives on young children with special needs.* Baltimore, MD: University Park Press.

Phillips, D., Lande, J., & Goldberg, M. (1990). The state of child care regulation: A comparative analysis. *Early Childhood Research Quarterly, 5,* 151-179.

Pinkerton, D. (1991). Substance exposed infants and children. Reston, VA: Clearinghouse on Handicapped and Gifted Children, Council for Exceptional Children.

Rab, V. Y., Wood, K. I., & Stanga, J. (1992). Training child care providers on the impact of the ADA. *Early Childhood Report, 3*(8), 5-8.

Radomski, M. A. (1986). Professionalization of early childhood educators: How far have we progressed? *Young Children, 41*(5), 20-23.

Salisbury, C. L. (1991). Mainstreaming during the early childhood years. *Exceptional Children, 58,* 146-155.

Seidel, J. F. (1992). Children with HIV-related developmental difficulties. *Phi Delta Kappan, 74,* 38-40, 56.

Sexton, D. (1990). Quality integrated programs for infants and toddlers with special needs. In E. Surbeck & M. F. Kelley (Eds.), *Personalizing care with infants, toddlers and families* (pp. 41-50). Wheaton, MD: Association for Childhood Education International.

Sexton, D., & Snyder, P. (1991). *Louisiana personnel preparation consortium project for Part H.* New Orleans, LA: University of New Orleans.

Shuster, C. K., Finn-Stevenson, M., & Ward, P. (1992). Family day care support systems: An emerging infrastructure. *Young Children, 47*(5), 29-35.

Snider, M. H., & Fu, V. R. (1990). The effects of specialized education and job experience on early childhood teachers' knowledge of developmentally appropriate practice. *Early Childhood Research Quarterly, 5,* 68-78.

Stevens, L. J., & Price, M. (1992). Meeting the challenge of educating children at risk. *Phi Delta Kappan, 74,* 18-23.

Surr, J. (1992). Early childhood programs and the Americans with Disabilities Act (ADA). *Young Children, 47*(5), 18-21.

U. S. Department of Education. (1990). *Twelfth annual report to Congress on the implementation of the Education for Handicapped Act.* Washington, DC: Office of Special Education and Rehabilitative Services.

U. S. Department of Education. (1991). *America 2000: An education strategy.* Washington, DC: Author.

Willer, B. (1987). Current reforms in early childhood education: Are we addressing the issues? *Young Children, 42*(6), 41-43.

Willer, B., & Bredekamp, S. (1990). Redefining readiness: An essential requisite for educational reform. *Young Children, 45*(5), 22-24.

Fourth-Grade Slump: The Cause and Cure

A new study reveals the impact of children's early childhood experience on their later achievement.

REBECCA A. MARCON

Rebecca A. Marcon is a developmental psychologist and associate professor of psychology at the University of North Florida in Jacksonville.

Parents, teachers, and administrators are often perplexed by what is often referred to as "fourth-grade slump." Why do so many bright, achieving children in the primary grades have difficulty making the transition to the upper elementary grades?

Although a number of ideas have been put forward, recent research suggests that the root of the difficulty lies in children's early childhood experiences, which influence how young children approach learning tasks. The impact is especially noticeable during the transition to fourth grade, which for many children is cognitively difficult because of increased expectations for independent thought, applications of previously learned concepts to new problems, and mastery of more complex skills and ideas. The transition can also be socially difficult because of increased expectations of maturity.

The latest results of an ongoing study in the District of Columbia Public Schools address this crucial transition period by comparing the outcomes of different models of early childhood education.

In the initial study, prompted by an unacceptably high first-grade retention rate, we set out in 1986–87 to examine the impact of different preschool models on the school success of inner-city, public school children. We studied the progress of four-year-olds enrolled in the District's prekindergarten or Head Start programs. The children were predominantly minority students (97 percent African American) and poor (76 percent qualified for subsidized lunch). More than two-thirds lived in single-parent families.

Three Early Childhood Models

A preliminary survey, based on classroom observations and teacher responses, identified three different preschool models operating in the D.C. school system:

- The *child-initiated* classrooms, called Model CI, had child-development-oriented teachers who allowed children to select the focus of their learning.
- The *academically directed* classrooms, or Model AD, had academically oriented teachers who preferred more teacher-directed instruction.
- The *middle-of-the-road* classrooms, called Model M, represented teaching beliefs and practices which fell between.

"Pushing children too soon into 'formalized academics' can actually backfire when children move into the later childhood grades where they are required to think more independently."

Our initial findings showed that children enrolled in the more child-development-oriented Model CI actually mastered more basic skills than those in Model AD or Model M classrooms. Furthermore, the Model M compromise approach did not work for any of the four-year-olds. By the end of the preschool year, Model M children were significantly behind the others in language, social, and motor development, as well as overall adaptive functioning and mastery of basic skills.

In the second and third years of the study, Model M children remained behind their peers as they moved into kindergarten and first grade, where Model CI children continued to excel while Model AD children's social development declined, along with their mastery of first-grade reading and math objectives.

As a result of the initial three-year study, we now knew that previous, inappropriate early learning experiences in many of the District's early childhood programs clearly hindered children's progress in the preprimary and primary years, and we had a clearer notion of the type of early childhood program that was needed.

Examining Fourth-Grade Transition

We continued to study the impact of early childhood experiences even as the District of Columbia system responded to the initial findings by instituting reforms in its early childhood programs. Having discovered ways to increase children's chances of making a successful transition from preschool to first grade, we now focused on the progress of the original study groups as they advanced through the primary grades.

The negative impact of overly academic early childhood programs on achievement and social development was clearly apparent by the fourth grade. Children who had attended Model AD prekindergarten programs were scoring noticeably lower in the fourth grade despite their adequate performance on third-grade standardized achievement tests. The Model AD children were also developmentally behind their peers and displayed notably higher levels of maladaptive behavior (*i.e.*, defiant behavior, anxiety, and distractibility).

As shown in *Figure 1*, children whose preschool experience was academically focused showed the greatest decline in school grades between third and fourth grades. At the same time, the long-term positive effects of a more active, child-initiated preschool experience showed up most clearly during this transition. Patterns of developmental change were more difficult to .identify, although children with overly academic preschool experiences had not advanced as rapidly in social development by the fourth grade.

In comparing children's academic progress since first grade, the study found that while all children's grades were typically lower by fourth grade, the three-year drop in performance was especially disconcerting for Model AD children. Their overall grade-point average dropped 22 percent from first to fourth grades, compared to only 5 and 6 percent for Model CI and M children. More specifically, Model AD grades decreased by 36 percent in math, 32 percent in reading and language, 30 percent in spelling and social studies, 23 percent in science, and 16 percent in health and physical education.

Ending Fourth-Grade Slump

Our findings show that fourth-grade slump can be traced back to inappropriate early childhood learning experiences for many children. The findings indicate that preschool programs are most successful when they correspond to children's level of development and natural approach to learning, and that children's academic and developmental progress through the elementary grades is enhanced by active, child-initiated early learning experiences.

The study also shows that later progress is slowed for most children when formal learning experiences are introduced too early. Pushing children too soon into "formalized academics" can actually backfire when children move into the later childhood grades where they are required to think more independently. This is because teacher-directed early childhood approaches that tell young children what to do, when to do it, and how to do it curtail development of autonomy.

According to developmental authority Constance Kamii, such teacher-directed approaches produce passive students who wait to be told what to think and do next. Therefore, it is not surprising that children who lack the early foundations of autonomy—the root of critical thinking and effective choice making—find the transition to fourth grade difficult.

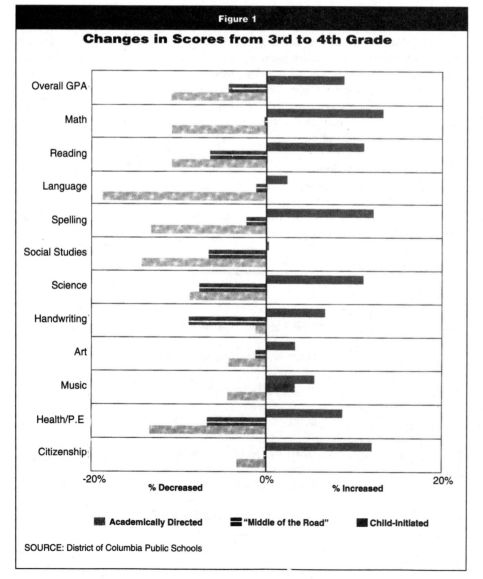

Figure 1

Changes in Scores from 3rd to 4th Grade

(Overall GPA, Math, Reading, Language, Spelling, Social Studies, Science, Handwriting, Art, Music, Health/P.E, Citizenship)

-20% — % Decreased — 0% — % Increased — 20%

Legend: Academically Directed · "Middle of the Road" · Child-Initiated

SOURCE: District of Columbia Public Schools

While the benefits of developmentally appropriate early childhood experiences may take a while to unfold, they become especially prominent by fourth grade, if not sooner. As we work to assure that all our children start school *ready to learn* by 2000, it is equally important that our schools be *ready to receive* these eager young learners. If we wish children to be independent and self-reliant, to choose wisely between options, and to think critically, our teaching styles and curricular focus must better reflect those desired outcomes. The early childhood years can either foster children's sense of autonomy or curtail it. As educators, the choice is ours.

REFERENCES

Elkind, D. "In Defense of Early Childhood Education." *Principal* 65:5 (May 1986): 6–9.

Kamii, C. "One Intelligence Indivisible." *Phi Delta Kappan* 65 (January 1984): 410–415.

Marcon, R. "Differential Effects of Three Preschool Models on Inner-city 4-year-olds." *Early Childhood Research Quarterly* 7:4 (1992): 517–530.

Marcon, R. "Socio-emotional Versus Academic Emphasis: Impact on Kindergartners' Development and Achievement." *Early Child Development and Care* 96 (December 1993): 81–91.

Marcon, R. "Doing the Right Thing for Children: Linking Research and Policy Reform in the District of Columbia Public Schools." *Young Children* 50:1 (November 1994): 8–20.

Schweinhart, L. J.; Barnes, H. V.; Weikart, D. P. *Significant Benefits: The High/Scope Perry Preschool Study through Age 27.* Ypsilanti, Mich.: High/Scope Educational Research Foundation, 1993.

Schweinhart, L. J.; Weikart, D. P.; Larner, M. B. "Consequences of Three Preschool Curriculum Models through Age 15." *Early Childhood Research Quarterly* 1:1 (1986): 15–45.

Sykes, M. R. "Creating a Climate for Change in a Major Urban School System." *Young Children* 50:1 (November 1994): 4–7.

Woods, C. "Responsive Teaching: Creating Partnerships for Systemic Change." *Young Children* 50:1 (November 1994): 21–28.

Zigler, E. "Should Four-year-olds Be in School?" *Principal* 65:5 (May 1986): 10–14.

A Blueprint for Change

During the school year 1986–87, the District of Columbia Public Schools responded to a high first-grade retention rate by initiating a three-year study to evaluate and determine the impact of early learning programs on children's long-term school success. The resulting 1990 report concluded that children enrolled in child-centered classrooms, where developmentally appropriate practices were implemented, had a higher passing rate in first grade than their peers in academically-oriented programs.

The district also authorized a three-year follow-up study that compared the previously studied children as they progressed from the primary to the upper elementary grades. This study indicated that by the age of 9 students from academically-oriented programs were clearly behind.

Because the evidence showed that child-initiated early childhood programs were effective, our next step was to develop a pilot project based on continuous progress and performance assessment. We began by allowing seven schools to replace skill-oriented academic programs with child-initiated, integrated, thematic learning programs from prekindergarten to third grade. The program has been expanded to include about half of our elementary schools and will eventually include all pre-K through third grades.

The program is success-oriented, capitalizing on the interests and capabilities of students while considering individual learning rates and styles. Our decision to emphasize social, emotional, and cognitive development in the early learning years is based on a growing body of evidence supporting such practices for young children, as well as increasing awareness that early retention is detrimental to a child's academic success.

Early on, we realized the need for authentic assessment instruments that would accurately reflect actual learning experiences while providing information about a child's overall development—social, emotional, physical, aesthetic, and cognitive. Research led us to the Work Sampling System developed by Samuel Meisels and others at the University of Michigan. The system's three-pronged performance assessment approach, which we've adapted, uses developmental checklists, portfolios, and summary reports. Because it provides a comprehensive overview of children's developmental progress, the system is not only highly effective, but popular with many teachers, students, and parents.

Overall, we have been pleased with our new approach to early childhood education. Based on the findings of our studies, we feel our youngest students will now be better prepared for the academic challenges ahead.

Franklin L. Smith
Superintendent
District of Columbia Public Schools

FOR FURTHER INFORMATION

The full report on which this article is based, *Early Learning and Early Identification Follow-Up Study: Transition from the Early to the Later Childhood Grades 1990-93,* by Rebecca A. Marcon, is available for $14 from the District of Columbia Public Schools, Center for Systemic Educational Change, 415 12th Street, N.W., Washington, D.C. 20004; (202) 724-4099.

Strategies for Teaching Children in Multiage Classrooms

Sandra J. Stone

Sandra J. Stone is Assistant Professor, Early Childhood/Literacy Education, Center for Excellence in Education, Northern Arizona University, Flagstaff.

The multiage classroom is becoming an increasingly popular way to restructure schools. Kentucky, for example, has mandated multiage classrooms in all primary grades (K-3). Mississippi and Oregon have similar mandates. Alaska, California, Florida, Georgia, New York, Pennsylvania, Tennessee and Texas are also considering implementation of multiage classrooms (Gaustad, 1992; Kentucky Department of Education, 1992; Lodish, 1992).

In a multiage classroom a group of mixed-age children stay with the same teacher for several years. Typical primary grade age groups are 5-6-7, 6-7-8 or 7-8-9. The children spend three years with the same teacher (Connell, 1987). While the current multiage movement generally focuses on the primary years, multiage classrooms are also being implemented in upper elementary classes with age groups of 8-9-10 and 9-10-11.

Multiage teachers are frequently asked, "How does one teach students with such a wide range of abilities?" The question implies that teaching several grades of children is impractical and too difficult. On the surface, teaching mixed ages does appear to be overwhelming.

Successful multiage classrooms require teachers to shift attention from teaching *curriculum* to teaching *children*. A multiage class requires teachers to consider children as individuals, each with his or her own continuum of learning. Teachers who try to teach grade-specific curriculum to multiple-grade classrooms may become frustrated and often return to same-age classrooms. Teachers who have instituted appropriate instructional strategies, however, find multiage classes to be exhilarating and professionally rewarding. What are some teaching strategies that will help make multiage classroom teaching successful?

Process Approach to Learning

A key factor in multiage classrooms' success is the use of a process approach to education. This approach emphasizes teaching children, rather than curriculum. Each child is treated as a whole person with a distinct continuum of learning and developmental rate and style. The teacher focuses on developing children's social skills and on teaching broad academic subjects such as reading, writing and problem-solving. Each goal reflects a developmental process, not the learning of discrete skills in a prescribed curriculum.

To facilitate the writing process, for example, the teacher provides daily opportunities to write. First, she models writing and includes broad-based writing conventions. The children's writing is based on their individual developmental continuum. The younger child may write one sentence, using only beginning sounds, while the older child may write paragraphs.

Rather than acting simply as the "giver of knowledge," she must facilitate each child's growth . . .

The teacher also provides daily opportunities for children to read. Children read independently and in large and small groups. In large groups, the teacher presents a shared reading experience and focuses on broad-based skills, such as recognizing initial consonants, predicting outcomes and finding compound words. In small groups, the teacher chooses teaching points to fit the children's individual needs, nurturing effective reading strategies and increased comprehension.

Opportunities for children to use math are also available. Children studying dinosaurs, for example, may choose to set up a dinosaur store. Younger children learn to distinguish between nickels and dimes or to compute how many dimes are needed to buy a 30-cent dinosaur. Older children may try more complex calculations, such as adding a series of numbers.

A teacher using the process approach provides opportunities, open-ended activities, experiences or projects in which all the children can participate on their own devel-

From *Childhood Education*, Winter 1994/95, pp. 102-105. © 1994 by the Association for Childhood Education International, 11501 Georgia Avenue, Suite 315, Wheaton, MD. Reprinted by permission.

opmental levels. The strategy is to provide the context where the learning process occurs. Children learn to read by reading, and to write by writing, in meaningful and relevant contexts. The process approach helps children to see themselves as progressive, successful learners.

Facilitator of Learning

The teacher must become a facilitator of learning in order to successfully implement a multiage classroom. A teacher must guide, nurture and support the learning process. Rather than acting simply as the "giver of knowledge," she must facilitate each child's growth in all areas according to individual developmental needs and interests. Therefore, teachers must *know the children*. A teacher can guide a younger child to use beginning sounds in writing only if she *knows* where the child is in the writing process. By facilitating learning, the teacher focuses on teaching children, not curriculum.

An Integrated Curriculum

Teachers choose an integrated curriculum in multiage classrooms that not only applies a holistic approach to learning, but also provides an excellent context for the process of learning. Teachers and/or children select a yearly, quarterly, monthly or even weekly theme. Children's reading, writing, problem-solving, graphing, measuring, painting and playing are based upon that thematic choice. As Connell (1987) notes, "integrating a curriculum around a theme allows children of different ages and stages to work together in a group as well as to practice skills at different levels" (p. 24).

Appropriate Learning Environment

The learning environment should permit all children to engage in the processes of learning. Such an environment includes active, hands-on learning experiences that are based on children's interests and choices. The center and/or the project approach is very effective in multiage

classrooms. Centers may include library, writing, listening, art, play, science, social science, social studies, math, drama and computers.

Using bears as a theme, children at the writing center might create stories based on a group reading of "Goldilocks and the Three Bears." At the listening center, children may choose from a selection of fictional and nonfictional stories about bears or related themes. Younger children at the science center could classify bears by type, while older children write descriptive paragraphs for each bear. At the play center, children of mixed ages can dramatize "Goldilocks and the Three Bears." Mixed-age groups could also design and build bear habitats or create a poster campaign to inform the public about endangered bear species.

Children choose their own open-ended activities and monitor their own time. The teacher is free to work with the children in small groups or individually as they become autonomous learners in charge of their own learning. The center and/or project approach allows children to be involved in active, hands-on learning within the social context of mixed ages.

Cross-age Learning

An effective multiage classroom encourages opportunities for cross-age learning. Social interaction in mixed-age groupings positively affects all areas of a child's development. Vygotsky (1978) suggests that children's learning can be enhanced by adults or more capable peers. In a multiage classroom where cooperation replaces competition, older

children become mentors to younger children. A multiage classroom is not effective if the children are predominantly isolated in same-age groups or even same-ability groups. Cooperative learning groups and peer tutoring are effective strategies. Collaboration through social interaction positively affects the children's learning.

Flexible Groupings

The predominant instructional strategy in multiage classrooms relies on small, flexible groupings. Children spend most of their class time in small groups, pairs or on their own.

While children participate in independent, cooperative groupings at centers or projects, the teacher works with small groups characterized by student needs or interests. For example, a teacher may conduct a literature study with a mixed-ability grouping, gather beginning readers together for support on using reading strategies and engage another group that showed interest in solving a particular problem. She may work individually with a child needing help in letter recognition. The breakdown of small groupings and independent study is not based on a predetermined, prescribed curriculum, but rather on the needs and interests of the children.

There is very little large-group instruction in the multiage classroom. Large group instruction times do provide a forum for broad-based skills. These instructional times allow for a wider curriculum presentation. Multiage teachers are amazed at how opening up the curriculum engages children to whom they ordinarily would not have presented certain concepts or skills.

Portfolio Assessment

Because the multiage classroom approach frees teachers to see children as individuals and relies on process learning, a new type of assessment is necessary. Portfolio assessment is an ideal strategy for documenting the progress of each

> **T**he center and/or project approach allows children to be involved in active, hands-on learning within the social context of mixed ages.

child. Children are assessed according to their own achievement and potential and not in comparison with other children (Goodlad & Anderson, 1987). The teacher holds different expectations for different children, does not grade portfolios and relies on using report cards that are narrative, rather than traditional.

Portfolios also help the teacher support and guide instruction. The authentic assessments in the portfolio enable teachers to know their students' strengths as well as areas that need further development. Portfolio assessment is an excellent tool for communicating with children and parents. It allows children to see themselves as successful learners and parents to better understand the learning process.

Conclusion

Strategies such as the process approach to learning, teacher as facilitator, appropriate learning environments, cross-age learning, flexible groupings and portfolio assessment all help teachers focus on teaching *children*. These strategies support the implementation of a successful and effective multiage program.

References and Other Resources

American Association of School Administrators. (1992). *The nongraded primary: Making schools fit children.* Arlington, VA: Author.

Anderson, R. H., & Pavan, B. N. (1993). *Nongradedness: Helping it to happen.* Lancaster, PA: Technomic Press.

Barbour, N. H., & Seefeldt, C. (1993). *Developmental continuity across preschool and primary grades: Implications for teachers.* Wheaton, MD: Association for Childhood Education International.

Bredecamp, S. (Ed.). (1987). *Developmentally appropriate practice in early childhood programs serving children from birth through age 8* (expanded edition). Washington, DC: National Association for the Education of Young Children.

Connell, D. R. (1987). The first 30 years were the fairest: Notes from the kindergarten and ungraded primary (K-1-2). *Young Children, 42*(5), 30–39.

Cushman, K. (1990). The whys and hows of the multi-age classroom. *American Educator, 14,* 28–32, 39.

Elkind, D. (1989). Developmentally appropriate practice: Philosophical and practical implications. *Phi Delta Kappan, 17*(2), 113–117.

Gaustad, J. (1992). Nongraded primary education: Mixed-age, integrated and developmentally appropriate education for primary children. *Oregon School Study Council Bulletin, 35*(7).

Goodlad, J. I., & Anderson, R. H. (1987). *The non-graded elementary school* (rev. ed.). New York: Teachers College Press.

Kasten, W. C., & Clarke, B. K. (1993). *The multiage classroom.* Katonah, NY: Richard C. Owen.

Katz, L. G., & Chard, S. C. (1989). *Engaging children's minds: The project approach.* Norwood, NJ: Ablex.

Katz, L. G., Evangelou, D., & Hartman, J. A. (1990). *The case for mixed-age grouping in early education.* Washington, DC: National Association for the Education of Young Children.

Kentucky Department of Education. (1992). *Kentucky's primary school: The wonder years.* Frankfort, KY: Author.

Lodish, R. (1992). The pros and cons of mixed-age grouping. *Principal, 71*(6), 20–22.

Oberlander, T. M. (1989). A nongraded, multiage program that works. *Principal, 68*(5), 29–30.

Vygotsky, L. S. (1978). *Mind in society: The development of psychological processes.* Cambridge, MA: Harvard University Press.

NURTURING KIDS'
Seven Ways *of* Being Smart

How to develop
your students'
multiple
intelligences

Kristen Nelson

KRISTEN NELSON *is a sixth-grade teacher at Ambuel Elementary in the Capistrano unified school district in Orange County, California. She is also a mentor teacher and consultant on multiple intelligences in the classroom.*

Throughout my teaching career I've been perplexed and fascinated by students who perform poorly in math and language activities, and appear unmotivated—yet thrive outside of the classroom. I'd see these "underachievers" in the streets after school, their faces lit with laughter and enthusiasm for whatever they were doing. They were engaged, expert, joyful—why couldn't I bring this out of them in class? Dr. Howard Gardner's Multiple Intelligences Theory nudged me toward the answer: I could reach many of these turned-off kids if I discovered their special ways of being smart.

You're probably familiar with Gardner's theory, but here's a refresher of his basic premise: Individuals don't have one fixed intelligence, but at least seven distinct ones that can be developed over time—linguistic, logical-mathematical, spatial, musical-rhythmic, bodily-kinesthetic, interpersonal, and intrapersonal. See the box ("The Seven Intelligences") and the clip-and-save chart [in this article] for more details about these seven kinds of smarts.

HOW MY TEACHING CHANGED

Gardner's theory is a dream come true for teachers—because it means intelligences can be nurtured. And with that in mind, I reinvented my curriculum and the way I taught it so that it met the needs of a wider range of learning styles—which, as educator Thomas Armstrong says, are "the intelligences put to work."

The strategies you can use to put the Multiple Intelligences Theory into play in your own classroom are limitless. To add to your thinking, here are two approaches that have had a big impact on my students' achievement: one is a focused unit that introduces kids to the concept of diverse strengths; the other is an open-ended exploration of the seven intelligences through classroom flow areas, which are similar to learning centers.

7 Smarts: An 8-Day Unit

Think a kindergartner will have trouble grasping the theory of Harvard psychologist Gardner? Think again. As a mentor teacher on multiple intelligences, I work with children throughout grades K–6, and even the youngest students naturally take to the idea that there are multiple ways of being intelligent.

I begin the unit by asking students what being smart

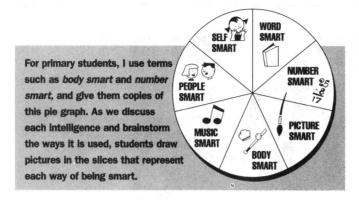

For primary students, I use terms such as *body smart* and *number smart,* and give them copies of this pie graph. As we discuss each intelligence and brainstorm the ways it is used, students draw pictures in the slices that represent each way of being smart.

means to them, and then list their replies on the board. Since their answers usually revolve around reading, writing, and math, we discuss the importance of these subjects in school success.

Next, I ask them to brainstorm other ways a person can be smart, conveying the idea that humans have proven time and again that although having strong math and language skills is important, it is not the only predictor of success in life. With grades 3 to 6, I discuss famous people who performed poorly in school but were smart in other ways. Albert Einstein and Pablo Picasso—who both disliked

school rules and dropped out to study under experts—are two good examples to use. With younger students, we talk about the fact that not everyone likes school all of the time.

As we continue our discussion, I give kids lots of examples of skills, activities, and professions that make use of each intelligence area.

EXAMINING STRENGTHS

After the introductory lesson, I focus on a different intelligence area for each of the next seven days. For example, on a spatial intelligence day with fourth graders, I might have students draw

floor plans of the Spanish mission we are studying and have them practice picturing numbers in their minds as we do oral calculations in math. On body-kinesthetic day, we role-play a scene from a novel we're reading, and learn a new sport. Each day, I also devote 45 minutes to exploring the famous people, book characters, and historical figures who are good role models in that intelligence.

By now, students are not only familiar with the different ways they're smart, but they are now ready and usually very willing to use their intelligences in daily work.

NURTURING KIDS ALL YEAR

After the opening unit, I integrate Multiple Intelligences Theory into my lesson plans for the rest of the year, adapting activities to meet various learning styles. For example, a child who is strong in spatial intelligence and is a visual learner can strengthen her reading and writing skills by drawing a picture before writing about a book she's reading. See the chart Draw Out Your Students' Strengths for

The Seven Intelligences

As you explore these seven intelligences with your students, keep in mind that Gardner's theory should not be used as another way to pigeonhole students as "spatial," "musical," and so forth. Students need to perceive themselves as having a combination of these intelligences, capable of growth in all areas.

Bodily-Kinesthetic: involves using the body to solve problems, create products, and convey ideas and emotions.

Interpersonal-Social: refers to the ability to work effectively with others; to understand them; and to notice their goals, motivations, and intentions.

Intrapersonal-Introspective: involves the ability to be deeply aware of inner feelings, intentions, and goals.

Logical-Mathematical: involves the ability to reason deductively or inductively and to recognize and manipulate abstract patterns and relationships.

Musical-Rhythmic: includes sensitivity to pitch, timbre, and rhythm of sounds, and responsiveness to music.

Verbal-Linguistic: involves ease with reading and writing skills, and sensitivity to the nuances, order, and rhythm of words.

Visual-Spatial: involves the ability to create visual-spatial representations of the world and to transfer those representations mentally or concretely—to think in pictures.

Adapted from "Seven Ways of Knowing" by David Lazear; *If Minds Matter: A Forward to the Future,* Vol. II (IRI/Skylight Publishing)

more ideas on how to build on your kids' multiple intelligences.

Flow Areas Foster Intelligence

Using multiple intelligences in your teaching has to go beyond detecting strengths in students and flexing just those intellectual muscles. You need to give students the opportunity to explore all seven domains. Setting up flow areas—which are centers organized around the seven intelligences—will help you accomplish this.

The concept of *flow* was developed by Mihaly Csikszentmihalyi, Ph.D., professor of human development at the University of Chicago, who describes flow as a state of complete absorption in something, to the point where one loses track of time. Csikszentmihalyi first observed flow when studying artists; he then looked for and found it in dancers, athletes, scientists, musicians, and talented people in many other fields.

In the classroom, flow areas provide students with the space, materials, time, and challenging activities that spark deep involvement while strengthening children's intelligences.

GO WITH THE FLOW

The very nature of flow areas is flexible, and they can be designed in numerous ways. Sometimes you'll want to set up flow areas for four to six weeks, and at other times just for a week or two. How you guide students to use them will vary, too. You'll want children to work in them solo, with partners, and in small groups; you can have children use them only when they're finished with their class work, or you can rotate students through the areas on a regular schedule. Try to block out a period of at least 30 minutes for kids, so they have a chance to get lost in their endeavor.

You can set up flow areas as centers independent of what students

are studying, or you can link them to your curriculum.

21 FLOW-AREA IDEAS
Verbal-Linguistic

1. Set up a language lab with a cassette player, cassettes, earphones, and talking books. Invite students to tape themselves reading a story or poem they've written, to share with others.
2. Establish a writing center with a computer, writing supplies, and examples of different types of writing. A fourth grader I taught used this area to write letters to local land developers to discuss her environmental concerns.
3. Organize a tutoring station where older children volunteer to help younger students with reading and writing. One sixth grader who lacked confidence in his reading gained more self-assurance when he helped a first grader learn to read.

CLIP AND SAVE

Draw Out Your Students' Strengths

Intelligence Area:	Is Strong In:	Likes to:	Learns Best Through:	Famous Examples:	Common Misbehaviors:
Verbal/ Linguistic	Reading, writing, telling stories, memorizing dates, thinking in words	Read, write, tell stories, talk, memorize, do word puzzles	Reading, hearing, and seeing words; speaking; writing; discussions	T. S. Eliot, Maya Angelou, Abraham Lincoln	Passing notes, reading during lessons
Logical/ Mathematical	Math, reasoning, logic, problem-solving, patterns	Solve problems, question, reason, work with numbers, experiment, use computers	Working with patterns and relationships, classifying, abstract thinking	Albert Einstein, John Dewey, Susanne Langer	Working on math or building things during lessons
Visual/ Spatial	Reading, maps, charts, drawing, puzzles, imagining things, visualization	Design, draw, build, create, daydream, look at pictures	Working with pictures and colors, visualizing, drawing	Pablo Picasso, Frank Lloyd Wright, Georgia O'Keeffe, Bobby Fischer	Doodling, drawing, daydreaming
Bodily/ Kinesthetic	Athletics, dancing, acting, crafts, using tools	Play sports, dance, move around, touch and talk, use body language	Touching, moving, processing knowledge through bodily sensations	Charlie Chaplin, Michael Jordan, Martha Graham	Fidgeting, wandering around the room
Musical/ Rhythmic	Singing, picking up sounds, remembering melodies, rhythms	Sing, hum, play an instrument, listen to music	Rhythm, melody, singing, listening to music and melodies	Leonard Bernstein, Mozart, Ella Fitzgerald	Tapping pencil or feet
Interpersonal/ Social	Understanding people, leading, organizing, communicating, resolving conflicts	Have friends, talk to people, join groups	Sharing, comparing, relating, interviewing, cooperating	Mohandas Gandhi, Ronald Reagan, Mother Teresa	Talking, passing notes
Intrapersonal/ Introspective	Understanding self, recognizing strengths and weaknesses, setting goals	Work alone, reflect, pursue interests	Working alone, self-paced projects, reflecting	Eleanor Roosevelt, Sigmund Freud, Thomas Merton	Conflicting with others

How to Enhance Your Teaching Smarts

☑ **Invite guest speakers.** Show students the relevance of each intelligence by inviting parents and community members as guest speakers—their professions can highlight specific intelligences. For example, a local architect described to my students how he designed a building they pass every day on their way to school—the kids were fascinated.

☑ **Create a video.** Have your students plan and execute a video to inform parents or other classes about the many ways of being smart.

☑ **Encourage individual projects.** Have students choose an intelligence area in which they would like to complete a one- to two-week project.

☑ **Honor overlooked intelligences.** Remember to recognize students that excel in bodily-kinesthetic, interpersonal, and intrapersonal intelligences.

☑ **Assess your own intelligences.** Think about how your strengths and weaknesses in the seven intelligences influence your teaching. Look at your lesson plans. Beside each activity, write the initials of the intelligences exercised—you will be able to see your dominant intelligence areas as well as the areas you need to enhance. Share your strengths and weaknesses with students.

☑ **Stretch yourself.** Instead of accepting the belief that you don't excel in certain areas, attend workshops and read books that can help strengthen these skills.

☑ **Team teach.** Use fellow teachers who have different intelligence strengths to plan lessons and activities. Rotating students can allow you to teach to your strengths and loves, while providing students with different styles of teaching and learning.

☑ **Update your professional portfolio.** Set your sights on having a portfolio that contains examples of lessons that use each intelligence area.

Math-Logic

4. Make a math lab with manipulatives, calculators, objects to measure and graph, and so on. My younger students love to use the area to classify pattern blocks, buttons, and coins. One older student calculated the expenses of an upcoming family trip and planned an itinerary.

5. Put together a science lab with simple hands-on experiments and science books. A flower-dissection lab—which I set up when we're learning about plant reproduction—is a favorite of my students.

6. Create a logic-challenge center. For example, I invited my fifth graders to develop a mystery-based board game. When I challenged my sixth graders to design a way to teach a blind person geometric shapes, they collected yardsticks and made giant squares, triangles, and parallelograms on the playground.

Spatial

7. Enrich an art area with paints, pencils, different types of paper, clay, and various objects students can use as models for still-life drawings. Display examples of famous artists' work for students to study. My students loved it when I brought in a large shell and invited them to do a painting of it in the style of Georgia O'Keeffe.

8. Stock a visual media center with a video camera, VCR, and videotapes. Invite groups of students to make a short classroom documentary. My students chose topics of concern to them, like getting along with parents.

9. Fill an architecture center with pencils, rulers, and large sheets of paper. Invite students to draw the floor plan of anything. A fourth grader planned, designed, and built a futuristic mission for space exploration.

Bodily-Kinesthetic

10. Put together a hands-on center with materials such as clay, blocks, and craft materials. While studying Michelangelo's sculpting style, my students decided to make chess sets out of clay.

11. Enrich a drama center with play books and ideas for student performances or puppet theater. One student wrote his own version of a Greek tragedy, selected his cast, and performed it for other classes.

12. Create an open space for creative movement (mini-trampoline, juggling equipment, drama area, and so on). Or set up an outside flow area that can be monitored by a parent volunteer. I've seen students use this area to learn how to juggle (which increases eye-hand coordination) and teach jazz and country dances to their peers.

Musical

13. Set up a music lab with cassettes, earphones, and various tapes to compare and contrast. For example, students can compare Mozart's "Symphony No. 39" with Garth Brooks's "The Thunder Rolls" and the Beatles' "Paperback Writer."

14. Display lyrics for students to analyze. Fill a listening lab with sound-related items such as a stethoscope, walkie-talkies, and a conch shell.

15. Invite students to compose their own songs and write the lyrics. A fourth grader composed a song for the violin that represented the tone

and feeling of the book *Where the Red Fern Grows* by Wilson Rawls.

Interpersonal

16. Create a flow area with a round table—to encourage group discussions. You can write curriculum-based discussion ideas on cards and place them in the center, or let students choose their own topics.

17. Establish a debate center where students form teams and choose a subject to debate. Give kids ten minutes to prepare for the debate. Rain-forest preservation versus local economic needs, and whether or not kids should be allowed to ride in-line skates to school are two topics that sparked heated discussions among students.

18. Give students an index card stating a common school-related problem. Challenge them to work together to come up with solutions. A group of second graders discussed how to resolve arguments that developed in their handball games. They wrote rules to share with other students.

Intrapersonal

19. Create a selection of self-esteem activities. For example, ask students to list ten of their strengths or have them write out specific ways they are a good friend to others. Encourage journal writing.

20. Invite kids to draw a picture that describes a mood or feeling. I've found this really helps older students to become aware of their fluctuating moods and to reflect on how their moods affect their daily lives.

21. Design study nooks for individual work. Use beanbag chairs to make them cozy spaces. A third grader who had difficulty controlling his anger used this nook often as a cooling-off location.

Personalized Learning

The biggest impact that the Multiple Intelligences Theory has had in my classroom is that it has helped me create an individualized learning environment. I no longer expect students to think exactly alike in order to be *right*. I am more comfortable with my students' individualistic thinking—and my own. In personalizing each student's education experience, I find that an increasing percentage of students discover their own strengths, put more effort into improving their weaker areas, and feel better about themselves.

The Challenges of Assessing Young Children Appropriately

In the past decade, testing of 4-, 5-, and 6-year-olds has been excessive and inappropriate. Given this history of misuse, Ms. Shepard maintains, the burden of proof must rest with assessment advocates to demonstrate the usefulness of assessment and to ensure that abuses will not recur.

Lorrie A. Shepard

LORRIE A. SHEPARD is a professor of education at the University of Colorado, Boulder. She is past president of the National Council on Measurement in Education, past vice president of the American Educational Research Association, and a member of the National Academy of Education. She wishes to thank Sharon Lynn Kagan, M. Elizabeth Graue, and Scott F. Marion for their thoughtful suggestions on drafts of this article.

PROPOSALS to "assess" young children are likely to be met with outrage or enthusiasm, depending on one's prior experience and one's image of the testing involved. Will an inappropriate paper-and-pencil test be used to keep some 5-year-olds out of school? Or will the assessment, implemented as an ordinary part of good instruction, help children learn? A governor advocating a test for every preschooler in the nation may have in mind the charts depicting normal growth in the pediatrician's office. Why shouldn't parents have access to similar measures to monitor their child's cognitive and academic progress? Middle-class parents, sanguine about the use of test scores to make college-selection decisions, may be eager to have similar tests determine their child's entrance into preschool or kindergarten. Early childhood experts, however, are more likely to respond with alarm because they are more familiar with the complexities of defining and measuring

development and learning in young children and because they are more aware of the widespread abuses of readiness testing that occurred in the 1980s.

Given a history of misuse, it is impossible to make positive recommendations about how assessments could be used to monitor the progress of individual children or to evaluate the quality of educational programs without offering assurances that the abuses will not recur. In what follows, I summarize the negative history of standardized testing of young children in order to highlight the transformation needed in both the substance and purposes of early childhood assessment. Then I explain from a measurement perspective how the features of an assessment must be tailored to match the purpose of the assessment. Finally, I describe differences in what assessments might look like when they are used for purposes of screening for handicapping conditions, supporting instruction, or monitoring state and national trends.

Note that I use the term *test* when referring to traditional, standardized developmental and pre-academic measures and the term *assessment* when referring to more developmentally appropriate procedures for observing and evaluating young children. This is a semantic trick that plays on the different connotations of the two terms. Technically, they mean the same thing. Tests, as defined by the *Stan-*

dards for Educational and Psychological Testing, have always included systematic observations of behavior, but our experience is with tests as more formal, one-right-answer instruments used to rank and sort individuals. As we shall see, assessments might be standardized, involve paper-and-pencil responses, and so on, but in contrast to traditional testing, "assessment" implies a substantive focus on student learning for the purpose of effective intervention. While *test* and *assessment* cannot be reliably distinguished technically, the difference between these two terms as they have grown up in common parlance is of symbolic importance. Using the term *assessment* presents an opportunity to step away from past practices and ask why we should try to measure what young children know and can do. If there are legitimate purposes for gathering such data, then we can seek the appropriate content and form of assessment to align with those purposes.

Negative History of Testing Young Children

In order to understand the negative history of the standardized testing of young children in the past decade, we need to understand some larger shifts in curriculum and teaching practices. The distortion of the curriculum of the early grades during the 1980s is now a familiar and well-documented story. Indeed, negative effects persist in many school districts today.

Although rarely the result of conscious policy decisions, a variety of indirect pressures — such as older kindergartners, extensive preschooling for children from affluent families, parental demands for the teaching of reading in kindergarten, and accountability testing in higher grades — produced a skill-driven kindergarten curriculum. Because what once were first-grade expectations were shoved down to kindergarten, these shifts in practice were referred to as the "escalation of curriculum" or "academic trickle-down." The result of these changes was an aversive learning environment inconsistent with the learning needs of young children. Developmentally inappropriate instructional practices, characterized by long periods of seatwork, high levels of stress, and a plethora of fill-in-the-blank worksheets, placed many children at risk by setting standards for attention span, social maturity, and academic productivity that could not be met by many normal 5-year-olds.

Teachers and school administrators responded to the problem of a kindergarten environment that was increasingly hostile to young children with several ill-considered policies: raising the entrance age for school, instituting readiness screening to hold some children out of school for a year, increasing retentions in kindergarten, and creating two-year programs with an extra grade either before or after kindergarten. These policies and practices had a benign intent: to protect children from stress and school failure. However, they were ill-considered because they were implemented without contemplating the possibility of negative side effects and without awareness that retaining some children and excluding others only exacerbated the problems by creating an older and older population of kindergartners.[1] The more reasonable corrective for a skill-driven curriculum at earlier and earlier ages would have been curriculum reform of the kind exemplified by the recommendations for developmentally appropriate practices issued by the National Association for the Education of Young Children (NAEYC), the nation's largest professional association of early childhood educators.[2]

The first response of many schools, however, was not to fix the problem of inappropriate curriculum but to exclude those children who could not keep up or who might be harmed. Readiness testing was the chief means of implementing policies aimed at removing young children from inappropriate instructional programs. Thus the use of readiness testing increased dramatically during the 1980s and continues today in many school districts.[3]

Two different kinds of tests are used: developmental screening measures, originally intended as the first step in the evaluation of children for potential handicaps; and pre-academic skills tests, intended for use in planning classroom instruction.[4] The technical and conceptual problems with these tests are numerous.[5] Tests are being used for purposes for which they were never designed or validated. Waiting a year or being placed in a two-year program represents a dramatic disruption in a child's life, yet not one of the existing readiness measures has sufficient reliability or predictive validity to warrant making such decisions.

Developmental and pre-academic skills tests are based on outmoded theories of aptitude and learning that originated in the 1930s. The excessive use of these tests and the negative consequences of being judged unready focused a spotlight on the tests' substantive inadequacies. The widely used Gesell Test is made up of items from old I.Q. tests and is indistinguishable statistically from a measure of I.Q.; the same is true for developmental measures that are really short-form I.Q. tests. Assigning children to different instructional opportunities on the basis of such tests carries forward nativist assumptions popular in the 1930s and

Illustration by Kay Salem

1940s. At that time, it was believed that I.Q. tests could accurately measure innate ability, unconfounded by prior learning experiences. Because these measured "capacities" were thought to be fixed and unalterable, those who scored poorly were given low-level training consistent with their supposedly limited potential. Tests of academic content might have the promise of being more instructionally relevant than disguised I.Q. tests, but, as Anne Stallman and David Pearson have shown, the decomposed and decontextualized prereading skills measured by traditional readiness tests are not compatible with current research on early literacy.[6]

Readiness testing also raises serious equity concerns. Because all the readiness measures in use are influenced by past opportunity to learn, a disproportionate number of poor and minority children are identified as unready and are excluded from school when they most need it. Thus children without preschool experience and without extensive literacy experiences at home are sent back to the very environments that caused them to score poorly on readiness measures in the first place. Or, if poor and minority children who do not pass the readiness tests are admitted to the school but made to spend an extra year in kindergarten, they suffer disproportionately the stigma and negative effects of retention.

The last straw in this negative account of testing young children is the evidence that fallible tests are often followed by ineffective programs. A review of controlled studies has shown no academic benefits from retention in kindergarten or from extra-year programs, whether developmental kindergartens or transitional first grades. When extra-year children finally get to first grade, they do not do better on average than equally "unready" children who go directly on to first grade.[7] However, a majority of children placed in these extra-year programs do experience some short- or long-term trauma, as reported by their parents.[8] Contrary to popular belief that kindergarten children are "too young to notice" retention, most of them know that they are not making "normal" progress, and many continue to make reference to the decision years later. "If I hadn't spent an extra year in kindergarten, I would be in __ grade now." In the face of such evidence, there is little wonder that many early childhood educators ask why we test young children at all.

Principles for Assessment And Testing

The NAEYC and the National Association of Early Childhood Specialists in State Departments of Education have played key roles in informing educators about the harm of developmentally inappropriate instructional practices and the misuse of tests. In 1991 NAEYC published "Guidelines for Appropriate Curriculum Content and Assessment in Programs Serving Children Ages 3 Through 8."[9] Although the detailed recommendations are too numerous to be repeated here, a guiding principle is that *assessments should bring about benefits for children, or data should not be collected at all.* Specifically, assessments "should not be used to recommend that children stay out of a program, be retained in grade, or be assigned to a segregated group based on ability or developmental maturity."[10] Instead, NAEYC acknowledges three legitimate purposes for assessment: 1) to plan instruction and communicate with parents, 2) to identify children with special needs, and 3) to evaluate programs.

Although NAEYC used *assessment* in its "Guidelines," as I do, to avoid associations with inappropriate uses of tests, both the general principle and the specific guidelines are equally applicable to formal testing. In other words, tests should not be used if they do not bring about benefits for children. In what follows I summarize some additional principles that can ensure that assessments (and tests) are beneficial and not harmful. Then, in later sections, I consider each of NAEYC's recommended uses for assessment, including national, state, and local needs for program evaluation and accountability data.

I propose a second guiding principle for assessment that is consistent with the NAEYC perspective. *The content of assessments should reflect and model progress toward important learning goals.* Conceptions of what is important to learn should take into account both physical and social/emotional development as well as cognitive learning. For most assessment purposes in the cognitive domain, content should be congruent with subject matter in emergent literacy and numeracy. In the past, developmental measures were made as "curriculum free" or "culture free" as possible in an effort to tap biology and avoid the confounding effects of past opportunity to learn. Of course, this was an impossible task because a child's ability to "draw a triangle"

or "point to the ball on top of the table" depends on prior experiences as well as on biological readiness. However, if the purpose of assessment is no longer to sort students into programs on the basis of a one-time measure of ability, then it is possible to have assessment content mirror what we want children to learn.

A third guiding principle can be inferred from several of the NAEYC guidelines. *The methods of assessment must be appropriate to the development and experiences of young children.* This means that — along with written products — observation, oral readings, and interviews should be used for purposes of assessment. Even for large-scale purposes, assessment should not be an artificial and decontextualized event; instead, the demands of data collection should be consistent with children's prior experiences in classrooms and at home. Assessment practices should recognize the diversity of learners and must be in accord with children's language development — both in English and in the native languages of those whose home language is not English.

A fourth guiding principle can be drawn from the psychometric literature on test validity. *Assessments should be tailored to a specific purpose.* Although not stated explicitly in the NAEYC document, this principle is implied by the recommendation of three sets of guidelines for three separate assessment purposes.

Matching the Why and How Of Assessment

The reason for any assessment — i.e., how the assessment information will be used — affects the substance and form of

> *The intended use of an assessment will determine the need for normative information or other means to support the interpretation of results.*

the assessment in several ways. First, the degree of technical accuracy required depends on use. For example, the identification of children for special education has critical implications for individuals. Failure to be identified could mean the denial of needed services, but being identified as in need of special services may also mean removal from normal classrooms (at least part of the time) and a potentially stigmatizing label. A great deal is at stake in such assessment, so the multifaceted evaluation employed must have a high degree of reliability and validity. Ordinary classroom assessments also affect individual children, but the consequences of these decisions are not nearly so great. An inaccurate assessment on a given day may lead a teacher to make a poor grouping or instructional decision, but such an error can be corrected as more information becomes available about what an individual child "really knows."

Group assessment refers to uses, such as program evaluation or school accountability, in which the focus is on group performance rather than on individual scores. Although group assessments may need to meet very high standards for technical accuracy, because of the high stakes associated with the results, the individual scores that contribute to the group information do not have to be so reliable and do not have to be directly comparable, so long as individual results are not reported. When only group results are desired, it is possible to use the technical advantages of matrix sampling — a technique in which each participant takes only a small portion of the assessment — to provide a rich, in-depth assessment of the intended content domain without overburdening any of the children sampled. When the "group" is very large, such as all the fourth-graders in a state or in the nation, then assessing a representative sample will produce essentially the same results for the group average as if every student had been assessed.

Purpose must also determine the content of assessment. When trying to diagnose potential learning handicaps, we still rely on aptitude-like measures designed to be as content-free as possible. We do so in order to avoid confusing lack of opportunity to learn with inability to learn. When the purpose of assessment is to measure actual learning, then content must naturally be tied to learning outcomes. However, even among achievement tests, there is considerable variability in the degree of alignment to a specific curriculum. Although to the lay person "math is math" and "reading is reading," measurement specialists are aware that tiny changes in test format can make a large difference in student performance. For example, a high proportion of students may be able to add numbers when they are presented in vertical format, but many will be unable to do the same problems presented horizontally. If manipulatives are used in some elementary classrooms but not in all, including the use of manipulatives in a mathematics assessment will disadvantage some children, while excluding their use will disadvantage others.

Assessments that are used to guide instruction in a given classroom should be integrally tied to the curriculum of that classroom. However, for large-scale assessments at the state and national level, the issues of curriculum match and the effect of assessment content on future instruction become much more problematic. For example, in a state with an agreed-upon curriculum, including geometry assessment in the early grades may be appropriate, but it would be problematic in states with strong local control of curriculum and so with much more curricular diversity.

Large-scale assessments, such as the National Assessment of Educational Progress, must include instructionally relevant content, but they must do so without conforming too closely to any single curriculum. In the past, this requirement has led to the problem of achievement tests that are limited to the "lowest common denominator." Should the instrument used for program evaluation include only the content that is common to all curricula? Or should it include everything that is in any program's goals? Although the common core approach can lead to a narrowing of curriculum when assessment results are associated with high stakes, including everything can be equally troublesome if it leads to superficial teaching in pursuit of too many different goals.

Finally, the intended use of an assessment will determine the need for normative information or other means to support the interpretation of assessment results. Identifying children with special needs requires normative data to distinguish serious physical, emotional, or learning problems from the wide range of normal development. When reporting to parents, teachers also need some idea of what constitutes grade-level performance, but such "norms" can be in the form of benchmark performances — evidence that children are working at grade level — rather than statistical percentiles.

To prevent the abuses of the past, the purposes and substance of early childhood assessments must be transformed. Assessments should be conducted only if they serve a beneficial purpose: to gain services for children with special needs, to inform instruction by building on what students already know, to improve programs, or to provide evidence nationally or in the states about programmatic needs. The form, substance, and technical features of assessment should be appropriate for the use intended for assessment data. Moreover, the methods of assessment must be compatible with the developmental level and experiences of young children. Below, I consider the implications of these principles for three different categories of assessment purposes.

Identifying Children with Special Needs

I discuss identification for special education first because this is the type of assessment that most resembles past uses of developmental screening measures. However, there is no need for wholesale administration of such tests to all incoming kindergartners. If we take the precepts of developmentally appropriate practices seriously, then at each age level a very broad range of abilities and performance levels is to be expected and tolerated. If potential handicaps are understood to be relatively rare and extreme, then it is not necessary to screen all children for "hidden" disabilities. By definition, serious learning problems should be apparent. Although it is possible to miss hearing or vision problems (at least mild ones) without systematic screening, referral for evaluation of a possible learning handicap should occur only when parents or teachers notice that a child is not progressing normally in comparison to age-appropriate expectations. In-depth assessments should then be conducted to verify the severity of the problem and to rule out a variety of other explanations for poor performance.

For this type of assessment, developmental measures, including I.Q. tests, continue to be useful. Clinicians attempt to make normative evaluations using relatively curriculum-free tasks, but today they are more likely to acknowledge the fallibility of such efforts. For such difficult assessments, clinicians must have specialized training in both diagnostic assessment and child development.

When identifying children with special needs, evaluators should use two general strategies in order to avoid confounding the ability to learn with past opportunity to learn. First, as recommended by the National Academy Panel on Selection and Placement of Students in Programs for the Mentally Retarded,[11] a child's learning environment should be evaluated to rule out poor instruction as the possible cause of a child's lack of learning. Although seldom carried out in practice, this evaluation should include trying out other methods to support learning and possibly trying a different teacher before concluding that a child can't learn from ordinary classroom instruction. A second important strategy is to observe a child's functioning in multiple contexts. Often children who appear to be impaired in school function well at home or with peers. Observation outside of school is critical for children from diverse cultural backgrounds and for those whose home language is not English. The NAEYC stresses that "screening should never be used to identify second language learners as 'handicapped,' solely on the basis of their limited abilities in English."[12]

In-depth developmental assessments are needed to ensure that children with disabilities receive appropriate services. However, the diagnostic model of special education should not be generalized to a larger population of below-average learners, or the result will be the reinstitution of tracking. Elizabeth Graue and I analyzed recent efforts to create "at-risk" kindergartens and found that these practices are especially likely to occur when resources for extended-day programs are available only for the children most in need.[13] The result of such programs is often to segregate children from low socioeconomic backgrounds into classrooms where time is spent drilling on low-level prereading skills like those found on readiness tests. The consequences of dumbed-down instruction in kindergarten are just as pernicious as the effects of tracking at higher grade levels, especially when the at-risk kindergarten group is kept together for first grade. If resources for extended-day kindergarten are scarce, one alternative would be to group children heterogeneously for half the day and then, for the other half, to provide extra enrichment activities for children with limited literacy experiences.

Classroom Assessments

Unlike traditional readiness tests that are intended to predict learning, classroom assessments should support instruction by modeling the dimensions of learning. Although we must allow considerable latitude for children to construct their own understandings, teachers must nonetheless have knowledge of normal development if they are to support children's extensions and next steps. Ordinary classroom tasks can then be used to assess a child's progress in relation to a developmental continuum. An example of a developmental continuum would be that of emergent writing, beginning with scribbles, then moving on to pictures and random letters, and then proceeding to some letter/word correspondences. These continua are not rigid, however, and several dimensions running in parallel may be necessary to describe growth in a single content area. For example, a second dimension of early writing — a child's ability to invent increasingly elaborated stories when dictating to an adult — is not dependent on mastery of writing letters, just as listening comprehension, making predictions about books, and story retellings should be developed in parallel to, not after, mastery of letter sounds.

Although there is a rich research literature documenting patterns of emergent literacy and numeracy, corresponding assessment materials are not so readily available. In the next few years, national interest in developing alternative, performance-based measures should generate more materials and resources. Specifically, new Chapter 1 legislation is likely to support the development of reading assessments that are more authentic and instructionally relevant.

For example, classroom-embedded reading assessments were created from ordinary instructional materials by a group of third-grade teachers in conjunction with researchers at the Center for Research on Evaluation, Standards, and Student Testing.[14] The teachers elected to focus on fluency and making meaning as reading goals; running records and story summaries were selected as the methods of assessment.

But how should student progress be evaluated? In keeping with the idea of representing a continuum of proficiency, third-grade teachers took all the chapter books in their classrooms and sorted them into grade-level stacks, 1-1 (first grade, first semester), 1-2, 2-1, and so on up to fifth grade. Then they identified representative or marker books in each category to use for assessment. Once the books had been sorted by difficulty, it became possible to document that children were reading increasingly difficult texts with understanding. Photocopied pages from the marker books also helped parents see what teachers considered to be grade-level materials and provided them with concrete evidence of their child's progress. Given mandates for student-level reporting under Chapter 1, state departments of education or test publishers could help develop similar systems of this type with sufficient standardization to ensure comparability across districts.

In the meantime, classroom teachers — or preferably teams of teachers — are left to invent their own assessments for classroom use. In many schools, teachers are already working with portfolios and developing scoring criteria. The best procedure appears to be having grade-level teams and then cross-grade teams meet to discuss expectations and evaluation criteria. These conversations will be more productive if, for each dimension to be assessed, teachers collect student work and use marker papers to illustrate continua of performance. Several papers might be used at each stage to reflect the tremendous variety in children's responses, even when following the same general progression.

Benchmark papers can also be an effective means of communicating with parents. For example, imagine using sample papers from grades K-3 to illustrate expectations regarding "invented spelling." Invented spelling or "temporary spelling" is the source of a great deal of parental dissatisfaction with reform curricula. Yet most parents who attack invented spelling have never been given a rationale for its use. That is, no one has explained it in such a way that the explanation builds on the parents' own willingness to allow successive approximations in their child's early language development. They have never been shown a connection between writing expectations and grade-level spelling lists or been informed about differences in rules for first drafts and final drafts. Sample papers could be selected to illustrate the increasing mastery of grade-appropriate words, while allowing for misspellings of advanced words on first drafts. Communicating criteria is helpful to parents, and, as we have seen in the literature on performance assessment, it also helps children to understand what is expected and to become better at assessing their own work.

Monitoring National and State Trends

In 1989, when the President and the nation's governors announced "readiness for school" as the first education goal, many early childhood experts feared the creation of a national test for school entry. Indeed, given the negative history of readiness testing, the first thing the Goal 1 Technical Planning Subgroup did was to issue caveats about what an early childhood assessment must *not* be. It should not be a one-dimensional, reductionist measure of a child's knowledge and abilities; it should not be called a measure of "readiness" as if some children were not ready to learn; and it should not be used to "label, stigmatize, or classify any individual child or group of children."[15]

However, with this fearsome idea set aside, the Technical Planning Subgroup endorsed the idea of an early childhood assessment system that would periodically gather data on the condition of young children as they enter school. The purpose of the assessment would be to inform public policy and especially to help "in charting progress toward achievement of the National Education Goals,

> *Beginning in 1998-99, a representative sample of 23,000 kindergarten students will be assessed and then followed through grade 5.*

and for informing the development, expansion, and/or modification of policies and programs that affect young children and their families."[16] Assuming that certain safeguards are built in, such data could be a powerful force in focusing national attention and resources on the needs of young children.

Unlike past testing practices aimed at evaluating individual children in comparison with normative expectations, a large-scale, nationally representative assessment would be used to monitor national trends. The purpose of such an assessment would be analogous to the use of the National Assessment of Educational Progress (NAEP) to measure major shifts in achievement patterns. For example, NAEP results have demonstrated gains in the achievement of black students in the South as a result of desegregation, and NAEP achievement measures showed gains during the 1980s in basic skills and declines in higher-order thinking skills and problem solving. Similar data are not now available for preschoolers or for children in the primary grades. If an early childhood assessment were conducted periodically, it would be possible to demonstrate the relationship between health services and early learning and to evaluate the impact of such programs as Head Start.

In keeping with the precept that methods of assessment should follow from the purpose of assessment, the Technical Planning Subgroup recommended that sampling of both children and assessment items be used to collect national data. Sampling would allow a broad assessment of a more multifaceted content domain and would preclude the misuse of individual scores to place or stigmatize individual children. A national early childhood assessment should also serve as a model of important content. As a means to shape public understanding of the full range of abilities and experiences that influence early learning and development, the Technical Planning Subgroup identified five dimensions to be assessed: 1) physical well-being and motor development, 2) social and emotional development, 3) approaches toward learning, 4) language usage, and 5) cognition and general knowledge.

Responding to the need for national data to document the condition of children as they enter school and to measure progress on Goal 1, the U.S. Department of Education has commissioned the Early Childhood Longitudinal Study: Kindergarten Cohort. Beginning in the 1998-99 school year, a representative sample of 23,000 kindergarten students will be assessed and then followed through grade 5. The content of the assessments used will correspond closely to the dimensions recommended by the Technical Planning Subgroup. In addition, data will be collected on each child's family, communi-

ty, and school/program. Large-scale studies of this type serve both program evaluation purposes (How effective are preschool services for children?) and research purposes (What is the relationship between children's kindergarten experiences and their academic success throughout elementary school?).

National needs for early childhood data and local needs for program evaluation information are similar in some respects and dissimilar in others. Both uses require group data. However, a critical distinction that affects the methods of evaluation is whether or not local programs share a

> *Fearing that "assessment" is just a euphemism for more bad testing, many early childhood professionals have asked, Why test at all?*

common curriculum. If local programs, such as all the kindergartens in a school district, have agreed on the same curriculum, it is possible to build program evaluation assessments from an aggregation of the measures used for classroom purposes. Note that the entire state of Kentucky is attempting to develop such a system by scoring classroom portfolios for state reporting.

If programs being evaluated do not have the same specific curricula, as is the case with a national assessment and with some state assessments, then the assessment measures must reflect broad, agreed-upon goals without privileging any specific curriculum. This is a tall order, more easily said than done. For this reason, the Technical Planning Subgroup recommended that validity studies be built into the procedures for data collection. For example, pilot studies should verify that what children can do in one-on-one assessment settings is consistent with what they can do in their classrooms, and assessment methods should always allow children more than one way to show what they know.

Conclusion

In the past decade, testing of 4-, 5-, and 6-year-olds has been excessive and inappropriate. Under a variety of different names, leftover I.Q. tests have been used to track children into ineffective programs or to deny them school entry. Prereading tests held over from the 1930s have encouraged the teaching of decontextualized skills. In response, fearing that "assessment" is just a euphemism for more bad testing, many early childhood professionals have asked, Why test at all? Indeed, given a history of misuse, the burden of proof must rest with assessment advocates to demonstrate the usefulness of assessment and to ensure that abuses will not recur. Key principles that support responsible use of assessment information follow.

• No testing of young children should occur unless it can be shown to lead to beneficial results.

• Methods of assessment, especially the language used, must be appropriate to the development and experiences of young children.

• Features of assessment — content, form, evidence of validity, and standards for interpretation — must be tailored to the specific purpose of an assessment.

• Identifying children for special education is a legitimate purpose for assessment and still requires the use of curriculum-free, aptitude-like measures and normative comparisons. However, handicapping conditions are rare; the diagnostic model used by special education should not be generalized to a larger population of below-average learners.

• For both classroom instructional purposes and purposes of public policy making, the content of assessments should embody the important dimensions of early learning and development. The tasks and skills children are asked to perform should reflect and model progress toward important learning goals.

In the past, local newspapers have published readiness checklists that suggested that children should stay home from kindergarten if they couldn't cut with scissors. In the future, national and local assessments should demonstrate the richness of what children do know and should foster instruction that builds on their strengths. Telling a story in conjunction with scribbles is a meaningful stage in literacy development. Reading a story in English and retelling it in Spanish is evidence of reading comprehension. Evidence of important learning in beginning mathematics should not be counting to 100 instead of to 10. It should be extending patterns; solving arithmetic problems with blocks and explaining how you got your answer; constructing graphs to show how many children come to school by bus, by walking, by car; and demonstrating understanding of patterns and quantities in a variety of ways.

In classrooms, we need new forms of assessment so that teachers can support children's physical, social, and cognitive development. And at the level of public policy, we need new forms of assessment so that programs will be judged on the basis of worthwhile educational goals.

1. Lorrie A. Shepard and Mary Lee Smith, "Escalating Academic Demand in Kindergarten: Counterproductive Policies," *Elementary School Journal*, vol. 89, 1988, pp. 135-45.

2. Sue Bredekamp, ed., *Developmentally Appropriate Practice in Early Childhood Programs Serving Children from Birth Through Age 8*, exp. ed. (Washington, D.C.: National Association for the Education of Young Children, 1987).

3. M. Therese Gnezda and Rosemary Bolig, *A National Survey of Public School Testing of Pre-Kindergarten and Kindergarten Children* (Washington, D.C.: National Forum on the Future of Children and Families, National Research Council, 1988).

4. Samuel J. Meisels, "Uses and Abuses of Developmental Screening and School Readiness Testing," *Young Children*, vol. 42, 1987, pp. 4-6, 68-73.

5. Lorrie A. Shepard and M. Elizabeth Graue, "The Morass of School Readiness Screening: Research on Test Use and Test Validity," in Bernard Spodek, ed., *Handbook of Research on the Education of Young Children* (New York: Macmillan, 1993), pp. 293-305.

6. Anne C. Stallman and P. David Pearson, "Formal Measures of Early Literacy," in Lesley Mandel Morrow and Jeffrey K. Smith, eds., *Assessment for Instruction in Early Literacy* (Englewood Cliffs, N.J.: Prentice-Hall, 1990), pp. 7-44.

7. Lorrie A. Shepard, "A Review of Research on Kindergarten Retention," in Lorrie A. Shepard and Mary Lee Smith, eds., *Flunking Grades: Research and Policies on Retention* (London: Falmer Press, 1989), pp. 64-78.

8. Lorrie A. Shepard and Mary Lee Smith, "Academic and Emotional Effects of Kindergarten Retention in One School District," in idem, pp. 79-107.

9. "Guidelines for Appropriate Curriculum Content and Assessment in Programs Serving Children Ages 3 Through 8," *Young Children*, vol. 46, 1991, pp. 21-38.

10. Ibid., p. 32.

11. Kirby A. Heller, Wayne H. Holtzman, and Samuel Messick, eds., *Placing Children in Special Education* (Washington, D.C.: National Academy Press, 1982).

12. "Guidelines," p. 33.

13. Shepard and Graue, op. cit.

14. The Center for Research on Evaluation, Standards, and Student Testing is located on the campuses of the University of California, Los Angeles, and the University of Colorado, Boulder.

15. *Goal 1: Technical Planning Subgroup Report on School Readiness* (Washington, D.C.: National Education Goals Panel, September 1991).

16. Ibid., p. 6.

The Challenge of Outcome-Based Education

Aiming for New Outcomes: The Promise and The Reality

John O'Neil

John O'Neil is Contributing Editor to *Educational Leadership*.

Just two years ago, the rhetoric supporting a massive American shift to an education system organized around student outcomes was cresting.

From Congress to the State House, politicians and educators advocated higher standards for student learning. One expert after another opined that consensus was needed on what students "should know and be able to do" at the culmination of their K–12 experience. Then, the thinking went, schools would refocus their programs to help students attain these desired outcomes. Ultimately, students would earn a diploma not by merely sitting through a series of required courses—they would have to demonstrate their proficiency in these common outcomes. "Outcome-based education" (OBE) was the label loosely applied to this results-oriented thinking.

The talk sparked a spate of activity. Acting on the impetus provided by national education goals, a national process was launched to describe outcomes in the major subject areas. State after state undertook to craft common learner outcomes, or to require districts to do so. One state, Pennsylvania, pledged to phase out the traditional Carnegie unit, saying that within several years the state's high school graduates would have to demonstrate attainment of outcomes, not merely accrue the necessary clock hours in required courses. If put into practice, the changes proposed in Pennsylvania and elsewhere would have marked a dramatic shift in the way schools do business.

> **Besieged by critics, supporters of outcome-based education are struggling to confront the implications of their philosophy.**

Since then, however, the OBE bandwagon has stalled. In Pennsylvania, the state was forced to curtail its ambitious OBE plan in the wake of fierce opposition, much of it mobilized by organized religious conservative groups. Among their criticisms, opponents claimed that the state's proposed outcomes watered down academics in favor of ill-defined values and process skills. Similar charges were lobbed against OBE plans in other states, and state officials in Minnesota, Ohio, Iowa, and Virginia have been forced to revise, delay, or drop their efforts.

In the face of the opposition, many OBE enthusiasts are retrenching, pondering how an idea that, on its face, appears so sensible, proved to be so controversial. "I think OBE is largely done for as a saleable public term," a former Pennsylvania official who played a key role in the state's OBE plan says darkly. "Now, nobody can use the O-word," jokes Bob Marzano, senior program director at the Mid-continent Regional Education Laboratory (McREL).

What Is OBE, Anyway?

One reason OBE has sparked differences of opinion is that many people—even within the camps of proponents and opponents—define the term differently.

At one level, outcome-based education is the simple principle that decisions about curriculum and instruction should be driven by the outcomes we'd like children to display at the end of their educational experiences.

Many OBE enthusiasts are retrenching, pondering how an idea that, on its face, appears so sensible, proved to be so controversial.

"It's a simple matter of making sure that you're clear on what teaching should accomplish ... and adjusting your teaching and assessing as necessary to accomplish what you set out to accomplish," says Grant Wiggins, director of programs for the Center on Learning, Assessment, and School Structure. "Viewed that way, nobody in their right mind would have objections to it." In this sense, outcome-based education is a process, and one could use it to come up with schools as unlike one another as Summerhill or one E.D. Hirsch dreamed up.

At another level, policymakers increasingly talk about creating outcome-driven education "systems" that would redefine traditional approaches to accountability. In policy-ese this means that schools should be accountable for demonstrating that students have mastered important outcomes (so-called "outputs") not for their per-pupil ratio or the number of books in the school library (so-called "inputs").

Both the outcome-based philosophy and the notion that schools should have more autonomy (site-based management) have been adopted as the new conventional wisdom guiding accountability, despite the lack of compelling research evidence supporting either reform, points out Thomas Guskey, professor of education policy studies at the University of Kentucky. Policy wonks love the crystal clear logic of OBE and Site-Based Management—at least on paper. "Outcome-based education gives them the 'what' and site-based management gives them the 'who' " in their accountability system, Guskey says.

Parents and educators familiar with a specific version of outcome-based education often equate all OBE with the model they've heard most about. But the models differ. The Johnson City, New York, public schools, for example, have gained a national reputation for their outcome-based education program. The Outcomes-Driven Developmental Model, as they refer to their model, has contributed to impressive gains in student achievement of desired outcomes over the past two decades. Another highly visible model of outcome-based education is that espoused by Bill Spady and the High Success Network.

The different interpretations of outcome-based education help explain why, even among those who support an outcomes-driven education system, sharp divisions persist over what it would look like. For example, business leaders and policymakers appear to strongly support the idea of outcome-based accountability systems. But their conception of desirable learning outcomes appears to be very different from that offered by educators.

The very nature of outcome-based education forces one to address inherently controversial issues. "The questions ultimately get down to the fundamentals—what's worth knowing and what's the purpose of schooling," says Jay McTighe, an observer of the

OBE movement who directs the Maryland Assessment Consortium. "Outcome-based education gets to the heart of the matter."

Current Conditions

Proponents of OBE suggest that an outcome-based education system would help to address some of the problematic conditions confronting contemporary schools.

Numerous experts, for example, believe that the currently expressed outcomes for student learning are neither sufficiently rigorous nor appropriate for the requirements of students' adult lives. One national study after another has shown that graduates of U.S. schools are able to demonstrate very basic levels of skill and knowledge, but that they lack higher-order thinking skills. Put simply, many students can (and do) make it through the education system without learning needed skills and knowledge, even though they've earned the requisite number of Carnegie units and passed minimum competency exams and classroom tests. Under OBE, students would be required to *demonstrate* these necessary outcomes before graduation. Just as pilots are required to demonstrate their facility at flying an aircraft (not merely sit through the required instruction), students would be pushed to display the outcomes society holds important.

This raises the related equity issue. The futures of many students are compromised because the outcomes held for them are low or unclear. As they progress through school, such students are frequently tracked into low-level courses where they are not held responsible for the outcomes necessary for success after graduation. As long as the credentialing system is based on seat time, one student may earn a diploma by taking advanced placement history and calculus, while another makes it through the system taking watered-down academic fare. Put another way, some students—and some schools—are held to high standards, while many others are not. According to the OBE philosophy, all students will

be held responsible for attaining common outcomes. And schools will be responsible for altering present conditions to prepare them to do it.

In addition, OBE can bring some needed focus to the way schools are organized. Currently, state and district regulations—including graduation requirements, competency tests, textbook adoption policies, local curriculum guides, special mandates to teach about AIDS or gun safety—combine in a patchwork of diffuse and oftentimes contradictory signals to which teachers must attend as they plan instruction. In the system envisioned by OBE enthusiasts, the desired learner outcomes become the foundation upon which decisions about curriculum, instruction, assessment, staff development, and so on are based. Presumably, such a system would be better aligned and focused and, thus, more efficient than the system now operating.

What Outcomes?

As promising an approach as OBE may be, even proponents have struggled to explain how schools can successfully act upon the implications

of their philosophy. Few schools appear to have actually reorganized their curriculum and overhauled their assessment and reporting schemes to reflect new, higher outcomes. More commonly, schools and districts draft outcomes based on the present curriculum or write ambitious and far-reaching new outcomes while changing the curriculum very little.

The reason seems to be that schools, districts, and states that have attempted to use OBE philosophy very quickly find themselves struggling with some difficult challenges.

The first is deciding what outcomes should form the heart of an OBE plan—and no aspect of OBE has proven quite so contentious. Opponents of OBE have consistently charged that traditional academic content is omitted or buried in a morass of pedagogic claptrap in the OBE plans that have emerged to date.

For example, a draft plan in Virginia, since shelved, contained six major areas of student outcomes: environmental stewardship, personal well-being and accomplishment, interpersonal relationships, lifelong learning, cultural and creative endeavors, work and economic well-being, and local and global civic participation. According to the draft, a student outcome for personal well-being and accomplishment was "a responsible individual who has a good sense of his or her abilities and needs, and uses that knowledge consistently to make choices likely to lead to a healthy, productive, and fulfilling life." A worthy aim, to be sure, but critics convinced the general public that such outcomes would lead to more "touchy-feely" exercises and less history and math in the schools.

Supporters of OBE find themselves in a precarious position. Many of them believe strongly that an educated graduate is not just someone who has absorbed a set of discrete experiences in the traditional academic domains. The OBE movement "has taken shape around the idea that the educational experience is too fragmented, and that important outcomes not easily pegged to typical subject area divisions and pedagogical approaches are falling through the cracks," says Wiggins. But architects of OBE plans find it extraordinarily difficult to weave the academic content into the broad outcomes. "If you say that the purpose of school is not control over the disciplines, but control over these more generic capacities," then there is a danger that traditional rigor will be diminished, says Wiggins. "Because if you now say that the purpose of a literature program, for example, is to teach people to communicate effectively, you are now saying, implicitly to some people, that it doesn't matter if you read Judy Blume or Shakespeare to accomplish that end."

OBE advocates have struggled mightily with the question of whether one set of outcomes will fit the needs of all students; those who will go on to Harvard as well as those who will clerk at K-Mart. One option would be to craft outcomes based on the kind of curriculum taken by students in the advanced college-prep track—outcomes derived from physics, U.S. history,

and so on—and push more students to attain such outcomes. But the more common approach taken by OBE planners has been to frame outcomes that describe students as "effective communicators" or "problem-solvers." Parents of high-achieving students, in particular, fear that such nebulous outcomes will result in less academic rigor in their children's program.

Good outcomes have to have three elements: the content knowledge, the competence (what the student is *doing*), and the setting (under what conditions the student is performing), says Kit Marshall, associate director and co-founder of the High Success Network, Inc. Content is *essential,* she says: "you can't demonstrate anything without the basics." But the field has fallen short in defining what a good outcome is, she says. "Many so-called outcomes are really more like goals, and they aren't assessable as such," says Marshall. "We have not clearly defined in a large enough sense what an outcome is, or what a demonstration of an outcome looks like. The field has not done that well enough."

The drafting of common outcomes for an OBE system requires enormous time and care. Even then, outcomes will appear too vague for some or too specific for others. If outcomes are too "global," McTighe notes, critics ask "Where's the beef?" But if a state specifies dozens or hundreds of outcomes, it is attacked for "prescribing the curriculum" and treading on local initiative.

How to Assess

A second major challenge facing any move to an outcome-based system is redesigning student assessment and reporting programs. Since OBE requires students to demonstrate their knowledge and skills, the assessments used to evaluate their performances become critically important.

But are the student assessments currently available up to the task? Although assessment experts know how to measure basic levels of skill and knowledge, they have less proven experience measuring higher-order outcomes within the subject area

Parents and educators familiar with a specific version of outcome-based education often equate all OBE with the model they've heard most about.

domains and almost no track record with the transformational, cross-disciplinary outcomes that some OBE plans envision.

Many experts say that performance-based assessments—not standardized, multiple-choice tests—are necessary to measure student attainment of outcomes. "Many outcomes demand a type of assessment that is more performance-oriented" because most current tests fail to measure the applications of knowledge described in new outcomes, says McTighe.

David Hornbeck, a former state school superintendent in Maryland who has advised states on outcome-based systems, believes the field is making progress on designing assessments that measure complex tasks. "We can measure much higher levels of knowledge and skills than we try to measure routinely now," he says, citing improvements in the assessment of student writing. But most experts agree that designing assessments linked to high-level and broadly written outcomes present enormous technical challenges.

One reason assessment is so critical, of course, is that OBE philosophy suggests that students should *demonstrate* their attainment of outcomes before receiving a diploma, a notion some experts referred to as "performance-based graduation." But even OBE proponents suggest moving very cautiously in considering whether to deny students a diploma based on their failure to demonstrate their proficiency on the assessments currently available. On certain outcomes, it's probably wise to give students feedback on their performance, but not to deny advancement or a diploma to students who fail, suggests Marzano.

Dubious outcomes and the prospect that assessment of those outcomes would be used in a high-stakes fashion fueled the criticisms about OBE in states such as Pennsylvania. But *not* holding students accountable to outcomes carries consequences, too. The Kentucky accountability system measures schools on their ability to help students to attain state-defined learner outcomes. Schools are held accountable (and can be taken over by the state if they show insufficient improvement), but students are not, says Guskey of the University of Kentucky. In fact, the state-required assessment of 12th graders is administered during the spring of their senior year, and is not connected with graduation requirements, "so students can just blow it off" without consequences, says Guskey.

Building School Capacity

A third major challenge facing those wishing to move to an OBE system involves building the capacity of schools to make the changes necessary for students to master required outcomes. On paper, OBE suggests that each school's curriculum and instruction would be re-organized to support agreed-upon student outcomes. In reality, many practices and traditions—mandatory standardized testing programs and college admissions requirements, for example—combine to create an inertia preventing local schools from changing very substantively in response to the precepts of OBE. This is true of other reforms besides OBE, notes Wiggins: faced with the prospects of a major new reform, educators often "retitle what they are already inclined to do."

For example, many of the schools claiming to practice OBE appear to offer the same set of courses as before, even though they've drafted new outcomes. A real tension exists between the curriculum educators might wish to implement and the one that responds to current conditions and

constraints. For example, "Right now, given our transitional education system, we've got to respect and respond to the fact that algebra is still a door to college," says Marshall. "So regardless of whether or not someone thinks that you'll ever use algebra, we've got to see to it that we're holding ourselves accountable, that we're expanding students' options, not limiting them."

Because drafting new outcomes and developing new assessments linked to them are such difficult tasks, they have drawn more attention than the question of what can be done to build schools' capacity to help students attain new outcomes, believes John Champlin, executive director of the National Center for Outcomes-Based Education and the former superintendent in Johnson City, New York "Outcomes are what we want, but what we have to do is to change the capacity of schools" to help students attain them. States need to place as much attention on the capacity-building side of outcome-based systems as on the accountability side, he says.

Future Directions

Although it's impossible to predict precisely what the future of outcome-based education is, there are several likely trends.

OBE plans will probably rely more heavily on outcomes defined in traditional subject areas, rather than the "transformational" outcomes that cross the disciplines. "The starting point and the emphasis should be on the academic disciplines," says Hornbeck. This is the model of the national standards for content and student performance, which are being crafted in all of the major disciplines and which will be published over the next year or two (mathematics standards have already been written). States that have defined outcomes within the subject areas, as in Kentucky, for example, have not encountered the same degree of opposition as states that attempted to create cross-disciplinary outcomes.

Another likely trend is that states will move slowly on attaching high

stakes to outcome-based education plans. Few states, for example, are likely to abolish the Carnegie unit as the basis for graduation, as Pennsylvania plans to do. Instead, bet on more states attempting to define learner outcomes, aligning assessment programs with those outcomes, and compiling student assessment data with other indicators of school performance as part of the accountability system. Until (and unless) performance-based assessments shore up their technical qualities, or the outcomes are more clearly defined, high-stakes uses are likely to be frowned upon.

A third trend is more systematic attempts to communicate with the public what outcome-based education is about. Educators substantially underestimated the degree of public confusion and disagreement with OBE in several of the states that attempted to launch programs. "There has to be an awful lot of attention to communicating in simple terms," says James Cooper, dean of the Curry School of Education at the University of Virginia. Virginia's OBE plan foundered, he says, in part because opponents convinced the middle ground of citizens that OBE (as defined in the state's proposed "common core" of learning outcomes) would mean lower academic standards. "The vagueness [of the plan] was a real political problem," says Cooper. State officials, "try as they might, could not say simply and clearly enough what this common core was. Then the opposition defined it in their terms as 'mushy-headed.'"

It may be that the public believes that the present performance of schools does not warrant the restructuring that would result from a true application of OBE's precepts. "People are really not that dissatisfied with what's going on" in schools, Cooper believes. "People are interested in school improvement, but not necessarily in break-the-mold schools or break-the-mold education." As a result, "major sweeping changes are exceedingly difficult," and modest, incremental changes seem the only plausible route.

Guiding and Supporting Young Children

No subject in early childhood education seems to attract the attention of teachers and parents more than how to guide behavior. New teachers are concerned that they will not be able to keep the children "under control." Mature teachers wrestle with the finer points of how to guide behavior positively and effectively. Parents have strong feelings on the subject of behavior, often based on their own childhood experiences. Teachers spend many hours thinking and talking about the best ways to guide young children's behavior: *What should I do about the child who is out of bounds? What do I say to parents who want their child punished? Is punishment the same as discipline? How do I guide a child who has experienced violence and now acts out violently?*

Dan Gartrell, in his article "Misbehavior or Mistaken Behavior?" clearly pictures two extremes of discipline—one based on punishment and the other on guidance. He cautions us to recognize the difference between the two and to choose the positive one. Because such terms as "misbehavior" make us think of punishment, a better term is "mistaken behavior." Gartrell sorts out three levels of mistaken behavior—strong needs, socially influenced, and experimentation—that identify the types of problems children are likely to experience. Giving alternatives is an effective way to guide children as worthwhile individuals who make mistakes.

"Behavior Management and 'The Five C's'" follows, providing a concise five-step plan for helping young children to learn appropriate behavior. David Almeida's plan calls for teachers to be clear by setting up a few well-chosen rules, then providing rewards for acceptable behavior and consequences for unacceptable behavior.

From their wealth of experience with young children, Donna Sasse Wittmer and Alice Sterling Honig provide

specific ways to encourage positive social development. Their article gives examples of modeling, redirecting, and assisting young children in gaining prosocial skills. This process is supported by the authors' belief that the ability

Unit 4

to relate to and interact with others is a vital aspect of development.

With so many families in America relocating each year, young children experience loss, and their education is sometimes fragmented. In "Helping Children to Cope with Relocation," Mary Renck Jalongo carefully analyzes the demands placed on children by relocation. She outlines a systematic approach for teachers to positively affect children's concepts about moving. She encourages the development of schoolwide policies that support new children. Her recommendations are important to consider in our highly mobile society.

The effect of domestic violence or abuse of young children is often inappropriate behavior or lack of control. Violent experiences can alter children's behavior and lower their self-esteem. In an early childhood setting, it is difficult for these children to cope with others and to express their emotions. Some children who have been affected by violence may be extremely angry and display unacceptable behaviors. Others may be pessimistic and act out in self-destructive ways.

Teachers find that guiding the behavior of children who have suffered abuse is a complicated task. Lorraine Wallach's article, "Breaking the Cycle of Violence," addresses ways teachers can successfully guide children who endure different types of violence. She advises us that the basis for working with these children is through relationships. Teachers must be models for affection and respect, communicating belief in children's abilities. Above all, consistency and care are necessary for children to learn. Wallach emphasizes the value of playing out bad experiences in order to learn to manage anger, fear, and anxiety. Dictating stories and art activities are also good outlets for feelings. Beyond the classroom,

Wallach calls for closer attention by community organizations to curbing violence. This comes about only when politicians and policy makers know that educators and families support efforts to fight crime and violence.

As with all areas of early childhood education, a high-quality, effective plan for guiding behavior does not arrive prepackaged for the teacher's immediate use. Guiding and disciplining are hard work, requiring careful attention to individual children and differing situations. The work is not complete until teachers examine their own sense of control and feelings about children's behavior. Anger and disrespect have no place in a positive environment. When feelings are brought out into the open and discussed calmly, teachers create an atmosphere where everyone is able to speak and act responsibly. This is the basis for a caring, helping environment for young children.

Looking Ahead: Challenge Questions

What is the difference between misbehavior and mistaken behavior? How is the difference reflected in a teacher's approach to classroom guidance?

What five or six basic rules are appropriate for a group of kindergarten children? What rewards and consequences would be powerful motivators for young children?

Give specific examples of positive discipline strategies and situations when you would use them.

How can the curriculum be used to help children build concepts about relocating? What school experiences could new students have to ease their transition?

In what ways is young children's emotional development jeopardized when they live with violence?

Misbehavior or Mistaken Behavior?

Dan Gartrell

Dan Gartrell, *Ed.D., a former elementary teacher in Ohio and Head Start teacher for the Red Lake Ojibwe in northern Minnesota, is a professor in early childhood education and director of the Child Development Training Program at Bemidji State University in Minnesota and author of Delmar's* A Guidance Approach to Discipline.

A common situation in early childhood classrooms is when two children argue over use of a toy car. In this scenario two teachers handle the situation differently. **Teacher one** arrives, takes the car, and declares that because the children are not using it appropriately, they will have to find something else to do. One child sits on a chair and looks sad; the other child sticks up an index finger (wrong finger) at the teacher's back as she puts the car on the shelf (Gartrell 1994).

Teacher two arrives, gets down on the children's level and holds the car. She says, "We have a problem. Please use your words so we can solve this problem." With a bit of coaching, the two

children determine that one child had the car first and the other wanted it. The teacher then helps the second child find "an almost new car that no one is using." The children play together using the two cars.

Traditional classroom discipline vs. conflict resolution and guidance

In their responses, the first teacher used traditional classroom discipline; the second used conflict resolution (Wichert 1989), an important technique in guidance. As commonly practiced, traditional discipline has failed to distinguish between

nonpunitive teacher intervention and punishment (Gartrell 1987; Reynolds 1990). The effects of punishment—diminished self-esteem, loss of enjoyment of learning, negative feelings toward self and others—make its use inap-

> **The difference between these two approaches is that traditional discipline criticizes children—often publicly—for unacceptable behaviors, whereas guidance teaches children positive alternatives, "what they can do instead."**

propriate in the classroom setting (Bredekamp 1987).

The difference between these two approaches is that traditional discipline criticizes children—often publicly—for unacceptable behaviors, whereas guidance teaches children positive alternatives, "what they can do instead." Traditional discipline punishes children for having problems they cannot solve,

From *Young Children*, July 1995, pp. 27-34. © 1995 by the National Association for the Education of Young Children. Reprinted by permission.

> The teacher who uses guidance is not permissive; she does not let children struggle vis-a-vis boundaries that may not be there. Instead, she provides guidance and leadership so that children can interact successfully within the reasonable boundaries of the classroom community.

while guidance teaches children to solve their problems in socially acceptable ways (Gartrell 1994).

One of the joys of teaching young children, despite a continuing lack of resources in the early childhood field, is the capacity of the professional to be fully nurturing within the teaching role. The practice of guidance, the creation and maintenance of a positive learning environment for each child, supports the nurturing function. Guidance connotes activism on the teacher's part (Gartrell 1994). The teacher who uses guidance is not permissive; she does not let children struggle vis-a-vis boundaries that may not be there. Instead, she provides leadership so that children can interact successfully within the reasonable boundaries of the classroom community.

"Misbehavior" makes us think of punishing

As classroom guidance continues to displace a reliance on traditional discipline, it is important that educators reevaluate other widely used terms and practices. One such term is misbehavior. Traditionally, misbehavior implies willful wrongdoing for which a child must be disciplined (punished). The term invites moral labeling of the child. After all, what kind of children misbehave? Children who are "naughty," "rowdy," "mean," "willful," or "not nice." Although teachers who punish "misbehavior" believe they are "shaming children into being good," the result may be the opposite. Because of limited de-

velopment and experience, children tend to internalize negative labels, see themselves as they are labeled, and react accordingly (Ginott 1975).

Greenberg (1988) makes the point that informed early childhood teachers do not think in terms of good or bad children but good or bad forms of discipline. When children act out, there are more important things to do than criticize the supposed character flaws of the child or fuss about the specific method of discipline to use. The teacher needs to consider the reasons for the behavior—was it a mismatch of the child and the curriculum, for instance, or trouble in the child's life outside school?

Equally important, the teacher needs to think about how to teach the child acceptable alternatives during and after the intervention. Many teachers of young children try to follow the prescription of Ginott: address the behavior; protect the personality (1975). As long as the teacher views mistaken acts as misbehavior, however, the avoidance of punishment and labeling becomes difficult, because of the moralistic baggage that the term carries (Gartrell 1994).

Probably the roots of the term misbehavior go back to the Middle Ages and the view that children, by nature, were "wayward" and "tending toward evil" (Osborn 1980). Historically, "beating the devil" out of children for misbehavior has been an accepted teaching practice. Berger (1991) and especially deMause (1974) establish that strict discipline,

based on obedience and corporal punishment, was common in schools into the 20th century. With modern permutations, "obedience or consequences" discipline still persists in schools today—to control children's "misbehavior."

"Mistaken behavior" makes us think of guiding and educating

In European American education, a moralistic attitude about the nature of children has been common. Another viewpoint has coexisted, however, that children have worth in and of themselves and, with guidance, tend toward good (Osborn 1980). Since the middle of the last century, this more benevolent perspective has manifested itself in the work of such educators and psychologists as Froebel, Montessori, Dewey, Piaget, Purkey, Ginott, and all major modern early childhood educators (Gartrell 1994). Common in the writings of these progressives are the ideas that

• the child is in a state of development;

• the processes of learning and developing are complex;

• through methods and curriculum, educators need to accommodate the developmental and experiential circumstances of each child; and

• guiding behavior is a big part of every teacher's job.

Certainly, this is the premise of the well-known 1987 NAEYC position statement on developmentally appropriate practice.

In her article "Avoiding 'Me Against You' Discipline," Greenberg (1988) frames the issue of

135

Illustration

I was in the classroom of a teacher who I knew used guidance. A child who had been having some difficulties said loudly to another, "You damn sunnamabitch!"

After comforting the second child for a moment, the teacher went to the first child and whispered in his ear. One of the things I heard her whisper was, "I'm proud of you." When she had gotten things settled, I went over and asked if what I thought I heard her whisper was correct. She smiled and said, "That's right, Dan. Un-til last week, when he got upset, he would hit or kick. We've been teaching him to use words instead. He did, and I'm proud of him! What you didn't hear me tell him were some different words to use that don't bother people" (Gartrell 1994).

The teacher here saw the child's use of words for what it was—neither a backslide nor a complete turnaround, but progress. By regarding the behavior as mistaken, she was able to use guidance to help the child continue to build upon his efforts.

---

teacher–child relations from the developmental perspective:

Some adults see each individual child as being at this moment "good" and at that moment "bad." It all adds up to a view of a child as, overall, either a "good child" or a "bad child": She's a good girl; he's a hateful child, a really naughty boy.

Other adults, and certainly those of us well educated in child development, think differently about children. We consider all infants, toddlers, and young children *potentially* good people, naive little people with a very small amount of experience on Earth, who have much to learn, and *a great deal of motivation to please, to be accepted, to be approved, to be loved, to be cared for.* We see young children as generally receptive to guidance and usually eager to "do it right." (24–25)

In the process of learning the complex life skills of cooperation, conflict resolution, and acceptable expression of strong feelings, children, like all of us, *make mistakes* (Gartrell 1987). The guidance tradition in early childhood education suggests that teachers who traditionally have considered problems in the classroom as misbehaviors think of them instead as mistaken behaviors (MnAEYC 1991). By considering behaviors as mistaken, the teacher is freed from the impediment of moral judgment about the child and empowered instead to meditate, problem-solve, and guide.

In the cognitive domain, a child who asks, "Is him going, too, teacher?" is not treated as though she has misbehaved. In an affirming manner, the teacher models the conventional usage, "Yes, Carlita, he is going, too." In the realm of behavior, the teacher also uses a positive approach. Children are not punished for the mistakes of words or deeds; they are helped to learn from their mistaken behavior. The concept of mistaken behavior fits well with the guidance approach.

Children's behavior poses higher emotional stakes for the teacher than most other teaching situations (Gartrell 1994). Matters of potential harm, disruption, and loss of control (by the adult as well as the child) are involved. This urgency factor makes accepting of the concept of mistaken behavior difficult for some teachers. The issue of intentionality also poses questions about the concept. If a child does something on purpose, is it still a mistaken behavior? The remainder of this article examines the concept of mistaken behavior.

Origins of the term "mistaken behavior"

Over the past 30 years, Rudolf Dreikurs (1968; Dreikurs, Grunwald, & Pepper 1982) has added much to our thinking about behavior management. Dreikurs's ideas, with which many readers are probably familiar, have been stepping stones to the concept "mistaken behavior." Dreikurs postulated that all behavior is

---

> In the process of learning the complex life skills of cooperation, conflict resolution, and acceptable expression of strong feelings, children, like all of us, make mistakes. Guiding behavior is a big part of every teacher's job.

---

purposeful, and the purpose of behavior is to achieve social acceptance. Dreikurs derived four goals of misbehavior: attention getting, power seeking, revenge seeking, and displaying inadequacy (1968). Usually pursued by the child in order, the four goals represent inappropriate ways of seeking social acceptance. **Dreikurs's landmark contribution was that he suggested nonmoralizing intervention** strategies, such as "logical consequences," to correct children's behavior (1968). He spoke of the importance of democratic leadership in the classroom—the need for teachers to earn, rather than try to force, respect (Dreikurs 1968). For educators and parents alike, Dreikurs has done much to raise the discussion of behavior above the level of moralization.

As important as his contributions are, Dreikurs wrote before recent findings surfaced about child development. As well, his views differ, in part, from those of the "self" psychologists of the 1960s and 1970s—Maslow, Rogers, Combs, Purkey, etc. (Gartrell 1994). For Dreikurs, social acceptance was the primary motivation in children's behavior. In contrast, both developmental and self psychologists see social acceptance as a foundation for full, balanced personal development rather than as an end in itself.

The concept of mistaken behavior draws from Dreikurs's nonmoralizing approach but draws more directly from the developmental and self psychologists. The concept of *mistaken* behavior, rather than misbehavior is an extension of the work of Steven Harlow (1975). Harlow integrated the thinking of Piaget, Erikson, Holt, and Riesman in his construct of *relational patterns*. Harlow explains,

By relational patterns, I mean ways in which children relate to situations, persons, and things in the school environment. (1975, 28)

Harlow writes about three levels of relational patterns, "which differ in their openness to experi-

If a child does something on purpose, is it still a mistaken behavior?

ence, maturity, and their capacity to operate freely" (1975, 28). The three levels are **survival, adjustment, and encountering.** Children may show different relational patterns in different situations. Harlow cautions against using such behavioral constructs in order to label; instead, the purpose is to help children progress in their personal and social development.

Three levels of mistaken behavior

From almost 30 years of teaching and observing in early childhood classrooms, I have identified three levels of mistaken behavior, based on Harlow's writings (Gartrell 1987, 1994). As Figure 1 illustrates, the levels of mistaken behavior share motivational sources with the relational patterns. The levels of mistaken behavior identify the types of problems children in the various relational patterns are likely to experience.

Level three: Strong-needs mistaken behavior

Children showing the survival relational pattern likely have experienced their environment as a "dangerous and painful place" over which they have little control (Harlow 1975). The behavior patterns of these children tend

to be rigid and exaggerated. To protect themselves, they resist change and continue the same behaviors in new situations, even if their patterns are extreme and inappropriate.

The child at the survival level is difficult for teachers to accept because of the nonsocial, at times antisocial, character of the child's behavior. Yet it is necessary for the teacher to establish a productive relationship, built on trust, in order to empower the child to progress to a higher relational level.

Children at the survival relational pattern show *level-three, strong-needs mistaken behavior.* Wherever it occurs, this level of mistaken behavior is the most serious. A sure sign that the mistaken behavior is at level three is that it continues over time. (Anyone, including teachers, can have an occasional "level three" day.) As Harlow suggests, strong-needs mistaken behavior results from psychological and/or physical pain in the child's life that is beyond the child's ability to cope with and understand. Often children show strong-needs mistaken behavior in the classroom because it is a safe haven in their environment. Through withdrawal or acting out, these children are asking for help in the only way they can (Gartrell 1994).

As the most serious level of mistaken behavior, the teacher takes a comprehensive approach with the child that usually involves other adults, especially parents or caregivers. The teacher

• intervenes nonpunitively;
• works to build a positive relationship with the child;

Children's behavior poses higher emotional stakes for the teacher than most other teaching situations. Matters of potential harm, disruption, and loss of control (by the adult as well as the child) are involved.

• seeks more information through observation;

• seeks more information through conversation with the child, other adults who work with the child, and parents or caregivers;

• creates a coordinated "individual guidance plan" in consultation with the other adults; and

• implements, reviews, and modifies the plan as necessary. (Gartrell 1994)

Sometimes level-three mistaken behaviors are symptoms of such deep problems in the child's life that the comprehensive guidance approach is not completely successful. Even when working with parents, the teacher cannot necessarily change life circumstances for a child, but he can make life easier—in ways that may have lasting beneficial effects.

Level two: Socially influenced mistaken behavior

Children who show the adjustment relational pattern have an increased ability to adapt to situations. Their criteria for doing so, however, is the judgment of significant others. "New ways of thinking and behaving are first sanctioned by an individual or reference group representing authority, before they are considered by the adjuster" (Harlow 1975, 30). Children at the adjustment level seek high levels of teacher approval, put off completing tasks because "I can't do it right," and may involve adults or other children in doing their projects for them. They lack the self-esteem and individual strength necessary to respond to a situation on its own terms.

Some teachers find gratification in the obedience and dependence of a child at the adjustment level. They may be reinforcing long-term, other-directed response tendencies in the child, however, that inhibit full personal development (Har-

---

Figure 1. **Common Sources of Motivation, Relational Patterns, and Levels of Mistaken Behavior**

Motivational source	*Relational pattern*	*Level of mistaken behavior*
Desire to explore the environment and engage in relationships	Encountering	One: Experimentation
Desire to please and identify with significant others	Adjustment	Two: Socially influenced
Inability to cope with problems resulting from health conditions or the school or home environment	Survival	Three: Strong needs

Courtesy of Delmar Publishers Inc. (Gartrell 1994, 38).

---

low 1975). Deprived of confidence in his own values and judgment, the child may continue to be influenced by others—especially peers—including toward self-destructive or oppressive mistaken behaviors (Gartrell 1994). With a child at the adjustment level, the task of the teacher is to nudge him toward autonomy (the encountering relational pattern) by helping him build self-esteem and proactive social skills (Harlow 1975).

Children showing the adjustment relational pattern are subject to *level-two, socially influenced mistaken behavior.* Level-two mistaken behaviors are "learned behaviors," reinforced in the child, intentionally or unintentionally, by other people important in the child's life. A child who uses an expletive in a classroom exactly as an adult would is showing a socially influenced mistaken behavior. Likewise, children who join others in calling a child "poopy butt" or "dorky" have been influenced by peers into a level-two mistaken behavior.

In responding to level-two mistaken behaviors, the teacher notes whether one child or a group of children are involved. When a group of children are involved, an effective technique, even with preschoolers (Hendrick 1992), is the class meeting.

Respecting the dignity of all concerned, the teacher points out the problem and, with the children, works out a solution. The teacher monitors progress and calls additional meetings, if necessary. If one child is involved, the teacher handles the situation privately; in a firm but friendly manner, explains what is unacceptable; and provides a guideline for an acceptable alternative. In either individual or group situations, the teacher follows up with encouragement and "compliment sandwiches"—two or three acknowledgments of progress along with one reminder of the agreed-to guideline (Gartrell 1994) (it is easier for us to change behaviors when others acknowledge our efforts).

By assisting children to learn alternatives to socially influenced mistaken behavior, the teacher helps them to understand that they have the capacity to evaluate, choose, and interact for themselves—essential life skills for a democracy (Wittmer & Honig 1994).

Level one: Experimentation mistaken behavior

Harlow's construct of relational patterns is built around the importance of autonomy—Piaget's term for the ability of the individual to make intelligent, ethical decisions

(Kamii 1984). Autonomy is the social relation pattern shown by children at the highest level, *encountering* (Harlow 1975).

Children at the encountering level are learning most effectively about themselves and the world; yet, because they are so open to new experience and because they are young, they are susceptible to mistaken behavior—and vulnerable to teacher criticism. About children at the encountering level, Harlow states,

In contrast with the adjustor and survivor, the encounterer is less concerned with security and certainty and much more occupied with what Erikson referred to as the inner mechanism that permits the individual to turn "passive into active" and to maintain and regain in this world of contending forces an individual sense of centrality, of wholeness, and of initiative. (1975, 30–31)

Children at the encountering relational pattern show *level-one, experimentation mistaken behavior*. The term *experimentation* is used because the child is learning through full engagement in the experiment of life. To cite previous illustrations, the two children who argued over use of a toy car were totally involved in that situation; they were demonstrating level-one mistaken behavior. Interestingly, perhaps in progressing from level three, the child who swore rather then hit also was showing level-one mistaken behavior. The experimentation can be "natural," through full involvement in the affairs of the classroom, or it can be "controlled," as in the case of a young child who, with a smile, uses an expletive in order to see the teacher's reaction.

The teacher responds in different ways to different situations. Sometimes he may step back and allow a child to learn from the experience; other times, he will reiterate a guideline and, in a friendly tone, teach a more appropriate alternative behavior. With children at level one, as with those at two and three, the teacher uses guidance and avoids the use of traditional discipline.

Understanding mistaken behaviors

An occasional misunderstanding about mistaken behavior is that some mistaken behaviors occur at only level one, others at level two, and still others at level three (Gartrell 1994). At each level, mistaken behaviors have distinct motivational sources. Behaviors that appear similar can be a result of differing motivations, and so be at different levels. The teacher must observe carefully to infer the motivation and the level of mistaken behavior in order to respond effectively. Figure 2 illustrates how similar mistaken behaviors can be at different levels.

At any relational level, the cause of mistaken behavior is insufficient understanding about how to act maturely in the complex situations of life. With a child's internal need to go forward and to learn—but limited ability to balance her own needs with those of others—mistaken behavior will occur. Knowledge of the relational patterns and the levels of mistaken behavior assists the teacher to understand and work with children when they make mistakes (Gartrell 1994).

The issue of intentionality

When people think about behavior, they may associate mistaken behavior with "accidents" and misbehavior with acts "done on purpose" (Gartrell 1994). Mistaken behavior includes both accidents and intentional behaviors. A young child on a trike who runs over the toe of another child by accident has shown level-one mistaken behavior. The accident was unintentional but was level one because it was a mistake that arose from involvement.

A child may run over another's foot for a second reason related to level one (Gartrell 1994). As a part of encountering social relations, the trike rider hits the other's foot "accidentally on purpose" to see what will happen. The lack of development of young children results in their difficulty understanding how another child would feel under such circumstances. The act was intentional but was done without full awareness of the consequences and so is level-one mistaken behavior. The importance of the term *mistaken behavior* is that it reminds the adult that the trike rider needs guidance about human feelings and the consequences of actions, not punishment for making a mistake.

Of course, hitting another child's foot might also be a level-two or level-three mistaken behavior (Gartrell 1994). At level two, one child follows another on a trike. The second rider sees the first swing close to a bystander and follows suit but strikes the bystander's foot. At level three, a trike rider who is harboring feelings of hostility acts out against an innocent child. When the teacher hypothesizes that level two or level three is involved, she reacts with increasing degrees of firmness, although she retains the element of friendliness, which is at the heart of guidance. If the trike rider's motives indicate that strong-needs mistaken behavior is present, the teacher should follow up as suggested for level three. The additional step is important because serious mistaken behaviors occur when children are the victims of life circumstances that are beyond their control. Even the mistaken behavior of aggression is a nonverbal request for assistance, not a situation requiring punishment.

It should be noted that whatever the level of mistaken behavior, the teacher reacts to the immediate situation by using guidance. She first gives attention to the victim, who deserves it. This action shows support for the wronged child (and also may help the teacher calm down). The teacher then speaks with the trike rider. She does some empathy building by pointing out that the trike hurt the other child and she cannot let anyone (including the trike rider) be hurt at school. She discusses with the trike rider how he could avoid having this problem next time. Although the teacher does not force an apology, she perhaps asks how the trike rider could help the child who was hurt feel better. The teacher then assists the trike rider back into positive activity, which often includes helping him to make amends. In guidance practice the teacher avoids the traditional discipline reaction. She does not lecture about how naughty the behavior was or automatically put the child in a time-out. The goal is to help the child learn from the mistake, not punish him for making it.

Again, the value of the term *mistaken behavior* is that it has different implications than the conventional term, *misbehavior*. Misbehavior tends to connote a judgment of character that leads to punishment rather than guidance. Mistaken behavior precludes character assessment and asks that the child be accepted as a person of worth (by virtue of being alive). The person may need to face consequences, but at the base of those consequences is guidance, so the possibility of change is maximized (Gartrell 1994).

A premise in the use of guidance is that even willful acts that are done "on purpose" still constitute mistaken behavior. A child who deliberately bites or intentionally

---

Figure 2. Classifying Similar Mistaken Behaviors by Level

Incident of mistaken behavior	Motivational source	Level of mistaken behavior
Child uses expletive	Wants to see the teacher's reaction	One
	Wants to emulate important others	Two
	Expresses deeply felt hostility	Three
Child pushes another off the trike	Wants trike; has not learned to ask in words	One
	Follows aggrandizement practices modeled by other children	Two
	Feels the need to act out against the world by asserting power	Three
Child refuses to join in group activity	Does not understand teacher's expectations	One
	Has "gotten away" with not joining in	Two
	Is not feeling well or feels strong anxiety about participating	Three

Courtesy of Delmar Publishers Inc. (Gartrell 1994, 49).

---

disobeys has made a mistake. The adult who is able to approach children as worthwhile individuals who make mistakes is in a philosophically strong position to assist them with healthy personal and social development.

References

Berger, S.K. 1991. *The developing person through childhood and adolescence.* New York: Worth.

Bredekamp, S., ed. 1987. *Developmentally appropriate practice in early childhood programs serving children from birth through age 8.* Exp. ed. Washington, DC: NAEYC.

deMause, L., ed. 1974. *The history of childhood.* New York: Peter Benrick Books.

Dreikurs, R. 1968. *Psychology in the classroom.* 2nd ed. New York: Harper and Row.

Dreikurs, R., B. Grunwald, & F. Pepper. 1982. *Maintaining sanity in the classroom.* New York: Harper and Brothers.

Gartrell, D.J. 1987. More thoughts... Punishment or guidance? *Young Children* 42 (3): 55–61.

Gartrell, D.J. 1994. *A guidance approach to discipline.* Albany: Delmar.

Ginott, H.G. 1975. *Teacher and child.* New York: Avon Books.

Greenberg, P. 1988. Ideas that work with young children. Avoiding "me against you" discipline. *Young Children* 44 (1): 24–29.

Harlow, S.D. 1975. *Special education: The meeting of differences.* Grand Forks, ND: University of North Dakota.

Hendrick, J. 1992. Where does it all begin? Teaching the principles of democracy in the early years. *Young Children* 47 (3): 51–53.

Kamii, C. 1984. Autonomy: The aim of education envisioned by Piaget. *Phi Delta Kappan* 65(6): 410–15.

Minnesota Association for the Education of Young Children (MnAEYC). 1991. *Developmentally appropriate guidance of children birth to eight.* Rev. ed. St. Paul: Author.

Osborn, D.K. 1980. *Early childhood education in historical perspective.* Athens, GA: Education Associates.

Reynolds, E. 1990. *Guiding young children: A child-centered approach.* Mountain View, CA: Mayfield.

Wichert, S. 1989. *Keeping the peace: Practicing cooperation and conflict resolution with preschoolers.* Philadelphia, PA: New Society.

Wittmer, D.S., & A.S. Honig. 1994. Encouraging positive social development in young children. *Young Children* 49 (5): 61–75.

Behavior Management and
"The Five C's"

*An effective five-step plan to help all students
learn appropriate behavior*

DAVID A. ALMEIDA

❝*In workshops
... I suggest a
five-step plan for
managing the
behavior of all
students, those
who have a his-
tory of behavior
problems and
those who do
not.***❞**

When asked how they feel about inclusion, many regular classroom teachers with whom I speak are concerned most about dealing with special students who have a reputation for being "behavior problems." The teachers worry that they'll be unable to handle the issues they feel are sure to arise when these students are included in the regular classroom.

While a great many teachers are confident that they have the resources, knowledge and energy needed to handle included students along with other exceptionalities, they indicate that they've received relatively little training and support as far as the "special ways" of handling behaviorally involved students are concerned.

Children today rarely act "appropriately" simply because the teacher expects them to. Rather, they act appropriately because of what they've learned either at home or in the classroom. Often, it's the teacher who must instruct children in appropriate behavior and who sets up a classroom environment that invites good behavior in children.

WAYNE TIRONE

A plan for all students. In workshops (or in preparation classes with my teacher trainees), I suggest a five-step plan for managing the behavior of all students, those who have a history of behavior problems and those who do not.

I call this plan "The Five C's" and I recommend it to all teachers, especially those who are in inclusive environments. The plan is easy to introduce and just as easy to carry out.

"The Five C's" of classroom behavior management are as follows: Clarity, Consequences, Consistency, Caring and Change. To see how they work together to form an effective plan to influence behavior, let's take a closer look at each of them.

1. Be clear. Clarity, the first C, speaks to the fact that all children must have a clear understanding of what constitutes acceptable and unacceptable behavior in the classroom.

Unacceptable behaviors must be described in the most concrete terms possible. Vague descriptions, such as "Children must be polite," are to be avoided. Why? Well,

David Almeida is an Assistant Professor of Education at Stonehill College, North Easton, MA.

"politeness" is an abstract term and one child's definition of politeness can be different from another child's definition.

If you wish, you can hang a chart listing unacceptable behaviors on the front wall of the classroom; however, I strongly recommend that no more than five "rules" be included on the chart. It has been my experience that classrooms where there are more than five basic rules are actually breeding grounds for behavior disorders since the atmosphere becomes too rigid for even the most structured child. Besides, more than five of anything is easily forgotten or ignored by children. Keep the rules clear, concrete and brief.

2. Provide consequences. The second C is for consequences. Behavior management is a delicate balance of rewards for acceptable behavior and consequences for unacceptable behavior.

Ever since your mother told you to "eat your peas if you want to go outside to play," you've been aware of how acceptable behavior increases the likelihood of rewards. Simply put, you'll work for something you want.

Critics may say this is pure manipulation and that it smacks of taking away the child's sense of individuality. Perhaps they're correct, but I've found that rewarding children for acting appropriately in the classroom is an exceptionally effective device.

Rewards don't always have to be tangible, of course. A simple "Thanks for doing so well today," given in a variety of ways many times throughout the day, reinforces within the child the concept that acceptable behavior garners rewards from others.

It should be remembered that, in turn, there must also be consequences for behavior which is unacceptable. Unacceptable behavior must produce an undesirable result.

In tandem, these two instruments are powerful motivators. Children learn quickly that if they act a certain way, they'll be given a reward; if they don't, they won't. Indeed, they may instead be given something they'd rather avoid.

3. Be consistent. The third C stands for consistency. You must be consistent in handing out rewards and consequences. When children act in an acceptable manner, make sure you acknowledge that fact – publicly, whenever possible.

Pay attention to students, validate their input and be genuine about the pleasure you take in their good behavior and active participation. The same holds true when dealing with unacceptable behavior. Be fair about the consequences, alter them if they're ineffective and be consistent about handing them out.

Remember, expected rewards and consequences presented immediately after behaviors occur are the most effective behavior change agents.

4. Be caring. The final two C's in the plan, caring and change, are perhaps the most important. First of all, teachers must care about their students as children. Children act the way they do because they're children. To get angry at them because they're acting the way children act makes little sense.

Teachers need to care more about their students as the focal point of the classroom, and less about the curriculum. Without question, the curriculum is important, but if students sense that you're more concerned about finishing a spelling lesson than you are about them, they'll be less likely to behave the way you'd like them to.

You're faced with another delicate balance – making sure the students learn the material while at the same time supporting their needs as children.

5. Be willing to change. This is where change, the final C, comes in. Teachers who are looking to create an environment where learning occurs and where behavior problems are kept at a minimum need to be willing to make changes for the sake of their students.

Structure and routine are important; however, teachers should be prepared to adapt or modify curriculum, change activities at a more frequent rate, and incorporate lots of movement and other types of hands-on activities into the school day.

So there you have them: "The Five C's." Taken together, they add up to a successful formula for behavior management that can be used in just about any of today's heterogeneous classrooms.

> **"**Often, it's the teacher who instructs children in appropriate behavior and who sets up a classroom environment that invites good behavior.**"**

Encouraging Positive Social Development in Young Children

Donna Sasse Wittmer and Alice Sterling Honig

Donna Sasse Wittmer, Ph.D., is assistant professor in early childhood education at the University of Colorado in Denver. She has had extensive experience directing, training in, and conducting research in early childhood care and education programs.

Alice Sterling Honig, Ph.D., professor of child development at Syracuse University in Syracuse, New York, was program director for the Family Development Research Program and has authored numerous books, including Parent Involvement in Early Childhood Education *and* Playtime Learning Games for Young Children. *She directs the annual Syracuse Quality Infant/Toddler Caregiving Workshop.*

Editor's note: *This two-part review presents techniques for teachers and parents, schools and communities, to promote young children's social development. Supportive research findings are often cited to back up the techniques suggested. In Part 1, suggestions refer to interpersonal interactions of caregivers with individual children or small groups of children. Techniques in Part 2 (. . . published in a subsequent issue of* Young Children*) target entire classrooms as well as broader systems, such as centers, schools, families, and communities.*

An earlier version of this article was presented at NAEYC's Annual Conference in Denver, Colorado, in November 1991. Portions of this article have been adapted from Prosocial Development in Children: Caring, Sharing, & Cooperating: A Bibliographic Resource Guide *by Alice Sterling Honig and Donna Sasse Wittmer (1992).*

A toddler, reaching for a toy, got his finger pinched in the hinge on the door of a toy shelf in his child care classroom. He cried loudly; his pacifier fell from his mouth. Another toddler, obviously distressed by the sounds of pain coming from his playmate, picked up the pacifier and held it in the crying toddler's mouth in an apparent attempt to help and comfort the injured toddler.

This example, shared by a child care provider, is one of many exciting prosocial events that have been observed in young toddlers, preschoolers, and primary-age children as they interact together in group settings. Caregivers of young children notice events such as the one above as they live and work with very young children. If adults implement curriculum that promotes interpersonal consideration and cooperation in children, we see even more of these behaviors.

Social development was seen as the core of the curriculum in nursery schools and kindergartens until a cognitive emphasis was brought into the field in the late 1960s; social development has recently been getting renewed attention by early childhood education leaders. Skilled teachers of young children implement prosocial goals for young children as they attempt to facilitate children's positive social interactions. Prosocial goals that teachers emphasize include

- showing sympathy and kindness,
- helping,
- giving,
- accepting food or toys,
- sharing,
- showing positive verbal and physical contact,
- comforting another person in distress,
- donating to others who are less fortunate,
- showing concern
- responding to bereaved peers,
- taking the perspective of another person,
- showing affection, and
- cooperating with others in play or to complete a task.

The adults in children's lives play an important role in helping children develop these prosocial attitudes and behaviors.

Not surprisingly, if caregivers and teachers take time to encourage, facilitate, and teach prosocial behaviors, children's prosocial interactions increase and aggression decreases (Honig 1982). In an interesting study, children who attended, from 3 months to kindergarten, an experimental child care program that focused on intellectual growth were rated by their kindergarten teachers as more aggressive than a control group of children who attended community child care programs during their preschool years for less amount of time (Haskins 1985). But when a prosocial curriculum entitled "My Friends and Me" was implemented, the next groups of child care graduates did not differ in aggression rates from control-group children. Emphasizing and encouraging prosocial behaviors made a difference in how children learned to interact and play with each other. A number of other intriguing research studies concerning teacher educators and curriculum intended to enhance positive social development in young children are described in our book *Prosocial Development in Children: Caring, Sharing, & Cooperating.*

© The Growth Program

Social development was seen as the core of the curriculum in nursery schools and kindergartens until a cognitive emphasis was brought into the field in the late 1960s; social development has recently been getting renewed attention by early childhood education leaders.

Focus on prosocial behaviors: Value, model, and acknowledge

Need it be said? What the adults who are important in children's lives value, model, and encourage in children influences them. What values do we value and encourage?

Value and emphasize consideration for others' needs. Children become aware at an early age of what aspects of life their special adults admire and value. Research on toddlers (Yarrow & Waxler 1976) and boys with learning disabilities (Elardo & Freund 1981) shows that when parents encourage their children to have concern for others, the children behave more prosocially.

As every experienced teacher knows, emphasizing the importance of children helping others whenever possible results in children undertaking more helping activities (Grusec, Saas-Kortsaak, & Simultis 1978). Children whose parents esteem altruism highly are more frequently considered

by peers as highly prosocial (Rutherford & Mussen 1968).

Model prosocial behaviors. "Practice what you preach," "Do as I say, not as I do," and "Monkey see, monkey do" are tried-and-true sayings that remind us that children model many behaviors that we do—and do not!—want them to imitate. Adults who model prosocial behaviors influence children's willingness to behave prosocially (Bandura 1986). A teacher who patiently tied his toddlers' shoelaces day after day observed that toddlers who saw a peer tripping over laces would bend down and try to twist their

friend's sneaker laces in an attempt to help. Bryan (1977) stresses that children imitate helping activities whether the models are living people or fictional characters. Over the years, modeling has proven more powerful than preaching. Traditionally we have called it *setting a good example.* How caregivers and parents act—kind, considerate, and compassionate, or cruel, thoughtless, and uncaring—influences young children to imitate them.

Children who frequently observe and are influenced by family members and teachers who behave prosocially will imitate those special adults. "Mama," ob-

---

If adults implement curriculum that promotes interpersonal consideration and cooperation in children, we see even more of these behaviors.

served 3-year-old Dana, "that was a very good job you did buckling my seat belt." How often Mama had used just such encouraging words with her preschooler!

Label and identify prosocial and antisocial behaviors. We all love it when our positive deeds are acknowledged. Notice the positive interactions, however small, that occur between children and encourage them through your comments. When adults label behaviors, such as "considerate toward peers" and "cooperative with classmates," children's dialogues and role-taking abilities increase (Vorrath 1985). Rather than just saying "That's good" or "That's nice" to a child, be specific in identifying prosocial behaviors and actions for children. Saying

"You are being helpful" or "You gave him a tissue, he really needed it to wipe his nose" will be most helpful to children.

Attribute positive social behaviors to each child. Attributing positive intentions, such as "You shared because you like to help others" or "You're the kind of person who likes to help others whenever you can," results in children donating more generously to people in need (Grusec, Kuczynski, Rushton, & Simultis 1978; Grusec & Redler 1980).

After 8-year-olds had shared their winnings from a game with "poor" children, the children who were given positive attributions (e.g., "You're the kind of person who likes to help others whenever you can"), as op-

posed to social reinforcers (just being told that it was good to share with others), were more likely to share at a later time (Grusec & Redler 1980).

Skilled teachers personalize attributions so that each child feels special. Say such things as "You are a very helpful person," "You are the kind of person who likes to stick up for a child who is being bothered," and "You really try to be a buddy to a new child in our class who is shy at first in finding a friend."

Children from punitive homes may need help understanding how to make attributions that are true rather than assuming that others have evil intentions. For example, you might ask, "Did your classmate step on your homework paper in the school-yard to be mean or to keep it from blowing away?" Focus children's thinking on attributes and intentions of others' actions as a way to prevent children from unthinkingly lashing out at others in angry response.

Notice and positively encourage prosocial behaviors, but do not overuse external rewards. In research by Rushton and Teachman (1978), social reinforcement for sharing increased sharing among young children even when the experimenter was no longer present. Goffin (1987) recommends that teachers notice when children share mutual goals, ideas, and materials, as well as when they negotiate and bargain in decision making and accomplishing goals. When caregivers and parents use external reinforcement too much, however, children's prosocial behaviors may decrease. Fabes, Fultz, Eisenberg, May-Plumlee, and Christopher (1989) reported that mothers who like using rewards may undermine their children's internalized *desire* to behave prosocially by increasing the salience of external rather than internal rewards.

Teachers have reported that offering stickers for prosocial be-

© The Growth Program

As every experienced teacher knows, emphasizing the importance of children helping others whenever possible results in children undertaking more helping activities. Children whose parents esteem altruism highly are more frequently considered by peers as highly prosocial.

haviors to one child in a classroom often backfires when other children become upset that they didn't also get stickers. A kindergarten child went home from school one day and told his grandmother, "I've got it figured out now. First you have to be bad, and then good, and then you get a sticker." Commenting on positive behaviors and attributing positive characteristics to children rather than using external rewards help young children internalize prosocial responses.

Encourage understanding of children's own and others' feelings and perspectives

Skilled teachers understand how to do these things:

Acknowledge and encourage understanding and expression of children's feelings. The ability to empathize with a peer who is experiencing sadness, anger, or distress may depend on a child having had a prior similar experience with those feelings (Barnett 1984). Children from ages 3 to 8 are becoming aware of *happy feelings* (3½ years), *fear* (3½ to 4 years), and *anger and sadness* (3 to 8 years) (Borke 1971).

Caregivers need to help children put feelings into words and to understand their feelings. Teachers can acknowledge and reflect children's feelings by making comments such as "It seems as if you are feeling so sad" or "You look like you are feeling angry. You want my attention *now*. As soon as I change Luanne's diaper, I can read to you." This calm observation by a child care provider wiped the thunder off a toddler's face. He looked amazed that his teacher had understood his feelings. He relaxed when she reassured him with a promise to come back in a few minutes and read with him.

Facilitate perspective- and role-taking skills and understanding others' feelings. Helping young children notice and respond to the feelings of others can be quite effective in teaching them to be considerate of others. A preschool teacher kneeled to be at eye level with a child who had just socked another child during a struggle for a bike. The teacher pointed out the feelings of the other child: "He's very sad and hurt. What can you do to make him feel better?" The aggressor paused, observed the other child's face, and offered the bike to the crying child.

A child's ability to identify accurately the emotional state of another, as well as the empathic ability to experience the feelings of another, contribute to prosocial behavior. Children who are altruistic and more willing to help others display more empathy and perspective-taking skills (a cognitive measure) (Chalmers & Townsend 1990).

Feshbach (1975) reported that two training techniques that promoted understanding in children of other children's feelings were *role playing* and *maximizing the perceived similarity* between the observer and the stimulus person. The latter is what antibias education is about.

Encourage children to act out stories dramatically. Children who act out different stories become aware of how the characters feel. Switching roles gives children a different perspective on the feelings and motives of each character. Acting out roles, as in "The Three Billy Goats Gruff" or "Goldilocks and the Three Bears" gives children a chance to understand each story character's point of view (Krogh & Lamme 1983). A first- or second-grade class may want to write a letter of apology from Goldilocks to the Bear family!

Trovato (1987) created the puppets "Hattie Helper," "Carl Defender," "Robert Rescuer," "Debra Defender," "Kevin Comforter," and "Sharon Sharer" for adults to use to help young children learn prosocial behaviors with other children. Crary (1984) also promotes the use of puppets for teachers and children to use in role playing different social situations that may arise in the classroom.

Perspective taking is not enough to ensure children's development of prosocial behaviors. Children who are low in empathy but high in perspective taking may demonstrate Machiavellianism (a tendency to take advantage in a negative way of knowledge concerning another person's feelings and thoughts) (Barnett & Thompson 1985). Although Howes and Farber's (1987) research with toddlers ages 16 to 33 months of in child care showed that 93% of toddlers responded prosocially to peers who showed distress, George and Main (1979) reported that abused toddlers looked on impassively or reacted with anger when a playmate was hurt or distressed. Vulnerable children urgently need help understanding and acknowledging their range of often very strong feelings and empathizing with other people's feelings.

Helping young children notice and respond to the feelings of others can be quite effective in teaching them to be considerate of others.

Use victim-centered discipline and reparation: Emphasize consequences. Other-oriented techniques focus a child on the effects of hurtful and antisocial behaviors, such as hitting or pinching. Results of a study of how children learned altruism at home revealed that parents of the most prosocial toddlers had emphasized the negative consequences of their toddlers' aggressive acts on other children (Pines 1979). Point out the consequences of the child's behavior. Emphasize to the aggressor the results of hurtful actions upon another person. Choose statements such as "Look—that hurt him!" "He is crying" and "I cannot let you hurt another child, and I do not want anyone to make you hurt; we need to help each other feel happy and safe in this class."

Help children become assertive concerning prosocial matters. If a child has high-perspective-taking skills and is assertive, then the child is likely to be prosocial. In contrast, if a child has high-perspective-taking skills and is timid, then the child is less likely to be prosocial (Barrett & Yarrow 1977). In the book *Listen to the Children* (Zavitkovsky, Baker, Berlfein, & Almy 1986, 42), the authors shared a true story about two young girls, Dolores and Monica, who were washing their hands before lunch. Eric was waiting for his turn to wash his hands. Out of the blue, he shouted crossly into Monica's face, "You're not pretty." The author and observer reported that out of the stillness came Dolores's firm voice, "Yes, she is. She looks just right for her." Dolores was demonstrating both perspective-taking skills—knowing that Monica's feelings were hurt—and prosocial defending skills. As teachers notice and acknowledge prosocial behaviors, children's self-confidence concerning prosocial interactions will increase.

Acknowledge and encourage understanding and expression of children's feelings. Facilitate perspective- and role-taking skills and understanding others' feelings.

© The Growth Program

Encourage problem solving and planfulness for prosocial behaviors

You have heard this before, but it takes time, effort, and planfulness to *do* it.

Encourage means–ends and alternative-solution thinking in conflict situations. Help children think through, step-by-step, their reasoning about how to respond when they are having a social problem with a peer. What are the steps by which they figure out how to get from the conflict situation they are in to peaceful, friendly cooperation or a courteous live-and-let-live situation?

Shure (1992) provides daily lessons for teachers to help children discover when their feelings and wishes are the *same* or *different* from other children's, or whether *some* or *all* of the children want to play the game that *one* prefers. Teachers who use these daily lesson plans with emphasis on encouraging children to think of alternative solutions to their social conflicts and to imagine the consequences of each behavior or strategy they think of can help aggressive and shy children become more positively social within three months. Increased positive social functioning is associated with children's ability to think of more strategies rather than with the quality of the social solutions they devise (Shure & Spivak 1978).

Use Socratic questions to elicit prosocial planfulness and recognition of responsibility. When a child is misbehaving in such a way as to disturb his own or class progress, quietly ask, "How does that help you?" This technique, recommended by Fugitt (1983), can be expanded to encourage group awareness by asking the child, "How is that helping the group?" or "How is that helping your neighbor?" This strategy is designed to help children recognize and take responsibility for their own behaviors.

Show pictured scenes of altruism, and ask children to create verbal scenarios. Show children pictured scenes of children being helpful, cooperative, generous, charitable, patient, courteous, sharing, and kind. Working with a small group of children, call on each child to make up a scenario or story about the child or children in the picture. Ask, "What do you think is happening here?" Be sure to help children become aware of how the child being helped feels and how the child who has been helpful or generous will feel about herself or himself.

Provide specific behavioral training in social skills. Cartledge and Milburn (1980) recommend defining skills to be taught in behavioral terms assessing children's level of competence. Then teach the skills that are lacking, evaluate the results of teaching, and provide opportunities for children to practice and generalize the transfer of these new social skills to other situations.

McGinnis and Goldstein use structured "skillstreaming" strategies to teach prosocial skills to preschool (1990) and elementary

© The Growth Program

Encourage means–ends and alternative-solution thinking in conflict situations. Help children think through, step-by-step, their reasoning about how to respond when they are having a social problem with a peer. What are the steps by which they figure out how to get from the conflict situation they are in to peaceful, friendly cooperation or a courteous live-and-let-live situation?

school (1984) children. Skills such as listening, using nice talk, using brave talk, saying thank you, asking for help, greeting others, reading others, waiting one's turn, sharing, offering help, asking someone to play, and playing a game are a few of the "beginning social skills" and "friendship making skills." Other skills help children deal with feelings and provide them with alternatives to aggression. Preschool

children who received training and were encouraged to (1) use politeness words, (2) listen to who is talking, (3) participate with a peer in an activity, (4) share, (5) take turns, and (6) help another person have fun were more sociable in the training classroom and at follow-up (Factor & Schilmoeller 1983).

Teaching concern for others is a familiar idea to teachers of children from infancy through 8 years!

Place a child who is experiencing social problems with a friendly, socially skilled playmate, preferably a younger one, to increase the social isolate's positive peer interactions.

Use positive discipline for promoting prosocial behaviors and less aggression

We have to educate children about socially desirable behaviors, as about many other things.

Use positive discipline strategies, such as induction and authoritative methods. When teachers use positive discipline techniques—such as reasoning, use of positive reinforcement, and empathic listening—and *authoritative* strategies (Baumrind 1977)—loving, positive commitment to the child plus use of firm, clear rules and explanations—children are more likely to behave prosocially. The more nonauthoritarian and nonpunitive the parent, the higher the child's level of reasoning (Eisenberg, Lennon, & Roth 1983). Discipline that is *emotionally intense but nonpunitive* is effective with toddlers (Yarrow & Waxler 1976).

Positive discipline: A protection against media violence. As one might guess, a relationship has been found between parents' positive discipline techniques and the effects of prosocial and antisocial television programs on children. Using Hoffman's terms to describe parenting styles, Abelman (1986) reported that parents who are most *inductive* (who use reasoning) and who rarely use love withdrawal or power assertion have children who are *most* affected by prosocial and *least* affected by antisocial television. The reverse is also true. Positive discipline, then, is a powerful buffer against the negative effects of antisocial media materials.

Respond to and provide alternatives to aggressive behaviors. This has been a basic principle of nursery and kindergarten education since their beginning. Writing much more recently, Caldwell (1977) advises caregivers not to ignore aggression or permit aggression to be expressed and assume that this venting will "discharge the tension." For example, bullying that is ignored does not disappear. Caldwell writes, "In order to control aggression, we must strengthen altruism" (1977, 9). Teach children what they can do to help others feel good.

Redirect antisocial actions to more acceptable actions. A child who is throwing a ball at someone may be redirected to throw a beanbag back and forth with another child.

Teach angry, acting-out children to *use words* to express feelings. When children are feeling aggrieved, tell them, "Use your words" instead of hurtful actions. Help children learn "I" statements to express their feelings or wishes and to express how they perceive a situation of distress or conflict (Gordon 1970). Give children words and phrases to use, such as "I feel upset when our game is interrupted," "I cannot finish my building if you take away these blocks," or "I was using that Magic Marker first. I still need it to finish my picture."

Ask children to restate classroom rules about not hitting or hurting others (Honig 1985). Preschool children, however, may interpret the rules from an egocentric viewpoint and not always understand the reasons for rules. Deanna, a preschooler, went home from school and told her mother, "Matthew pinched me." After talking about the classroom rule, "Don't pinch or hit back," Deanna's mother tried to get Deanna to problem-solve other solutions to the problem, such as telling Matthew that it hurt when he pinched. The next day, when her mom picked her up from school, Deanna reported angrily, "Matthew pinched me back." When asked why she pinched him, Deanna restated the classroom rule, "That doesn't matter; he's not supposed to pinch me back."

Offer children choices. This is another "basic" of professional work with young children. Toddlers and preschoolers struggling to assert newly emergent autonomy cooperate more easily with caregiver requests if they feel empowered to make choices. Adults can decide on the choices to be offered. For the toddler having trouble settling at naptime, the offer "Would you like to sleep with your head at this end of your cot or the other end?" may empower him enough to decide cheerfully just how he wants to lie down for naptime. Gilligan observed that "The essence of the moral decision is the exercise of choice and the willingness to accept responsibility for that choice" (1982, 58). Often adults forget that if they carefully craft choices, children may more readily cooperate in the home and in the classroom. During snacktime adults can offer a choice of "darker or lighter toast," "apple or orange juice" to the finicky eater who generally resists food simply set down without her being allowed some choice. When children want to practice throwing a small basketball into a preschooler-size net, discuss the need for a turn-taking rule and offer a choice: "Do you want to take two or three throws for your turn?" Later, comment on how the children followed the rule. Ask them how they think the rule helped their game go more peaceably.

Provide opportunities for social interactions through play—pair "social isolates" with sociable children

Place a child who is experiencing social problems with a friendly, socially skilled playmate, preferably a younger one, to increase the social isolate's positive peer interactions (Furman, Rahe, & Hartup 1978). Pair an assertive, gregarious, but gentle child (who is the recipient of many prosocial overtures and is likely to offer help and friendliness) with a very shy child.

Create good adult–child relationships

Children learn to enjoy being with other people when they experience adults who are positive, caring, loving, and responsive. When adults respond to a child in affectionate, kind, empathetic ways, the child learns how to be a communicative partner who knows how to take turns, listen, negotiate, and help others; common sense tells us that this is logical. Park and Waters (1989)

found that two children who had experienced affirmative first relationships with their mothers engaged in more harmonious, less controlling, more responsive, and happier play together than did children who had not experienced positive first relationships.

Provide body relaxation activities

Create a relaxed classroom climate to further harmonious interactions. Relaxation exercises can restore harmony when children are fussy or tense. Back rubs help. Sand play and water play promote relaxation in some children who have a difficult time acting peaceably.

Children may lie down on mats and wiggle each limb separately, in turn, to relax and ease body tension. Many classical music pieces, such as the Brahms *Lullaby* or Debussy's *Reverie*, can be useful in helping children imagine peaceful scenes. Focused imagery activities can reduce tensions. Have children close their eyes and imagine being in a quiet forest glade, listening to a stream flow nearby and feeling the warm sunshine on their faces.

Group movement to music adds another dimension of relaxation. Dancing partners need to tune in to each other's motions and rhythmic swaying as they hold hands or take turns imitating each other's gestures.

Use technology to promote prosocial behaviors

Unlike most of the familiar principles for promoting social development reviewed in this article, *this* idea will be new to many teachers. Videotape children who are behaving prosocially to facilitate sharing. A video camera in the classroom can help promote altruism. Third-grade children viewed videotapes of themselves and models in situations involving sharing. This technique was effective in increasing sharing immediately following training and one week later (Devoe & Sherman 1978). Maybe some teachers who like trying new things will try this idea with *younger* children.

Conclusion

As teachers focus on and facilitate prosocial behaviors, the whole ambience of a classroom may change. As teachers model kindness and respect, express appreciation for prosocial actions, promote cooperation, teach children how their behaviors affect others, point out each child's prosocial behaviors with admiration to the other children, and encourage children to help each other, prosocial deeds and attitudes will

© The Growth Program

Offer children choices. This is another "basic" of professional work with young children. Toddlers and preschoolers struggling to assert newly emergent autonomy cooperate more easily with caregiver requests if they feel empowered to make choices. Adults can decide on the choices to be offered.

increase. Adults' interactions with young children make a powerful difference in the atmosphere and climate of the classroom.

References

Abelman, R. 1986. Children's awareness of television's prosocial fare: Parental discipline as an antecedent. *Journal of Family Issues* 7: 51–66.

Bandura, A. 1986. *The social foundation of thought and action: A social cognitive theory.* Englewood Cliffs, NJ: Prentice Hall.

Barnett, M. 1984. Similarity of experience and empathy in preschoolers. *The Journal of Genetic Psychology* 145: 241–50.

Barnett, M., & S. Thompson. 1985. The role of perspective-taking and empathy in children's Machiavellianism, prosocial behavior, and motive for helping. *The Journal of Genetic Psychology* 146: 295–305.

Barrett, D.E., & M.R. Yarrow. 1977. Prosocial behavior, social inferential ability, and assertiveness in young children. *Child Development* 48: 475–81.

Baumrind, D. 1977. Some thoughts about childrearing. In S. Cohen & T.J. Comiskey (Eds.), *Child development: Contemporary perspectives.* Itasca, IL: F.E. Peacock.

Borke, H. 1971. Interpersonal perception of young children: Egocentrism or empathy? *Developmental Psychology* 5: 263–9.

Bryan, J.H. 1977. Prosocial behavior. In H.L. Hom, Jr., & P.A. Robinson, eds. *Psychological processes in early education.* New York: Academic.

Caldwell, B. 1977. Aggression and hostility in young children. *Young Children* 32 (2): 4–14.

Cartledge, G., & J.F. Milburn, eds. 1980. *Teaching social skills to children.* New York: Pergamon.

Chalmers, J., & M. Townsend. 1990. The effects of training in social perspective taking on socially maladjusted girls. *Child Development* 61: 178–90.

Crary, E. 1984. *Kids can cooperate: A practical guide to teaching problem solving.* Seattle, WA: Parenting Press.

Devoe, M., & T. Sherman. 1978. A microtechnology for teaching prosocial behavior to children. *Child Study Journal* 8 (2): 83–92.

Eisenberg, N., R. Lennon, & K. Roth. 1983. Prosocial development: A longitudinal study. *Developmental Psychology* 19: 846–55.

Elardo, R., & J.J. Freund. 1981. Maternal childrearing styles and the social skills of learning disabled boys: A preliminary investigation. *Contemporary Educational Psychology* 6: 86–94.

Fabes, R.A., J. Fultz, N. Eisenberg, T. May-Plumlee, & F.S. Christopher. 1989. Effect of rewards on children's prosocial motivation: A socialization study. *Developmental Psychology* 25: 509–15.

Factor, D., & G.L. Schilmoeller. 1983. Social skill training of preschool children. *Child Study Journal* 13 (1): 41–56.

Feshbach, N. 1975. Empathy in children: Some theoretical and empirical considerations. *The Counseling Psychologist* 5: 25–30.

Fugitt, E. 1983. *"He hit me back first!" Creative visualization activities for parenting and teaching.* Rolling Hills Estates, CA: Jalmar.

Furman, W., D.F. Rahe, & W.W. Hartup. 1978. Rehabilitation of low-interactive preschool children through mixed-age and same-age socialization. In H. McGurk, ed., *Issues in childhood social development.* Cambridge: Methuen.

George, C., & M. Main. 1979. Social interactions of young abused children: Approach, avoidance, and aggression. *Child Development* 50: 306–18.

Gilligan, C. 1982. *In a different voice.* Cambridge, MA: Harvard University Press.

Goffin, S.G. 1987. Cooperative behaviors: They need our support. *Young Children* 42 (2): 75–81.

Gordon, T. 1970. *Parent effectiveness training.* New York: Wyden.

Grusec, J.E., & E. Redler. 1980. Attribution, reinforcement, and altruism. *Developmental Psychology* 16: 525–34.

Grusec, J., P. Saas-Kortsaak, & Z. Simultis. 1978. The role of example and moral exhortation in the training of altruism. *Child Development* 49: 920–3.

Grusec, J., J. Kuczynski, P. Rushton, & Z. Simultis. 1978. Modeling, direct instruction, and attributions: Effects on altruism. *Developmental Psychology* 14: 51–7.

Haskins, R. 1985. Public school aggression among children with varying day care experience. *Child Development* 56: 689–703.

Honig, A.S. 1982. Research in review. Prosocial development in children. *Young Children* 37 (5): 51–62.

Honig, A.S. 1985. Research in review. Compliance, control, and discipline. Part 1. *Young Children* 40 (2): 50–8.

Honig, A.S., & D.S. Wittmer. 1992. *Prosocial development in children: Caring, sharing, & cooperating: A bibliographic resource guide.* New York: Garland.

Howes, C., & J. Farber. 1987. Toddlers' responses to the distress of their peers. *Journal of Applied Developmental Psychology* 8: 441–52.

Krogh, S., & L. Lamme. 1983 (January–February). Learning to share: How literature can help. *Childhood Education* 59 (3): 188–92.

McGinnis, E., & A. Goldstein. 1984. *Skillstreaming the elementary school child: A guide to prosocial skills.* Champaign, IL: Research Press.

McGinnis, E., & A. Goldstein. 1990. *Skillstreaming in early childhood. Teaching prosocial skills to the preschool and kindergarten child.* Champaign, IL: Research Press.

Park, K., & E. Waters. 1989. Security of attachment and preschool friendships. *Child Development* 60: 1076–81.

Pines, M. 1979. Good Samaritans at age two? *Psychology Today* 13: 66–77.

Rushton, J.P., & G. Teachman. 1978. The effects of positive reinforcement, attributions, and punishment on model induced altruism in children. *Personality and Social Psychology Bulletin* 4: 322–5.

Rutherford, E., & P. Mussen. 1968. Generosity in nursery school boys. *Child Development* 39: 755–65.

Shure, M.B. 1992. *I can problem solve: An interpersonal cognitive problem-solving program.* Champaign, IL: Research Press.

Shure, M., & G. Spivack. 1978. *Problem-solving techniques in childrearing.* San Francisco: Jossey-Bass.

Trovato, C. 1987. Teaching today's kids to get along. *Early Childhood Teacher* 34: 43.

Vorrath, H. 1985. *Positive peer culture.* New York: Aldine.

Yarrow, M.R., & C.Z. Waxler. 1976. Dimensions and correlates of prosocial behavior in young children. *Child Development*, 47: 118–25.

Zavitkovsky, D., K.R. Baker, J.R. Berlfein, & M. Almy. 1986. *Listen to the children.* Washington, DC: NAEYC.

Helping Children To Cope with Relocation

Mary Renck Jalongo

Mary Renck Jalongo is Professor, Department of Professional Studies in Education, Indiana University of Pennsylvania, Indiana, Pennsylvania.

Marlene Sanchez, a 15-year veteran teacher, stops by the elementary school office before classes officially begin to pick up her class list. As she scans the children's names—most of them are unfamiliar—she remembers when the lists represented with reasonable accuracy the class composition for the entire school year. Today, 6 million American families relocate each year, forcing teachers to deal with higher student turnover rates than ever before (Olkowski & Parker, 1992). Educator Nancy Larrick describes the current situation:

> The weakening job market and scarcity of housing for low-income families have dislocated hundreds of thousands of households. This means frequent moves, often as many as four different schools for a child in one year. In my small town . . . elementary teachers have learned to expect a 47 percent turnover in their classes each year. (Larrick, 1992, pp. 245-246)

What policies have schools established to deal with the consequences of our "highly mobile society?" Neither school administrators nor classroom teachers have had consistent access to theory, research or expert opinion to guide their daily interactions with children and families who are moving away or settling in.

One reason for this information gap is the literature's fragmented nature. The topic of moving has been covered by educators, sociologists, child psychologists, military personnel, corporate mobility experts and the United States Census Bureau.

The author provides a critical synthesis of literature about moving, including recent, authoritative and often surprising findings about the effects of moving on children and families. Also, the author recommends school-wide policies and classroom practices designed to facilitate the child's adjustment to moving.

The Adaptive Demands of Relocation

Many adults tend to characterize moving as either negative or positive, without much evidence to support their point of view other than popular wisdom or direct experience. *Every* move places adaptive demands on the child and family (Kyrios & Prior, 1990; Stroh & Brett, 1988). Even when a child perceives a move to be generally positive, the necessary adjustments are disruptive and create additional pressures. Adults frequently gauge the adaptive demands of relocation by the distance from their previous homes, while children—especially young ones—place less relevance on this variable because they exert less control over their surroundings (Jalongo, 1985).

Consider the situation of 5-year-old Justin. After his parents separated, he and his mother moved from their rural home to an urban apartment. Although the apartment is just one hour away from his old house, his situation has been radically altered. In one year, Justin became part of a single-parent family; fell below the poverty line; left his teacher, school and friends; moved farther away from his grandparents and other relatives; lost his outdoor play area and had to give away his puppy. Justin's experience exemplifies the significant losses that may accompany moving.

Effects of Moving on Peers

One finding of relocation research that is generally overlooked is that all children are affected by a move, particularly the ones who are left behind when a friend moves away (Field, 1984). This conclusion makes sense when we consider that young children fear separation and abandonment above all else and that teenagers' stated primary reason for attending school is to see their friends (Goodland, 1984; Wolman, 1978). Even adults who are sensitive to children's needs sometimes overlook the fact that both the best friend who leaves and the best friend who remains behind have to start all over again. In fact, research suggests that, among preschoolers, the children who are left behind may be more agitated for a longer period of time (Field, 1984). As Joanne Hendrick (1984) explains,

> Sometimes teachers underestimate what it means to a child when a friend moves away . . . But children often feel quite depleted and adrift when this occurs . . . As in working through any kind of separation, the leaver's and the leftbehind's feelings of grief, apprehension, and sometimes anger need to be recognized and honored. (p. 224)

From *Childhood Education*, Winter 1994/95, pp. 80-85. © 1994 by the Association for Childhood Education International, 11501 Georgia Avenue, Suite 315, Wheaton, MD. Reprinted by permission.

Individual Responses

Adaptive responses to a move are a highly individual matter. Although children are encouraged if other family members demonstrate an attitude of hopeful anticipation about the move, each person in the family interprets and responds to the situation in different ways.

Consider, for example, two sisters in secondary school. When their father accepted a promotion that required relocation, they left their 300-student high school for one with 3,000 students. They were both miserable at first and even stopped eating lunch so that they could avoid the public humiliation of sitting alone in the cafeteria. About five months later, the younger sister, a 10th-grader, adjusted after she established friendships. But the older sister, whose senior year, prom plans and summer job were sacrificed to the move, remained depressed all year. Although these two young women were roughly the same age and had family, school and move in common, their perspectives were entirely different. The 12th-grader interpreted the move as a denial of her personhood and as a sign of indifference from her father, while the 10th-grader ultimately regarded it as an inescapable part of life and a challenge met.

Loss of a Natural Habitat

Children experience moving as loss of their natural habitat (Gabarino, 1987). Even if the relocation does not involve great distance, it can mean losing a network of people who know, respect and trust the child. Vance Packard (1983) once said that we have to re-establish our credentials every time we move. The familiar ways of interacting with close friends seldom work well with new acquaintances. Strangers may view directness as arrogance, silliness as weirdness, teasing as a threat. Reestablishing credentials is a time-consuming and often frustrating process. Therefore, experts estimate that a child needs at least a year to make an overall adjustment to relocation (Current Health, 1985).

The child who changes culture and country as well as residence is more than the "new kid" at school; he or she is an expatriate (Jalongo, 1983). Such was the case for 5-year-old Korean twins who were adopted by a wealthy American family in Maine. Accustomed to living in rural poverty, the girls had never been on an airplane and were terrified by the escalator and the moving walkway at the airport. Having never even seen a television, they refused to go outdoors after watching a nature program because they were fearful of being attacked by wolves. Before the move, they had never been in the company of more than a handful of village children at once; now they were boarding a school bus with children of all ages who did not speak their language. The girls found themselves in an unpredictable environment, one in which it was exceedingly difficult to distinguish between positive change and dangerous threats.

Effects of Moving on Academic Achievement

Some evidence indicates that the academic performance of children who move repeatedly often declines. A study conducted by the Denver Public Schools revealed that approximately 95 percent of students who remained in the district graduated, while just 30 percent of the students who moved three or more times during their public school careers eventually graduated (Olkowski & Parker, 1992). Statistics such as these should be interpreted cautiously, however, taking into consideration some important variables. Families that live at or below the poverty line—such as migrant workers or the homeless—are apt to be overrepresented in moving statistics because they move more frequently overall and are much more likely to move within the same calendar year (Strong & Tenhouse, 1990). Also, family moves are often connected to severe family stress, such as a divorce or death. Therefore, relocation may be only one factor affecting children's academic achievement.

New Roles for Teachers and Schools

Teachers, parents, administrators and other support personnel can help reduce the adaptive demands of relocation on children by:

■ *Providing inservice training, observation guidelines and support for staff.* Recognize that the adjustments necessary during relocation can influence children's self-confidence, behavior and physical health, as well as their response to neighborhoods and peers, teachers and schools (Field, 1984; Gabarino, 1987). Too often, new students feel like they are an imposition. Typically, when a new student appears, the teacher stops the lesson, scrounges around for a desk, bids a hasty welcome and leaves the child to "sink or swim."

Educators must understand that a child's reaction to the stress of relocation is frequently delayed. Children tend to progress through five stages: 1) contact—feeling excited about exploring the new setting; 2) disintegration—contrasting the old and new environments and feeling disoriented, isolated or depressed; 3) reintegration—rejecting the new environment and feeling anxious, angry, suspicious or hostile; 4) autonomy—regaining balance and feeling less like an outsider as confidence returns; and 5) independence—accepting and appreciating differences between the environments as the adjustment is made (Adler, 1975; Walling, 1990).

Educators can provide additional patience and support by contacting parents and referring children to school counselors or psychologists when appropriate. Finally, educators can help by learning more about the topic through professional reading and inservice training (National

Association of School Psychologists, 1992).

■ *Responding to children's common questions and concerns.* Too often, adults treat moving as a purely logical, logistical matter, whereas children more commonly experience it as an emotional, social matter. When surveyed, 2,500 elementary and middle school students identified their major questions about moving and school as: What will the new kids be like? Will I be able to make friends? What will my new school be like? Will my teacher be nice or mean? Will my work be harder? What if I can't find my way around school? What is there to do there? (Mullen, 1989; Olkowski & Parker, 1992).

Providing information is one of the best ways that schools can address such questions. Ideally, children will learn all they can about a school before they attend. School newspapers, calendars, publications describing school policies or a collection of children's writings can be used to alleviate many common concerns. Ask older children to welcome a new student with information from the Chamber of Commerce and from their favorite hang-outs, such as the skating rink, the ice cream shop and the record store. Don't forget that one simple photograph can speak volumes. Relocation experts point out that a class picture may ease fears about being ostracized because of different hairstyles and fashions (Ervin, 1990).

■ *Using the curriculum to help children build concepts about moving.* Learning about, and coping with, moving can be a basic survival skill for today's children. Therefore, school curriculum should integrate experiences about moving into all subject areas. Young children might benefit from a play center with a moving theme or a class project on the moving van. The following concepts may soothe very young children's fears about moving:

- People live in homes for different lengths of time
- Sometimes people leave their homes temporarily to live somewhere else (when they visit, camp or travel)
- Sometimes people leave one home and move to a new home
- People have different feelings about moving
- Moving involves packing and transporting people, pets and possessions
- When people move, they often leave familiar people, places and things
- People who move discover new people, places and things
- Some things about a new home are very different from the old home, while other things are very much the same
- Sometimes people visit their old neighborhood and/or communicate with the people who live there
- People move for different reasons (Kostelnik, 1991).

School-age children's concepts about moving can be positively affected if they learn about geographical names, locations and the relocation process. Teachers can develop simulations, such as planning the classroom arrangement or creating maps and models of the community (Beem & Prah, 1984). Middle and high school students could plan a hypothetical move, obtaining literature from several moving companies in order to compare the services and costs.

After some coaching on interviewing techniques, children could interview a guest from another country, a representative from a local moving company or a real estate agent. The school counselor is a source of information about common concerns related to moving

One of the best ways to gain insight about the child's perspective on moving is to encourage self-expression.

and can provide professional advice on dealing with these issues. In addition, many excellent books deal with the issue of moving. A list of recommended books on relocation, arranged by grade level, follows this article.

One of the best ways to gain insight about the child's perspective on moving is to encourage self-expression. Children can come to terms with the stresses of moving by using creative thinking strategies such as fantasizing, brainstorming, making analogies and inventing metaphor; children who find it difficult to communicate in other ways often find drawing, writing, music, dance and puppetry to be effective outlets for their feelings (Mancus & Mancus, 1976).

■ *Developing school-wide policies that support children and families who are new to the school.* When new families arrive in a community, school personnel are usually among their first contacts. Too often, the parents are greeted by a handful of forms pushed across a counter and the children by a roomful of unfamiliar faces. But every child and family need kind, supportive treatment and substantive information about the new school during their adjustment period. Naturally, it will be more difficult if families do not communicate with the school in advance. At the very least, new students ought to make preliminary school visits to meet their teachers and have a chance to tour the school before meeting the other children (Jalongo, 1993).

Young children should be encouraged to bring familiar objects to the new school. A favorite toy or a photograph of parents may help assuage the fears of preschoolers. Older children might bring a map that charts their travels or a collection of items that can be used to introduce others to their interests and hobbies. Schools with high turnover rates could institute small, grade-level support groups for children who have moved recently.

One team of school counselors developed a special program for newcomers that included public service announcements on the radio, a home visit and a school visit, a newcomers' picnic and an orientation program (Keats, Crabbs & Crabbs, 1981). Responses to a follow-up survey of parents and children revealed that 77 percent of children felt that they benefited from meeting a school staff member before attending classes, 90 percent of families appreciated the home visit and 95 percent of families felt more comfortable in the new school after going to the picnic (Keats, Crabbs & Crabbs, 1981). All or some of these strategies could be implemented on a regular basis, particularly in schools with high turnover rates.

■ *Putting children in charge of welcome and departure rituals.* Children could share in developmentally appropriate responsibilities for contacting new classmates before and after they arrive at school. Very young children can draw pictures to send to a newcomer, while older children can serve on a welcoming committee and assemble information packets. Welcoming banners, balloons or receptions prepared by classmates will communicate the message, "We're glad you're here." All the children should be coached in how to welcome new classmates by showing them around, sitting with them at lunch, answering questions and serving as peer tutors. This approach allows teachers to assign various students to work with a new child and increases the likelihood that social relationships will be formed. Older children, once they get settled,

could be interviewed by peers for a profile in the school or class newspaper. Student-managed activities such as these can be very effective ways to help a child feel welcome, while at the same time building every child's interpersonal skills.

While school staff may be reluctant to address the departure of one of their students, these children need empathy and encouragement in order to get mentally prepared for a move. Teachers who have worked with transient families in

While school staff may be reluctant to address the departure of one of their students, these children need empathy and encouragement . . .

the military recommend waiting for a quiet moment to say: "I know that you feel sad about leaving your friends here. We will miss you, too, and we will think about the good times that we had together here. Just think of how lucky your new friends and teacher will be to have you for a friend" (Long & Brant, 1979).

Peers should become involved in the departure rituals, as well. The children could create a keepsake book that addresses what will happen when the child moves and includes photos of the old and new house, old and new school, friends and teachers (Beem & Prah, 1984). Such books could also serve as home-school communication devices as families can use them to prepare the child for the move. Often, a keepsake book becomes the first thing that a child will share with the new class—and a vehicle for re-establishing those credentials that were lost in the move.

Educators who understand the effects of relocation on the child can

institute classroom practices and school-wide policies that support every child during these important transitions. In this way, they can make an important contribution to building a sense of community in our ever-changing society.

References

Adler, P. (1975). Transitional experience: An alternative view of culture shock. *Journal of Humanistic Psychology*, 13–23.

Beem, M., & Prah, W. (1984). When I move away, will I still be me? *Childhood Education*, 60(5), 310–314.

Dowd, F. A. (1987). Strategies and materials for teachers and parents helping children adjust to geographic relocation. *Journal of Youth Services in Libraries*, 1(1), 65–78.

Ervin, N. J. (1990, February). It's not easy being a teen. *Mobility*, 35–36.

Field, T. (1984). Separation stress of young children transferring to new schools. *Developmental Psychology*, 20(5), 786–792.

Gabarino, J. (1987). The human ecology of early risk. In S. Meisels & J. Shonkoff (Eds.), *Handbook of early intervention*. New York: Cambridge University Press.

Goodlad, J. I. (1984). *A place called school: Prospects for the future.* New York: McGraw Hill.

Hendrick, J. (1984). *The whole child: Early education for the eighties* (3rd ed.). St. Louis, MO: Mosby.

Jalongo, M. R. (1983). Promoting peer acceptance of the newly immigrated child. *Childhood Education*, 60(2), 117-124.

Jalongo, M. R. (1993). Packed and moved but not settled in: How moving affects children. *PTA Today*, 19(2), 17-19.

Jalongo, M. R. (1985). When young children move. *Young Children*, 40, 51-57.

Keats, D. B., Crabbs, M. A., & Crabbs, S. K. (1981). Facilitating the adjustment process of new students. *Elementary School Guidance and Counseling*, 15, 319-323.

Kostelnik, M. J. (Ed.). (1991). *Teaching young children using themes.* Glenview, IL: GoodYear.

Kyrios, M., & Prior, M. (1990). Temperament, stress and family factors in behavioral adjustment of 3- to 5-year-old children. *International Journal of Behavioral Development*, 13(1), 67-93.

Larrick, N. (1992). Reflections on children and books. In D. Burleson (Ed.), *Reflections: Personal essays by 33 distinguished educators* (pp. 245-267). Bloomington, IN: Phi Delta Kappa.

Long, I., & Brant, L. (1979). *Moving: United States Air Force child care program activity guide.* (ERIC Document Reproduction Service No. ED 213 500).

Mancus, D. S., & Mancus, P. M. (1976). *How is a moving van like a camel? Creative strategies for helping a child deal with anxiety.* (ERIC Document Reproduction Service No. ED 243 584).

Moving right along. (1985). *Current Health, 11*(2), 12-13.

Mullen, E. (1989, March). Assessing the needs of the relocating child. *Mobility,* 21-22.

National Association of School Psychologists. (1992). *Kids on the move: Meeting their needs.* Silver Spring, MD: Author.

Olkowski, T. T., & Parker, L. (1992). *Helping children cope with moving.* York, PA: William Gladden Foundation.

Packard, V. (1983). *Our endangered children: Growing up in a changing world.* Boston: Little, Brown.

Stroh, L. K., & Brett, J. M. (1988). *Corporate mobility: Effects on children.* (ERIC Document Reproduction Service No. ED 307 061).

Strong, J. H., & Tenhouse, C. (1990). *Educating homeless children: Issues and answers* (Fastback # 313). Bloomington, IN: Phi Delta Kappa.

Walling, D. R. (1990). *Meeting the needs of transient students.* (Fastback # 304). Bloomington, IN: Phi Delta Kappa.

Wolman, B. (1978). *Children's fears.* New York: New American Library.

Children's Books About Relocation

Mary Renck Jalongo, Melissa Renck and Jyotsna Pattnaik, compilers

In preparing this bibliography, we have selected books that deal sensitively with the adaptive demands of geographic relocation for children. Both fiction and nonfiction titles are included; contemporary as well as historical accounts are represented on the list. Many of these books deal with more "routine" moves while other titles deal with the special circumstances of homelessness, the newly immigrated, the children of migrant workers or dramatic changes in family structure and relationships that precipitate a move.

Preschool/Primary

Aliki. (1984). *We are best friends.* New York: Greenwillow.

Asch, F. (1980). *Goodbye house.* New York: Simon & Schuster.

Altman, L. J. (1993). *Amelia's road.* New York: Lee & Low.

Bourke, L. (1981). *It's your move: Picking up, packing up, and settling in.* Reading, MA: Addison-Wesley.

Bunting, E. (1991). *Fly away home.* Boston: Houghton Mifflin.

Carlstrom, N. (1990). *I'm not moving!* New York: Macmillan.

Danziger, P. (1994). *Amber Brown is not a crayon.* New York: Putnam.

Giffard, H. (1992). *Red fox on the move.* New York: Dial.

Greenwood, P. D. (1993). *What about my goldfish?* New York: Clarion.

Hughes, S. (1979). *Moving Molly.* Englewood Cliffs, NJ: Prentice-Hall.

Johnson, A. (1992). *The leaving morning.* New York: Orchard.

Johnston, T. (1992). *The quilt story.* New York: Putnam.

Kinsey-Warnock, N. (1992). *Wilderness cat.* New York: Dutton.

Komaiko, L. (1987). *Annie bananie.* New York: Harper.

Kuklin, S. (1992). *How my family lives in America.* New York: Bradbury.

O'Kelley, M. L. (1991). *Moving to town!* Boston: Little, Brown.

Sharmat, M. W. (1978). *Mitchell is moving.* New York: Macmillan.

Shefelman, J. (1992). *A peddler's dream.* Boston: Houghton Mifflin.

Slater, H. (1992). *I move to a new house.* New York: Smithmark.

Smith, J. L. (1981). *The monster in the third dresser drawer and other stories about Adam Joshua.* New York: Harper & Row.

Stolz, M. (1991). *King Emmett the second.* New York: Greenwillow.

Thomas, A. (1993). *Lily.* New York: Henry Holt.

Tobias, T. (1976). *Moving day.* New York: Knopf.

Turner, A. W. (1991). *Stars for Sarah.* New York: Harper & Row.

Waber, B. (1988). *Ira says goodbye.* Boston: Houghton Mifflin.

Watson, W. (1978). *Moving.* New York: Harper & Row.

Wild, M. (1993). *Space travelers.* New York: Scholastic.

Woodruff, E. (1991). *The wing shop.* New York: Holiday House.

Ziefert, H. (1988). *A clean house for mole and mouse.* New York: Viking.

Breaking the Cycle of Violence

Lorraine B. Wallach

Lorraine B. Wallach is a Distinguished Service Professor Emerita at the Erikson Institute in Chicago, Illinois.

Violence is epidemic in the United States today. The public at large and the media have finally taken notice of the brutality that has permeated our families and our communities. Of particular concern is the toll crime and violence are taking on the lives of our children (Kotlowitz (1991). In increasing numbers, children are the victims of violence both inside and outside their homes. They are the casualties of the chaos and destructiveness that have engulfed many neighborhoods.

Besides being the victims of violence, children are witnesses to the crime and brutality of the streets, and in their homes they see parents fighting and siblings being beaten. Research has shown that children suffer the consequences of witnessing violence as well as experiencing it directly (Pynoos & Eth, 1985, Tulsa World, August 4, 1994).

Perhaps the most alarming statistic is the increasing number of children who themselves engage in criminal acts. Adolescent gangs are the obvious wrongdoers in many communities, but increasingly younger children are guilty of many acts of brutality. We now have

children killing children (Illinois Criminal Justice Information Authority, 1992).

What can educators and child development professionals do to lessen the toll violence is taking on today's youngsters? Before seeking solutions, it is necessary to understand how living with violence penalizes healthy development.

The bonding of infants with care givers and the development of trust in the world are the major tasks of the early years (Erikson, 1950). These tasks are jeopardized when families live in stressful environments. When danger lurks outside and people are not safe in their own homes, families cannot provide the kind of consistent and predictable climate that is required for healthy child rearing. They do not have the emotional energy to meet the infants' needs in a warm, nurturing, and responsive manner.

At the toddler stage children are learning to walk and then to run and jump. In order to perfect these new skills they need safe space, which is found in parks, playgrounds, and community play areas. Toddlers have an inner push toward physical activity. They also have an inner push to do things their own way. This is the "no" and the "me do" stage (Brazelton, 1974). Toddlers who are confined to small, indoor quarters with

many restrictions on their activities can become difficult to manage. The combination of their drive toward physical exercise and the wish to do things their own way can cause friction with their caregivers. This interruption of the relationship between toddler and care giver is one more factor that can lead to physical punishment, and even abuse.

As children become preschoolers, their developmental goal is to reach out to people beyond their families (Erikson, 1950). They try to gain knowledge about how others live and relate to each other. They begin to know that there are different ways of doing things. When preschoolers cannot go out and there are restrictions on their activities, socialization can be jeopardized. Their understanding of the adult world is limited and children learn that outsiders are to be feared rather than trusted. Although such a lesson may be necessary in many communities, it interferes with learning how to get along with others.

School-age children must leave home to go to school, which means they must venture into the community each day. In school they are expected to gain the academic skills that will help them become capable workers, as well as the social skills that will make them effective members of society. Many children who grow up in households and communities

From *Children Today,* Vol. 23, No. 3, 1994-95. Reprinted by permission of *Children Today,* a publication of the Administration for Children and Families, U.S. Department of Health and Human Services.

beset by stress and violence have not learned the skills necessary to function well in school. They do not come prepared to learn and have difficulty meeting the demands of the school setting. If, in addition, they do not feel safe, academic and social learning are compromised. The strategies many children develop to protect themselves from fear of the outside world and from their inner tensions can include shutting out external stimuli, which interferes with learning the lessons school offers (A. Freud, 1937). Children are not open to learning to read, write, and to do arithmetic. In addition, they are not available to learn social skills and cooperative group behavior.

What can professionals do to break the cycle of violence that has overtaken us? There is no one simple answer, but those who care for and educate children on a daily basis can make a difference in the lives of those children. They can supplement what families can not, or do not, provide.

First, teachers and child care workers must be ready to deal with difficult children. They must be ready to start where the children are, and not expect them to be where the textbooks say they are (Donovan & McIntyre, 1990). If some children in third grade are reading at a first grade level, those children must be taught at that level. However, children must be approached with the expectation that they are capable of learning and the adults are there to help them. The same approach can be applied to children's behavior. If they do not have inner controls, they must be provided with firm, but benign, limits. It must be made clear, however, that children are expected to learn to control their own behavior.

The basis for all work with children who are at risk for pathological development is through relationships (Alexander, 1948). Adults must be ready to form meaningful relationships with children so that the children can alter their views of the world and of themselves. This is best done through identification with caring adults who provide models for behavior and learning, who communicate belief in the children's abilities, and who offer affection and respect. Most children get

these benefits from their families during their formative years. Those who are not so lucky have to get them later if they are to succeed in life. People who work with children are in the best position to compensate for such deficits.

This task is not an easy one because children who need extra help are the very ones who have difficulty forming meaningful relationships with adults. They have to be met more than half-way, and adults must be willing to spend the extra time and emotional energy necessary to succeed in this undertaking (Coopersmith, 1967).

In order to do this, those in responsible positions must redefine their roles. Professionals can no longer see themselves in the traditional roles of teachers,

---

Children who do not have adult models who express feelings in socially acceptable ways are in particular need of activities that encourage them to communicate their feelings.

---

social workers, nurses, or group workers. They must be ready to relate to children in a different way and on a deeper level. The first grade teacher must do more than teach children how to read and write, although those skills are essential. She must be ready to listen to the stories

children tell and to accept those stories, even when they are filled with violence and gore. In addition to teaching them the skills they need, the teacher who can accept children and their feelings will provide both a model for the children and an antidote to the hopelessness and despair offered by their communities.

Individual staff members can not do it alone. Programs must support their efforts by providing schedules that allow staff the extra time necessary to develop one-to-one relationships. Consistency of personnel must be a priority so that each child is encouraged and supported in getting close to one adult (Garbarino, Dubrow, Kostelny, Pardo, 1992).

Consistency and care are often lacking for children who live in stressful environments. Service programs can fill that gap in the children's lives by providing continuity in staff, stability in programs, and unvarying expectations. This does not mean that people and programs always have to be exactly the same. Of course, there will be changes, and there will be times when it is more important to be spontaneous than to rigidly adhere to a plan. However, it is essential for children to learn that they can count on some part of their world that will not change erratically, without warning.

Care is another ingredient that adults can give children. Children need to know that people care for them and about them (Cooperment, 1967). They need to know there are adults who are concerned enough to make efforts to help and support them. Care includes clear expectations and limits, which are most important for youngsters who live in chaos. All children need to know what is expected of them, but children who have not experienced consistency in their lives are in particular need of established rules of behavior. Even when they resist discipline, it is necessary to hold the line. If the expectations are appropriate to the children's stages of development and take into account individual differences, they provide a necessary structure. As children internalize the rules that are part of their daily lives, they begin to establish inner controls.

Discipline helps children learn what is right and what is wrong, but they need to learn constructive ways of expressing their feelings (Wallach, 1993). Children who do not have adult models who express feelings in socially acceptable ways are in particular need of activities that encourage them to communicate their feelings. They can benefit from dramatic play, a variety of art activities, and storytelling.

Play is very important for younger children. They can use stuffed animals and dolls as an outlet for their anger. If they are lonely, they can imagine that they have many friends. If they are frightened, they can pretend to be big and strong. Through play, they can transform bad experiences into scenarios with happy endings (Garbarino & Stott, 1990. Play also lets children relive the difficult times in their lives. The need to replay traumas occurs in children as well as adults (Terr, 1981). Grownups talk about traumatic events; children play them out. Sometimes they change the endings so that they are the winners and not the losers, or the transgressors and not the victims. In other words, they can pretend they are active instead of passive; they are in charge of things. Through play children can come to grips with the emotional residue of the difficulties they have experienced. Gradually, they learn to manage the anger, anxiety, and other feelings that are difficult to cope with by reenacting them time and again.

There is currently a controversy among child care and education professionals about whether or not to allow children to play with guns or to play war games. Each program has to decide for itself what is best for its children and families, and then convey that policy clearly to staff and parents. Consideration should be given to what guns and fighting mean in the community in which children live. The policy ought to spell out the difference between what staff provides for the children and what is produced by the children because of their own needs.

When programs offer guns to children, it may encourage aggressive play, and children may think aggression is sanctioned by adults. However, when children create their own aggressive games, they are seeking release of affect or are symbolically working out their own questions. If the adults who care for them accept their play while teaching them other ways of behaving, children will get the message that adults accept their feelings but do not approve of behavior that hurts others or destroys property. When there is a decision to

---

Those aspects of our society that breed violence must be changed, while the violence that presently exists must be restrained.

---

restrict guns or aggressive play, alternative means for expressing hostility and anger must be provided so that children have an outlet for their emotions.

Dictating stories is an excellent way for young children to relive the difficulties in their lives and to come to grips with their feelings (Garbarino & Stott, 1990). Because the stories children invent are private and are not observed by other children, they allow great leeway for communicating the traumas they are experiencing—and they do not have negative effects on other children. If the adults who are sharing the storytelling with them accept what the children have to say, the children have an opportunity to work through their problems. Even if it makes adults uncomfortable, it is important for them to accept children's ideas and feelings. While adults may need to limit children's

behavior, they should respect their feelings.

Older children can write their own stories. Putting ideas and feelings on paper offers each child the opportunity for emotional release. It also gives opportunities for children to take more objective views of what they are experiencing. It gives them a chance to stand aside and observe from the outside in. It gives them an observing ego.

Art activities can also be an outlet for children. The younger ones get a release from the sensory experience of playing with the materials. Paints, clay, crayons, sand, and water all offer ways for children to express feelings. Older children can use art materials to illustrate their stories or to spell out ideas and feelings through drawing, painting, or sculpting. What some children may find difficult to put into words may be expressed through the symbolism of their artwork (Garbarino) .

In addition to providing children with outlets for their feelings, programs can offer them social settings that are not filled with violence and hate. The social fabric of the children's group can be designed to promote cooperation, acceptance of individual differences, and non-violent ways of resolving conflicts. Starting with the youngest, children can be taught to get along with each other.

The first principle of teaching social skills is through modeling them. Adults should provide examples for the children. They have to demonstrate their acceptance of all the children, even those who cause difficulty or are aggressive with others. It does not mean letting unruly children run slipshod over everyone, but it does mean providing firm limits without being harsh or demeaning. Usually the children who have the most trouble accepting reasonable limits are the ones who suffer from poor self image. They do not value themselves, therefore they cannot value others. These children need to have their self esteem bolstered, not torn down.

Children also need to be taught the specific skills it takes to get along with one another. A recent book by Vivian Paley (1992) describes a method she used to help kindergarten children learn to function in a group without excluding anyone. The book is called *You Can't Say You Can't Play,* and describes her approach to encouraging children to learn new techniques for getting along with each other. The experiment was a great success, resulting in new social skills for both those children that excluded others and those who were excluded.

Professionals working in programs for children who are at risk have a most important task when it comes to helping parents and family members. In order to break the cycle of violence, teachers, child care workers, and social workers must give parents non-violent ways of disciplining their children. Harsh physical punishment has proven to be ineffective in helping children gain firm inner controls (Dorr, Zax, & Bonner lll, 1983). Physical abuse increases children's anger, making it harder for them to control themselves. It also provides a poor model of behavior. It has been demonstrated that violence begets violence.

Parents must be offered alternatives to physical punishment so they can provide firm controls without resorting to violence. Many parents think that beating children is the only way to make them behave. But children can be taught to behave without using violent means. !t is, of course, more difficult to set clear rules and hold to them in a consistent manner when there is no support from other families in the neighborhood. If families can get together and set standards of behavior and support each other in holding to those rules, parents will find it easier to relinquish physical punishment as their only means of discipline.But it is impossible to expect individual families or small programs to battle gangs and drug dealers alone. Curbing community violence requires a major effort on the part of every neighborhood. Programs for children and families can work together and with other community organizations, including local governmental agencies, to coordinate efforts to combat neighborhood violence.

Part of the effort to fight crime and violence on the neighborhood level must include letting politicians and policy makers know that educators and child care professionals support all attempts to reduce crime through gun control, the curbing of drugs, the restriction of gang activity, and any other means available. Policy makers must also be made aware of professional support for efforts to fight crime and violence through prevention: by providing jobs, decent housing, first rate education, and curbing discrimination.

Reducing violence in this country is going to take efforts in all directions. The cycle of violence must be broken at many points. Those aspects of our society that breed violence must be changed, while the violence that presently exists must be restrained. Children must be cared for so they do not perpetuate the cycle by growing into violent adults.

The task is a formidable one, but if crime can be reduced in one neighborhood, if one child or one family can be saved, the first battle in the war on violence will have been won.

References

Alexander, Franz (1948). Fundamentals of Psychoanalysis. New York: W.W. Norton.

American Bar Association Report finds child abuse root of major social problems. (1994, August 8). Tulsa World, p.7.

Brazelton, T. Berry (1974). Toddlers and Parents. New York: A Delta Book.

Coopersmith, Stanley (1967). The Antecedents of Self-esteem. San Francisco: W.H. Freeman Co.

Donovan, D.M., McIntyre, D (1990). Healing the Hurt Child. New York: W.W. Norton.

Dorr, D, Zax, M., Bonner 111, J.W. (1983). The Psychology of Discipline. New York: International University Press, Inc.

Erikson, Erik (1950). Childhood and Society. New York: W.W. Norton.

Freud, Anna (1937). The Ego and the Mechanisms of Defense. London: Hogarth Press.

Garbarino, J. & Stott, F. (eds.). (1990) What Children Can Tell Us. Chapter 8, San Francisco: Jossey-Bass Publishers.

Garbarino, J., Dubrow, N., Kostelny, K., Pardo, C. (1992) Children in Danger: Coping with the Consequences of Community Violence. San Francisco: Jossey-Bass Publishers.

Kotlowitz, A. (1991) There Are No Children Here. New York: Doubleday.

Paley, Vivian G. (1992). You Can't Say You Can't Play. Cambridge, MA: Harvard University Press.

Pynoos, R. & Eth, S. (1985). Children Traumatized by Witnessing Personal Violence: Homicide, Rape or Suicide Behavior. In S.Eth & R. Pynoos(Eds.), Posttraumatic Stress Disorder in Children (pp. 19-43). Washington, DC: Journal of American Psychiatric Press.

Terr, L. (1981). Forbidden Games: Posttraumatic Stress Disorder in Children. Journal of American Academy of Child Psychiatry, 20, 741—760.

Wallach, Lorraine B. (1993). Helping Children Cope with Violence. Young Children, 48(4), 4-11.

Additional Reading

The Friendly Classroom for a Small Planet by Priscilla Prutzman, Lee Stern, M. Leonard Burger, Gretchen Bodenhamer, New Society Publishers. A Handbook on Creative Approaches to Living and Problem Solving for Children.

Teaching Children to Care: Management in the Responsive Classroom by Ruth Sidney Charney.

Creating Conflict Resolution by William J. Kreidler. More Than 200 Activities for Keeping Peace in the Classroom.

Elementary Perspectives: Teaching Concepts of Peace and Conflict by William J. Kreidler.

Supporting Victims of Child Abuse

**Classroom teachers have a unique opportunity
to identify abused children and to start the healing
process that will restore safety to their lives.**

Thelma Bear
Sherry Schenk
Lisa Buckner

Thelma Bear coordinates district public school programs for students and works with women survivors of abuse as a psychotherapist in private practice. **Sherry Schenk** works as a school psychologist with elementary and middle school children and has worked with sexually abused children. **Lisa Buckner** has a B.S. in psychology and is a school bus driver. The authors may be reached at Weld County School District Six, 811 Fifteenth St. Greeley, CO 80631.

Survivors' Voices

Before I started kindergarten, I knew that I could not believe what people said. My father would say, "I know you like this," as he touched me in sexual ways that I did not like or that caused great physical pain. My early years were a real struggle. Because I could not trust what I heard, it was hard to learn sound-letter associations, memorize isolated facts, or learn anything I had heard and not seen.

The messages I received from my perpetrators were intended to prevent my telling what they were doing to me. To keep the horrible secret I learned to be silent, and the silence became my prison. I felt that I was the only child who had ever experienced such bad things. I thought I was so bad that I should separate myself from everyone. It was lonely.

Since I felt I could not talk, I did all kinds of quiet acting out in the hope that someone would notice that something was terribly wrong in my life. My behaviors were either ignored or I was told to behave, to be a good girl. During 3rd and 4th grade, I repeatedly sawed on or cut my wrist with a little knife. I wore bizarre clothing, laughed excessively, and withdrew from others.

Today I am a school psychologist. I have overcome the academic hurdles, but I continue to experience some of the emotional pain of abuse.

—*Sherry Schenk*

The messages about my abuse were also intended to keep me quiet, to protect my perpetrators. I was quiet and shy, but I would also do daring things with little regard for my physical safety. They called me "accident prone." I was told I was crazy and that if I ever told, "someone" would take me away and I would never see anyone in my family again ... or I would be killed. These were terrifying threats to me.

I was a very good student, usually at the top of my class. Looking back now, I was afraid to be anything but perfect. I was afraid of what would happen at home. School became a safe haven, and I worked hard to keep it that way by staying silent about my abuse. I remember more than once trying to get teachers to take me home with them.

I am currently a school bus driver and enjoy daily contact with children in a less-structured environment. When I see symptoms of child abuse, I report what I hear and observe. I would always rather err on the side of the child. I would rather make the report than to ignore what I know.

—*Lisa Buckner*

In 1987, when I was asked to facilitate groups for survivors of abuse at a University Counseling Center, I knew little about the incidence or results of abuse. The frequency of women who had been abused as children was much greater than we had thought. We soon had 4 groups and more than 50 names on a waiting list. I learned about the tremendous cost of keeping the family secret. I learned of the emotional pain that can result from feeling different. As an educator I was appalled at my previous lack of awareness of the consequences of abuse. I vowed to somehow assist in giving a voice to those survivors who can teach us what it was to live with abuse and how to help today's children.

—*Thelma Bear*

Our varied roles as therapist, educator, school psychologist, school bus driver, student, and administrator have provided us with the experience and education on which this article is based. This is a new field, an area in which all of us are searching for facts, understanding, and ways to help those who have been and continue to be abused. The combined perspectives we share from personal, professional, and academic experiences have added to our knowledge in ways that have been valuable to us as people who care a great deal about children.

Probably no adult is more trusted by children who have been abused than a beloved and caring teacher. Teachers have an opportunity afforded few adults to identify abused children and to start a process that will restore safety in the child's world. However, many teachers have not been adequately prepared to deal with the complex social issues that have so strongly affected abused children. We want to give teachers a knowledge base about child abuse, describe possible interventions, and communicate an understanding of the emotional issues involved.

The Incidence of Child Abuse

Although the statistics are overwhelming, professionals in the mental health field generally accept that the incidence of child abuse is much greater than that reported.

In 1979, Geiser advised that 200,000 children were sexually abused each

Figure 1

	Physical Indicators	Behavioral Indicators	
Physical Abuse	■ unexplained bruises (in various stages of healing), welts, human bite marks, bald spots ■ unexplained burns, especially cigarette burns or immersion-burns (glove-like) ■ unexplained fractures, lacerations, or abrasions	■ self-destructive ■ withdrawn and aggressive—behavioral extremes ■ uncomfortable with physical contact ■ arrives at school early or stays late as if afraid	■ chronic runaway (adolescents) ■ complains of soreness or moves uncomfortably ■ wears clothing inappropriate to weather, to cover body
Physical Neglect	■ abandonment ■ unattended medical needs ■ consistent lack of supervision ■ consistent hunger, inappropriate dress, poor hygiene ■ lice, distended stomach, emaciated	■ regularly displays fatigue or listlessness, falls asleep in class ■ steals food, begs from classmates ■ reports that no caretaker is at home	■ frequently absent or tardy ■ self-destructive ■ school dropout (adolescents)
Sexual Abuse	■ torn, stained, or bloodied underclothing ■ pain or itching in genital area ■ difficulty walking or sitting ■ bruises or bleeding in external genitalia ■ venereal disease ■ frequent urinary or yeast infections	■ withdrawn, chronic depression ■ excessive seductiveness ■ role reversal, overly concerned for siblings ■ poor self-esteem, self-devaluation, lack of confidence ■ peer problems, lack of involvement ■ massive weight change	■ suicide attempts (especially adolescents) ■ hysteria, lack of emotional control ■ sudden school difficulties ■ inappropriate sex play or premature understanding of sex ■ threatened by physical contact, closeness ■ promiscuity
Emotional Maltreatment	■ speech disorders ■ delayed physical development ■ substance abuse ■ ulcers, asthma, severe allergies	■ habit disorders (sucking, rocking) ■ antisocial, destructive ■ neurotic traits (sleep disorders, inhibition of play)	■ passive and aggressive—behavioral extremes ■ delinquent behavior (especially adolescents) ■ developmentally delayed

Adapted in part from: D. D. Broadhurst, M. Edmunds, and R. A. MacDicken. (1979). *Early Childhood Programs and the Prevention and Treatment of Child Abuse and Neglect*. The User Manual Series. Washington, D.C.: U.S. Department of Health, Education, and Welfare.

year with victims as young as two months. "Nightline's" Forrest Sawyer (1989) stated that 2 million cases of child abuse are reported in the United States every year. In its newsletter, the National Organization for Victims' Assistance (1989) indicated that 2.2 million children are reported physically or sexually abused each year. Many cases are closed after a cursory investigation; many cases remain unreported.

Of the cases reported, many are young children. Among Blume's (1990) statistics were:

■ 35 percent of all reported child sex abuse cases in 1988 were of girls under 6.

■ Dr. Michael Durfee of the Los Angeles Department of Health Services reported in 1984 that more sexual abuse was reported on 2-year-olds than any other age group; 3- and 4-year-olds were next.

Kantrowitz (1988) gave the following numbers:

■ More than 2 million cases of child abuse were reported in 1986, compared with 669,000 in 1976.

■ More than 1,200 children die each year through child abuse and neglect.

■ Parents who were abused as children were six times more likely to abuse their own children.

Goodwin (1982) reported that:

■ 5 to 20 percent of psychiatric outpatients were women who had experienced incest.

■ 4 out of 10 mothers of children who died of physical abuse were incest victims.

According to Butler (1978), a much greater incidence of incest occurred among affluent, middle-, and upper-class families than was reported. Of reported sexual abuse, she asserted that 75 percent of the incidents were committed by someone the child trusted. Butler (1978) added that:

■ One-half to three-fourths of adult male sexual offenders had been sexually abused.

■ Sexual abuse was one of three reasons children ran away from home.

■ In a questionnaire sent to 1,800 college students, one-third indicated that they had been sexually abused.

Research on child abuse is a fairly

recent development. Only in the last two decades has the subject appeared in professional journals. It is urgent that all personnel in public schools become educated and make every effort to break the continuing cycle of abuse.

Types of Abuse

How is child abuse defined? The Colorado Department of Education (1988) describes four types:

1. *Physical abuse*: nonaccidental physical injury to a child. Examples include slapping, shaking, hitting, kicking, burning, pushing, smothering, restraining (physical or chemical), and torture (may be related to ritualistic abuse and/or satanic worship). A few forms of abuse may be attributed to lack of knowledge on the part of the parent—for instance, neurological damage can result from shaking a child. Physical abuse should be suspected if the following are present: bruises, burns, broken bones, and/or internal injuries. Further, a child who appears fearful or who startles easily may be the victim of abuse.

2. *Emotional maltreatment*: the constant belittling and rejecting of a child, the absence of a positive emotional atmosphere. Examples include verbal abuse, inadequate or inappropriate parenting, and neglect. Any of these can destroy a child's self-esteem and weaken self-concept. The "failure to thrive" syndrome is an example of the results of emotional maltreatment. Delays in emotional development and immature behavior may indicate emotional neglect.

3. *Physical neglect*: failure on the part of the child's caretaker to provide adequate food, clothing, shelter, or supervision. The extreme form of neglect is abandonment of a child with no regard or concern for his or her welfare.

4. *Sexual abuse*: sexual exploitation, molestation, or prostitution of a child (p. 1). Sgroi, Porter, and Blick (1982) define child sexual abuse as a sexual act imposed on a child who lacks the emotional, maturational, and cognitive development to understand what is happening and to protect him- or

Probably no adult is more trusted by children who have been abused than a beloved and caring teacher.

herself. Sexual abuse may be overt or covert. Examples of overt abuse include unwanted touching of any part of the body, such as hugs or kisses presented as innocent signs of affection. More obvious examples include any penetration of the body with objects or body parts. Unexplained infections or diseases and external or internal injuries are symptoms that require investigation for the possibility of sexual abuse.

Covert sexual abuse is more difficult to recognize. Since this type of abuse does not include physical contact, the perpetrator may rationalize the behavior as innocent. Examples may include voyeurism, asking the child to watch inappropriate sexual behaviors, invading the child's privacy, and/or behaving in a seductive manner toward the child.

Most adults who have not been abused would rather not accept the reality of the number of children who have been abused. Many prefer to think of physical injury, terrorizing, and psychological torture as atrocities that only happen to hostages imprisoned in foreign countries. They do not want to accept that these abominations occur to nearly 2.7 million children in this country ("Study Finds ..." 1992). Figure 1 lists physical and behavioral indicators of these four types of abuse.

A Safe Classroom Environment

There is no escape for children caught in a world where silence often seems the only way to survive. And there is no escape from confronting the issues for those who work with children.

Teachers who educate themselves about abuse will find many opportunities to support children who have neither the experience nor the maturity to unravel the turmoil they face.

Although the academic environment is structured for learning, the ability to learn is dependent on a child's arriving at school with basic needs met. Children who have been abused have had the basic requirements for healthy development withheld and violated. Getting physiological needs met, as well as those for safety, belonging, trust, and love, maximizes the child's development as a learner. The classroom teacher has the opportunity to provide an environment where the child can begin to succeed and recognize that he or she is capable and valued.

The most important ingredient in a safe classroom is the teacher's attitude toward students. The most crucial belief a teacher must have is that the child is not to blame. There is nothing that a child can do to prevent or stop the abuse. The discrepancy between the power of a child and that of an adult is too great. However, it is important to remember that these children are strong. They have developed coping mechanisms that have helped them to survive traumatic experiences. An accepting, caring attitude by the teacher will allow the child to trust enough to make the first steps toward developing a saner life.

Each of us needs a personal space into which others do not intrude without permission (Blume 1990). Victimized children have not learned that it is okay to say no, nor do they know how it feels to have personal and physical space honored. The teacher should help an abused child to set healthy boundaries and to know that he or she will be respected. Before the child can believe in his or her ability to set personal boundaries, he or she may need to be taught to trust personal judgments, feelings, and perceptions (Blume 1990).

Part of establishing healthy boundaries is understanding that confidentiality within the school is honored by staff and students. If a student confides in classmates and teachers, the information must be handled with great care in order to protect the vulnerability of the child. At times, the disclosure of information about the abuse may be unintentional. Some of the ways the secret may accidentally be disclosed are observations by the teacher or others, physical injuries or conditions discovered in a doctor's examination, and/or inappropriate sexual behaviors by the child (Sgroi et al. 1982).

To offer support, the teacher must, first, be approachable. If an abused child begins to tell what is happening, positive body language will encourage the child to continue. The teacher must also watch for cues about how to respond. The child may either want to be comforted physically or may not want to be touched. At this point, it is more important to actively listen than to comment or ask questions. Listening to those who will talk is important; however, some students will be unable to share verbally what is happening. In these instances, the teacher must be observant. The indicators listed in Figure 1 may help teachers in attempting to decide if abuse should be suspected.

Drawings, too, may provide clues to students who have been sexually abused. Hillman and Solek-Tefft (1988) list five themes to ask a child about if they are drawn repeatedly: stark sexual images, phallic symbols, general symbols (broken hearts, rain, black skies), self-image distortions, and general confusion (p. 107).

Girls and boys who have been abused attempt both to keep the secret of what is happening and to control the emotional turmoil they feel inside. As a result, the child may act out, or he or she may become the epitome of the "good" child. Both of these behaviors may disguise the problem. A child who behaves as a perfect student may be seen as having no problems, while acting out may cover the real issues, making the child appear to be the problem. Teachers should listen to their gut response to a child, particularly if that feeling is based on a suspicion that something is wrong.

> If an abused student confides in classmates and teachers, the information must be handled with great care to protect the vulnerability of the child.

Occasionally a child will spontaneously disclose an episode of abuse. Although a teacher may doubt the story, it is vitally important to believe the child (Besharov 1990). The child is taking a significant step in trusting the teacher enough to tell what is happening. To betray that trust would repeat the betrayal experienced when an adult abused the child and failed to serve as a protector. Even though the explanation may be fragmented, teachers should listen supportively and ask open-ended questions to fill in gaps. Sometimes after telling the secret, the child may recant the story due to fear, threats, or acceleration of the abuse (Sgroi et al. 1982). Most experts agree that children do not have the ability or knowledge to make up complex lies, especially lies related to adult sexual behavior (Besharov 1990, Conerly 1986, Crewdson 1988).

How to Support an Abused Child

In addition to creating a safe classroom environment, there are other ways teachers can help support an abused child. Most of these behaviors and attitudes are familiar ones.

1. *Expectations*. Teachers can honor the strength and courage of these children by having high expectations for them. Emotionality may interfere with thinking; therefore, it is important to set reasonable goals and to provide the support needed for the child to feel confident in his or her abilities. School can be a place where children rebuild their self-esteem, assert themselves, and see themselves as successful.

2. *Structure*. Abused children may feel powerless to control much in their environment. To cope, they may: (a) refuse to even try to control what happens around them; (b) strive to manipulate everything they can by bossing peers and controlling belongings; and (c) express disproportionate feelings whenever they feel threatened. When these children fly off the handle with little provocation, they may be doing so to try to establish control. To help the child feel a sense of control in a positive manner, teachers should give accurate information and build trust. Allowing expression of feelings when appropriate through art, music, drama, and/or creative writing will also help the child to feel less controlled by pent-up emotion.

3. *Identity*. Children who have been abused in ways that met an adult's needs and denied the child's needs have little sense of personal identity. Teachers can help by pointing out the child's strengths. Statements such as "You are a hard worker," "You are a good friend when you help a classmate with a problem," and "People in this classroom like you because you are fun to be with" will help the child understand how others perceive him or her. Teachers can also help abused children gain a sense of personal identity by asking questions that help them formulate a position on issues, administering interest inventories, and teaching decision-making and problem-solving skills. These skills will assist in interpersonal relationships as well as in self-understanding.

4. *Self-esteem*. Abused children have little self-esteem. Teachers can help them learn that they are valued, accepted, and capable by fostering an environment that honors each child's uniqueness. Valuing differences will enable children to begin to see themselves as having something to contribute that others appreciate.

With each successful completion of a classroom task, the child's sense of competency will be fostered.

5. *Sense of belonging.* Abused children think they did something wrong and that they are bad. Because they have kept a secret from everyone, they assume there is a reason for them to be isolated from others. To facilitate a sense of belonging, the teacher may provide designated places for possessions, display work in the classroom, and make a conscious attempt to include these children in classroom activities. Support through teaching social skills individually, in small group settings, and through cooperative learning will also help abused children practice interacting in a nonthreatening atmosphere.

6. *Social skills.* Because abused children have not learned to listen to their inner selves, they may focus on pleasing and meeting the needs of others while neglecting their own needs. Having been introduced to the adult world through an abusive relationship, the child may have learned inappropriate behaviors and language. The child may feel unworthy to interact on an equal basis with others and may fear rejection. A classroom climate that fosters caring, appreciation for differences, consistent rules and boundaries, and recognition for small successes will nurture a child who has been discounted at home.

7. *Tolerance of differences.* Because each child will respond in a unique way to abuse, classroom behaviors may be variable. Some of the feelings an abused child may experience are anxiety, guilt, embarrassment, depression, anger, and resolution (Hillman and Solek-Tefft 1988). The checklist (fig. 1) may help teachers identify emotions and behaviors that might be explained by abuse. Consultation with a school psychologist, social worker, counselor, or nurse may also help teachers understand unexplainable

> Teachers have the opportunity to give an abused child gifts that cannot be measured in any monetary or quantitative way.

behaviors and emotions of their students.

8. *Consistency.* Teachers can support a child's need for structure by maintaining a consistent daily schedule, by having clear expectations for performance in both behavioral and affective areas, and by allowing the child to provide structure in his or her own way. A child's need for structure can restrict the depth of his or her encounter with the world. Teachers may respond to this need by encouraging risk-taking in ways that will encourage success and personal worth.

Although teachers are not responsible for investigation of child abuse, they are legally obligated to report suspected abuse. When abuse is suspected, the teacher can compare the child's behaviors with those of other students at the same developmental level, review the child's past and present behaviors, and refer to indicators such as those listed in Figure 1. To report any suspicions, the teacher should contact the school district child abuse team or the Department of Social Services. The appropriate agencies will assess the situation and decide how to keep the child safe.

Working with children who have suffered abuse is a skill that every teacher possesses. Given a few guidelines and accurate information, the teacher's natural concern and caring for students will promote the process of healing. Teachers have the opportunity to give an abused child the hope of a childhood, the joy of play, and the sense of being cared for by others. Those are gifts that cannot be measured in any monetary or quantitative way.

References

Besharov, D. (1990). *Recognizing Child Abuse.* New York: The Free Press.
Blume, E. (1990). *Secret Survivors.* New York: The Free Press.
Butler, S. (1978). *Conspiracy of Silence.* San Francisco: New Glide Publications.
Colorado Department of Education (1988). *The School's Role in the Prevention/Intervention of Child Abuse and Neglect.* Denver: Colorado Department of Education.
Conerly, S. (1986). "Assessment of Suspected Child Sexual Abuse." In *Sexual Abuse of Young Children,* edited by K. MacFarlane, pp. 30-51. New York: The Guilford Press.
Crewdson, J. (1988). *By Silence Abused.* New York: Harper & Row.
Geiser, R. (1979). *Hidden Victims: The Sexual Abuse of Children.* Boston: Beacon Press.
Goodwin, J. (1982). *Sexual Abuse: Incest Victims and Their Families.* Boston: John Wright.
Hillman, D., and J. Solek-Tefft. (1988). *Spiders and Flies.* Lexington, Mass.: Lexington Books.
Kantrowitz, B. (December 1988). "A Tale of Abuse." *Newsweek,* pp. 56-59.
National Organization for Victims' Assistance. (March 1989). Newsletter.
Sawyer, F. (Journalist). (1989). *Nightline* television program, ABC.
Sgroi, S., F. Porter, and L. Blick. (1982). "Validation of Child Sexual Abuse." In *Handbook of Clinical Intervention in Child Sexual Abuse,* edited by S. Sgroi, pp. 39-79. Lexington, Mass.: Lexington Books.
"Study Finds Child Care Increasing." (April 1992). *The Greeley Tribune,* p. A-11.

Curricular Issues

At the end of a busy day, most teachers would relish the thought of walking into a restaurant where they would not have to make any choices about what to eat or do any of the shopping and cooking. All the food would be prepared by others and set before the hungry teachers to consume. Sounds wonderful! Maybe for two or even three nights the idea would be appealing, but come the fourth night, some teachers really would not like what was being served, or would cook it differently. In this restaurant, there are no opportunities for customer suggestions.

Does this sound like some classrooms? The adults choose the topic of study and spend frantic weeks preparing the materials and activities. The teachers then lay everything out in front of the children and wait for them to eagerly lap up the information and activities prepared by the teacher. Unfortunately, this is how many classrooms operate.

Teachers in these classrooms do all the work, with no input from the children, their families, or their environment. Topics of study are often decided months in advance. A strict schedule is adhered to so that all the teacher-chosen topics can be covered in a particular time frame. Each year, themes are covered at the same time, and little, if any, deviation from the master calendar occurs. Unknowingly, teachers are making more work for themselves by ignoring the ideas and expertise that children and their families could contribute. During the big snowstorm of January 1996, children up and down the East Coast had questions such as, "How much snow really came down?" or "What will happen when all this snow starts to melt?" Teachers who drew their curriculum from the interests of their class helped the children to discover the answers to these questions and others through experiments inside and outside of the classroom. But some classes returned to school after days off to be greeted with only a brief discussion on the snowstorm before launching into a unit preplanned by the teacher. That preplanned unit could have been put on hold. There were important questions to be answered by the children! The skills children acquire, such as investigating, predicting, and hypothesizing, can be more useful in future learning than knowing specific facts about a particular topic.

The articles in this unit deal with developing a child-centered curriculum. Just as teachers want a say in what they eat and how it is prepared, children want a chance to investigate topics they are curious about, like which vegetable has the most seeds. Or they may want to explore sea life, because a classmate has just returned from the Cayman Islands, where she swam with stingrays. A child-centered curriculum offers possibilities for investigating, exploring, predicting, and collaborating, among other skills that are the benchmarks of a successful school experience. In "Project Work with Diverse Students," Shareen Abramson, Roxanne Robinson, and Katie Ankenman describe a project-based approach to learning. Children living in an area where it snows can

do many experiments inside and outside with the snow to answer questions.

In "A Framework for Literacy" and "Read Me a Story: 101 Good Books Kids Will Love," the reader is presented with valuable information on the benefits of a quality literacy program. Many of the books on the list will be recognized as classics we remember from childhood. Reread a favorite, or check out an unknown title and enjoy it with a child. Make reading to and with children a ritual both in and out of the classroom.

A truly child-centered curriculum in a developmentally appropriate program is constantly changing, just like the children who attend that program. It is the job of the teachers and caregivers to keep pace with the children's needs and interests as they grow and learn.

Looking Ahead: Challenge Questions

How are the processes of learning to read and write connected? What can facilitate these processes in the classroom?

What role do the diverse lifestyles of the children in a classroom play in the development of the curriculum?

After reading "Early Childhood Physical Education: Providing the Foundation," describe some fundamental movement skills that are most appropriate for preschool children.

How can curriculum webs be built with input from the children?

What should teachers or parents consider when choosing literature for children?

What are the benefits of an inquiry approach to curriculum development?

Diversity:
A Program for All Children

Suzanne M. Winter

Suzanne M. Winter is Assistant Professor, Early Childhood Education, University of Texas at San Antonio.

One of the most intriguing challenges facing educators today is providing programs that present *all* children with opportunities to flourish. Multicultural education and the inclusive education model have important implications for educators confronting this challenge. These approaches have significantly increased teachers' awareness of the inequities that can undermine their efforts to provide a quality education for all children. Many teachers seeking ways to implement a program for all children, however, are discovering that there is no quick fix. Children represent a multiplicity of family types, ethnic groups, cultures and abilities. Creating an atmosphere in which both harmony and diversity can reign presents a considerable challenge. The author intends to clarify the concept of "programs for all children" and to propose a framework of practical strategies for implementation.

Confusing Terminology

Educators developing a program for all children must have knowledge of multicultural education and inclusion. Unfortunately, the confusing terminology used in professional literature can impede full understanding. Terms such as "anti-bias," "bias-free," "diversity," "bicultural education," "acculturation," "cross-cultural education," "mainstreaming" and "inclusion" often have different connotations, depending upon the author. One can easily become sidetracked by trying to decipher terminology. Instead, educators should focus upon the more important underlying theories and philosophies that support meeting children's diverse educational needs.

Defining Multicultural Education

Multicultural education, once associated primarily with providing equal educational opportunities to culturally or linguistically diverse children, has developed a broader scope. Multicultural education now seeks to recognize a host of other individual differences, including race, ethnicity, religion, gender (Dean, Salend & Taylor, 1993), socio-economic class, age, ability (York, 1991) and family lifestyle (Jones & Derman-Sparks, 1992).

Educators have tried a variety of approaches. Some emphasize achieving racial and ethnic equity (Banks, 1993), while others stress social cooperation and the establishment of positive human relationships (Sleeter & Grant, 1987; York, 1991). The global education approach adds an international perspective to the knowledge base of children (Begler, 1993). For some, global education must also include an element of environmental responsibility (Hopkins & Winters, 1990). Although considered to be a relative newcomer to the multicultural education arena, global education has already influenced the curriculum of some local and state education systems (Wooster, 1993).

Another well-known approach to multicultural education is the anti-bias approach pioneered by Louise Derman-Sparks and the ABC Task Force (1989). This approach incorporates the ideals of democracy into the classroom by encouraging teachers to regularly involve children in planning and decision-making processes. The anti-bias approach stresses that children must develop skills for effectively functioning in their own society and in those across the globe (Derman-Sparks, 1993/94). Activism is another important tenet of this approach. Children learn not only to be more aware of injustices, but also to act to correct such situations as a means of achieving a more equitable society (Derman-Sparks & ABC Task Force, 1989; York, 1991).

The Inclusive Education Model

In order to serve all children, advocates of the inclusive education model believe that children with disabilities belong in classrooms with their normally developing peers. While the terms "mainstreaming" and "integration" are often used synonymously for "inclusion," the concepts are not the same. "Mainstreaming" implies that children with special needs have not previously been part of the mainstream of society and "integration" means children must meet certain criteria for enrollment in a class (Deiner, 1993). A better term is "inclusion," which implies a sense of "belonging" rather than simply "placement."

Legal mandates have provided

much of the impetus for the inclusive education movement. The Education for All Handicapped Children Act (EHA) of 1975 (P.L. 94-142) required not only the availability of free and appropriate public education for school-age children with disabilities, but also specified that education had to be provided in the "least restrictive" environment. The Education of the Handicapped Act Amendments of 1986 (P.L. 99-457) mandated services for preschool children with disabilities. In 1990, EHA was renamed the Individuals with Disabilities Education Act (IDEA) (P.L. 101-476).

The inclusive education movement also received support from provisions in the 1990 Americans with Disabilities Act (ADA) (P.L. 101-336) and further IDEA amendments. The Individuals with Disabilities Education Act Amendments of 1991 (P.L. 102-119) required that, when appropriate, early intervention for children with special needs should be provided in "natural environments," meaning homes and community programs serving typical children (Deiner, 1993; Sexton, Snyder, Sharpton & Stricklin, 1993). In 1992, another provision of ADA became effective, making it illegal to prohibit children with special needs from attending any home or center-based child care or nursery school facility that accommodates the public (Surr, 1992).

These legal mandates make it clear that including children with special needs must be a part of our plans to serve all children. The implementation methods are, however, still a source of debate among professionals in the fields of early childhood and early childhood special education (Bredekamp, 1993; Carta, Atwater, Schwartz & McConnell, 1993; Carta, Schwartz, Atwater & McConnell, 1991; Johnson & Johnson, 1992; Johnson & Johnson, 1993; McLean & Odom, 1993). Until a body of research develops in this fledgling field, teachers will have to rely on a common sense approach.

Implementation Strategies

A comparison of the multicultural and inclusive education perspectives reveals a number of common denominators from which to propose strategies for implementing a program for all children.

Meet Individual Needs

■ *Understand each child as a unique individual.* Recognizing the unique characteristics and learning styles of each child is a vital step in determining the most effective teaching methods. Children's verbalizations during play and learning activities can help identify their preferences, strengths and weaknesses (Allen, 1992; Beaty, 1994). Families are another valuable source of information. Holding family conferences at school is one way to establish effective communication. Home visits may yield even richer information about the family's structure (Wellhousen, 1993), values and traditions.

■ *Plan for individually appropriate learning.* All young children share a common need to learn through active, "hands-on" discovery with concrete materials, including children with special challenges, linguistic differences and diverse cultural heritages (Deiner, 1993; King, Chipman & Cruz-Janzen, 1994). A teacher must plan learning activities that are also matched to the individual abilities and specific needs of each child. Flexible activities make such individually appropriate learning possible without sacrificing a child's opportunities for social interaction. For example, Chai, a 1st-grader with limited English proficiency, can work with his classmate, Brad, to measure items in the math center. Both boys can accomplish the lesson's objective while benefiting from language sharing as they name the objects in their own first language.

Create an Atmosphere of Acceptance

■ *Personalize the classroom.* Acceptance is an important aspect of inclusive programs. A personalized classroom can be created by

Recognizing the unique characteristics and learning styles of each child is a vital step in determining the most effective teaching methods.

viewing the classroom environment through the eyes of individual children. This strategy can help create a classroom environment that is more comfortable and familiar for children (York, 1992). On a visit to Keesha's home, for example, her teacher noticed several batik decorations that inspired her to develp a batik art project for the class. Families can help children become more comfortable with diversity by sharing their traditions, family photographs and items reflecting their cultural heritage (Derman-Sparks & ABC Task Force, 1989). A personalized classroom must include children with special challenges. Such children will feel more accepted when the physical space of the classroom has been adjusted to allow them a choice of learning experiences with their peers (Winter, Bell & Dempsey, 1994).

■ *Introduce a "diversity perspective."* Children need opportunities to become familiar with a broad range of people who vary in their customs, languages and abilities. Be careful to avoid depicting people in a token or stereotypical manner (Derman-Sparks & ABC Task Force, 1989). For example, children should learn that modern Native Americans do not conduct their daily activities in full ceremonial attire. The presence of children with special needs and challenges in classrooms provides very natural opportunities for children to gain a different perspective. Children's natural curiosity will lead them to learn about the special challenges facing some of their classmates. Activities and adaptive equipment designed to help children understand disabilities can further enhance their diversity perspective (Deiner, 1993). The real litmus test of the "diversity perspective" within a classroom is the extent to which each learning opportunity promotes better understanding and a sense of community.

Address Personal Biases

■ *Identification and understanding of personal biases.* Honestly evaluate your feelings to ensure that personal biases do not jeopardize your relationships with each child (Derman-Sparks, 1993/94). York (1992) has developed a number of exercises that allow teachers to introspectively examine their attitudes and identify possible biases. Teachers must strive to understand the source of biased attitudes and work to develop greater acceptance. A teacher support group is one way to learn greater acceptance (Derman-Sparks & ABC Task Force, 1989; York, 1991).

■ *Gain a different perspective.* Talking with persons who have special challenges or a cultural heritage different from your own can help you recognize your own personal biases and evaluate your level of empathy (Derman-Sparks & ABC Task Force, 1989). Mike, a special education teacher who is profoundly deaf, helped me to better understand his life. He described the frustration of faculty meeting discussions that were too fast-paced and of colleagues who failed to seriously consider his ideas.

Promote Attitudes of Acceptance

■ *Foster social interactions.* Creating programs for all children depends upon first helping children to develop accepting attitudes (Dean, Salend & Taylor, 1993; Derman-Sparks, 1993/94). Fostering social interactions and friendships among children is one strategy for accomplishing this goal. Well-organized,

cooperative learning activities can increase positive social interaction in multilingual classrooms (Enright & McCloskey, 1988). Also, cooperative learning may provide the context for enhancing literacy skills (Meloth, 1991) and developing a sense of community and identity (Enright & McCloskey, 1988).

Social interaction is also important in inclusive classrooms. While empirical evidence suggests that some type of adult intervention may be necessary to facilitate friendships among children with special challenges and their peers, the exact nature of this intervention remains speculative (Guralnick, 1993; Peterson & McConnell, 1993). Hanline (1985) recommends arranging classroom space into small group areas and selecting materials that are conducive to interaction.

■ *Model respect and acceptance.* Whether children are different in ability, ethnicity or culture, evidence suggests that a teacher's own accepting behavior may encourage children to develop more tolerant, accepting dispositions (Buswell & Schaffner, 1992; King, Chipman & Cruz-Janzen, 1994). In fact, the teacher may be such a strong socializing agent that simply reinforcing the cooperative play of children with special challenges and their peers can encourage repeated social interactions (Hanline, 1985).

Encourage Open Communication

■ *Offer honest, well-informed explanations.* Open communication is an essential ingredient for successful inclusive programs. The teacher must be willing to address sensitive issues concerning inclusion, anti-bias and cultural diversity. Children, curious by nature, will notice and subsequently ask questions about the differences among people. Recognizing the differences while emphasizing the similarities will promote positive attitudes toward diversity (Derman-Sparks & ABC Task Force, 1989; Hanline, 1985). Do not ignore a child's disability; candid

explanations will help eliminate any possible misconceptions, confusion or fears that children may have regarding classmates with special challenges (Derman-Sparks & ABC Task Force, 1989).

■ *Encourage critical thinking.* A primary goal in providing open communication is to encourage children's critical thinking. Consider the following conversation between 3-year-old Amy and her teacher:

Amy: "Do you like Ninja turtles?"
Teacher: "No, I don't."
Amy: "Well, I guess boys just like boys' stuff and girls like girls' stuff."
Teacher: "Amy, it's okay for girls and boys to like the same things. I don't happen to care for Ninja turtles because they fight so much."

Amy's teacher modeled critical thinking, which may help Amy to recognize bias in the future (Derman-Sparks, 1993/94).

Build the Competence of Children

■ *Plan ways to build children's self-esteem.* Teachers should seize every opportunity to help children build skills and competencies by planning ways for children to achieve success each day. Also, teachers should convey expectations for the child's success (Marion, 1995). Such expectations may be influenced, however, by teachers' perceptions of each child's abilities. Therefore, educators must try to be free of bias related to the child's ethnicity, gender, language or program placement (Sosa, 1993).

Children, especially those with special challenges, need recognition of their competencies. Second-grade math problems may stump Lisa, who has learning disabilities, but she remembers song lyrics. Her music teacher recognizes Lisa's competency by asking her to help Stephanie learn the chorus for the PTA program. Emphasizing children's strengths and their similarities to others may create a basis for greater acceptance (Derman-Sparks, 1989).

Activities that help develop group identity, both ethnic and cultural, are also important. Children should be given chances to learn about themselves in relation to their heritage (Derman-Sparks & ABC Task Force, 1989). King, Chipman and Cruz-Janzen (1994) warn that even subtle devaluing of cultural or ethnic membership may result in significant damage to children's self-esteem.

■ *Use effective guidance techniques.* Consistent implementation of effective guidance techniques will prepare children to live more peacefully in a world of diversity. All children should learn to cooperate and to resolve conflicts peacefully through negotiation. Adults may need to provide suggestions and support to help children achieve these goals. Very young children, or children with communication disorders, may find it difficult to adequately express their emotions (Derman-Sparks & ABC Task Force, 1989; Marion, 1995). In such cases, teachers will need to play a substantial role in guiding the conflict to resolution. Conflicts stemming from cross-cultural differences in values (Gudykunst & Kim, 1992) may require teacher mediation in order to heighten each child's awareness of the dispute's underlying issues (Enright & McCloskey, 1988).

Incorporate Instructional Technology

■ *Use media events to make the lifestyles of other people "come alive."* The value of instructional technology should not be ignored. Television and video allow students to visit other countries and explore lifestyles without leaving the classroom. Teachers must be sure, however, that people are presented in typical, not ceremonial or stereotypical, situations. Children should be able to vicariously experience a realistic "slice of life." Follow-up activities

could give children opportunities to experience first-hand the dress, food and activities of other cultures.

*T*eachers should seize every opportunity to help children build skills and competencies by planning ways for children to achieve success each day.

■ *Computers and other electronics help children function on a more equitable level.* Computer technology offers children equal opportunities for success in inclusive programs. Educators are just beginning to see how computers can help second-language learners in multilingual classrooms (Enright & McCloskey, 1988). With computers and other electronics, children with special challenges can write, problem-solve and collaborate more effectively with their peers (Storeygard, Simmons, Stumpf & Pavloglou, 1993).

■ *Computers serve as a "common bond" to facilitate friendships.* Children's differences are often less obvious when they work together on the computer. Many software programs offer creative games and exercises for which there are no wrong answers. Thus, computers can serve as a medium for social interaction. The best software packages for enhancing social interaction are ones that emphasize cooperative learning and shared responsibility of group members (Male, 1994). More research is needed to further illuminate the social ramifications of increased computer use in inclusive classrooms. At this point, however, computer technology appears to hold great promise as a tool for improving the social inclusion of children with special challenges.

Conclusion

Implementing programs for all children requires teachers to evalu-

ate both their attitudes toward diversity and the instructional strategies they choose to employ in the classroom. At the heart of a program for all children is the flexibility to adapt lessons to more closely fit children's individual needs. The program's goals and implementation strategies should be continuously evaluated and adjusted to reflect changes in the classroom's composition. The framework of practical strategies presented in this article is intended to serve as both a guide for implementation and a tool for monitoring progress.

References

Allen, K. E. (1992). *The exceptional child: Mainstreaming in early childhood education* (2nd ed.). Albany, NY: Delmar.

Banks, J. A. (1993). Multicultural education for young children: Racial and ethnic attitudes and their modification. In B. Spodek (Ed.), *Handbook of research on the education of young children* (pp. 236-250). New York: Macmillan.

Beaty, J. J. (1994). *Observing development of the young child* (3rd ed.). New York: Macmillan.

Begler, E. (1993). Spinning wheels and straw: Balancing content, process, and context in global teacher education programs. *Theory into Practice, 32*(1), 14-20.

Bredekamp, S. (1993). The relationship between early childhood education and early education special education: Healthy marriage or family feud? *Topics in Early Childhood Special Education, 13*(3), 258-273.

Buswell, B., & Schaffner, B. (1992). Building friendships—an important part of schooling. ED 348-806, OSERS (U.S. Office of Special Education and Rehabilitation Services) *News in Print, IV*(4), 5-9.

Carta, J. J., Atwater, J. B., Schwartz, I. S., & McConnell, S. R. (1993). Developmentally appropriate practices and early childhood special education: A reaction to Johnson and McChesney Johnson. *Topics in Early Childhood Special Education, 13*(3), 243-254.

Carta, J. J., Schwartz, I., Atwater, J. B., & McConnell, S. R. (1991). Developmentally appropriate practice: Appraising its usefulness for young children with disabilities. *Topics in Early Childhood Special Education, 11*(1), 1-20.

5. CURRICULAR ISSUES

Dean, A. V., Salend, S. J., & Taylor, L. (1993). Multicultural education: A challenge for special educators. *Teaching Exceptional Children, 26*(1), 40-43.

Deiner, P. (1993). *Resources for teaching children with diverse abilities* (2nd ed.). Fort Worth, TX: Harcourt Brace College Publishers.

Derman-Sparks, L., & ABC Task Force. (1989). *Anti-bias curriculum: Tools for empowering young children.* Washington, DC: National Association for the Education of Young Children.

Derman-Sparks, L. (1993/94). Empowering children to create a caring culture in a world of differences. *Childhood Education, 70*(2), 66-71.

Enright, D. S., & McCloskey, M. L. (1988). *Integrating English: Developing English language and literacy in the multilingual classroom.* Reading, MA: Addison-Wesley.

Gudykunst, W., & Kim, Y. (1992). *Communicating with strangers: An approach to intercultural communication* (2nd ed.). New York: McGraw-Hill.

Guralnick, M. J. (1993). Developmentally appropriate practice in the assessment and intervention of children's peer relations. *Topics in Early Childhood Special Education, 13*(3), 344-371.

Hanline, M. F. (1985). Integrating disabled children. *Young Children, 40*(2), 45-48.

Hopkins, S., & Winters, J. (Eds.). (1990). *Discovering the world: Empowering children to value themselves, others and the earth.* Philadelphia, PA: New Society Publishers.

Johnson, J. E., & Johnson, K. M. (1992). Clarifying the developmental perspective in response to Carta, Schwartz, Atwater, and McConnell. *Topics in Early Childhood Special Education, 12*(4), 439-457.

Johnson, K. M., & Johnson, J. E. (1993). Rejoinder to Carta, Atwater, Schwartz, and McConnell. *Topics in Early Childhood Special Education, 13*(3), 255-257.

Jones, E., & Derman-Sparks, L. (1992). Meeting the challenge of diversity. *Young Children, 47*(2), 12-18.

King, E., Chipman, M., & Cruz-Janzen, M. (1994). *Educating young children in a diverse society.* Boston: Allyn and Bacon.

Male, M. (1994). *Technology for inclusion: Meeting the special needs of all students.* Boston: Allyn & Bacon.

Marion, M. (1995). *Guidance of young children* (4th ed.). Englewood Cliffs, NJ: Prentice-Hall.

McLean, M. E., & Odom, S. L. (1993). Practices for young children with and without disabilities: A comparison of DEC and NAEYC identified practices. *Topics in Early Childhood Special Education, 13*(3), 274-292.

Meloth, M. (1991). Enhancing literacy through cooperative learning. In E. H. Hiebert (Ed.), *Literacy for a diverse society: Perspectives, practices, and policies* (pp. 172-183). New York: Teachers College Press.

Peterson, C. A., & McConnell, S. R. (1993). Factors affecting the impact of social interaction skills interventions in early childhood special education. *Topics in Early Childhood Special Education, 13*(1), 38-56.

Sexton, D., Snyder, P., Sharpton, W. R., & Stricklin, S. (1993). Infants and toddlers with special needs and their families. *Childhood Education, 69*(5), 278-286.

Sleeter, C. E., & Grant, C. A. (1987). An analysis of multicultural education in the U.S. *Harvard Educational Review, 57,* 421-44.

Sosa, A. (1993). *Thorough and fair: Creating routes to success for Mexican-American students.* Charleston, WV: ERIC Clearinghouse on Rural Education and Small Schools.

Storeygard, J., Simmons, R., Stumpf, M., & Pavloglou, E. (1993). Making computers work for students with special needs. *Teaching Exceptional Children, 26*(1), 22-24.

Surr, J. (1992). Early childhood programs and the Americans with Disabilities Act (ADA). *Young Children, 47*(5), 18-21.

Wellhousen, K. (1993). Children from nontraditional families: A lesson in acceptance. *Childhood Education, 69*(5), 287-288.

Winter, S. M., Bell, M. J., & Dempsey, J. D. (1994). Creating play environments for children with special needs. *Childhood Education, 71,* 28-32.

Wooster, J. S. (1993). Authentic assessment: A strategy for preparing teachers to respond to curricular mandates in global education. *Theory into Practice, 32*(1), 47-51.

York, S. (1991). *Roots & wings: Affirming culture in early childhood programs.* St. Paul, MN: Redleaf Press.

York, S. (1992). *Developing roots & wings.* St. Paul, MN: Redleaf Press.

Project Work with Diverse Students

Adapting Curriculum Based on the Reggio Emilia Approach

Shareen Abramson, Roxanne Robinson, and Katie Ankenman

Shareen Abramson is Professor, Early Childhood Education Program, Department of Literacy and Early Education and Director of the Early Education Center, California State University, Fresno. Roxanne Robinson and Katie Ankenman are student teachers, Early Education Program, California State University, Fresno.

The preschools of Reggio Emilia, Italy, have generated excitement among early childhood educators in the U.S. and throughout the rest of the world. Presentations at professional conferences concerning these Italian schools draw standing-room-only crowds (Weissman, Saltz & Saltz, 1993). Visitors to Reggio Emilia schools marvel at the exceptional quality of the programs; the dedication, sensitivity and intelligence of the teachers and staff; the depth and sophistication of the project work; and the remarkable evidence of learning that is taking place (Bredekamp, 1993; Katz, 1990; New, 1990; Rankin, 1992).

Some educators in the United States are now attempting to adapt the Reggio Emilia approach (Forman, Moonja, Wrisley & Langley, 1993; Fyfe & Caldwell, 1993; LeeKeenan & Nimmo, 1993). The community of Reggio, however, tends to be culturally homogeneous. Although all socioeconomic levels exist in the area, the compre-

hensive social services limit the effects of poverty. Could Reggio Emilia principles and practices be translated into a community that, like so many in the U.S., is culturally, economically and linguistically diverse? Could it be implemented successfully with older elementary students as a means for promoting their development? Could student teachers apply the Reggio Emilia approach as they develop curriculum for diverse students?

These are the questions that the authors sought to address during a course on integrated curriculum in the Early Childhood Education Program at California State University, Fresno.

Reggio Emilia Approach

Preschools in Reggio Emilia demonstrate a number of exemplary and innovative education practices. The approach is discussed in detail in *The Hundred Languages of Children* (Edwards, Gandini & Forman, 1993). Key features of this approach include:

Community Commitment. Over the last 30 years, Reggio Emilia has created a publicly supported system of early childhood education centers that serve 35 percent of infants/toddlers and 47 percent of preschoolers in the community (Gandini, 1993b).

Supportive Relationships. Parents founded the Reggio Emilia schools at the end of World War II

(Gandini, 1993b). Loris Malaguzzi, the director of these schools for 40 years, engaged staff, parents, children and the community in the continuing development and management of programs (Malaguzzi, 1993b; Rinaldi, 1993; Spaggiari, 1993). Reciprocity and interaction characterize relationships among these participants. "Our goal is to create an amiable school—that is, a school that is active, inventive, livable, documentable and communicative ... a place of research, learning, revisiting, reconsideration and reflection ... where children, teachers and families feel a sense of well-being ..." (Malaguzzi, 1993c, p. 9). Staff members collectively participate in decision-making and teachers work in pairs. In addition, schools have an "atelierista" (artist) and a "pedagogista" (curriculum specialist) who work with teachers on curriculum development. A parent advisory council at each school helps facilitate an active home-school partnership. Because children stay with the same teacher for three years, these relationships are further enhanced.

A Unique Philosophy. The Reggio Emilia philosophy draws upon a number of constructivist theories, including those of Vygotsky and Piaget, but is most often described in terms of the "image of the child" (Gandini, 1993b; Malaguzzi, 1993b; Rinaldi, 1993). Reggio educators view each child as an individual with rights and potentials. They reject a portrayal of children as dependent or needy.

The authors are grateful for the suggestions of Lella Gandini, the U.S. liaison for Reggio Emilia schools, in the preparation of this manuscript.

5. CURRICULAR ISSUES

Preparation of the Environment. Reggio teachers recognize that the environment has teaching functions. The environment can be both a "container" for experiences and "content" for study and exploration (Gandini, 1993a). Teachers pay careful attention to all aspects of the environment, looking for ways to increase children's educational, aesthetic and social opportunities (Gandini, 1993b). All of the schools have unusual, open-ended, creative play structures and spaces that are often related to projects. School interiors and grounds are beautiful and a source of pride for children, teachers, parents and the community.

Atelier (Studio/Resource Room). Each school has a large atelier staffed by an artist who works with teachers and parents in planning, implementing and documenting project work (Vecchi, 1993). The atelier offers an incredible variety of supplies for children's use. Each classroom has a "mini-atelier" for additional experiences.

Project-based Curriculum. Much of the curriculum in Reggio Emilia schools centers around projects, which are unique in several important ways. Their distinguishing aspects include:

- the teacher role of both facilitator and partner in learning
- topic selection based on student interests and experiences
- collaboration among students, teachers and parents
- project content emerging from students' evolving understanding and not from a set of prepackaged activities
- multiple experiences with media to represent understandings
- repetition of activities for different purposes
- extended period of time devoted to a project
- small-group rather than whole-class projects

- project documentation (Edwards, 1993; Gandini, 1993b; Katz, 1993; New, 1990; Rankin, 1993).

Rather than "covering" the curriculum or a project, teachers and children together "uncover" a project (LeeKeenan & Nimmo, 1993). This project work helps all children develop their language, literacy, scientific, mathematical and social knowledge.

Collaboration. Educators in Reggio Emilia prefer using small groups because they provide a social context that fosters meaningful dialogue, collaborative problem solving and productive cognitive conflict (Malaguzzi, 1993c). Working together as a group takes precedence over individual efforts when children collaborate on large-scale projects such as creating murals or building a dinosaur. Parents interact frequently with teachers, formally and informally, and are involved in curriculum development activities, discussion groups and special events.

Multiple Languages. Echoing Howard Gardner's (1985) theory of "multiple intelligences," Reggio educators believe that children have the capacity for representing ideas in a wide variety of symbolic and graphic modes, what Malaguzzi called the "hundred languages of children" (Malaguzzi, 1993a). Gardner identified seven sources of intelligence: linguistic, musical, logico-mathematical, spatial-aesthetic, bodily kinesthetic, interpersonal and intrapersonal. An approach that recognizes multiple paths of expression and intellectual performance is especially effective with students whom the standard curriculum often fails to reach. Reggio educators believe the visual arts are not "a separate part of the curriculum but . . . [are] inseparable from the whole cognitive-symbolic expression of the developing child" (Gandini & Edwards, 1988, p. 15). Pretend play is another manifestation of the symbolic functioning es-

sential to children's development (Malaguzzi, 1993c). Children's expression of knowledge through musical performance, drama and manipulative constructions provides adults with a potent means for accessing children's perception and understanding of their world.

Documentation. Children's conceptual development can be documented over time, creating a basis for evaluating and planning future activities (Vecchi, 1993). Teachers can combine photographs, audiotape transcripts, videotapes, notes and products of children's project work to create a detailed, visual display of learning. This documentation serves as an individual and collective "memory" of activities, a method for reflecting on learning that leads to new experiences, a way to share learning with parents and others and a mechanism for capturing growth and development (Vecchi, 1993). Documentation displays are everywhere in Reggio Emilia schools. While many are of current project work, other displays are historical in nature—in effect, the collective "memory" of former students and their families.

All of the above principles have profound implications for educational practice. The use of projects and recognition of multiple languages seem to be especially relevant to the needs of diverse learners.

Projects as a Teaching Strategy for Diverse Students

Teaching strategies for linguistically diverse learners are undergoing dramatic changes. While earlier methods emphasized rote learning and drill, newer approaches to teaching a second language are based on a holistic view that gives primacy to both language as meaningful communication and to students' own experiences as the source for language development (Abramson, Seda & Johnson, 1990; Enright, 1986; Enright & McCloskey, 1985; Hudelson, 1984).

Projects that relate to students' experiences and interests, as in the Reggio Emilia approach, can be ideal ways to encourage language and conceptual development.

Allen (1986), for example, describes how an extended project began with a reading of *Strega Nona* (De Paola, 1975). Linguistically diverse children, ages 8 to 10, tested "magic" objects and powders, examined different types of pasta, and planned and prepared a pasta lunch. As Allen notes, these related experiences help children develop vocabulary, acquire scientific and mathematical ideas and refine their literary skills.

Melvin and Stout (1987) urge teachers of the linguistically diverse to rely more heavily on authentic materials. In the project "Discover a City," for example, students view an introductory slide show or videotape of city scenes, locate sights of interest on a map, contact the tourist bureau for additional information, create an itinerary for a four-day visit to the city and calculate costs for transportation, meals and other activities. Such activities provide a real and motivating context for language use.

Crawford (1993) believes that diverse learners are greatly interested in themes with multicultural dimensions. She describes an investigation of folktales that begins by introducing students to new concepts through bulletin board displays, audiovisual and community resources and dramatic experiences. Subsequent activities develop direction and organization for the study and include techniques such as brainstorming, semantic maps and prediction guides. Finally, students explore the theme or topic through various learning activities, develop generalizations and culminate the study. This project approach demonstrates the power of projects as a teaching strategy for diverse students and the value of adapting the Reggio Emilia approach.

Multiple Languages and Diverse Students

Reggio schools give prominence to the visual languages. Educators there view creative production as a nonverbal and alternative mode of expression that affords insights to an individual's level of understanding, perceptions and feelings. For linguistically diverse learners, such activities free them from the need to express ideas in a language that may be new and unfamiliar. Moreover, expressive activities give linguistically diverse students equity and a common ground with others.

According to Clay (1986), talking, reading, writing, thinking, drawing and making are all constructive processes in which the learner attempts to make sense of experience. She distinguishes "constructive" learning activities that involve relating, thinking and problem solving from those involving rote learning and repetitive tasks. She argues that "when instruction requires each child to shift to a constructive mode of thinking, to link the current task with personal knowledge, then any competency that the child has is allowed to contribute to the output" (p. 768).

Drawing on the work of Howard Gardner (1985), Shier (1990) makes a case for the importance of the visual arts for teaching linguistically diverse learners. According to Shier, both Project Zero and Arts Propel, initiatives begun at Harvard University and based on Gardner's theory of multiple intelligences, are examples of programs that successfully utilize creative expression and demonstrate the interrelatedness of cognitive and affective processes. Shier finds that such a curriculum promotes language development, enhances an appreciation of cultural differences and increases creative and thinking skills. Visual arts, literary arts, video and theater, as well as visits by guest artists and trips to art museums, have enormous po-

tential for expanding the learning horizons of linguistically diverse children.

Seely and Hurwitz (1983) reviewed a summer program serving Asian, Mexican, Caribbean and European immigrant children ranging in age from 6 to 17. An art teacher, drama teacher and language specialist worked together to use visual arts and drama as a means for developing language. The students' use of creative expression not only supported their English language development, but also affirmed their sense of themselves as productive, inventive and active learners. The teachers believed that creative endeavors enhanced students' attitudes of risk-taking, spontaneity and self-confidence that then carried over into their language learning.

Student Teachers Learn About the Reggio Emilia Approach

The Early Childhood Education Program at the authors' university includes a course on "Integrated Curriculum." The course examines research and uses projects based on an adaptation of the Reggio Emilia approach. Instead of turning in an elaborate final project, student teachers work in the practicum classroom, representing the progress of the project over the semester with photo-documentation, examples of student work, observational notes and reflections, as well as lesson plans.

In the practicum, student teachers are assigned to a public elementary school that has a highly diverse student population. Approximately 70 percent of the students are classified as limited-English-proficient. Student teachers are placed in groups of three to encourage collaborative learning and create a support system during the practicum.

After observing in their classrooms and talking with students and their cooperating teacher, the student teachers think about broad topic areas that might interest the students. They introduce these topics to the whole class, sharing ideas, books and materials and exploring related questions. Children sign up for projects, ranking the topics in order of their interest. Working individually, with their class group and with one another, student teachers identify some of the topic's conceptual dimensions through brainstorming and "webbing" sessions (Workman & Anziano, 1993).

It is important to note that these first student teacher projects are not yet of the same caliber as ones seen in Reggio Emilia schools. Beginning student teachers in the United States are, however, making use of insights from the work of Reggio educators, as well as other information sources, in developing curriculum for diverse students.

Projects in Diverse Classrooms

The student teachers' projects covered a broad range of topics and activities. The teachers and children, for example, of a 1st-grade class decided to pursue a project on sand. As part of the project, the group played in the sand box. Before and after this activity, the children drew pictures of sand. After the sandbox visit, Pavi, who was only beginning to learn English, drew an elaborate picture showing one child building a sand castle and another child with a bucket and shovel digging nearby. While Pavi could say only "sand, sand" when asked to tell about it, his picture graphically demonstrated a great deal more knowledge than he was able to verbalize.

As project activities developed, student teachers adapted to the Reggio Emilia approach by listening to students' conversations, looking at their pictures and generating questions. Some of these activities included: examining rocks, shells and sand through a magnifying glass; counting and grouping rocks into various categories; identifying the rocks that were collected; comparing sand to other similar sub-

Photo courtesy of the authors

Students make sand in a jar by mixing sand, rocks and water.

stances such as sugar, flour, salt, cornmeal, popcorn kernels, oatmeal, baking powder and birdseed; studying the effects of mixing water with sand and other substances; reading the story *Sand Cake* (Asch, 1979) and making an edible "sand" cake; and finally, building a sand castle. During these activities, students often conversed with others in their native language, thereby promoting their conceptual development (Abramson, Seda & Johnson, 1990; Enright & McCloskey, 1985).

Initially, many students appeared confused about the nature and origin of sand. The children's questions about sand inspired a sand-making activity. After trying a number of different methods, the children discovered that they could create sand if they combined rocks and shells in containers filled with water and then shook them.

The teachers gave students unlimited time to explore and digress, providing invaluable opportunities for collaborative problem solving and scientific inquiry. Students were concerned when some of the containers in the sand-making experiment leaked at the lid after a hard shake. The student teacher recorded their discussion on tape:

Outhay: We need to put tape around the lid so it doesn't leak.

Vue: We need to hold paper towels around it.

Tasha: I'm not going to shake mine at the top. If you don't make the water go to the top, it won't leak out.

Leticia: We need to make the lids tighter.

The students were allowed to try all the solutions. The tape worked until it became too wet to adhere. The children closely examined one of the containers that did not leak, discovering that the lid had an interior rubber seal. The student teacher and children discussed how to make a better seal for the other containers, eventually deciding upon putting a rubber band at the screw top. This technique worked very well, and the children experienced a strong sense of accomplishment. Working on this problem was closer to the children's interests and more rich than a teacher-initiated lesson might have been.

Keeping written records and photographic documentation, as Reggio educators do, helped the student teachers follow the children's progress, reflect on the learning and plan future activities. The children enjoyed looking at their photographs and sharing them with their classmates. They often conversed in their native language about the activities captured by the photographs.

In a 4th-grade classroom, a study of "Homes" led to a different type of project. While such a project might not be especially interesting to young children (LeeKeenan & Nimmo, 1993), the older students soon immersed themselves in home studies. When asked about their interest, several students explained that they already knew something about the topic, which made them confident. The student teachers developed a "KWL" (Know/ Want to learn/ Learned) chart (Tompkins & Hoskisson, 1991) to find out what the students knew. The resulting list mainly included things that are found in homes, such as bedrooms, bathrooms, sinks and doors.

A graphic representation activity also revealed students' knowledge of homes. Asked to draw a home or to make one with clay, the students drew very similar pictures: a classic, "flat" drawing of a box with a triangle on top, two square windows and a door in the middle. Clay representations also were similar, as most students flattened the clay and used a pencil to draw a house, suggesting perhaps a limited familiarity with this media.

To help students gain a three-dimensional understanding of how a home is constructed, the student teacher suggested that the students try to create a "standing" home from available materials, including drinking straws and pipe cleaners. Although most students began by working on their own, they were soon discussing construction strategies with one another, explaining how they had connected the walls or added the ceiling. They tried a large number of different ways to create house frames. Some students twisted pipe cleaners around

the end of the straws to connect them. Others inserted the pipe cleaners into the straws and bent them to create joints. Through collaboration and demonstration, they identified the most effective ways for constructing their models.

As the project continued, the students discussed different types of homes, especially homes in other cultures. Before going to the library to research cultures, the teachers paired strong readers with less proficient students who shared the same interest. The students recorded the information they found on a data chart (Tompkins & Hoskisson, 1991). They were excited by many of their discoveries. The students studying the Navajos, for example, could not believe that *hogans* were made from mud and grass. Two students who chose to study the Southeast Asian culture were surprised by the many different styles of homes found in that culture. Cooperation was high among the students as they gathered information for each other and shared books that could help other groups. Ultimately, the students used the completed data charts to write research reports.

After the research was done, the students were eager to build models. Model building, like some of the earlier activities, required problem solving, creativity and collaboration. The students expanded upon their learning from the earlier home-building activity. Concerned with the accuracy of their model, students who built a Navajo *hogan* with wood sticks reexamined the photograph of a modern-day *hogan*. One of the group members said, "It's not quite right. Look, they have grass covering their walls." The group then collected dried grass and twigs to glue on the walls, and dirt to create the surrounding environment.

On the final day of the project, the students set up a "Home Exhibit" that included their models, a name card identifying the culture each house represented, the names

of the students who worked on the model and the written reports. Parents were invited to the exhibit, where they had a chance to join students in viewing the different homes, reading about the cultures and asking questions.

Conclusion

The above examples prove the benefits of adapting Reggio Emilia principles to teaching culturally diverse elementary-age students. These students responded enthusiastically to projects that were interesting and meaningful. Project experiences that encouraged expression in multiple modes or "languages" helped to build concepts and bridge language differences. The projects enabled the students to achieve curriculum objectives in ways that were far more meaningful than using a textbook. Students learned to collaborate, conduct research and create representations of their learning. Their thinking was extended and deepened by having more time to explore and solve problems. Documentation allowed them to examine their own progress.

Student teachers were successful in utilizing strategies from Reggio Emilia schools to design an enriching curriculum. In doing so, they discovered the power of the Reggio Emilia approach to reach all children, especially the culturally and linguistically diverse.

References

Abramson, S., Seda, I., & Johnson, C. (1990). Literacy development in a multilingual kindergarten classroom. *Childhood Education, 67*, 68-72.

Allen, V. G. (1986). Developing contexts to support second language acquisition. *Language Arts, 63*, 61-66.

Asch, F. (1979). *Sand cake.* New York: Parents Magazine Press.

Bredekamp, S. (1993). Reflections on Reggio Emilia. *Young Children, 49*(1), 13-17.

Clay, M. M. (1986). Constructive processes: Talking, reading, writing, art, and craft. *Reading Teacher, 39,* 764-770.

Crawford, L. W. (1993). *Language and literacy learning in multicultural classrooms.* Boston: Allyn & Bacon.

De Paola, T. (1975). *Strega nona.* Englewood Cliffs, NJ: Prentice Hall.

Edwards, C. (1993). Partner, nurturer and guide: The roles of the Reggio teacher in action. In C. Edwards, L. Gandini, & G. Forman (Eds.), *The hundred languages of children: The Reggio Emilia approach to early childhood education* (pp. 151-169). Norwood, NJ: Ablex.

Edwards, C., Gandini, L., & Forman, G. (Eds.). (1993). *The hundred languages of children: The Reggio Emilia approach to early childhood education.* Norwood, NJ: Ablex.

Enright, D. S. (1986). "Use everything you have to teach English": Providing useful input to young language learners. In P. Rigg & D. S. Enright (Eds.), *Children and ESL: Integrating perspectives* (pp. 113-162). Washington, DC: TESOL Publications.

Enright, D. S., & McCloskey, M. L. (1985). Yes, talking! Organizing the classroom to promote second language acquisition. *TESOL Quarterly, 15,* 431-453.

Forman, G., Moonja, L., Wrisley, L., & Langley, J. (1993). The city in the snow: Applying the multisymbolic approach in Massachusetts. In C. Edwards, L. Gandini, & G. Forman (Eds.), *The hundred languages of children: The Reggio Emilia approach to early childhood education* (pp. 233-250). Norwood, NJ: Ablex.

Fyfe, B., & Caldwell, L. (1993). In P. Weissman, R. Saltz, & E. Saltz (Eds.), *Innovations in Early Education: The International Reggio Exchange, 1*(2) (p. 6-7). Detroit, MI: Merrill-Palmer Institute.

Gandini, L. (1993a). Educational and caring spaces. In C. Edwards, L. Gandini, & G. Forman (Eds.), *The hundred languages of children: The Reggio Emilia approach to early childhood education* (pp. 135-149). Norwood, NJ: Ablex.

Gandini, L. (1993b). Fundamentals of the Reggio Emilia approach to early childhood education. *Young Children, 49*(1), 4-8.

Gandini, L., & Edwards, C. P. (1988). Early childhood integration of the visual arts. *Gifted International, 5*(2), 14-17.

Gardner, H. (1985). *Frames of mind: The theory of multiple intelligences.* New York: Basic Books.

Hudelson, S. (1984). Kan yu ret an rayt en Ingles: Children become literate in English as a second language. *TESOL Quarterly, 18,* 221-238.

Katz, L. G. (1990). Impressions of Reggio Emilia preschools. *Young Children, 45*(6), 11-12.

Katz, L. G. (1993). What can we learn from Reggio Emilia? In C. Edwards, L. Gandini, & G. Forman (Eds.), *The hundred languages of children: The Reggio Emilia approach to early childhood education* (pp. 19-37). Norwood, NJ: Ablex.

LeeKeenan, D., & Nimmo, J. (1993). Connections: Using the project approach with 2- and 3-year-olds in a university laboratory school. In C. Edwards, L. Gandini, & G. Forman (Eds.), *The hundred languages of children: The Reggio Emilia approach to early childhood education* (pp. 251-267). Norwood, NJ: Ablex.

Malaguzzi, L. (1993a). No way. The hundred is there. In C. Edwards, L. Gandini, & G. Forman (Eds.), *The hundred languages of children: The Reggio Emilia approach to early childhood education* (pp. vi). Norwood, NJ: Ablex.

Malaguzzi, L. (1993b). History, ideas and basic philosophy. In C. Edwards, L. Gandini, & G. Forman (Eds.), *The hundred languages of children: The Reggio Emilia approach to early childhood education* (pp. 41-89). Norwood, NJ: Ablex.

Malaguzzi, L. (1993c). For an education based on relationships. *Young Children, 49*(1), 9-12.

Melvin, B. S., & Stout, D. F. (1987). Motivating language learners through authentic materials. In W. M. Rivers (Ed.), *Interactive language teaching* (pp. 44-56). Cambridge: Cambridge University Press.

New, R. (1990). Excellent early education: A city in Italy has it. *Young Children, 45*(6), 4-10.

Rankin, B. (1992). Inviting children's creativity—A story of Reggio Emilia, Italy. *Child Care Information Exchange, 85,* 30-35.

Rankin, B. (1993). Curriculum development in Reggio Emilia: A long-term curriculum project about dinosaurs. In C. Edwards, L. Gandini, & G. Forman (Eds.), *The hundred languages of children: The Reggio Emilia approach to early childhood education* (pp. 189-211). Norwood, NJ: Ablex.

Rinaldi, C. (1993). The emergent curriculum and social constructivism. In C. Edwards, L. Gandini, & G. Forman (Eds.), *The hundred languages of children: The Reggio Emilia approach to early childhood education* (pp. 101-111). Norwood, NJ: Ablex.

Seely, C., & Hurwitz, A. (1983). Developing language through art. *School Arts, 82*(9), 20-22.

Shier, J. H. (1990). Integrating the arts in the foreign/second language curriculum: Fusing the affective with the cognitive. *Foreign Language Annals, 23,* 301-314.

Spaggiari, S. (1993). The community-teacher partnership in the governance of the schools. In C. Edwards, L. Gandini, & G. Forman (Eds.), *The hundred languages of children: The Reggio Emilia approach to early childhood education* (pp. 91-99). Norwood, NJ: Ablex.

Tompkins, G. E., & Hoskisson, K. (1991). *Language arts: Content and teaching strategies.* New York: Macmillan.

Vecchi, V. (1993). The role of the atelierista. In C. Edwards, L. Gandini, & G. Forman (Eds.), *The hundred languages of children: The Reggio Emilia approach to early childhood education* (pp. 119-127). Norwood, NJ: Ablex.

Weissman, P., Saltz, R., & Saltz, E. (Eds.). (1993). *Innovations in Early Education: The International Reggio Exchange, 1*(2). Detroit, MI: Merrill-Palmer Institute.

Workman, S., & Anziano, M. C. (1993). Curriculum webs: Weaving connections from children to teachers. *Young Children, 48*(2), 4-9.

Curriculum Webs: Weaving Connections From Children to Teachers

Susan Workman and Michael C. Anziano

Susan Workman, Ed.D., is director of the San Juan College Child Development Center, a lab school and child care facility for two- to eight-year-olds. Susan holds a doctorate in early childhood education from Syracuse University.

Michael C. Anziano, Ph.D., is director of early childhood education and associate professor of psychology at San Juan College. Michael's current work involves strategies for early intervention.

In one preschool classroom a group of three- through six-year-old children take turns tracing one another's bodies as they move in a variety of poses. The teacher observes their fascination with posing and extends their interest the following day by placing mirrors in the art area. Several days later, on a walking field trip, children begin to explore the concept of "puddles." The teacher draws their attention to the puddle: "Look in the puddle and tell me what you see." As the children respond she helps them connect their experience with the reflection in the puddle to their experience with mirrors. They return to the classroom and search the art boxes for reflective materials. Aluminum foil on cardboard becomes lakes and puddles, and children explore the idea of reflections in the block corner as they construct houses.

Throughout these activities children are expanding their understanding of the concepts of self, water, and houses. The teacher's skill in extending children's interests and experiences is supported by a webbed curriculum—one that was developed by observing children and documenting their recurring interests and the themes of their activities. The possibilities and connections inherent in the series of related webs this teacher uses provide an unending resource for curriculum development.

Connecting concept webs

Semantic webbing, especially the integration and *connections* among webs, may become the central feature of any curricular approach. Developmentally appropriate activities and outcomes for children result from teachers responding to the children's interests. The preschooler thinks about the world primarily in terms of actions that can be performed, so the choice of concepts must provide for action-oriented, child-initiated plans and activities. In our case, teachers spent an entire semester observing and documenting children's interests. The result was a set of basic concepts—earth, air, water, houses, and self—which could be developed as webs. The child begins with a specific problem, for example, constructing a house. In constructing a house, symbolic media chosen by the child will vary from three-dimensional blocks to paper and pencil, clay, sand, or a computer program (e.g., "Town Builder"). A child could begin with a different problem, such as moving water from one place to another. Each basic concept can be represented by a content web,

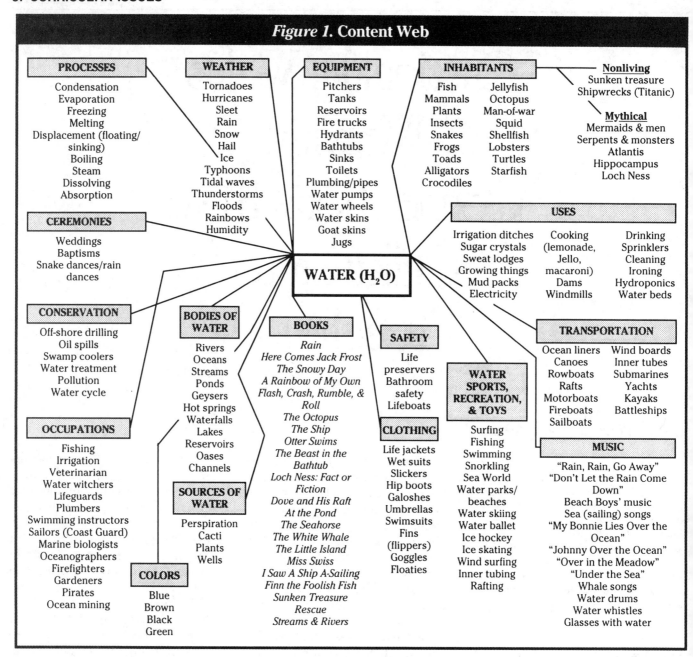

Figure 1. Content Web

PROCESSES
Condensation
Evaporation
Freezing
Melting
Displacement (floating/
sinking)
Boiling
Steam
Dissolving
Absorption

CEREMONIES
Weddings
Baptisms
Snake dances/rain
dances

CONSERVATION
Off-shore drilling
Oil spills
Swamp coolers
Water treatment
Pollution
Water cycle

OCCUPATIONS
Fishing
Irrigation
Veterinarian
Water witchers
Lifeguards
Plumbers
Swimming instructors
Sailors (Coast Guard)
Marine biologists
Oceanographers
Firefighters
Gardeners
Pirates
Ocean mining

WEATHER
Tornadoes
Hurricanes
Sleet
Rain
Snow
Hail
Ice
Typhoons
Tidal waves
Thunderstorms
Floods
Rainbows
Humidity

EQUIPMENT
Pitchers
Tanks
Reservoirs
Fire trucks
Hydrants
Bathtubs
Sinks
Toilets
Plumbing/pipes
Water pumps
Water wheels
Water skins
Goat skins
Jugs

INHABITANTS
Fish   Jellyfish
Mammals   Octopus
Plants   Man-of-war
Insects   Squid
Snakes   Shellfish
Frogs   Lobsters
Toads   Turtles
Alligators Starfish
Crocodiles

Nonliving
Sunken treasure
Shipwrecks (Titanic)

Mythical
Mermaids & men
Serpents & monsters
Atlantis
Hippocampus
Loch Ness

WATER (H$_2$O)

USES
Irrigation ditches   Cooking   Drinking
Sugar crystals   (lemonade,   Sprinklers
Sweat lodges   Jello,   Cleaning
Growing things   macaroni)   Ironing
Mud packs   Dams   Hydroponics
Electricity   Windmills   Water beds

BODIES OF WATER
Rivers
Oceans
Streams
Ponds
Geysers
Hot springs
Waterfalls
Lakes
Reservoirs
Oases
Channels

SOURCES OF WATER
Perspiration
Cacti
Plants
Wells

COLORS
Blue
Brown
Black
Green

BOOKS
Rain
Here Comes Jack Frost
The Snowy Day
A Rainbow of My Own
*Flash, Crash, Rumble, &
Roll*
The Octopus
The Ship
Otter Swims
*The Beast in the
Bathtub*
*Loch Ness: Fact or
Fiction*
Dove and His Raft
At the Pond
The Seahorse
The White Whale
The Little Island
Miss Swiss
I Saw A Ship A-Sailing
Finn the Foolish Fish
*Sunken Treasure
Rescue*
Streams & Rivers

SAFETY
Life
preservers
Bathroom
safety
Lifeboats

CLOTHING
Life jackets
Wet suits
Slickers
Hip boots
Galoshes
Umbrellas
Swimsuits
Fins
(flippers)
Goggles
Floaties

WATER SPORTS, RECREATION, & TOYS
Surfing
Fishing
Swimming
Snorkling
Sea World
Water parks/
beaches
Water skiing
Water ballet
Ice hockey
Ice skating
Wind surfing
Inner tubing
Rafting

TRANSPORTATION
Ocean liners   Wind boards
Canoes   Inner tubes
Rowboats   Submarines
Rafts   Yachts
Motorboats   Kayaks
Fireboats   Battleships
Sailboats

MUSIC
"Rain, Rain, Go Away"
"Don't Let the Rain Come
Down"
Beach Boys' music
Sea (sailing) songs
"My Bonnie Lies Over the
Ocean"
"Johnny Over the Ocean"
"Over in the Meadow"
"Under the Sea"
Whale songs
Water drums
Water whistles
Glasses with water

and Figure 1 illustrates the content web for the concept of water.

By working with several webs simultaneously, children are encouraged to see connections among the concepts. Houses, animals, and babies were three of our initial concept webs. Children began to think in terms of relationships that fostered their understanding that animals—including themselves—live in houses, or that a nest is a particular kind of house that holds babies. Children's ideas about concepts like houses,

earth, air, and water are often derived from the central concept of self, as activities in each web begin with the children's own experience. Figure 2 presents the content web for the concept of self.

The natural interrelations among these webs support the developmental interaction approach of Biber (1977), who, along with others, has advocated for preschool curricula in which cognitive, affective, and social processes are all interdependent. The child's intellectual energy and the

growth of cognitive functions like judging, comparing, reasoning, and problem solving are always interacting with motivational and interpersonal processes. In thinking about concepts like water, earth, and air, the child engages in the environment, transforms materials, and has opportunities to feel competence by observing his effect on materials like water and earth. At the same time social processes are facilitated by opportunities to share, cooperate with others, tutor one's peers, and learn

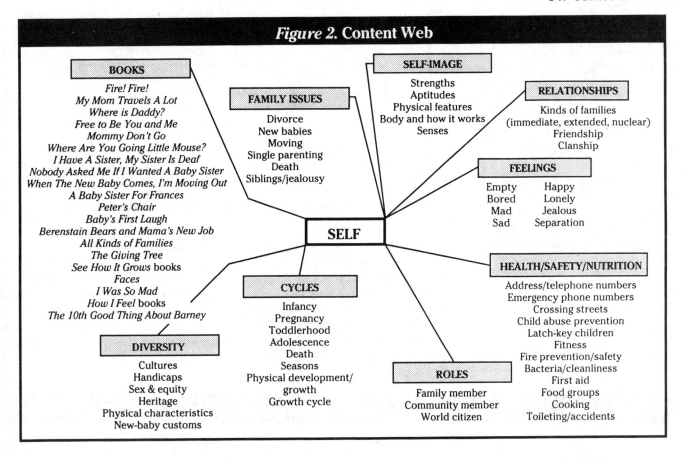

Figure 2. Content Web

BOOKS

Fire! Fire!
My Mom Travels A Lot
Where is Daddy?
Free to Be You and Me
Mommy Don't Go
Where Are You Going Little Mouse?
I Have A Sister, My Sister Is Deaf
Nobody Asked Me If I Wanted A Baby Sister
When The New Baby Comes, I'm Moving Out
A Baby Sister For Frances
Peter's Chair
Baby's First Laugh
Berenstain Bears and Mama's New Job
All Kinds of Families
The Giving Tree
See How It Grows books
Faces
I Was So Mad
How I Feel books
The 10th Good Thing About Barney

DIVERSITY
Cultures
Handicaps
Sex & equity
Heritage
Physical characteristics
New-baby customs

FAMILY ISSUES
Divorce
New babies
Moving
Single parenting
Death
Siblings/jealousy

SELF-IMAGE
Strengths
Aptitudes
Physical features
Body and how it works
Senses

RELATIONSHIPS
Kinds of families
(immediate, extended, nuclear)
Friendship
Clanship

FEELINGS
Empty   Happy
Bored   Lonely
Mad   Jealous
Sad   Separation

SELF

CYCLES
Infancy
Pregnancy
Toddlerhood
Adolescence
Death
Seasons
Physical development/
growth
Growth cycle

ROLES
Family member
Community member
World citizen

HEALTH/SAFETY/NUTRITION
Address/telephone numbers
Emergency phone numbers
Crossing streets
Child abuse prevention
Latch-key children
Fitness
Fire prevention/safety
Bacteria/cleanliness
First aid
Food groups
Cooking
Toileting/accidents

about other cultures. An activity in our earth web, for example, involves small groups of children working together to make a papier mâché globe. The globe can be adapted into a piñata and used as part of a Hispanic celebration, such as Cinco de Mayo. Children also interrelate important emotional and affective content through the expression of feelings surrounding a concept like self, which may include discussions or dramatic play involving themes such as a new baby or sibling rivalries. The webbed approach, then, allows for the natural integration of expanding intellectual functions with emotion, attitude, and feeling.

The interrelation of concept webs is an important extension of Levin's (1986) approach. Levin presents some fine examples of a series of activities based on webs such as "rocks" and "gerbils." Our approach focuses on the development of webs and also devotes particular attention to the rela-

tions and connections among various webs. In the next section we describe our approach to curriculum and give examples and applications of these ideas as they are carried out in our laboratory preschool.

Creating a curriculum web

The first step in organizing a webbed curriculum is to identify concepts from children's interests to serve as a starting point. Choose ideas that are small (bread, for example, would be fine; seasons would not) in order to make the task manageable. The concepts should be able to be related to one another. They also should lend themselves to being part of a cycle that can be returned to again and again. "Spring" is difficult to return to, but houses can always be explored. Finally, choose children's ideas that are universal. They are more likely to mesh

with one another, and they facilitate the integration of ideas and customs from diverse cultures. Ongoing concepts in our classrooms are self, houses, air, water, and earth.

Then the fun begins! Groups of four or five staff members brainstorm each topic, listing as many headings and subheadings as their understanding and experience allows. Their observations of children's interests and ideas are critical to a successful, inclusive web. Evaluation is delayed as the collective knowledge of the group is outlined on paper. Each web becomes a source of endless possibilities for active exploration of a concept (see Figure 2). In addition, the relationships among the webs provide flexibility, richness, and depth. Figure 3 illustrates the interactive relationships possible among the basic concepts.

Another critical step in the process is to assure that each web contains possibilities for children

5. CURRICULAR ISSUES

to have experiences related to program goals or learner outcome. These goals can be listed and numbered, and the original web can be coded to indicate possibilities for each outcome. Then webs are reorganized according to goals, thus allowing staff to look at a topic from both a concept view and a process view. Figure 4 gives an example of this process, using our program's goals as "learner outcome." It is important to remember, however, that learning is in the hands of the child and may take many directions depending on her developmental level and the individual interests she has.

Curriculum in action

How do teachers and children

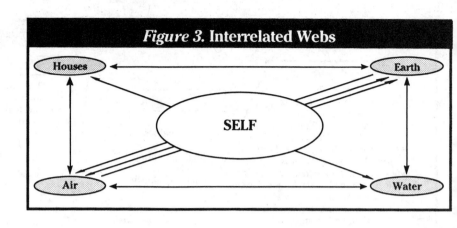

Figure 3. Interrelated Webs

collaborate to weave the classroom curriculum? This process is an example of the art and the science of good teaching. First, each activity is viewed as a launching pad for extending children's ideas and understanding; for example, a child's interest in houses might

extend to houses for dogs, houses for worms (earth), and houses for birds. Each of these options is viable and can serve as a jumping-off place for exploring other concepts. Worms and earth might lead to creating terrariums; terrariums might spark interest in a trip to

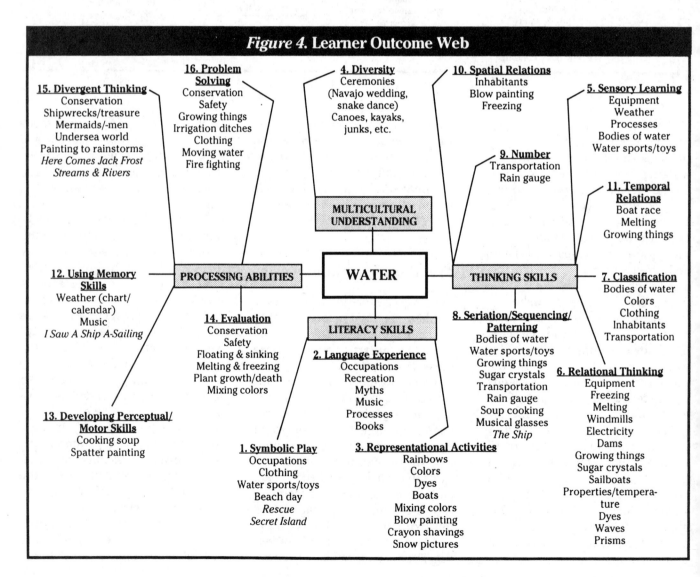

Figure 4. Learner Outcome Web

15. Divergent Thinking
Conservation
Shipwrecks/treasure
Mermaids/-men
Undersea world
Painting to rainstorms
Here Comes Jack Frost
Streams & Rivers

16. Problem Solving
Conservation
Safety
Growing things
Irrigation ditches
Clothing
Moving water
Fire fighting

4. Diversity
Ceremonies
(Navajo wedding, snake dance)
Canoes, kayaks, junks, etc.

10. Spatial Relations
Inhabitants
Blow painting
Freezing

5. Sensory Learning
Equipment
Weather
Processes
Bodies of water
Water sports/toys

9. Number
Transportation
Rain gauge

11. Temporal Relations
Boat race
Melting
Growing things

12. Using Memory Skills
Weather (chart/calendar)
Music
I Saw A Ship A-Sailing

MULTICULTURAL UNDERSTANDING

PROCESSING ABILITIES

WATER

THINKING SKILLS

7. Classification
Bodies of water
Colors
Clothing
Inhabitants
Transportation

14. Evaluation
Conservation
Safety
Floating & sinking
Melting & freezing
Plant growth/death
Mixing colors

LITERACY SKILLS

8. Seriation/Sequencing/Patterning
Bodies of water
Water sports/toys
Growing things
Sugar crystals
Transportation
Rain gauge
Soup cooking
Musical glasses
The Ship

2. Language Experience
Occupations
Recreation
Myths
Music
Processes
Books

6. Relational Thinking
Equipment
Freezing
Melting
Windmills
Electricity
Dams
Growing things
Sugar crystals
Sailboats
Properties/temperature
Dyes
Waves
Prisms

13. Developing Perceptual/Motor Skills
Cooking soup
Spatter painting

1. Symbolic Play
Occupations
Clothing
Water sports/toys
Beach day
Rescue
Secret Island

3. Representational Activities
Rainbows
Colors
Dyes
Boats
Mixing colors
Blow painting
Crayon shavings
Snow pictures

the greenhouse. For another child, or in another classroom, the progression of activities will be very different. At each point the child can be helped to make connections: "Do you remember when . . . ?" "How is this like . . . ?"

Second, webbing assures that both teachers and children see relationships. A cornerstone for curriculum development is the idea of relationships. Relationships are the connections that enable children to organize and make sense of their world, build concepts, and think about things in new ways. The experiences and environments we plan with children, therefore, should be organized in such a way that the connections between ideas and events are apparent to the children—easily grasped and able to be represented from their point of view. This representation—whether through language, drawing, block building, or dramatic play—enables the teacher to observe the connections children are making and plan the best way to extend children's interest and understanding (New, 1990).

Third, these relationships are woven by children and teachers together. Teachers are careful observers of children; they listen and help to clarify children's ideas: "What are your ideas about rain and where it comes from?" "I'm wondering if there's another way to move the water from the water table to the bucket." Teachers extend opportunities for children by helping them make connections to previous experiences: "How is what you see in the puddle like what you saw in the mirror? How is it different?" The teacher's open-ended questions encourage the process of comparing and help children construct notions of similarities and differences. Teachers might share their wonderings—"I wonder if there's a way to make the foil float"—and encourage children's ideas—"How can we find out?" This reflective thinking becomes part of the curriculum development process for teachers and children as they weave a design among the curriculum webs.

The possibilities inherent in a webbed curriculum are virtually limitless. Each time a teacher or child creates an interesting question or sees a relationship that he is interested in pursuing, the follow-up exploration can be documented and added to enrich the repertoire of possibilities for other children and teachers at other times. It becomes possible to document curriculum as it emerges uniquely (see, for example, Jones, 1989) with each group of children and teachers and to add it to the available idea pool for others to use. In this way the curriculum is not a static set of materials but a living, growing resource.

For further reading

National Association for the Education of Young Children & National Association of Early Childhood Specialists in State Departments of Education. (1991). Guidelines for appropriate curriculum content and assessment in programs serving children ages 3 through 8. *Young Children, 46*(3), 21–38.

Workman, S., Bradley, S., Nipper, C., & Workman, D. (1991). *Myself and my surroundings: An early childhood curriculum resource.* Farmington, NM: San Juan College.

References

Biber, B. (1977). A developmental interaction approach: Bank Street College of Education. In M.C. Day & R.K. Parker (Eds.), *The preschool in action* (2nd ed.) (pp. 423–460). Boston: Allyn & Bacon.

Jones, E. (1989, November). *Curriculum can be more than what happens: Three approaches to developing appropriate curriculum for young children.* Paper presented at the annual conference of the National Association for the Education of Young Children, Atlanta, GA.

Levin, D.E. (1986). Weaving curriculum webs: Planning, guiding and recording curriculum activities in the day care classroom. *Day Care and Early Education, 13*(4), 16–19.

New, R. (1990). Excellent early education: A city in Italy has it. *Young Children, 45*(6), 4–10.

Voice of Inquiry: Possibilities and Perspectives

Clint Wills

Clint Wills is an education consultant.

"You could count their claws and teeth," Michael said when asked to think like a mathematician about dinosaurs. Twenty-three more 1st-graders nodded their approval at this suggestion. I wondered aloud, "How would you do that?" Michael took some time to think about it.

"Well, when they roar you would just look real quick!"

As I noted this answer, Michael's classmates offered their solutions. The discussion and debate picked up momentum.

"When they roar, you might not have time to count, so you could jam a stick in their mouth."

"Uh-uh, it might break!"

"Not if it's a big stick, like a little tree."

This line of thinking diverged when Kelly offered, "You could tie their mouth open with a rope." The moment of silence that ensued while the children considered the possibility was short-lived.

"They might cut through it with their teeth."

"Wait! You could use some wire, like some *big* wire!"

The discussion diverged again when Vanessa said, "You could count the teeth in the skull of a dead dinosaur."

"Yeah!" exclaimed Michael, "and we could really do that, too."

"Even with a picture," David added.

Others voiced support for Vanessa's strategy and I wrote it on the chart tablet, adding to the growing list of mathematical ways to think about dinosaurs.

This lively conversation took place as my 1st-graders helped plan a dinosaur study we had undertaken. It is significant to note that the students played a role in creating a curriculum in which we operated as a group of researchers. In fact, it was the inclusion of students' voices in the curriculum that caused me to take my first serious look at the use of inquiry in my classroom.

Beginning with my first day of undergraduate classes, countless teachers, mentors and friends urged me to make my classroom a democracy by planning my curriculum with the help of my students. Intuitively, I agreed with these exhortations; I left each exchange filled with enthusiasm, eager to achieve democracy in my classroom. I always fell short of these goals.

While I had become very good at knowing what I should be doing, I still had very little understanding of *how* to do it. In other words, I was long on belief and short on practice.

During my third year as a 1st-grade teacher, my fifth year in the classroom, I heard Carolyn Burke explain inquiry-driven curriculum (Burke, 1991) and something important dropped into place for me. Now I could see a practical, sensible way to collaborate with my students.

Curricular Structures: Four Models

Inquiry is sometimes referred to as the newest version of thematic teaching, and in some ways this is true. A comparison of four curricular models (Prescriptive, Thematic, KWHL and Inquiry) reveals some logical relationships, and a progressive pattern emerges.

The characteristic unifying these (and other) curricular models is this: learning progresses from the known to the unknown. Once we have acknowledged this basic similarity, however, a more pronounced division emerges. A strong connection exists between the prescriptive and thematic models and between the KWHL and inquiry models, but these two subsets are fundamentally different.

A close look reveals that most thematic models have evolved from a linear view of learning, which identifies knowledge as a static, immutable, quantifiable entity. The inquiry model has evolved from a

It was the inclusion of students' voices in the curriculum that caused me to take my first serious look at the use of inquiry in my classroom.

circular or recursive perspective that presupposes the tentative, dynamic nature of knowledge. In order to better understand Inquiry as curriculum, it is helpful to examine its evolution and its relationship to the three other curricular structures.

The Prescriptive Model

The original prescriptive model (see Figure 1), one still widely used, is found in countless programs and the common denominator is the DPTT continuum (i.e., **D**iagnose, **P**rescribe, **T**each and **T**est). Ideally, this continuum allows for learning programs that fit the needs of individual students, with little or no wasted instructional time for the teacher and little or no "busy work" for the student. The teacher administers a pretest to determine student ability, prescribes a course of study, teaches these skills, then administers a retest to determine progress.

Even when used correctly, however, this model casts the teacher as the active transmitter of knowledge and the child as the passive receiver (Weaver, 1990). Furthermore, the knowledge being transmitted is often lifted verbatim from an outside source, such as a teacher's manual. This practice effectively keeps the expertise in the hands of the "program" from which the manual came.

The prescriptive model views learning from a very linear perspective, much like a train racing along a railroad track. The course is predetermined and no detours are allowed. The only variable is the speed with which the journey is made. An unusually quick trip denotes a child whose learning ability is above grade level; an on-time arrival denotes a child at grade level. All educators are familiar with the many labels for those who arrive late. Of course, many of those late arrivals never complete the trip, eventually choosing to jump from the train.

This linear nature frequently prevents teachers from implementing the DPTT curriculum as a collection of individually tailored learning programs. The school year takes on the characteristics of a race; teachers feel intense pressure to hurry the students along toward the finish line. It seems there is not enough time in the school year to test, teach, retest and reteach. In such a classroom, Vanessa's brilliant strategy for exploring dinosaurs would be left unspoken, because if I invited such seemingly random conversations, our train would be derailed and the race could be lost.

The Thematic Model

Ironically, most "thematic approaches" are closely tied to the prescriptive model. While thematic models (see Figure 2) attempt to make learning more authentic by drawing connections between the disciplines, these connections are usually in the form of prescribed activities designed to teach the same predetermined skills as the prescriptive model. Progress is still essentially linear: the sequence, duration and composition of the themes are predetermined by the teacher or grade level.

Themes may be independent of the children's interests (and, often, the teacher's as well) and they frequently have no connection to each other. As in the prescriptive model, curriculum (knowledge) is viewed as predetermined and finite and thus is transmitted to the child. Because the school year still frames a curricular race, little or no provision is made for the transaction of new questions or insights generated by the child (Weaver, 1990). Yet a cursory glance appears to show a curriculum that is more integrated, and therefore more authentic.

Prescriptive Model

Each subject is autonomous, with its own linear sequence of skills.

	Diagnose	Prescribe	Teach	Test
Reading	||||||||||	|||||||||||||	||||||	|||>
		Skills		
Spelling	||||||||||	|||||||||||||	||||||	|||>
		Skills		
Mathematics	||||||||||	|||||||||||||	||||||	|||>
		Skills		
Science	||||||||||	|||||||||||||	||||||	|||>
		Skills		
Art	||||||||||	|||||||||||||	||||||	|||>
		Skills		

Figure 1

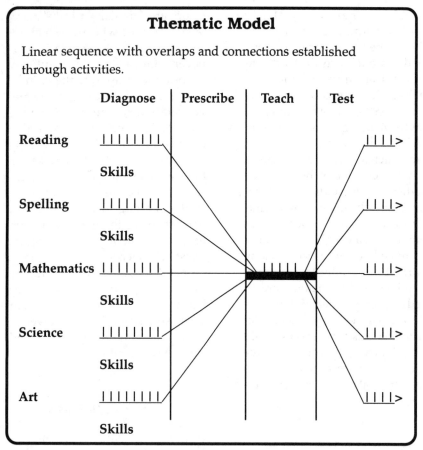

Thematic Model

Linear sequence with overlaps and connections established through activities.

Figure 2

More simply, prescriptive models tell the student what to learn, while KWHL models ask the student what he or she would like to learn.

The Inquiry Model

To understand how KWHL differs from inquiry, it is helpful to look at the general structure of a unit from an inquiry perspective (see Figure 4).

I begin the school year by asking the children what they would like to know more about. The questions and topics we generate are displayed on a bulletin board and serve as a curricular guide for the rest of the year. This strategy gives me access to two of the three primary influences on my curriculum, which are the children's interests, my own interests and the units I am required to teach.

My curriculum is a negotiation, a balance that I achieve among these three sources of input. Part of my job is to streamline the topics we will cover, combining and unifying when possible. This unification process, which often begins by simply observing, "Hey, that's kind of like . . . ," is an authentic means of connecting knowledge. All that is required is an open forum for discussion and a teacher who is willing to listen to the children and

The KWHL Model

The third model is called KWL or KWHL (see Figure 3), which is an acronym for: What do you already **K**now? **W**hat would you like to know? **H**ow will you find out? What did you **L**earn? While this process utilizes inquiry techniques, KWHL is used primarily as a means for guiding student research. Inquiry addresses student research, but also includes dimensions of curricular construction and professional growth.

Like the prescriptive and thematic models, KWHL progresses from what is known to the unknown, and has a means of accounting for new learning. Prescriptive models, however, progress from pre-test to post-test while KWHL models progress from "What do you already know?" to "What did you learn?"

This critical difference puts the responsibility for learning on the stu-

dent, allowing for the value of experience, self-directed questioning, familiarity with research procedures and self-evaluation or reflection.

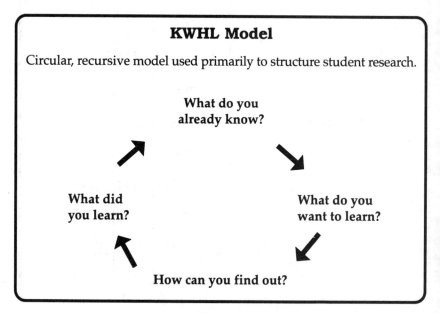

KWHL Model

Circular, recursive model used primarily to structure student research.

What do you already know?

What do you want to learn?

How can you find out?

What did you learn?

Figure 3

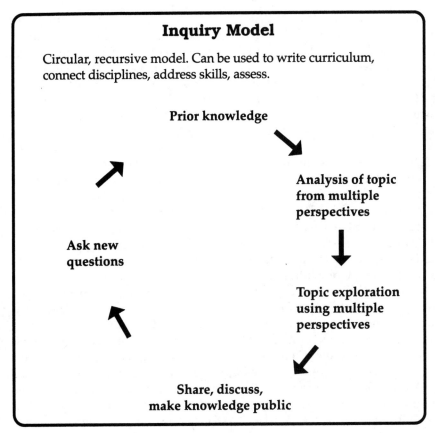

Inquiry Model

Circular, recursive model. Can be used to write curriculum, connect disciplines, address skills, assess.

Prior knowledge

Analysis of topic from multiple perspectives

Ask new questions

Topic exploration using multiple perspectives

Share, discuss, make knowledge public

Figure 4

learn from them. After establishing the areas of interest, we begin our studies. I have found that our questions most often fit into the curricular definitions of science, social studies and health.

Most of our units progress according to the following plan, which is very closely based on ideas presented by Carolyn Burke (1991):

■ *Organize a text set.* I assemble all resources available from the library, my own collections, students, other teachers, etc. I gather any and all artifacts related to the topic, including, but not limited to, books.

■ *Hold a book browse.* When most or all of my resources are in the classroom, I place them on the four tables where the children sit. The children then spend about 15 minutes looking at the resources, discussing them, playing with them, etc. After 15 minutes, the groups move to new tables and the

process is repeated until, at the end of an hour, each group has visited each table and is back "home."

■ *Create graffiti boards.* Upon returning to their original seats, students help to clear the desktops. Each group is then given one large sheet of bulletin board paper (large enough to cover the entire table) and each child writes and/or draws everything he or she knows about the topic. In this alternative to webbing and mapping, the students are responsible for their own efforts and do not need the teacher as a mediator. The exercise is usually fairly noisy as comments, questions and small group discussions accompany the drawing and writing. These discussions can be illustrated on the graffiti board. A child whose idea stems from the drawing or writing of another child can draw lines connecting the two ideas. The finished product should be covered with words, pictures and lines.

■ *Share graffiti boards.* When the graffiti boards are completed, each student explains his or her contribution. During this process, I usually record the key points on a chart tablet. A good title for this chart is "What We Think We Know," which gives the document the characteristics of a rough draft and avoids possible conflicts over "facts." This also gives me the chance to cull the information, eliminating repetition and creating a reference source that will be posted for the duration of the study.

■ *Hold a sign system/knowledge domain discussion.* This terminology, which seems complex at first glance, represents a very basic and simple premise that is central to the Inquiry model. It is simply another way of saying that sign systems are how we communicate and knowledge domains are what we communicate. There are five main sign systems: language, art, music, drama and mathematics. Each system is non-redundant; that is, each system, when used to convey knowledge of a topic, could yield different information. Knowledge domains are a bit more complex and there are many more of them. Philosophy, biology, geography, nutrition, quantum physics—all of these are knowledge domains. Every subject area, every discipline and every school of thought can be a knowledge domain, each offering a different perspective.

The opening dialogue is an example of 1st-graders using the mathematic sign system to think about dinosaurs. While seated at the chart tablet, I had asked the students to talk about things a mathematician might do to show others what he or she knows about dinosaurs. As they responded, I recorded their ideas. Eventually, we had a set of math activities to pursue in large groups, small groups or individually. Repeating this process while considering art, music, language and movement gave us activities in those curricular areas. Expanding this process to include some basic knowledge domains would give us science, social studies or health activities. The net result is a unit planned by, and with, the children.

I ask the children to consider three types of questions for each sign system or knowledge domain:

- What would an artist say about this topic (or a picture depicting the topic)? This question generates a list of things the children already know (prior knowledge, or the "K" of KWHL).
- What would an artist ask about this topic? This generates a list of questions or things we want to know (the "W" of KWHL).
- What would an artist do to show others what he or she knows about the topic? This generates a list of activities for us to do (part of the "H" of KWHL).

Conduct explorations (large group, small group and individual). I post the lists we create and incorporate them into my lesson plans. They serve as jumping-off points for discussions, field trips, guest speakers, class-made books, research projects and so on. Some of the questions lend themselves to individual research projects, while some are better suited to be answered by a field trip. Some activities demand that we walk outside for a whole-class experience; some are perfect for a small-group response. I trust my own judgment, with input from my students, in making these decisions.

Share insights, discuss, ask new questions. This step, which sounds like a final procedure, actually occurs throughout the study. It is the evaluative component that offers the student a chance to self-evaluate while giving the observant teacher insight into the child's use of skills and strategies. The key to realizing the full potential of this process is the teacher's ability to fa-

cilitate sharing in a way that is naturally respectful of the children's ideas. This single element may be the most elusive and difficult aspect of an inquiry (or indeed any) curriculum. It requires teachers to be listeners and learners in a profession that has trained them to be talkers and authority figures.

Teachers need to believe that the class absolutely cannot function effectively without sharing ideas and asking new questions. This process is so fundamental that, if used properly, students' observations and questions will connect the curriculum in ways far more subtle, sophisticated and authentic than our own clumsy, agenda-laden efforts to force a vestige of each discipline into every activity. The sophisticated connections that students make are part of a process known as reflexivity (Watson, Burke & Harste, 1989). This process occurs when we apply our knowledge in one area to other areas, making new connections and increasing our understanding of the relationships between knowledge.

Reflexivity differs from reflection. For instance, a child who has studied dinosaurs might reflectively say, "Tyrannosaurus ate Triceratops." The same child might then reflexively say, "Hey, that's like how lions eat zebras." The child has applied a knowledge of one predator/prey relationship to another, making a reflexive connection. For the observant teacher, this is an event to be documented. It is also a wonderful springboard into other questions and research.

Conclusions

My purpose in this article was not to elevate the status of one curricular model at the expense of others; the realities of teaching today often necessitate finding a balance among these and other models. We should, however, have a clear understanding of the implications, applications and characteristics of the curricular models we choose to utilize.

After so much talk of inquiry and other models, it would be appropriate to conclude by mentioning whole language, a model to which inquiry is quite closely related (Harste & Leland, 1994). A fundamental trust in children as capable decision-makers drives the philosophy and practices we call whole language. This same trust also drives inquiry. Belief that children make sense, make connections and seek literacy forms the foundation of whole language, as well as inquiry. Whole language trusts teachers to be autonomous experts capable of valid, authentic assessment and insightful evaluation of developing language strategies. Inquiry demonstrates a trust in teachers to be expert researchers, learners and leaders. So close are these connections and so prevalent are the principles of whole language in other disciplines that many contend it is time for a change to the term whole literacy.

By any name, what I strive for is a democratically constructed curriculum that respects all voices of the learning community; values questions, ideas and opinions; treats assessment and evaluation as a natural part of the learning process; and enables children to feel happy and secure. I am quite certain that the struggle to achieve this matters far more than the achievement itself.

References

Burke, C. (1991, October). *Keynote address*. Paper presented at the Eisenhower Grant Meeting, Columbia, SC.

Harste, J., & Leland, C. (1994). Multiple ways of knowing: Curriculum in a new key. *Journal of Language Arts, 71*(5).

Watson, D., Burke, C., & Harste, J. (1989). *Whole language: Inquiring voices*. New York: Scholastic.

Weaver, C. (1990). *Understanding whole language*. Portsmouth, NH: Heinemann.

ALL ABOUT ME

*Are We Developing Our
Children's Self-Esteem
or Their Narcissism?*

LILIAN G. KATZ

*Lilian G. Katz is professor of early childhood education
at the University of Illinois, director of the ERIC Clearinghouse on Elementary and Early Childhood Education, and president of the National Association for the
Education of Young Children.*

DEVELOPING AND strengthening young children's
self-esteem typically is listed as a major goal in state
and school district kindergarten curriculum guides. Early
childhood education has long been blessed with a variety of curriculum approaches that emphasize and advocate diverse goals and methods. In spite of this diversity,
the one goal all the approaches agree is important is that
of helping children to "feel good about themselves." The
terms applied to this goal include: self-esteem, self-
regard, self-concept, feelings of self-worth, self-confidence, and often, "feeling good about oneself."

For example, in a 1990 document titled "Early Childhood Education and the Elementary School Principal,"
the National Association of Elementary School Principals
issued "Standards for Quality Programs for Young Children." The first of twelve characteristics given for "quality early childhood programs" is that they "develop a positive self-image."[1]

Many other books, kits, packets, and newsletters urge
teachers to help children gain positive self-concepts.
Here's a typical example of this view:

> . . . the basis for *everything we do* is self-esteem.
> Therefore, if we can do something to give children
> a stronger sense of themselves, starting in
> preschool, they'll be [a lot wiser] in the choices
> they make.[2]

Along similar lines, the prestigious Corporation for
Public Broadcasting issued a twenty-page pamphlet,
directed to teenagers, entitled "Celebrate Yourself. Six
Steps to Building Your Self-Esteem."[3] The first main section, "Learn to Love Yourself Again," asserts that, as
babies, we all loved ourselves, but as we grew up, "we
found that not everyone liked everything we did," so we
"started picking on ourselves." The pamphlet lists six
steps toward self-celebration: The first is "Spot Your Self-
Attacks"; The second step, "See What Makes You Special," includes a recommended "Celebration List," suggesting that the reader compile a 22-item list of all the
"good things about me." The twenty-two items recommended under the heading "My Talents" include: thinking fast, playing trivia, and babysitting. The twelve items
under "My Body" include physical attributes such as
smile, hair, strength, legs, etc. Among eight items under
"My Achievements" are: something special I made; a
grade I got; a compliment I got; an award I won; and so
forth. The third step of the celebration is "Attack your
Self-Attacks." The fourth, "Make Loving Yourself a Habit,"
is illustrated by a cartoon character admiring itself in a
mirror. The final two steps are "Go for the Goal" and
"Lend a Hand to Others." This last step is subtitled "Love
Grows When You Give It Away."

It is perhaps just this kind of literature that accounts
for a large poster I came across in the entrance hall of a
suburban school: Pictures of clapping hands surround
the title, "We Applaud Ourselves." While the sign's probable purpose is to help children "feel good about themselves," it does so by directing their attention inward. The
poster urges self-congratulation; it makes no reference to
other possible ways of earning applause—by consider-

From *American Educator,* Summer 1993, pp. 18-23. Reprinted with permission from *American Educator,* the quarterly journal
of the American Federation of Teachers.

ing the feelings or needs of others, for example. Many schools display posters that list the Citizen of the Week, Person of the Week, Super Spellers, Handwriting Awards, and other such honors that seem to encourage showing off.

I also noted a sign over an urban elementary school principal's office that says: "Watch your behavior, you are on display!" Although its purpose may be to encourage appropriate conduct, it does so by directing children's attention to how they *appear* to others rather than to any possible functions of appropriate behavior. What I am suggesting by these examples is, that as commendable as it is for children to have high self-esteem, many of the practices advocated in pursuit of this goal may instead inadvertently develop narcissism in the form of excessive preoccupation with oneself.

It was while observing a first-grade class in an affluent suburb of a large midwestern city that I first became aware of the ways in which self-esteem and narcissism can be confused. Working from dittoed pages prepared by the teacher, each student had produced a booklet called "All about Me." The first page asked for basic information about the child's home and family. The second page was titled "What I like to eat"; the third was called "What I like to watch on TV"; the next was "What I want for a present," and another was "Where I want to go on vacation," and so forth.

On each page, attention was directed toward the child's own inner gratifications. Each topic put the child in the role of consumer—of food, entertainment, gifts, and recreation. Not once was the child asked to assume the role of producer, investigator, initiator, explorer, experimenter, wonderer, or problem-solver.

These booklets, like many others I have encountered around the country, never had pages with titles such as "What I want to know more about," or "What I am curious about," or ". . . want to explore, . . . to find out, . . . to solve, . . . to figure out" or even "to make." Instead of encouraging children to reach out in order to investigate or understand phenomena around them worthy of their attention, the headings of the pages turned their attention inward.

Since first encountering these booklets, I have learned from teachers that the "All about Me" exercise is intended to make children "feel good about themselves" and to motivate them by beginning "where they are." The same intentions, however, could be satisfied in other, better ways. Starting "where children are" can be accomplished by providing topics that (1) encourage children to be curious about others *and* themselves, and, (2) reduce the emphasis on consummatory activities, and (3) at the same time, strengthen the intellectual ethos of the classroom.

Indeed, starting "where the children are" can just as easily be satisfied by pooling class data in a project entitled "All about *Us*." The individual data can be collected, summarized, graphed, compared, and analyzed in a variety of ways that minimize focusing the children's attention exclusively on themselves.

Several years ago, I saw this kind of project put into practice in a rural British infant school. The title of a large display on the bulletin board was: "We Are a Class Full of

Why should children's attention so insistently be turned inward?

Bodies"; just below the main heading was "Here Are the Details." The display space was filled with bar graphs showing birth dates, current weight and height, eye color, number of lost teeth, shoe sizes, etc., in which data from the entire class were pooled. The data started "where the children were." As the children worked in small groups to take measurements, prepare graphs, help one another to post displays of their analyses of the students' individual characteristics, the teacher was able to create an ethos of a community of researchers looking for averages, trends, and ranges.

I observed another example of practices intended to foster self-esteem that may instead contribute to self-preoccupation in a suburban kindergarten in which the comments made by the children about their visit to a dairy farm were displayed on a bulletin board. Each of the forty-seven children's sentences listed on the bulletin board began with the words "I liked. . . ." For example, "I liked the cows," ". . . the milking machine," ". . . the chicks," etc. There were no sentences that began "What surprised me was. . . ," "What I want to know more about is. . . ," or "What I am curious about. . . ."

The children's sentences can be analyzed on many levels. For the purposes of this article, their salient characteristic is the exclusive focus on gratification and the missed opportunity to encourage the natural inclination of children to examine worthwhile phenomena in the world around them. Surely there were features of the farm visit that might have aroused some children's curiosity and sparked further investigations of the real world. Such responses were not solicited and were therefore unlikely to have been appreciated and strengthened.

Another common example of a practice intended to enhance self-esteem but unlikely to do so, was a display of kindergartners' work that consisted of nine large identical paper-doll figures, each having a balloon containing a sentence stem that began "I am special because. . . ." The children completed the sentence with the phrases: ". . . I can color," ". . . I can ride a bike," ". . . I like to play with my friends," ". . . I know how to play," ". . . I am beautiful," ". . . I am learning to read," ". . . I can cut," ". . . everybody makes me happy." These children surely are not likely to believe for very long that they are special because they can color, ride a bike, or like to play. What might these children think when they discover just how trivial these criteria for being special are? The examples described above are not unusual; similar work can be found in schools all over the country.

WHY SHOULD children's attention so insistently be turned inward? Can such superficial flattery really boost self-esteem; and are young children's minds being intellectually engaged by such exercises? Can a child's propensity to explore and investigate worthwhile topics be strengthened by such activities? Is it possible the cumulative effect of such practices, when used frequently, undermines children's perceptions of their teachers as being thoughtful adults, worthy of respect?

Many books and kits for teachers recommend similar exercises that help children "feel good about themselves." One typical example is a booklet with tear-out worksheets called *Building Self-Esteem with Koala-Roo.*[4] One page is bordered by the phrase "YOU ARE SPECIAL!", which appears fourteen times, in capital letters. In the page's upper left-hand corner is a drawing of a smiling koala bear waving one paw, while holding a heart that says "I love you" in the other. The heading on the page is "You Are Special." Below the heading is a line for a child's name following the phrase "You are Special!" again. This is followed by "I am very glad that I have been your X grade teacher." No space is provided for the teacher's own name. This line is followed by text that reads "There's no one else quite like you," "You're one of a kind," "unique," and so forth.

I doubt whether the complete text of the page just described meets the readability index for kindergartners, first graders, or any children young enough to be taken in by such excessive pandering. It would be surprising (and disappointing) if children old enough to read these pages are inspired by their content.

Another example of the genre can be found advertised in a popular teachers' magazine. Titled "Excellence in Early Childhood," the ad promotes a unit of activities called "I Am Special" for 3-, 4- and 5- year-olds. The kit being offered includes a student activity book filled with colorful hands-on projects and illustrated stories, and a teacher guide for twenty-nine lesson plans, stories, and finger plays designed to promote "feeling good abut oneself." In answer to the question of what children will learn from the "I Am Special" kit, the advertisement claims that children "become aware that they are created in a very special and unique way," and "see themselves as good and worthwhile individuals." These illustrations are just two examples from among many similar teaching aids I have seen in early childhood classrooms all over the U.S.

The concept of specialness expressed in these activities seems, by definition, contradictory: If everybody is special, nobody is special. Furthermore, frequent feedback about how special a child is might even raise some doubt along the lines of "Methinks thou dost protest too much"!

In similar fashion, it is not clear whether the traditional "show-and-tell" (or "bring and brag") activity used in traditional early childhood programs does as much to enhance self-esteem as it does to encourage children to be unduly concerned about the impressions they make on others or to learn the techniques of one-upmanship. Many early childhood specialists justify the practice on the grounds that it gives children a chance to practice an early form of public speaking and thereby to strengthen their verbal expressive skills. Some teachers also hope children will sharpen their listening skills as they watch their peers show and tell. However, it is not clear what happens to children who feel that what they have to show and tell cannot compete with their peers' contributions. Furthermore, my observations of such group sessions suggest that more than a few children seem to be tuning out their peers rather than learning to listen to them.

I believe there are other more meaningful and intellectually defensible ways for children to speak to groups of their peers. For example, children can report discoveries and experiences derived from their own efforts, ideas, and real accomplishments.[5]

THE TREND toward overemphasizing self-esteem and self-congratulation may be due to a general desire to correct earlier traditions of eschewing compliments for fear of making children conceited. However, the current practices described above seem to me to be over-corrections of such traditions.

Although there is little doubt that many children arrive at preschool and school with less than optimum self-esteem, telling them otherwise is not likely to have much effect. Feelings cannot be learned from direct instruction. Furthermore, constant messages about how wonderful one is may raise doubts about the credibility of the message and the messenger.

Self-esteem is most likely to be fostered when children have challenging opportunities to build self-confidence and esteem through effort, persistence, and the gradual accrual of skills, knowledge, and appropriate behavior. In addition, adults can show their esteem for children in more significant ways than the awarding of gold stars and happy faces. Esteem is conveyed to children when adults and peers treat them with respect, ask them for their views and preferences (even if they are not acceded to), and provide opportunities for real decisions and choices about those things that matter to the children. Young children's opinions, suggestions, and preferences should be solicited respectfully and considered seriously. To be sure, some children come up with wild or silly notions, and their peers will quickly tell them so. In the course of discussion, however, teachers can gain insight into how children understand the matters at hand and can make sound decisions about which children need their help.

Cheap success in a succession of trivial tasks most likely will not foster self-esteem. Young children are more apt to benefit from real challenge and hard work than from frivolous one-shot activities.

For example, in many early childhood programs, the amount of time and effort given to activities related to holidays seems excessive. Although festive occasions alleviate the routine of daily life, like anything else, they can be overdone. Early childhood educators traditionally have emphasized that play is children's natural way of learning.[6] Indeed, a large body of research and years of practical experience attest to the powerful role of play in all facets of learning in the early years.

It is just as natural, however, for young children to learn through investigation. Children are born natural-and social scientists. Like anthropologists, they devote much time and energy to investigating and making sense of their environments. During the preschool and early school years, teachers can capitalize on this in-born disposition by engaging children in investigations through project work. In-depth investigations of real topics, real environments, events, and objects are worthy of children's attention and understanding.

In the course of such undertakings, children negotiate with their teachers to determine the questions to be answered, the studies to be undertaken, and ways to represent their findings in media such as paintings, drawings, and dramatic play. Project work provides children with ample opportunity for real discussion, decision making, cooperation, initiative, negotiation, compromise, and evaluation of the outcomes of their efforts. In this way, children learn the criteria of self-esteem. This self-esteem can be related to their contribution to the work of the group, to the quality of the effort, and its results.

Most of the tasks offered to young children in early childhood classes allow for individual effort and achievement. However, the interpersonal processes that foster healthy self-esteem require the amount of individual work to be balanced with group work in which each child can contribute to the total group effort through cooperation with other students.

EARLY CHILDHOOD practitioners are right to be diligent in encouraging children through the use of frequent positive feedback. The distinction between praise and flattery is often blurred however. Gushing over a child's fingerpainting may be accepted by the child with pleasure. But, it is difficult to know when frequent praise begins to lose its value and is dismissed by children as empty teacher talk. If children become accustomed to frequent praise, some of them will think its inevitable occasional absence is a rebuke—even when this is not intended. It is difficult for adults to maintain a constant flow of meaningful praise. And, if a child's sense of self-worth can be raised by simple flattery from one person, it just as easily can be deflated by another.

A large body of evidence indicates that children benefit from positive feedback. But, praise and rewards are not the only methods of reinforcement. Another kind of positive feedback is *appreciation*. By appreciation I mean positive reinforcement related explicitly and directly to the *content* of the child's interest and effort. If a child poses a thoughtful question, a teacher might, for example, come to class the next day with a new reference book. Or, she might share with the children ideas generated from reflecting on problems they had raised concerning procedures to try. In these ways, the teacher treats children's concerns with respect, thereby deepening interest in the issues they have raised and providing positive feedback without deflecting children from the content. The important point here is that the teacher shows in a positive way that she appreciates their concerns *without taking their minds off the subjects at hand or directing their attention inwards.* When children see that their concerns and interests are being taken seriously, they are more likely to raise them in the next discussion, and to take their own ideas seriously. Teachers can strengthen children's disposition to wonder, reflect, raise questions, and generate alternative solutions to practical and intellectual problems. Certificates, gold stars, stickers, and trophies also provide children with positive feedback, but the salience of such devices

Cheap success in a succession of trivial tasks most likely will not foster self-esteem.

is likely to deflect the children's and teacher's attention from the content of the work at hand.

Another form of frequent praise stems from teachers' eagerness to reinforce cooperative behavior among young children. Teachers often praise children's efforts by saying such things as "I was really glad when you used your words to get your turn. . . ." or "It made me happy to see you share your wagon with Sally." Such strategies may be helpful when first teaching children how to use verbal strategies for conflict resolution. But, like all strategies, they can be overdone, especially as children reach the preschool years. At issue here is the hypothesis that frequent praise can be taken by children to mean that the praised behavior is not expected—as though the unspoken end of these kinds of elliptical sentences is ". . . because I never expected you to." It may be that children sense our unspoken expectations, and will, indeed, frequently live up to them. Such teacher responses also may imply that the rationale for the desirable behavior is to please the teacher.

It would seem more appropriate for teachers to exercise a quiet and calm authority by stating clearly and respectfully precisely what behavior is expected as occasions arise. Because young children are in the early stages of acquiring interactive and conflict-resolution skills, teachers will have to exercise patience in using this strategy.

ANOTHER APPROACH that teachers might use to make children less dependent upon praise from others is to help them develop and apply their own evaluation criteria.

For example, rather than have children take their work home every day, encourage them to collect it in a special folder or portfolio for a week or so. Then at some point, encourage children to select an item they want to take home and discuss with them the criteria for selection they might apply. The emphasis should not be on whether a child likes a piece of work, or whether it is good or bad. Instead, guide children to think about whether a piece of work includes all they want it to, or whether it is sufficiently clear or accurate, or whether it shows progress compared to the last item they took home, and so forth. At first, parents might be disappointed when the flow of paintings, collages, and worksheets is interrupted; but teachers can help parents to engage their children in fruitful discussion about the criteria of selection used, thus encouraging children to take seriously their own evaluations of their work.

Similarly, when children are engaged with others in project work, they can evaluate the extent to which they have answered the questions they began with, and assess the work accomplished on criteria developed with their teacher concerning the accuracy, completeness, and interest value of their final products.[7] The children should be encouraged to discuss what they might do the next time they undertake an investigation, thus strengthening the propensity to vary their strategies and use their own experience as a source from which to improve their next undertakings. Applying such criteria to their own efforts helps children to become engaged in their work. It also helps them to gain understanding and competence rather than drawing their attention toward themselves or to the image they project to others.

When children are engaged in challenging and significant activities, they are bound to experience some failures, reverses, and rebuffs. Parents and teachers have an important role to play—not in avoiding such events—but in helping children cope constructively when they fail to get what they want—whether it's a turn with a toy or success at a task. In such incidents, the teacher can say something like "I know you're disappointed, but there's tomorrow, and you can try again." As long as the teacher accepts a child's feelings and responds respectfully, the child is more likely to learn from the incident than to be harmed by it. Children are able to cope with rebuffs, disappointments, and failures when adults acknowledge and accept their feelings of discouragement and at the same time tell children they can try again another time.

Another approach is to teach children how to use what they have learned from their own experiences as a source of encouragement. A teacher might, for example, help a child recall an earlier incident when he or she struggled with a task or situation and eventually mastered it.

Learning to deal with setbacks, and maintaining the persistence and optimism necessary for childhood's long and gradual road to mastery: These are the real foundations of lasting self-esteem. Children who are helped to develop these qualities will surely respect themselves—though they probably will have better things to think about.

References

[1] National Association of Elementary School Principals. 1990. *Early Childhood Education and the Elementary School Principal. Standards for Quality Programs for Young Children.* Arlington, Va.: NAESP.

[2] Sandy McDaniel quoted in "Political Priority #1: Teaching Kids to Like Themselves," *New Options,* issue no. 27, April 28, 1986.

[3] Corporation for Public Broadcasting. 1991. *Celebrate Yourself. Six Steps to Building Your Self-Esteem.* Washington, D.C.: Corporation for Public Broadcasting.

[4] Femdel, L. and B. Ecker. 1989. *Building Self-Esteem with Koala-Roo.* Glencoe, Ill.: Scott, Foresman and Co.

[5] Katz, L.G. and S.C. Chard. 1989. *Engaging Children's Minds: The Project Approach.* Norwood, N.J.: Ablex Publishing Corp.

[6] Isenberg, J. and N.L. Quisenberry. 1988. *Play: A Necessity for All Children.* A position paper of the Association for Childhood Education International. Wheaton, Md.: Association for Childhood Education International.

[7] Katz and Chard, op. cit.

A Framework for Literacy

Don't try to <u>tell</u> them – <u>show</u> them just exactly what whole language really is

MARY HOPKIN

Mary Hopkin teaches at the Saudi Arabia International Schools, Dhahran, Saudi Arabia.

In the May 1995 issue of *Teaching K-8*, Maryann and Gary Manning highlighted the most difficult obstacle to whole language implementation: the education of parents and other concerned stakeholders as to just what whole language is and what it's not.

> *On pages 197–198, two reproducible pages you can use that will show your children and their parents how specific learning tasks evolve into literacy.*

Parents, as well as some educators, are confused by whole language because they can't quite grasp how it fits into the existing structure to which they've grown accustomed. They hear so many conflicting defin- itions and criticisms that they're hesitant to accept this common-sense approach to teaching literacy, no matter how strongly enthusiastic teachers advocate it.

No easy task. As the Mannings point out, the task of whole language advocates is to articulate the whole language philosophy in user-friendly terms within the context of a reasoned and logical instructional frame- work. This is no easy task.

After many attempts to discuss the mer- its of whole language with colleagues and parents, a group of my comrades-in-arms and I put our heads together and developed a schematic framework to present the phi- losophy in a clear, succinct format. The framework has become a practical, function- al tool for use throughout the curriculum implementation process. The more we use it, the more uses we find for it. It is presently:

1. a process-productive instrument kept in the student's portfolio and used by the students themselves to observe and docu- ment their learning in process;

2. a tool used in conferencing to focus par- ticipants on the student's learning occur- ring within the context of our specified expectations;

Schematic A – The Flow

Belief Statement → Program Outcomes → Integrated Topics → Specific Objectives → Exhibitions of Literacy

Reprinted with permission from *Teaching K-8*, October 1995, pp. 52-56. © 1995 by Early Years, Inc., Norwalk, CT 06854.

Schematic B – Translating Beliefs into Expected Program Outcomes

Belief statement: "We believe that literacy enhances personal career achievement and provides a source of enrichment and joy in life."

The Language Arts Curriculum Overview: Early Stages Through Elementary Fluency

The central focus of our elementary literacy program is the broad curricular area which we call language arts. The language arts consist of the development of reading, speaking, listening and writing skills, and are integrated with all other curricular subjects. A variety of resources are utilized in the process of learning to construct meaning from language, including periodicals, textbooks, reference books, children's experiences and thoughts, technology and a large collection of children's literature.

READING OUTCOMES: EARLY STAGES THROUGH ELEMENTARY FLUENCY

Language Development

As a result of our language arts program, we expect our students to:
> enjoy shared reading experiences
> acquire adequate vocabulary
> relate sounds to letters
> use contextual clues
> construct meaning from text

Emergent Reading

As a result of our language arts program, we expect our students to:
> enjoy shared reading experiences
> decode new words
> read orally with consequence
> detect sequences
> predict outcomes
> experience the making of books
> understand the relationship of reading to writing and thinking

Reading Fluency

As a result of our language arts program, we expect our students to:
> share reading for pleasure
> enjoy a variety of literature
> read with expression/clarity
> draw logical conclusions
> identify main ideas
> locate/research data
> read for both information gathering and pleasure

WRITING OUTCOMES: EARLY STAGES THROUGH ELEMENTARY FLUENCY

Pre-Writing Skills

As a result of our language arts program, we expect our students to:
> develop fine motor coordination
> form letters in conventional ways
> relate sounds to letters
> experience thoughts written down
> experience teacher model-writing

Emergent Writing

As a result of our language arts program, we expect our students to:
> use sight words appropriately
> use spelling approximations
> space words correctly
> write legibly
> write short sentences
> sequence written ideas logically

Writing Fluency

As a result of our language arts program, we expect our students to:
> generate ideas to communicate
> write first draft
> revise/edit first draft
> use conventional spelling, grammar and punctuation
> publish final draft
> write for particular audiences

LISTENING AND SPEAKING OUTCOMES: EARLY STAGES THROUGH ELEMENTARY FLUENCY

Sharing Information

As a result of our language arts program, we expect our students to:
> participate in group discussions
> communicate ideas with clarity
> respond appropriately in discussions
> follow and relay oral directions
> enjoy sharing in the group process

Critical Listening

As a result of our language arts program, we expect our students to:
> follow oral directions
> draw logical conclusions
> distinguish facts
> analyze oral information
> evaluate oral information
> listen selectively for main ideas

Speaking Fluency

As a result of our language arts program, we expect our students to:
> use expressive words
> articulate words and thoughts
> present information with clarity
> communicate effectively
> demonstrate self-confidence and poise in group speaking

3. a tool to orient new members quickly to our mission, values and instructional goals, and the direction we are moving in order to get there;
4. a documentation tool which ensures that our transferring students have a clear and accurate record of their achievements within our specified curriculum framework.

More of the same. The first time we sat down with a group of parents and presented our process tool, the sense of reassurance and understanding on their faces brought us an enormous sense of pride and satisfaction. And when we presented the framework to our colleagues, their predictable reaction was, "Well, what else is new? We've been doing this for years." Exactly. Of course we

Schematic C – Grade 3 Integrated Curriculums

The theme for the year is *Voyages from Past to Present*. The theme was chosen for its flexibility in allowing maximum integration across the curriculum. After reviewing the instructional topics offered in grades 2 and 4, the grade 3 team identified the following thematic topics for the 1995-96 school year. The chosen topics provide continuity from grade 2 and preparation for grade 4. The five boldfaced headings below represent the major topics for the year; the activities and content listed below the headings relate to the curriculum outcomes specified for grade 3 (*Schematic D*).

Traveling Through Time
Our Planet
The oceans
Land forms
Rocks/fossils/minerals
Making a timeline
Weather
Matter and composition
Civilization
Early communities
Needs of people
Ancient civilizations
Simple machines
Explorations
Keeping a journal
Bartering and money
Telling time
Great explorers
The Mayflower voyage
Settling in the New Regions
Getting along
Historical fiction
Remembering the past
Early schools

Folktales Around the World
Historical Perspectives
Origins of folktales
Fun and fanciful tales
Folklore
International communities
Geographical Perspectives
Locating countries on maps
and globes
Seasons
Winter diorama
A snow day
Writing short stories
Human Needs
Families and friends
Giving and receiving
Expressions of thought
writing poetry
writing short stories
reading for pleasure
telling stories
Celebrations and holidays
international feast

Fact or Fiction
Shared Inquiry
Research skills
Making timelines
Measurement
Geometric shapes
Multiplication/division
True-to-life fiction
Sharing novels
Problem solving
Collaborative projects
Independent Research
Locating information
Information Processing
Drawing conclusions
Critical Thinking
Analyzing oral information
Evaluating information
Identifying facts
Developing strategies for
solving problems
Listening selectively
Presenting ideas
Revisiting Fantasy

Our World Today
Research Projects
Using reference tools
Collecting data
Organizing data
Recording data
Writing essays
Reading non-fiction
Reading statistics
Using decimals/fractions
Using graphs/tables
Applying critical thinking
Sharing information
Making observations
Recording observations
Global Responsibility
Eco-systems
Endangered species
Habitats

Adaptation
Climate
Problem-solving
Map-making
Earth Day

Planning for Our Future
Being a person
Body systems
Health and nutrition
Emotions and stress
Adaptation
People We Admire
Autobiographies
Biographies
Our Personal Best
Presentations/exhibitions
Personal responsibility
Making choices
literature
writing
presentations
Assessing the Year
Taking achievement tests
Portfolio review

have! Now let's do more of the same and document that we're doing it.

Although the framework has evolved into a more refined and functional tool through the years, it remains my most trusted strategy in convincing skeptics that whole language isn't just a frivolous waste of valuable instructional time, but is instead a way of looking at our curriculum and what we do in terms of our literacy goals and just what our expectations are for the students as a result of our interaction with them.

Schematics A, B, C and D are parts of the framework I share with parents and new teachers. We begin by defining the framework in terms of observable program expectations (*Schematic A*). In other words, what do we expect our students to be able to do in this broad area we call literacy (*Schematic B*)? Only after we have defined what it is can we integrate our beliefs into our instructional program (*Schematic C*). Finally, we want parents and students to see specific learning tasks evolving into literacy through practical applications of language experiences (*Schematic D*).

The schematics clearly and succinctly define our beliefs, our program outcome

Schematic D – Specific Learning Objectives

We believe that literacy enhances personal and career achievement, and provides a source of enrichment and joy in life. ***Language Arts Curricular Outcomes*** ***This Is What I Can Do in Grade Three***	*My Name* *My Class* *The Day I Began* *The Day I Finished*

On the Way to Reading Fluency

R 1 Specific Reading Outcomes	Date	I Can Do It!	I Saw You Do It!
R 1.1 *I enjoy listening to chapter stories.*			
R 1.2 *I choose to read independently.*			
R 1.3 *I choose to explore unfamiliar resources.*			
R 1.4 *I share creatively about books I have read.*			
R 1.5 *I share my feelings about books.*			
R 1.6 *I can re-tell stories in sequence.*			
R 1.7 *I can recall facts from informational books.*			
R 1.8 *I can re-read for details.*			
R 1.9 *My English language experience is OK for reading.*			
R1 .10 *I recognize the basic sight words.*			
R1 .11 *I enjoy reading a variety of literature.*			
R 2 Oral Reading Fluency			
R 2.1 *When I read aloud, I observe punctuation.*			
R 2.2 *I read with confidence and expression.*			
R 3 Reading Attitudes			
R 3.1 *I choose to read because I enjoy reading.*			
R 3.2 *I can select books that I enjoy and can read.*			
R 3.3 *I like to share reading materials with others.*			

On the Way to Writing Fluency

W1 The Conventions of Handwriting	Date	I Can Do It!	I Saw You Do It!
W 1.1 *I can form letters correctly.*			
W 1.2 *I can join letters correctly in cursive writing.*			
W 1.3 *I can space my words correctly.*			
W 1.4 *I write so others can read what I have to say.*			
W 2 The Conventions of Punctuation in Writing			
W 2.1 *I can use capital letters at the right times.*			
W 2.2 *I can use periods at the right times.*			
W 3.3 *I can use commas at the right times.*			

(Continued on next page)

expectations, how we integrate our topics and the way we involve our learners in their own learning.

The final products are the student's personal exhibitions of learning, the portfolio of achievement. Our whole language framework shows an obvious link between our mission and beliefs and the processes in place to provide the opportunities for our students to achieve literacy competence and fluency.

Writing Fluency *continued from page 197*

The Conventions of Punctuation (continued)	Date	I Can Do It!	I Saw You Do It!
W 2.4 I can use question marks at the right times.			
W 2.5 I can use exclamation marks when I need to.			
W 2.6 I can use quotation marks at the right times.			
W 3 The Conventions of Spelling in Writing			
W 3.1 I follow phonetic rules when they work.			
W 3.2 I can use basic sight words.			
W 3.3 I can use a dictionary or spell check to check.			
W 4 Creative Writing			
W 4.1 I can pre-plan my writing tasks.			
W 4.2 I can sequence my ideas logically.			
W 4.3 I can form paragraphs with main ideas.			
W 4.4 I can use interesting and colorful words.			
W 4.5 I can proofread and edit my first drafts.			
W 4.6 I can write short stories.			

On the Way to Listening Competency

L. 1 Specific Listening Skills	Date	I Can Do It!	I Saw You Do It!
L 1.1 I enjoy listening to my teacher read.			
L 1.2 I enjoy listening to my classmates read.			
L 1.3 I listen attentively when my teacher talks.			
L 1.4 I listen attentively when my classmates talk.			
L 1.5 I follow instructions.			
L 1.6 I enjoy talking in a small group.			
L 1.7 I enjoy participating in large group discussions.			
L 1.8 I enjoy a variety of listening activities.			

On the Way to Speaking Fluency

S 1 Specific Speaking Skills	Date	I Can Do It!	I Saw You Do It!
S 1.1 I like to give information to others.			
S 1.2 I like to talk to my teacher.			
S 1.3 I like to talk with other students.			
S 1.4 I speak with appropriate grammar.			
S 1.5 I can speak my thoughts fluently and confidently.			

General Observations and Comments

Read me a story: 101 good books kids will love

Experts agree that there are many benefits to reading to children. One important one: It takes time to read a book. What better gift can we give a child than time?

By **Joan Garvey Hermes**, *the mother of six and a freelance writer who also teaches English at Bishop McNamara High School in Kankakee, Illinois.*

We've made many mistakes raising our children—on a family vacation several years ago we left two of them behind in a Pizza Hut in Minocqua, Wisconsin, a fact that is still the subject of many a guilt trip. But I know we've done one thing right. We read to them.

Goodnight Moon, The Fuzzy Duckling—the list of books we read would be familiar to many young parents; so would our motives for reading: We love books, and we wanted to share this love with our children. We enjoyed the quiet time a book provided, and, at day's end, we liked the ritual of bath, books, prayers, and bed for them—followed by some time alone for us.

As time passed and our son and daughters grew and changed, our reasons for reading to them did the same. We still enjoyed the quiet time, but something else was added. The books we read often enhanced Tom's or Maggie's pleasure in the things he or she had seen that day. Sometimes the very titles Annie or Kate would choose would give us, as parents, a clue to something that had been important to them that day. Martha and Molly, as did their older siblings before them, would often find, in books, a certain comfort to soothe a worry or hurt that had been part of their day.

Much has been written about the value of books. Reading books and being read to at an early age develops literacy, enhances vocabulary and grammar skills, instructs the reader about the world close at hand and far away, and encourages creativity and imagination. Being read to establishes a never-to-be-forgotten sense of security in providing a ritual, a period of time during which a child and reader sit together and attend to a story.

As I look back over the years of reading, being read to, and reading to, I remember many of the books that are part of me as a result of these experiences. It gives me pleasure to think of the many books that are also part of our children's histories.

Most of us read to our children for the sheer fun of it. It gives us pleasure to pass on to our children the stories we loved when we were their age. We enjoy discovering with them stories that are new to us and them. Often, too, a story can say for us the things we feel inadequate to express in our own words. Even those who are not big readers themselves choose to read to their children because educators stress the benefits of reading, particularly early reading, to children. There are also subtle reasons to read to our children, and these are perhaps the most important of all.

When we read, we have to slow down. We gather our child or children to ourselves, and we spend time with them. We give, they receive. Sometimes they give as they make their own observations about the story being read. We establish a ritual, and rituals provide security. We establish a tradition, and this leads to another important reason to read to our children.

Parents pass a culture to their children. As parents we do this whether we want to or not. What we choose to do, or not to do, conveys a message to our children. When we read to our children, we teach them that they are important to us. Books are a relatively inexpensive treat, and public libraries provide them for free. But we do spend time when we read. It takes time to sit down to read a book. What better gift can we give our child than the gift of time?

Because books teach as they are enjoyed, they provide a near perfect way to say what is important to us. Children might soon lose interest in a lecture about the importance of honesty or kindness, yet they will spend hours listening to stories.

Reading provides an oasis in a world too busy and too active at times to stop and take note of what really matters. This, too, is why it continues to be of value to read to our children long after they have learned to read themselves. Two years ago when one daughter in our house was making her way through Ray Bradbury's *Fahrenheit 451*, I read the book to her. As an honors English student, she was more than capable of reading the book herself, but we enjoyed moving through it together and talking about the ideas. I hope that experience remains for her as pleasant as it does for me. And I am sure there are older parents who continue, as mine do when we talk on the phone or visit, to say, "What are you reading?" or "Have you read . . . ?" While we can no longer curl up on the couch together, we can still share our love of books and the ideas they hold.

Perhaps the best reason for reading to children is the reason that motivates our own reading as well: We read because it is good for the soul. . . . Reading can remind us that we are not alone in thinking certain values are important. They can put us in the presence of families who are working to be good people. Books can remind us that it is important to be kind, accepting, and to stand up for what is right.

Feel free to browse

What follows is a look at books for children. . . . Books are subtle. They can teach without preaching. The titles have been chosen in a less-than-scientific manner. I began and ended my research at my children's bookshelves. I also spent time in the juvenile sections of Stuart Brent and Waterstone's bookstores in Chicago, and I spoke with lovers of books—adult friends of mine and the high-school students I teach.

One thing to bear in mind: I hold a prejudice so deeply seated that it feels like a universal truth that books and television are mutually exclusive. Period. A family that truly enjoys books will keep television viewing to such a minimum that it will be virtually nonexistent. It's difficult to maintain the attention of a toddler who has been raised on a diet of images that change every few seconds. It is virtually impossible to expect a child of early school age to settle in with a book and adapt to the challenge of following the words if that child has grown accustomed to receiving his or her entertainment in a passive manner. Turn off the television.

A second point. Children's books come with a recommended reading level. While this idea is well intentioned, it can be a mistake. Author Robertson Davies said it best in his speech "The Conscience of a Writer." "There are," Davies says, "no absolutes in literature that can be applied without reference to personal taste and judgment. The great book for you is the book that has the most to say to you at the moment when you are reading. I do not mean the book that is the most instructive, but the book that feeds your spirit. And that depends on your age, your experience, your psychological and spiritual need."

Taking this into account, then, the books that follow have been loosely grouped into even looser categories, and these categories overlap. Books have been listed from younger to older readers, starting with books that are often read aloud to children, continuing to the junior-high-school level, after which point we can assume that the child is making almost all reading choices fairly autonomously.

Listen, my children

It is possible to read to a very small child. Children old enough to sit in a lap can look at pictures as the pages of a book are turned for them. This establishes a ritual and teaches the skill of sitting while looking at brightly colored pictures. While the littlest readers may not understand the actual words themselves, the ritual of words and their rhythm is a wonderful introduction to reading. Little children love the idea of ritual. Equally important to them is security.

Children also have an early aesthetic sense and can enjoy the feel, texture, and color of a book at a very young age. Anyone who has observed a baby playing endlessly with his or her fingers and toes knows that this person has a developing capacity for enjoying intellectual stimulation. The following books are colorful, pleasant to look at, repetitive in tone, and provide a chance to look at the world inside and out of the house.

Goodnight Moon by Margaret Wise Brown: A little bunny says goodnight to the familiar objects in his room. *Pat the Bunny*, a tactile "look" at the child's world by Dorothy Kunhardt. *Each Peach, Pear, Plum* by Janet and Allan Ahlberg, with its charming illus-

trations and rhymes, invites a baby to play a game of "I Spy." *Are You My Mother?* by Philip D. Eastman and *A House Is a House for Me* by Mary Ann Hoberman: repetition promotes a sense of security. *Peter's Chair* (which also deals with the arrival of a new baby), *The Snowy Day*, and almost any book by Ezra Jack Keats use colorful yet gentle illustrations that put a child in a world of people doing pleasant things together and on their own. *The Baby* by John Burningham and *Grandmother and I* by Helen E. Buckley give a look at family members young and old. . . .

Finally, the following classics need little description. Their longevity is testimony enough to the fact that they answer a need in the children to whom they are read: *Scuffy the Tugboat* by Gertrude Crampton (Scuffy is also brave and resourceful), *Tawny, Scrawny Lion* by Kathryn Jackson and *Saggy, Baggy Elephant, Poky Little Puppy* by Janet S. Lowrey, *The Little Engine That Could* by Watty Piper ("I think I can, I think I can . . ."), *Carrot Seed* by Ruth Krauss, and *Harold and the Purple Crayon* by Crockett Johnson.

The Runaway Bunny by Margaret Wise Brown should be in a category all by itself because this one does it all. A little bunny asks what his mother would do were he to run away. With beautiful words and even more beautiful illustrations, she convinces him that there is no place on earth he could go that she would not be there to protect him. An all time favorite. Brown has also given us the ultrasatisfying *Home for a Bunny*. Another type of book that can be included in a selection of books for babies is any Mother Goose book. Children love the security of repetition and the humor inherent in these rhymes. These books act as a child's first introduction to poetry. Choose your own favorites—two from this house are *Classic Mother Goose* and an edition illustrated by Tomie de Paola.

Very first reading experiences will include titles that will change depending on the child being read to. Parents are advised not to discount books that have some story line. Many times the pleasure of the rhythm of the words means as much to a child as would knowing their literal meaning. Books without words can be enjoyed by a child who enjoys time alone with books. The following books provide a way for a child to "read" on his or her own, but can be enjoyed with an adult as well: *Babies* by Gyo Fujikawa, *The Snowman* by Raymond Briggs, *Seasons* by

Once upon a time

THE FOLLOWING STORIES are timeless and appealing because they are both comforting and empowering. Good is rewarded and evil punished; size and age mean nothing if one is clever; magic is possible. These stories come in many forms, with varied text and illustrations. A subtle benefit of folk tales is the window they provide into different cultures.

Paul Galdone:
The Three Bears
The Three Little Pigs
Peter Asbjornsen:
The Three Billy Goats Gruff
Marcia Brown:
Stone Soup
Robert McCloskey:
Andy and the Lion
(an updated version of the traditional *Androcles and the Lion*).
Wanda Gag:
Millions of Cats
Esphyr Slobodkina:
Caps for Sale
The Brothers Grimm:
Bremen Town Musicians
Rumpelstiltskin
Shoemaker and the Elves

Charles Perrault:
Little Red Riding Hood
Cinderella
Ezra Jack Keats:
Over in the Meadow
Jacob Grimm:
Frog Prince
Hans Christian Anderson:
The Ugly Duckling
The Princess and the Pea
The Emperor's New Clothes
Thumbelina
Arlene Mosel:
Tikki Tikki Tembo
Oscar Wilde:
The Selfish Giant
Peter Parnall:
The Great Fish
Arthur Ransome:
The Fool of the World and the Flying Ship
Margot Zemach:
It Could Always Be Worse
Harve Zemach:
Salt: A Russian Tale
William Steig:
Caleb and Katie
The Amazing Bone
Brave Irene
Tiffky Doofky
Gerald McDermott:
Anansi the Spider: A Tale from Ashanti
Tomie de Paola:
The Legend of the Indian Paintbrush
The Legend of the Bluebonnet
The Legend of Old Befana

John Burningham, *Ah-Choo* by Mercer Mayer (and also by Mayer, *Four Frogs in a Box* and *A Boy, a Dog, a Frog, and a Friend*), *Deep in the Forest* by Brinton Turkle (a twist on the story of the three bears), *Blackboard Bear* by Martha Alexander, and *Moonlight* by Jan Ormerod, a delightful look at a family putting a reluctant child to bed.

Relative adjustments

The following books present young children with loving and sometimes imperfect families. In *Go and Hush the Baby* by Betsy Byars, Will hushes the baby with a cookie and a story among other things, before the baby finally falls asleep. *Jeremy Isn't Hungry* by Barbara Williams shows how a big brother "helps" his harried mother by looking after baby brother Jeremy. *A Birthday for Frances* and *Bedtime for Frances* by Russell Hoban— time spent in the company of this very human little-girl badger is time well spent and never to be forgotten. In these two favorites, Frances prepares for her sister's birthday and for bed respectively. *Big Brother* by Charlotte Zolotow is dependably satisfying, as are all Zolotow's books. *And My Mean Old Mother Will Be Sorry, Blackboard Bear* by Martha Alexander and *Someday, Said Mitchell* by Barbara Williams give us children who are angry, but know they are loved. Maurice Sendak's classic *Where the Wild Things Are* does the same, and perhaps the paradigm of this type is William Steig's *Spinky Sulks*. When Spinky gets teased one time too often, he takes to his hammock until his family's love is proved to his satisfaction.

Papa Small is a classic Lois Lenski look at a father. *Lyle, Lyle Crocodile* by Bernard Waber continues the adventures of Lyle and his adopted human family from *The House on East Eighty-Eighth Street* and *Lyle Finds His Mother*, which reunites this fetching crocodile with his biological mother. Beverly Cleary's *Two Dog Biscuits* gives us ordinary children and an ordinary day, and the beauty of *Owl Moon* by Jane Yolen lies in its ability to take us with an ordinary parent and child as they experience the extraordinary beauty of a perfect night for "owling."

Sylvester and the Magic Pebble by William Steig gives us a donkey whose parents are reunited with him even though he has been transformed into a rock, and Rosemary Well's *Hazel's Amazing Mother* gives us a mother who acts for mothers everywhere

> While the littlest readers may not understand the actual words themselves, the ritual of words and their rhythm is a wonderful introduction to reading.

when she swoops down on some nasty little children who are tormenting her beloved Hazel. Finally *Fay and Delores* by Barbara Samuels are two appealingly human sisters.

Hey, what about me?

All children need acceptance. The following books introduce the reader to families and friends who come to accept someone. Perhaps the classic case of the need for acceptance can be seen in sibling rivalry. In *A Baby Sister for Frances*, Russell Hoban, lets us watch Frances as she comes to love baby sister Gloria. *Alexander and the Terrible, Horrible, No Good, Very Bad Day* and *I'll Fix Anthony* are two Judith Viorst tales to which any siblings can relate. *I'll Be the Horse If You'll Play With Me* and *Nobody Asked Me If I Wanted a Baby Sister* by Martha Alexander show older and younger-aged children respectively as they adjust to the problems and pleasures of living with a sibling. And no look at sibling rivalry would be complete without (my favorite) Rosemary Well's *Noisy Norah*. You simply must meet Norah, an absolutely gorgeous little spitfire of a mouse who does what it takes to get the familial attention she needs.

Other kinds of acceptance within the family can be seen in *Poinsettia and Her Family* by Felicia Bond, wherein a little pig from an overcrowded house comes to see her family is not so bad to have around; *Dinner at Alberta's* by Russell Hoban, with a funny family who accommodate one another, as do family members at William's House in Charlotte Zolotow's *William's Doll*.

Leo the Late Bloomer by Robert Kraus and *Gregory the Terrible Eater* by Mitchell Sharmat give us a lion whose parents love him enough to accept him as he is and a goat who reaches a compromise with his loving parents. In *Fish Is Fish*, Leo Lionni advises self-acceptance as a fish learns this important truth. *Thy Friend Obadiah* by Brinton Turkle has Obadiah, the charming little Nantucket Quaker who reluctantly befriends a ubiquitous seagull, just as Molly's friend in Kay Charao's *Molly's Lies* befriends the little kindergartner and thus inspires her to stop fibbing. *Ferdinand* by Munro Lief is the sweet, classic story of a gentle bull, and *Oliver Button Is a Sissy* by Tomie de Paola gives us Oliver who, having been teased for taking dance lessons, shows his schoolmates that those lessons can be impressive.

Acceptance can sometimes take the form of forgiveness. Kevin Henkes' *Chrysanthemum* is a sweet little mouse who loves her name, until classmates make fun of it. They get their comeuppance, though, and Chrysanthemum is gracious about it. Again, Maurice Sendak's *Where the Wild Things Are* features Max, who, while wearing his wolf suit, is sent to bed by his mother, yet it all works out in the end. I hope Richard Scarry's book *The Naughty Bunny* is still in print. It tells the story of a bunny who puts his mother through a harrowing day. Of course she forgives him. And the paradigm for all of us who need forgiveness is the beloved *Curious George*.

Though there are some pallid later versions, the original H. A. Rey books—*Curious George Rides a Bike* and the first title above—must be on every child's bookshelf. There is nothing this adventuresome little monkey will not try, and the man in the yellow hat forgives him unconditionally. You'll also want to make the acquaintance of Oliver and Amanda pig in Jan Van Leeuwen's *Oliver Pig at School*. Children can read Else Holmeskund Minarick's *Little Bear* books to themselves or enjoy them with an adult. *No Fighting! No Biting!* by the same author encourages a gentler approach to living. Wendell, in Kevin Henkes' *A Weekend With Wendell*, isn't easy to love as he teases and torments his hosts for the weekend, but his hostess comes to find him endearing. You will, too.

Mole and Troll by Tony Johnston and *Frog and Toad* by Arnold Lobel are great friends, as are *George and Martha*, a hippopotamus couple from James Marshall. Tomie de Paola's *Bill and Pete*, a crocodile and his little bird friend, are not to be missed; neither are *Strega Nona*, de Paola's little "grandma witch" and Big Anthony, her helper, who is in constant need of forgiveness. . . .

And they all lived happily . . .

As children grow and move a bit away from the protective circle of home and family, they have a need to feel competent. Children like to be reminded that things usually turn out just fine in the long run. . . . Here are some books that place our children in the presence of people, things, and animals who are making their way successfully through the world. *Frederick* is Leo Lionni's little mouse who provides for his fellow mice by giving them something they didn't know they needed. *Swimmy* by the same author tells the story of one tiny black fish, who, united with his fellow fish, finds strength and protection.

Virginia Lee Burton gives us *Katy and the Big Snow*, wherein a valiant little snowplow digs an entire town out after a blizzard. I have memorized the words to Burton's *Mike Mulligan and His Steam Shovel*, having read it almost daily to a parade of children eager to hear one more time how Mike and his machine dug the cellar of the new town hall in record time. Ivan Sherman's *I Am Giant* reminds the reader of just how powerful a little girl giant can be. William Steig's *Brave Irene* delivers a dress for her ailing seamstress mother despite the obstacle of a raging blizzard. *Lentil* saves the day for Robert McCloskey's town filled with people waiting to welcome home a local hero.

McCloskey has given us so many unforgettable books. The mallard family in his *Make Way for Ducklings* has become so famous that Boston's Public Gardens have a statue of them. *Blueberries for Sal* ends happily despite the crisis of mistaken identities that happens when a mother bear and Sal's mother unknowingly swap offspring. *One Morning in Maine* features this same family. A tooth has been lost, then lost again, but all works for the best in the end.

Parents will love *Oh Were They Ever Happy!* by Peter Spier, which tells the tale of thoughtful children painting the house while the parents are gone for the day. Mercer Mayer's Little Critter runs into a little trouble himself when he tries to help out in *Just For You*. Don Freeman gives us a little bear who solves a problem in *A Pocket for Corduroy*.

Marjorie Flack's classic *The Story About Ping* takes us to China, where we meet Ping as he is separated from, and reunited with, his family. In *A Bargain for Frances*, Hoban brings Frances back again, this time to solve the problem of a friend who has tricked Frances out of her favorite tea set. Shel Silverstein's *The Missing Piece* finds its soul mate. The little boy in his book *The Giving Tree* finds wisdom. And James Marshall's Miss Nelson, from several titles beginning with *Miss Nelson is Missing*, finds a way to discipline her unruly class of school children when she must be away from school.

The illustrations in Lore Segal's *Tell Me a Mitzi* are unusual yet captivating in this series of stories, the first one following Mitzi

> Children like to be reminded that things usually turn out just fine in the long run.

In times of trouble

Some things are too painful to talk about. Watching others move through similar situations can provide comfort.

Death:

Nana Upstairs, Nana Downstairs by Tomie de Paola

The Tenth Good Thing about Barney by Judith Viorst

The Dead Bird by Margaret Wise Brown

Living with a single parent:

Mushy Eggs Adrienne Adams

I Love My Mother by Paul Zindel

A Father Like That by Charlotte Zolotow

Illness:

The Sick Story by Linda Hirsch

A Visit to the Hospital by Francine Chase

Just Awful by Alma Whitney

War:

Potatoes, Potatoes by Anita Lobel

War and Peas by Michael Foreman

Millions of Cats by Wanda Gag. The best of the best—not to be missed.

Brave Soldier Janosh by Victor Ambrus

Drummer Hoff by Barbara Emberley

---

as she puts in a full day's work before her parents are even out of bed. *Mr. Popper's Penguins* by Richard and Florence Atwater has captivated children for ages as it follows the ups and downs of Mr. Popper as he tends to these creatures. The idea of caring for something or someone is beautifully realized in Lynn Reid Bank's series featuring *The Indian in the Cupboard*. Omri discovers that a cabinet he has received is magic as the plastic toy he has placed inside it comes to life. The three books that follow Omri and his magic cupboard are not to be missed.

Perfect the Pig by Susan Jeschke provides magic of another sort as we watch Perfect, a lovely little winged pig, get stolen and reunited with his friend Opal. *Lost in the Storm* reunites a boy and his dog after an island storm. *Left Behind* by Carol Carrick reunites a boy with his classmates after they become separated on a class trip. Well before its time is Marjorie Flack's *The Easter Bunny and the Little Gold Shoes*. Not only is this feminine Easter Bunny able to provide a kindness for a sick little boy, but she has filled her position only after overcoming social

prejudice and managing to get her household of numerous little bunnies in order by giving them all household chores to tend to.

Another wonderful role model with a slightly older reading level is Carol Ryrie Brink's *Caddie Woodlawn*. Caddie is brave, resourceful, and compassionate as she grows up in her native Wisconsin. Like Laura Ingalls Wilder's wonderful *Little House* books, Brink's book is based on family history. . . .

The end never comes

Books take us out of ourselves to a world we might not otherwise see. They introduce us to people worth meeting. They put us in the presence of virtues worth imitating. The youngest child can enjoy a book, and that very book, enjoyed before even the first day of school, may speak to the child on such a profound level that it comes to mind years later when it is needed. Children will lead us, and later lead themselves, to the books that speak to them. These will stay with them forever.

Early Childhood Physical Education:

Providing the Foundation

Arlene Ignico

Arlene Ignico is an associate professor of elementary physical education at Ball State University, Muncie, IN 47306.

Preschool educators must provide children with developmentally appropriate motor skill instruction in an effort to build a foundation for successful participation in later childhood and adult physical activities.

A developmentally appropriate curriculum for preschool children provides experiences which encourage development in the psychomotor, affective, and cognitive areas. If any of these areas has been neglected in the past, it is perhaps the psychomotor area. Historically, early childhood educational programs have focused more on academic readiness skills and less on motor skill instruction. Psychomotor goals have been addressed by providing learning centers with gender stereotypical play equipment (e.g., kitchens, dolls, fire trucks, tools), sandboxes, and swings. Recently, however, many positive changes have been taking place in preschools throughout the nation as a result of the efforts of several professional organizations.

Among the recommendations proposed by the National Association for the Education of Young Children (Bredekamp, 1987), the Council on Physical Education for Children (COPEC) (1994), and U.S. Department of Health and Human Services (1992) is to provide physical education for students enrolled in preschool programs. This recommendation is based in part on the assumptions that

school physical education assures a minimum amount of physical activity for children and that it encourages continued physical activity beyond the school years. It is based also on the evidence that physical activity is essential for children to develop an understanding of the movement concepts and to refine skills such as striking, jumping, and balancing (Bredekamp, 1987; COPEC, 1994).

Perhaps more convincing is the evidence suggesting that school physical education programs for young children can have a significant, positive effect on children's fundamental motor skill performances (Ignico, 1992a, 1992b) and health-related fitness (Ignico, 1990). In two studies, I found that preschool children who received a 10-week motor skill instructional program showed significant improvement in fundamental motor skills as measured by the Test of Gross Motor Development (Ignico, 1992a, 1992b). In my study examining fitness levels of children enrolled in daily and weekly physical education programs (1990), I reported that children enrolled in daily physical education programs obtained a sufficient amount of moderate to vigorous

physical activity to achieve Physical Best fitness standards. Furthermore, these children performed significantly better on tests of health-related fitness than children enrolled in twice-weekly physical education programs.

COPEC recommends that preschool children receive daily instruction in fundamental motor skills, movement concepts, and activities which are designed to help them understand and value the basic concepts of fitness (1994). There is considerable support, therefore, for the inclusion of fundamental motor skill instruction and daily gross motor activities in every preschool program.

Fundamental Motor Skills and Movement Concepts

The content of physical education in preschool programs consists of both fundamental motor skills and movement concepts. Motor skills are the "action verbs" and movement concepts are the "modifiers." In other words, motor skills are the movements (e.g., hop, kick, throw) and movement concepts provide the how, where, with whom, or with what a movement will be performed (Gallahue, 1993; Graham, Holt-Hale, & Parker, 1993; Sanders, 1992). Fundamental motor skills are commonly classified into three categories: locomotor, manipulative, and stability (table 1). The three categories of movement concepts are space, effort, and relationships (table 2).

Children are ready to begin learning these basic motor skills and movement concepts by age three or four (Gallahue, 1989; Sanders, 1992). Complex skills required for participation in most games and sports are comprised of adaptations, combinations, and refinement of these fundamental movement skills. Acquiring these basic movement patterns increases a child's potential for learning more advanced sport skills (Seefeldt & Haubenstricker, 1982) and lifetime physical activities. In fielding a ground ball in softball, for example, a player must be able to efficiently use the locomotor skill of sliding and the manipulative skills of catching and throwing. If a child receives appropriate instruction and practice in each of these fundamental motor skills, then she or he can be successful in a game situation. Similarly, if a child receives sufficient instruction in aquatics and racquet skills, then she or he may be encouraged to participate in lifetime activities such as swimming and tennis.

Learning fundamental motor skills may also have a positive effect on self-concept and social skill development (Gallahue, 1989; Williams, 1983). Everyday observation indicates that competency in movement skills can have a positive influence on children's self-esteem and peer interactions. In fact, movement is critical in early self-concept development because it plays a dominant role in a child's everyday life. Both girls and boys perceive competence in physical activities as extremely valuable which indicates a strong link between skill level and social status in children (Harter, 1982; Weiss, 1987).

According to Lever (1976, 1978), children develop many social skills through their play experiences. The social skills developed in team sports and games, however, are far more valuable than those developed in games not requiring proficiency in fundamental motor skills. Sports and games are characterized by distinct roles, many players and rules, and player interdependence. Consequently, participation in sports and games promotes the development of leadership skills, independence, assertiveness, and confidence (Lever, 1978).

Participation in sports and games may also substantially contribute to cognitive development. Emmot (1985) proposed that sports and games requiring fundamental motor skill ability promote the development of visual-spatial abilities and field-independence. Since field-independence correlates highly with performance in mathematics, participation in sports and games may indirectly influence subsequent academic performance.

Although biological factors can create certain physical limitations, most researchers agree that sociocultural factors play a greater role in children's motor skill development.

Specifically, parents, teachers, and peers contribute largely by providing encouragement, instruction, and practice opportunities (Gallahue, 1989). Teachers can have an increasingly important effect on children's motor skills during the early school years (Greendorfer, 1980). Therefore, preschool educators must provide children with developmentally appropriate motor skill instruction in an effort tc build a foundation for successful participation in later childhood and adult physical activities.

Health-Related Physical Fitness

The topic of health-related fitness in young children has generated considerable attention and interest among public health professionals, researchers, and parents. Although few studies have examined preschool children's fitness, researchers investigating elementary school children have suggested that these children have low aerobic endurance and high levels of body fat (Kuntzleman & Reiff, 1992; Updyke & Willett, 1989). In fact, at least 25 percent of all elementary school children exceed desirable weight standards, and this figure is steadily increasing (Bar-Or, 1987). Two primary factors contribute to this unfortunate trend: first, children between the ages of 2 and 12 watch approximately 25 hours of television per week. Second, they spend less than 2 percent of the day participating in high intensity physical activity. Of greatest concern is that low fit and overweight children show early signs of coronary heart disease, high cholesterol levels, and high blood pressure (Sallis & McKenzie, 1991; Williams et al., 1992).

Health-related fitness components include aerobic endurance, muscular strength and endurance, flexibility, and body composition. Based on the assumption that these components improve with regular physical activity, national organizations have targeted school-based programs as a means to increase children's physical activity. This strategy is reflected in the *Healthy Children 2000* (U.S.

Table 1. Fundamental Movement Skill Themes

Skills

Locomotor ⇒	walking
	running
	jumping
	galloping
	sliding
	hopping
	leaping
	skipping
Stability ⇒	stretching
	curling
	bending
	twisting
	body rolling
	dodging
	balancing
	inverted supports
Manipulative ⇒	dribbling
	throwing
	catching
	kicking
	punting
	trapping
	volleying
	striking

Table 2. The Movement Concepts

Effort	Space	Relationships
Force	**Levels**	**Objects/People**
strong	high/medium/low	over/under
light		in/out
	Directions	between/among
Time	forward/backward	in front/behind
fast	diagonally/sideways	above/below
slow	up/down	through/around
sudden		
sustained	**Pathways**	**People**
	straight	mirroring
Flow	curved	shadowing
free	zigzag	in unison
bound		together/apart
	Ranges	solo
	body shapes	partner/group
	body spaces	
	body extensions	

Department of Health and Human Services, 1992) objectives which recommend daily physical education for preschool children.

Most preschool teachers would agree that specific fitness training is neither necessary nor developmentally appropriate for preschool children. In fact, simply providing children with developmentally appropriate play experiences will produce acceptable levels of fitness during the preschool years. A play environment which is large enough for children to move freely and safely will encourage children to remain active. This kind of play environment not only promotes regular physical activity but also provides a place to practice fundamental motor skills.

Providing preschool children with daily fundamental motor skill instruction and gross motor play will undoubtedly require additional training for preschool teachers. In light of the significant benefits of a developmentally appropriate physical education program, however, the rewards would far exceed the investment. The National Association for Sport and Physical Education (1992) defines the physically educated person as someone who demonstrates competence in a variety of manipulative, locomotor, and nonlocomotor skills and who participates regularly in physical activity. With this definition in mind, preschool educators can plan developmentally appropriate learning activities that will promote motor skill acquisition, fitness development, and a lifetime of physical activity.

References

Bar-Or, O. (1987). A commentary to children and fitness: A public health perspective. *Research Quarterly for Exercise and Sport, 58,* 304-307.

Bredekamp, S. (Ed.). (1987). *Developmentally appropriate practice in early childhood programs serving children from birth through age 8.* Washington DC: National Association for the Education of Young Children (NAEYC).

Emmot, S. (1985). Sex differences in children's play: Implications for cognition. Special Issue: Sex roles and sex differences and androgyny. *International Journal of Women's Studies, 8,* 449-456.

Council on Physical Education for Children. (1994). *Developmentally appropriate physical education practices for young children.* Reston, VA: AAHPERD Publications.

Gallahue, D. (1993). *Developmental physical education for today's children.* Dubuque, IA: Brown & Benchmark.

Gallahue, D. (1989). *Understanding motor development.* Carmel, IN: Benchmark.

Greendorfer, S. (1980). Gender differences in physical activity. *Motor Skills: Theory into Practice, 4,* 83-90.

Graham, G., Holt-Hale, S., & Parker, M. (1993). *Children Moving.* Mountain View, CA: Mayfield.

Harter, S. (1982). Development perspectives on self-esteem. In E.M. Hetherington (Ed.), *Handbook of child psychology: Socialization, personality, and social developments* (Vol. IV). New York: John Wiley and Sons.

Ignico, A. (1990). A comparison of the fitness levels of children enrolled in daily and weekly physical education programs. *Journal of Human Movement Studies, 18,* 129-139.

Ignico, A. (1992a). Effects of a competency-based instruction on kindergarten children's gross motor development. *Physical Educator, 48,* 188-191.

Ignico, A. (1992b). Physical education for Head Start children: A field-based study. *Early Child Development and Care, 77,* 77-82.

Kuntzleman, C., & Reiff, G. (1992). The decline in American children's fitness levels. *Research Quarterly for Exercise and Sport, 63,* 107-111.

Lever, J. (1978). Sex differences in the complexity of children's play and games.

American Sociological Review, 43, 471-483.

Lever, J. (1976). Sex differences in the games children play. *Social Problems, 23,* 478-487.

National Association for Sport and Physical Education (1992). *The physically educated person.* Reston, VA: AAHPERD Publications.

Sallis, J., & McKenzie, T. (1991). Physical education's role in public health. *Research Quarterly for Exercise and Sport, 62,* 124-137.

Sanders, S. (1992). *Designing preschool movement programs.* Champaign, IL: Human Kinetics.

Seefeldt, V., & Haubenstricker, J. (1982). Patterns, phases, or stages: An analytical model for the study of developmental movement. In J.A.S. Kelso & J.E. Clark (Eds.), *The development of movement control and coordination* (pp. 309-318). New York: John Wiley & Sons.

Updyke, W., & Willett, M. (Eds.). (1989). *Physical fitness trends in American youth.* Washington, DC: Chrysler-AAU Physical Fitness Program.

U.S. Department of Health and Human Services. (1992). *Healthy children 2000.* Boston, MA: Jones and Bartlett.

Weiss, M. (1987). Self esteem and achievement in children's sport and activity. In D. Gould & M. Weiss (Eds.), *Advances in pediatric sport sciences* (Vol. 1). Champaign, IL: Human Kinetics.

Williams, D., Going, S., Lohman, T., Harsha, D., Srinivasan, S, Webber, L., & Berenson, G. (1992). Body fatness and the risk of elevated blood pressure, total cholesterol and serum lipoprotein ratios in children and adolescents. *American Journal of Public Health, 82,* 358-363.

Williams, H. (1983). *Perceptual and motor development.* Englewood Cliffs, NJ: Prentice-Hall.

Reflections

Early childhood education is gaining more and more of America's attention. National panels grapple with issues relating to young children and release strong words urging support and developmentally appropriate practices. Popular magazines, like *Working Mother,* annually publish a listing of states where working parents can get the best care for their children. Political candidates include positions on early childhood in their platform statements. Much of this attention has come in the past five years. Yet it is amazing to recognize that the present state of early childhood education is an outgrowth of our heritage. Much that is considered contemporary practice and curriculum came from the early days of child care and kindergartens.

Dorothy Hewes, a prominent historian of early childhood education, points out in her article the long-standing connection between child care and sponsorship of centers outside the home. Kindergartens began to spread in an era when people were concerned about social policies to improve the nation. This fortunate timing ensured child care as a factor in reform through the decades. To Hewes, kindergarten has never been sentimental, for it has made a strong impact on our nation.

"The Movers and Shapers of Early Childhood Education" continues our theme of reflecting on heritage to understand the present. In concise form, Roger Neugebauer presents vignettes of 30 people who have contributed to the profession and influenced its direction into the future. They are researchers, educators, gurus, and bureaucrats, the "movers and shapers" of early childhood education. Some are prolific writers or leading speakers, while others are community activists or hard-working practitioners. It is important to know who has shaped the profession, for their expertise has made it strong and influential.

One kindergarten teacher who has made an impact on her students and innumerable teachers-in-training is Vivian Paley. For 24 years, she taught at the historic University of Chicago Lab School, the experimental school begun by John Dewey. Barbara Mahany's article, "Mrs. Paley's Lessons," teaches us a simple, profound lesson—we must take seriously what children say and what we say to them. Through a series of "snapshots" of Mrs. Paley's classroom, we learn that teaching is a moral act. Through the years, this great teacher has been a philosopher and transcriber of what children say. "Mrs. Paley's Lessons" is a rich, full portrait of a teacher who truly respects children.

In an article with a broad focus on services to children, Sharon Kagan uses the United States as a case study to explore how nations allocate responsibility for children and families. She provides evidence that the U.S. government has supported children and families only in times of national crisis. The result of scattershot responsibility through the decades is inadequate, fragmented services. Kagan concludes that responsibility for children is shared by numerous entities, resulting in a new type of family support system. With the passage of the Family Support and Family Preservation Act in 1993, governmental support is strengthening. These are positive signs of national commitment to share responsibility for children and families.

The final article of this year's *Annual Editions: Early Childhood Education* is a report on a study of the relationships among cost of child care, quality of care experiences, and effects on children. In a major nationwide

higher standards, encourage investment in training staff, and ensure adequate financial support.

The United States has a rich heritage of early care and kindergartens. It has produced many early childhood educators and leaders. National government continues to make subtle, yet important advances in taking responsibility for children and families. Still, we need the nation to pay even more attention to early childhood. We close by highlighting the recommendation made in "Cost, Quality, and Child Outcomes in Child Care Centers: Key Findings and Recommendations": *The nation must commit to improving the quality of child care services and to ensuring that all children and their families have access to good programs—that is, good-quality child care must become a merit good.*

Looking Ahead: Challenge Questions

Other than meeting children's immediate needs, what was the community value of the early kindergartens in the United States?

What writers, researchers, or gurus in early childhood education have influenced you?

A teacher can learn a lot by listening to young children. What important things could young children teach you?

Throughout our nation's history, which of these entities has had the most responsibility for children: neighborhood, parents, nation, family, kin, community? How has this line of responsibility changed?

What five essential characteristics should parents look for in choosing child care?

How high is the quality of child care centers in your area? What evidence do you use to rate their quality?

survey, the quality of child care was found to be poor to mediocre. The quality ratings included provisions for health and safety, support from adults, and learning experiences. Infant and toddler rooms, in particular, were of poor quality. Child care in centers is costly to provide, and tuition is not subsidized. Based on the findings, four recommendations for centers are advocated: communicate information about high-quality programs, implement

Starting · Points ·

Executive Summary of the Report of the Carnegie Corporation of New York Task Force on Meeting the Needs of Young Children

Our nation's infants and toddlers and their families are in trouble. Compared with most other industrialized countries, the United States has a higher infant mortality rate, a higher proportion of low-birthweight babies, a smaller proportion of babies immunized against childhood diseases, and a much higher rate of babies born to adolescent mothers. Of the 12 million children younger than age 3 in the United States today, a staggering number are affected by one or more risk factors that undermine healthy development. One in four lives in poverty. One in three victims of physical abuse is a baby younger than age 1.

These numbers reflect a pattern of neglect that must be reversed. It has long been known that the first years of life are crucial for later development, and recent scientific findings provide a basis for these observations. We can now say, with greater confidence than ever before, that the quality of young children's environment and social experience has a decisive, long-lasting impact on their well-being and ability to learn.

The risks are clearer than ever before: an adverse environment can compromise a young child's brain function and overall development, placing him or her at greater risk of developing a variety of cognitive, behavioral, and physical difficulties. In some cases these effects may be irreversible. But the opportunities are equally dramatic: adequate pre- and postnatal care, dependable caregivers, and strong community support can prevent damage and provide a child with a decent start in life.

Researchers have thoroughly documented the importance of the pre- and postnatal months and the first three years, but a wide gap remains between scientific knowledge and social policy. Today, changes in the American economy and family, combined with the lack of affordable health and child care and the crumbling of other family supports, make it increasingly difficult for parents to provide the essential requirements for their young children's healthy development.

More than half of mothers of children younger than age 3 work outside the home. This is a matter of concern because minimal parental leave is available at the time of birth, and child care for infants and toddlers is often hard to find and of poor quality. Most parents feel overwhelmed by the dual demands of work and family, have less time to spend with their children, and worry about the unreliable and substandard child care in which many infants and toddlers spend long hours. These problems affect all families, but for families living in poverty, the lack of prenatal and child health care, human services, and social support in increasingly violent neighborhoods further stacks the deck against their children.

These facts add up to a crisis that jeopardizes our children's healthy development, undermines school readiness, and ultimately threatens our nation's economic strength. Once a world leader and innovator in education, the United States today is making insufficient investments in our future workforce—our youngest children. In contrast to all the other leading industrialized nations, the United States fails to give parents time to be with their newborns, fails to ensure pre- and postnatal health care for mothers and infants, and fails to provide adequate child care.

The crisis among our youngest children is a quiet crisis. After all, babies seldom make the news. Their parents—often young people struggling to balance their home and work responsibilities—tend to have little economic clout and little say in community affairs. Moreover, children's early experience is associated with the home—a private realm into which many policymakers have been reluctant to intrude.

The problems facing our youngest children and their families cannot be solved through piecemeal efforts; nor can they be solved entirely through governmental programs and business initiatives. All Americans must take responsibility for reversing this quiet crisis. As the risks to our children intensify, so must our determination to enact family-centered programs and policies to ensure all of our youngest children the decent start that they deserve.

From *Young Children*, July 1994, pp. 58-61. © 1994 by the Carnegie Corporation of New York. Reprinted by permission.

Recommendations for action

The task force concluded that reversing the quiet crisis calls for action in four key areas that constitute vital starting points for our youngest children and their families.

Promote responsible parenthood

Our nation must foster both personal and social responsibility for having children. To enable women and men to plan and act responsibly, we need a national commitment to making comprehensive family planning, preconception, prenatal, and postpartum health services available, and to providing much more community-based education about the responsibilities of parenthood. To promote responsible parenthood, the task force recommends

• planning for parenthood by all couples to avoid unnecessary risks and to promote a healthy environment for raising a child;

• providing comprehensive family planning, preconception, prenatal, and postpartum services as part of a minimum health care reform package;

• delaying adolescent pregnancy through the provision of services, counseling, support, and age-appropriate life options;

• expanding education about parenthood in families, schools, and communities, beginning with the elementary school years but no later than early adolescence; and

• directing state and local funds to initiate and expand community-based parent education and support programs for families with infants and toddlers.

Guarantee quality child care choices

For healthy development, infants and toddlers need a continuing relationship with a few caring people, beginning with their parents and later including other child care providers. If this contact is substantial and consistent, young children can form the trusting attachments that are needed for healthy develop-ment throughout life. Infants and toddlers should develop these relationships in safe and predictable environments—in their homes or child care settings. To guarantee quality child care choices, the task force recommends

• strengthening the Family and Medical Leave Act of 1993 by expanding coverage to include employers with fewer than 50 employees, extending the 12-week leave to four to six months, and providing partial wage replacement;

• adopting family-friendly workplace policies, such as flexible work schedules and assistance with child care;

• channeling substantial new federal funds into child care to ensure quality and affordability for families with children under 3 and making the Dependent Care Tax Credit refundable for low- and moderate-income families;

• providing greater incentives to states to adopt and monitor child care standards of quality;

• developing community-based networks linking all child care programs and offering parents a variety of child care settings;

• allocating federal and state funds to provide training opportunities so that all child care providers have a grounding in the care and development of children under 3; and

• improving salary and benefits for child care providers.

Ensure good health and protection

When young children are healthy, they are more likely to succeed in school and, in time, to form a more productive workforce and become better parents. Few social programs offer greater long-term benefits for American society than guaranteeing good health care for all infants and toddlers. Good health involves more than health care services. Being healthy means that young children are able to grow up in safe homes and neighborhoods. To ensure good health and protection, the task force recommends

• making comprehensive primary and preventive care services, including immunizations, available to infants and toddlers as part of a minimum benefits package in health care reform;

• offering home-visiting services to all first-time mothers with a newborn and providing comprehensive home-visiting services by trained professionals to all families who are at risk for poor maternal and child health outcomes;

• expanding the Women, Infants and Children (WIC) nutritional supplementation program to serve all eligible women and children;

• making the reduction of unintentional injuries to infants and toddlers a national priority;

• expanding proven parent education, support, and counseling programs to teach parents nonviolent conflict resolution in order to prevent child abuse and neglect, and implementing community-based programs to help families and children cope with the effects of living in unsafe and violent communities; and

• enacting national, state, and local laws that stringently control the possession of firearms.

Mobilize communities to support young children and their families

Broad-based community supports and services are necessary to ensure a decent start for our youngest children. Unfortunately, community services for families with children under 3 are few and fragmentary. To reverse the crisis facing families with young children, the old ways of providing services and supports must be reassessed, and broad, integrated approaches must be found to ensure that every family with a newborn is linked to a source of health care, child care, and parenting support. To mobilize communities to support young children and their families, the task force recommends

• focusing the attention of every community in America on the needs of children under 3 and their families by initiating a community-based strategic planning process;

• experimenting broadly with the creation of family-centered communities through two promising approaches: creating family and child centers to provide services and supports for all families, and expanding and adapting the Head Start model to meet the needs of low-income families with infants and toddlers;

• creating a high-level federal group, directed by the president, to coordinate federal agency support on behalf of young children and to remove the obstacles faced by states and communities in their attempts to provide more effective services and supports to families with young children;

• funding family-centered programs through the Community Enterprise Board in order to strengthen families with infants and toddlers; and

• establishing mechanisms, at the state level, to adopt comprehensive policy and program plans that focus on the period before birth through the first three years of a child's life.

A call to action

The task force calls upon all sectors of American society to join together to ensure the healthy development of our nation's youngest children.

• We ask the *president* to direct a high-level federal group to review the findings of this report and to ensure the adequacy, coherence, and coordination of federal policies and programs for families with young children.

• We urge *federal agencies* to identify and remove the obstacles that states and communities encounter as they implement federally funded programs or test innovative solutions.

• We call upon *states* to review their legislative and regulatory frameworks, particularly with regard to child care, in order to raise the quality of services for children younger than age 3.

• We call upon *community leaders* to assess the adequacy of existing services for families with young children (especially those with multiple risks), to recommend steps to improve and coordinate services, and to introduce mechanisms for monitoring results.

The Quiet Crisis

Of the 12 million children younger than age 3 in the United States today, a staggering number are affected by one or more risk factors that make healthy development more difficult.

Changes in family structure are troubling

• In 1960, only 5% of all births in the United States were to unmarried mothers; by 1988, the proportion had risen to 26%.

• About every minute, an American adolescent has a baby; every year, about 1 million adolescents become pregnant.

• Divorce rates are rising: In 1960 less than 1% of children experienced their parents' divorce each year; by 1986 the percentage had more than doubled, and by 1993 almost half of all children could expect to experience a divorce during childhood and to live an average of five years in a single-parent family.

• Children are increasingly likely to live with just one parent, usually the mother: In 1960 fewer than 10% of all children younger than age 18 lived with one parent; by 1989 almost a quarter of all children lived with one parent. Fathers are increasingly absent from the home.

Many young children live in poverty

• One in four infants and toddlers younger than age 3 (nearly 3 million children) live in families below the federal poverty level.

• While the number of children younger than age 6 increased by less than 10% between 1971 and 1991, the number of poor children younger than age 6 increased by more than 60%.

More children live in foster homes

• In a mere four years, from 1987 to 1991, the number of children in foster care jumped by more than 50%—from 300,000 in 1987 to 460,000 in 1991.

• Babies younger than age 1 are the fastest growing category of children entering foster care, according to a study conducted in New York and Illinois.

Infants and toddlers are spending less time with their parents

• Pressures on both parents to work mean that they have less time with their young children; more than half of mothers of infants now work outside the home.

• More than 5 million children younger than age 3 are in the care of other adults while their parents work. Much child care for infants and toddlers is of substandard quality, whether it is provided by centers, family child care homes, or relatives.

Health data are discouraging

• In the United States, 9 of every 1,000 infants die before age 1—a mortality rate higher than that of 19 other nations.

• The mortality rate is higher for infants born in minority families: African American babies are twice as likely to die within the first year of life as are White babies.

• In 1992, rates of immunization against common childhood diseases among 2-year-olds were only 30% in some states; in most states they were less than 60%.

Physical abuse, neglect, and unintentional injury are common

• One in three victims of physical abuse is a baby—less than a year old. In 1990 more 1-year-olds were maltreated than in any previous year for which we have data.

• Almost 90% of children who died of abuse and neglect in 1990 were younger than age 5; 53% were less than a year old.

• The leading cause of death among children age 1 to 4 is unintentional injury.

• We call upon the ***private and philanthropic sectors,*** including foundations, to pay more attention to families with children under 3 and to expand their support of initiatives that give our youngest children a decent start in life.

• We urge ***educators*** to incorporate services to children under age three in their plans for the schools of the 21st century, to increase their efforts to educate young people about parenthood, and to provide more training and technical assistance to child care providers.

• We call upon ***health care decision makers*** to include, in any plan for national health care reform, comprehensive prenatal care for expectant mothers and universal primary and preventive care for young children and to consider establishing a specific standard of coverage and service for young children.

• We urge ***service providers*** in child care, health, and social services to work together by taking a family-centered approach to meeting the needs of young children and the adults who care for them. We ask them to offer staff, parents, and other caregivers opportunities to learn more about the needs of families with young children, about child development, and about promoting children's health and safety.

• We call upon ***business leaders*** to support policies that result in family-friendly workplaces for businesses of every size, for example strengthening the Family and Medical Leave Act of 1993 and introducing flexible work schedules.

• We call upon the ***media*** to deliver strong messages about responsible motherhood and fatherhood, to promote recognition of the importance of the first three years, and to give us all insight into the quiet crisis.

• We call upon ***mothers and fathers*** to secure the knowledge and resources they need to plan and raise children responsibly. When these resources are not available, we urge them to make their needs known to government representatives, community leaders, and service providers.

All Americans must work together, in their homes, workplaces, and communities, to ensure that children younger than age 3—our most vulnerable citizens—are given the care and protection they need and deserve. Nothing less than the well-being of our society and the future of its vital institutions is at stake.

Sisterhood and Sentimentality—America's Earliest Preschool Centers

Dorothy W. Hewes, Ph.D.

Dorothy Hewes, professor emeritus of the Department of Child and Family Development at San Diego State University, has been involved with varied aspects of early education over the past half century. She coordinates the History Seminar at the NAEYC annual conference and is currently finishing a history of parent participation preschools.

America's "oldest child care centers" were started during a period of economic growth and intellectual turbulence. Although there were a few wealthy families during the 18th century, someone described the nation as having "pyramids of money in a desert of want." By the mid-1800s, however, professional and business men began to prosper. As the morally superior gentler sex, middle-class wives improved their minds and discharged obligations to the unfortunates of society through church, club, and literary groups. There was no unifying sense of sisterhood, no mutual faith or endeavor.

When the German kindergarten of Friedrich Froebel became known to English-speaking Americans during the 1870s, women became energized by his idea that within each child lies the potential for self-realization and self-learning, a potential developed not through stern discipline but by "learning by doing" in a joyous play school. Parents abandoned old beliefs in children's innate depravity to promote development of their innate goodness through the kindergarten system. Three to six year olds could learn morality and citizenship while they enjoyed educational games and songs or busied themselves with bead stringing, block building, paper folding, and the construction of "forms of beauty" with wooden slats or parquetry blocks. Mothers could extend their domestic role by assisting the teachers in the classroom, learning new methods to apply at home.

There were less than a dozen kindergartens in 1870, all dependent upon parent fees. Ten years later, when there were about 400 in 30 states, most of them had some form of outside financial support. Early sponsors included the New England Women's Club, Sorosis, and the Women's Christian Temperance Union (with its motto of "Prevention, Not Reform—the Kindergarten Not the Prison is True Philanthropy").

Women of all social classes, religious denominations, and political orientations banded together to promote both charity and fee-paid kindergartens. Affluent matrons gave generously to the cause. Jane Stanford contributed $30,000 to San Francisco's Golden Gate Kindergarten Association by 1887 and a later endowment of $100,000. . . . Pauline Agassiz Shaw, who used some of the profits from her husband's copper mining interests to underwrite 31 Boston kindergartens by 1882, objected to the term "charity" because it was demeaning to the recipients. Names like Armour, Vanderbilt, and Hearst are also on the donor lists, but some kindergarten association members pledged 50¢ a month, saved penny by penny.

Whatever their financial status, these women shared more than a faith in Froebel's system; they shared inferior status in a society that was controlled by men. Even in the National Education Association, the Kindergarten Department represented a chasm between genders that was greater than any distinctions based upon professional training.

The expansion of charity kindergartens, many of them in churches, supplemented or replaced some of the custodial day nurseries for poor working mothers. In her history of kindergartens, Nina Vandewalker wrote that "the new institution became recognized as the most valuable of child-saving agencies, with mission kindergarten work so valuable among wealthy young women as to be almost a fad."

Although about half of the country's 4,000 kindergartens were philanthropic when the 1893 depression began, mere numbers cannot capture the evangelical fervor contained in letters and publications of the period; Ross aptly called it "The Kindergarten Crusade."

Kindergarten advocates were often considered to be "sentimental," but this term can mean the use of sensitivity and emotions rather than logical processes. It was a feminine strategy that made a strong impact during an era when people were concerned with the moral, social, and political aspects of good citizenship; a clearly rational approach would never have gained momentum. However, extravagant claims were often made—as when Mary Mann wrote that entire neighborhoods were transformed if "little minds" were "fertilized" by the kindergarten. "Fathers found entertainment in the children's singing to keep them home from the grog shop" and the beer money went into a savings fund.

American enthusiasts also added their own interpretations to the original German writings. For example, Froebel devised the "Snail Game" as a transition from active outdoor play to indoor activities. Children were to join hands with the teacher, who slowly turned so that the line formed a spiral and then uncoiled to become a circle. The American translation ended with the mystical interpretation that this symbolized the wholeness of humanity but missed its practical intention.

Critics could easily point to writings like these to condemn the whole system—and to provide a basis for their own *advanced* ideas. But to children in the urban missions, on the Indian reservations, at places like the Colorado Fuel and Iron Company where there were 27 home languages, or in countless parlors where mothers presided over a cluster of young neighbors, the hours in kindergarten were filled with delightful activities.

The negative inheritance from those early kindergarten enthusiasts persists in the expectation that psychic rewards are adequate compensation, that work with young children and their parents is so fulfilling that any mention of higher salaries or public funding somehow defiles its sentimental sanctity.

Our list of oldest child care organizations includes a substantial number that originated in settlement houses that were established as multipurpose service centers in urban poverty areas. One of the first was in Detroit, opening in 1881; but the best known was Jane Addams' Hull House in Chicago. Its kindergarten, opened in 1889 as a model of beauty and convenience, had competent staff assisted by students from Alice Putnam's training classes. Many others were equally excellent, but some were so horrible that the first child care licensing laws were developed as an attempt to control the worst of them.

In the early kindergartens, teachers conducted a morning class for about 15 children and made social calls on families during the afternoon. The children were taught to address the teachers as "Auntie" to emphasize her sisterly relationship with their mothers.

By the late 1890s, men with advanced degrees in the "new sciences" like psychology and sociology began to propound a logical and unsentimental approach to education and the problems of poverty. Organizations like the National Conference of Charities and Corrections professionalized and systematized philanthropy, thus creating paid administrative positions and promoting "Friendly Visitors" to make certain that their funds were well spent. The resulting philanthropic kindergartens often had larger classes and a more structured program than the more informal groups of the early years. In the public school kindergartens, also efficiently administered, teachers not only had large classes but were expected to teach double sessions.

OUR HERITAGE FROM THE PAST CENTURY

Much of today's equipment and methodology has been an outgrowth of those early kindergartens. We may schedule *circle time* with finger plays and action games just as Froebel did in 1837. We have plastics and play dough instead of wood and natural clay, but we still believe that "what a child imitates, he begins to understand." This didn't just happen. After kindergartens became public school classes for five year olds, Progressive Froebelians maintained the philosophy of learning through play by developing nursery schools for the younger children and by organizing the Committee on Nursery Schools, now the National Association for the Education of Young Children (NAEYC), in the 1920s.

Our heritage goes beyond methods and materials. The United States has always had some sort of other-than-mother care, as Geraldine Youcha and other writers have pointed out; but the first public concern about standards and salaries began in the kindergarten era. By 1908, when there were about 400 settlement house and mission kindergartens, Vandewalker reflected popular opinion when she criticized those "whose purpose is served if the children are kept clean, happy, and off the streets. . . . The large number of children enrolled, the economy exercised in the use of material, the low salaries paid, these and other conditions that too frequently prevail in philanthropic work have done much to obscure the real educational value of the kindergarten. . . . The teacher often undertook her work as a labor of love and asked for no remuneration. If salaries were paid, they were wholly out of proportion to the services rendered (p. 126)."

The negative inheritance from those early kindergarten enthusiasts persists in the expectation that psychic rewards are adequate compensation, that work with young children and their parents is so fulfilling that any mention of higher salaries or public funding somehow defiles its sentimental sanctity. As we prepare to enter the 21st century, it is time to move beyond charity, sentimentality, and sisterhood with evidence that child care is a worthwhile public investment.

6. REFLECTIONS

SUGGESTIONS FOR FURTHER READING

Addams, Jane. *Twenty Years at Hull House*. New York: Macmillan, 1920.

Braun, S. J., and E. P. Edwards. *History and Theory of Early Childhood Education*. Belmont, CA: Wadsworth, 1972.

Hewes, Dorothy W. "Patty Smith Hill." *Young Children* (May) and ERIC EJ148709 PS505187, 1976.

Hewes, Dorothy W. "NAEYC's First Half Century." *Young Children* (September) and ERIC EJ148709 PS505187, 1976. (This publication is scheduled to be reprinted later this year.)

Hewes, Dorothy W. "Compensatory Early Childhood Education: Froebelian Origins and Outcomes." ERIC ED264980 PS015596, 1985.

Hewes, Dorothy W. "Early Childhood Exhibit Controversies: 1890 and 1990." ERIC ED330431 PS019280, 1990.

Kelley, Mary. *Woman's Being, Woman's Place: Female Identity and Vocation in American History*. Boston: G. K. Hall, 1979.

Ross, Elizabeth. *The Kindergarten Crusade: The Establishment of Preschool Education in the United States*. Athens, OH: Ohio University Press, 1976.

Rothman, David J. *Poverty, USA: The Charitable Impulse in Eighteenth Century America*. New York: Arno, 1971.

Vandewalker, Nina C. *The Kindergarten in American Education*. New York: Macmillan, 1908.

Weber, Evelyn. *The Kindergarten: Its Encounter with Educational Thought in America*. New York: Teachers College Press, 1969.

Williams, Leslie R., and Doris Fromberg. *Encyclopedia of Early Childhood Education*. New York: Garland, 1992.

Youcha, Geraldine. *Minding the Children—Child Care in America from Colonial Times to the Present*. New York: Scribner, 1995.

A tribute to some of the many VIPs of child care

The Movers and Shapers of Early Childhood Education

Roger Neugebauer

We recently invited a random selection of our readers to tell us who they see as the key people who have shaped our profession. Their response was overwhelming — they chronicled the contributions of over 200 individuals. We have selected 30 of these individuals to represent the rich diversity of very important people in our profession.

These people have much in common — most began their careers as preschool teachers, many were active in the early days of Head Start, many have served in leadership roles in NAEYC, and all have remained steadfast advocates for children for more than three decades. However, they followed many paths and bring diverse talents and interests to the profession. This mix of common interests and varied contributions represents the norm in this profession and is what makes it so strong and vibrant....

— Scholars —

Most veterans in the early childhood profession cut their teeth on the works of **Urie Bronfenbrenner**, professor of child development at Cornell University. He not only has influenced generations of adults with his teaching and writing, but he also has influenced millions of children by actively participating in the launching of Head Start.

Constance Kamii, an internationally renowned proponent of Piagetian theory, now teaches at the University of Alabama where she is actively experimenting with Piagetian approaches to math education. Her career includes studying and teaching under Jean Piaget at the University of Geneva, as well as participating in the landmark Perry Preschool Project.

For over three decades, **Bernard Spodek**, as professor of early childhood education at the University of Illinois, has worked tirelessly to promote an understanding of how children develop. He has lectured extensively throughout the world. His writings include the popular *Foundations of Early Childhood Education* (Prentice Hall, 1991), co-authored with Olivia Saracho.

— Researchers —

When the demand for child care was poised to explode in the mid-1960s, research of **Bettye Caldwell** at Syracuse University on the effects of child care was instrumental in shaping the direction of Head Start, as well as the direction of most professionally oriented child care. She continues to be a strong child advocate at the University of Arkansas.

Alice Sterling Honig was a partner in research with Bettye Caldwell at Syracuse University and has remained there to focus her attention on the youngest children. Through her prolific writing and her engaging presentations, she has become the leading authority on caring for infants in group settings.

In 1960, **David Weikart** launched the Perry Preschool Project to demonstrate the impact of a carefully designed curriculum. Over three decades later, this project is still influencing our profession as advocates promote its positive research results, and as practitioners shape their programs around the High/Scope curriculum which evolved from this research.

When Head Start was launched, many of our profession's top thinkers were tapped to give it direction. **Edward Zigler** was a key player among these. His continuing research on child development as sterling professor of psychology at Yale University has kept him in the forefront of the profession. He remains an active advisor to Head Start as it grows and evolves.

— Translators —

No single instrument has had more impact on the early childhood centers than the *Early Childhood Environment Rating Scale* (Teachers College Press, 1980) of which **Thelma Harmes** is the first author. This tool is accepted by researchers as a standard for evaluation and is widely employed by centers as a guide to improving service delivery.

Joanne Hendrick has educated early childhood teachers both as a professor, currently at the University of Oklahoma, and as the author of popular texts on early childhood education which concisely translate current thinking on child development into principles and practices to apply in the classroom.

A mentor for generations of early childhood teachers, **James L. Hymes, Jr.** began his career as head of two Kaiser Child Service Centers in Portland, Oregon, during World War II. He has influenced the direction of our field as an educator, a writer, a lecturer, and as president of NAEYC. He now serves as a chronicler of the profession with his *Year In Review* publications.

There is no more effective explicator of early childhood teaching practices than **Lilian Katz**. She is respected worldwide for her writing and speaking on teacher training and curriculum development. Currently, she serves as director of the ERIC Clearinghouse on Elementary and Early Childhood Education and as professor of early childhood education at the University of Illinois.

— Educators —

Anyone who has heard **Barbara Bowman** speak soon recognizes that she combines an uncommon grasp of child development and learning theory with an extraordinary eloquence. She was one of three founders of the Erikson Institute for the Advanced Study in Child Development, a leading early childhood teacher training institution. Now, three decades later, she serves as its president.

Countless early childhood professionals have had their careers enriched and inspired by **Elizabeth Brady**. Her influence has been felt in the classrooms of the University of California, in countless AEYC workshops and retreats, as well as in individual program consultations. She touches students of all ages with a quick wit and a deep commitment to quality education.

Shirley Moore's first day as an early childhood teacher was nearly her last as she was assigned to supervise nap time and chaos ensued. Fortunately for the profession, she persevered, and 50 years later she is still educating and inspiring new teachers. The past 30 years she has worked at the University of Minnesota, first at the lab school and currently as professor emeritus at the Institute of Child Development.

Over half a century ago, **Joan Swift** studied at the Iowa Welfare Station where pioneering research on child development was taking place. In this pioneering spirit, she authored one of the earliest literature reviews on the effects of early childhood education programs, established one of the first paraprofessional training programs, and provided impetus to the establishment of six laboratory preschools in Chicago.

— Practitioners —

For decades, **Mozelle Core** operated high quality child care centers, including the Donner Belmont Demonstration Child Care Center in Nashville, Tennessee. She inspired generations of early childhood professionals in Tennessee as a mentor and model in her center as well as through her active involvement in professional organizations.

When **Grace Mitchell** had her first child, she also gave birth to Mrs. Bailey's Nursery School in Waltham, Massachusetts. Sixty years later, she is still working hard on behalf of children and early childhood professionals. Today, she keeps active by sharing her insights in books and by traveling to visit centers and give inspirational keynotes.

Winona Sample, like James Hymes, began her career during World War II providing child care for Army wives. She continued her career as a preschool teacher and director, and later became active in providing services for migrant workers and later for Native Americans in Head Start. Currently, she shares her expertise as a Head Start trainer and consultant.

Docia Zavitkovsky is known as the storyteller of the early childhood community. She uses her endless collection of classroom stories not only to entertain but, more importantly, to educate and to inspire. Her wealth of stories flows from her decades of work as a teacher and director — most recently as director of Santa Monica's child development programs.

— Bureaucrats —

When **Bertha Campbell** had her first child, she realized she didn't know enough about young children and pursued a masters degree in child development. Years later, having earned two more masters degrees as well as a doctorate in education, she was hired by the state of New York as a program and staff development specialist. She recently retired as chief of the Bureau of Child Development.

Not many of us think of **Polly Greenberg**, the editor of *Young Children*, as a bureaucrat. However, during the Kennedy years, she was one of "Bobby's Guerrillas." She wrote an early position paper on Head Start for Sargent Shriver. When Head Start was launched, she was appointed to head the southeast region where she worked aggressively to recruit Head Start providers and to support parent participation in these programs.

Jenni Klein began her career as a preschool teacher in the 1950s. When Head Start was launched, she was appointed educational specialist in the Head Start Bureau. For over a decade, she rose steadily in the Bureau, all the while remaining active and influential in NAEYC and other professional organizations.

Jeannette Watson is known as "Mrs. Early Childhood Education of Texas." For 17 years, starting in the late 1940s, she directed a child care center in Austin. In 1971, she was appointed director of early childhood development for the state of Texas. In this position, and through professional associations, she has implemented many innovative programs for children and families.

— Advocates —

T. Berry Brazelton has been called the "pediatric guru of the 1980s."

He is well known for his insights on child development and parenting. In addition, he has given countless hours traveling across the country promoting the value of properly funded early childhood programs.

Asa Hilliard, III, a moving lecturer and an articulate writer, has used these talents to deliver hundreds of papers and keynotes on the nature of diversity education, the validity of current testing practices for black children and teachers, quality teaching of black children, and the historical roots of black Americans. The huge success of National Black Child Development Institute (NBCDI), which recently celebrated its 25th anniversary, can be attributed to the dedication of its founder and current executive director, **Evelyn K. Moore**. NBCDI serves as a gathering place for all those concerned about the future of African American children; it regularly informs the American public on the status of these children, and it advocates actively for legislation meeting the needs of all poor and disadvantaged children.

— Gurus —

Millie Almy began her career as a teacher and director of nursery schools in the late 1930s. For the past 50 years, she has inspired thousands as a professor, most recently at the University of California. Not only is she a great teacher of teachers, she also helps professionals see the key role the director plays in supporting the development and performance of teachers.

In 1943, **Dorothy Hewes** received a

degree in institution management. Throughout her career, she has built on this training, first as a center director and currently as a professor at San Diego State University, to professionalize center administration. Her books and articles were among the first to focus in-depth attention on the work of the center director.

Gwen Morgan is the Jacqueline of all trades in early childhood education. She has been a vocal advocate for federal funding, has promoted coordination efforts at the state level, and has focused attention on improving state licensing laws. In addition, in providing summer seminars for directors at Wheelock College for 25 years, she has personally trained many of the current leaders in the field.

Day Care as a Child-Rearing Environment (NAEYC, 1972), by **Elizabeth Prescott**, was a landmark publication. It looked at centers not as a collection of classrooms but as self-standing organizations influenced by leadership styles and structural patterns. This publication and subsequent creative work by Prescott and her peers at Pacific Oaks College inspired an entire generation of directors to look at their work in a new light.

These are but a few of the many individuals who have shaped, and continue to impact, the early childhood profession. In communities across the world, countless individuals with a wide range of talents, resources, and interests have supported the development of much needed early childhood services.

Mrs. Paley's Lessons

*The only kindergarten teacher to receive a MacArthur grant has a
message for you from her pupils*

Barbara Mahany

Boiled down, a day in one particular kindergarten amounts to this:

Two tummyaches of undetermined origin. A bunny that breakfasts on pink paper hearts and a teacher's brown shoelace after that. A breathless report of a wiggly tooth surrendered to the tooth fairy the night before, and, offered as proof, a curled-up dribbling tongue poking through the now vacant space. A broken piggy bank to tape back together, and a little boy's broken heart with it. Twenty-one heads to count, milk cartons to fetch and, on the playground, two sets of tears, first to wipe, then to referee. A 5-year-old curled up in a ball, refusing to come out from the cubby hole. A squeaky old heating vent that must be slapped and slapped, and still it won't stop its whine.

At lunchtime, it's a little boy who won't eat what's packed: bored, he protests, with peanut butter-and-jelly day after day after day. After lunch, it's a little girl who says she feels sick to her stomach and then proves it.

And just about 2 o'clock, when the chief arbiter, healer and repairwoman in this classroom is seated at the very edge of her teeny-tiny chair turning the teeny-tiny pages of a child's hand-drawn storybook, called an "Eensy Book" around here and narrated publicly by its young illustrator, someone from the back of the story circle yells, "I can't hear!" "If you concentrate you can hear even if there's a hurricane outside," calls back the one turning the pages, prompting this: "What's a hurricane?" "It's like a tornado," offers a more learned little someone, who then provides a fairly convincing imitation of a twister at full-throttle.

So goes the cacophony of kindergarten.

All that and in between, oh, somewhere around 100 or so yankings at one rolled-up oxford cloth sleeve, followed every time by the insistent and unrelenting "Teacher! Teacher!", a refrain that not once all day, all week, in Room 284 of the University of Chicago Laboratory Schools went unheard, unanswered, unexplored.

You see, until the final school bell rang three weeks ago Wednesday, ending a 36-year teaching career—two dozen of those years at the grand old Lab Schools, the last six in that very classroom—Room 284 was that of Vivian Gussin Paley.

And long ago in those kindergartens, Paley, 66, taught herself to hear not what some would call the noise, the nonsense, of 5- and 6-year-olds at the work of play. No, Paley has heard beyond all that. Far, far beyond.

She has learned the essential lesson, and from her little schoolroom in Hyde Park she's taught it to a generation of teachers and parents and caretakers of children around the globe. It is this: Take very seriously the things that children say, and take equally seriously the things you say to children.

What's coming from the mouths of kindergartners is often the truest truth, the uncluttered voice of the soul, and none of us can afford not to listen. Likewise, what's seeded in those nascent souls, through the words we choose to speak to them, may well take root and change forever the way the next and the next generations see and shape the world.

Nothing less is at stake in the kindergarten, what Paley calls "the official start of public life," and where the classroom, in the end, is the moral laboratory and the social experiments done there the most everlasting. For, if you begin at the beginning—when consciousness and conscience are taking form—with a curriculum that soars beyond reading and writing and counting to 99 and seeks to draw the best from human nature, creating in kindergartners a sense of fairness and rightness for life, then the "children's garden" is not some romping ground for ring-around-the-rosy but the crucible for hope. And teaching there, says Paley, is every bit a "moral act."

What she hears from kindergartners slips by most of us. Some can only wish to hear it. Some can't imagine it's there.

But it is, this magic, this poetry, what Paley calls "literature in every sense; the simplicity of their stories nonetheless miraculously reveals the deepest of human emotions."

Twenty years ago, not long after moving back to the city where she'd grown up and not long after accepting a position at the Lab Schools, which just happened to be hiring that first summer and just happened to be walking distance from the

Hyde Park tri-level she'd moved into with her husband, Irving, and two nearly grown sons, David and Bobby, Paley picked up a borrowed tape recorder and marched back into her classroom.

She was determined, after years of not really hearing the dialogue all around her, to absorb every last word of the scripts being unspooled by these young dramatists, philosophers and, oh yes, theologians in her care.

She'd gotten an inkling that these were "the genuine intellectual people," the ones building block cities and cradling baby dolls all around her. She set out to prove it—first, to herself; later, to anyone who cared to turn an ear.

Immersed in this gathering of child thought, Paley came upon a novel means of eliciting even more storytelling, that is, letting the children spin aloud their own dramas and mysteries and fairy tales. She began every day taking dictation from the little story weavers, taking down two-sentence, three-sentence, sometimes notebook-page-long narratives. And then she made it a practice to have the young thespians act out their works in the daily story circle.

So grew the volume of the dialogue, and so too the wisdom of the children's transcriber, stage director and master of ceremonies.

Since then Paley has poured what she's heard onto the pages of eight remarkable books, the latest, "Kwanzaa and Me: A Teacher's Story," published in February by Harvard University Press. Each book tackles a single central question of classroom life—the racism, the stories, the gender differences, the children's development, the outsider and the struggle to belong, the ethics, and the ways in which classrooms dismiss the differences, and thus the heart, of the children who make up their rosters. With each, Paley probes the question as it unfolds among a community of children over the course of a school year. (In "Kwanzaa," though, Paley takes her question cross-country to the lectures and workshops that fill her weekends' calendar.)

Each book reads in part like passages from a teacher's journal, the source from which the musings and commentaries and self-analyses are drawn. And, too, each volume gives the reader the sense that he or she, like Paley, is perched at the doll corner door, listening in—hearing about and seeing the world, not for the first time, of course, from the mouths and through the eyes of a 3- or 4- or 5- or 6-year-old child.

Along the way, and probably a good bit of the reason she was awarded a MacArthur Foundation "genius" award in 1989—the only elementary teacher and one of only two classroom teachers so honored—Paley has given all of us not just snapshots of the minds and souls of preschoolers and kindergartners but full-blown portraits of how they think, what they feel and the ways in which they imagine, complete with all the shadings and brush strokes that can be born only of a child's most intimate, unguarded revelations.

Listen in:

Wally: I know all about Jonas. He got swallowed by the whale.
Fred: How?
Wally: God sent him. But the whale was asleep so he just walked out.
Fred: How did he fly up to God? I mean how did he get back to shore if it was so deep?

Wally: He didn't come from the sky. But he could have because there's an ocean in the sky. For the rain to come down.
Fred: Oh yeah. That's for the gods. When they go deep they never drown, do they?
Wally: Of course not. They're just going nearer to Earth.
Jill: How does the ocean stay up?
Fred: They patch it up. They. . . .
Wally: They take a big, big, big bag and put it around the ocean.
Fred: It's a very, very, very big bag.
Eddie: Which reminds me. Do you know how many Christmas trees God gets? Infinity.
Teacher: Who gives him Christmas trees?
Eddie: He makes them.
Wally: When people burn them. . . . You see he's invisible. He takes up the burned parts and puts them together.
Rose: Are there decorations?
Wally: Invisible decorations. He can see them because he's invisible. If you tell him there's an invisible person here, he believes it.
Eddie: You can't fool God.
Wally: Sure you can. It's a good trick. You can say, "I'm here," and you're really not, but he can't see you. You can fool him.
Eddie: But he hears you.
Wally: Right. He hears you talk. He talks, too. But you have to ask him. He talks very soft. I heard him.
Eddie: You know, 353 years ago everyone could see God. He wasn't invisible then. He was young, so he could stay down on Earth. He's so old now he floats up in the sky. He lived in Uganda and Egypt.
Fred: That's good, because everyone in Egypt keeps. They turn into mummies.

Paley and her players keep at it, page after page, explaining away in kindergarten terms the mysteries of the universe.

There's Wally, again, who observes in one of his wiser moments: "You can never take a picture of thinking." And there's Rose, who suddenly wonders as the class readies a pile of vegetables for a dramatization of the children's classic "Stone Soup." "Do stones melt?" "They will if you cook them," informs Lisa. "If you *boil* them," corrects Eddie, who soon presides over the lowering of three stones into a pot of boiling water as the class decides to test his hypothesis.

There's Deana, who swears she bumped into the tooth fairy at the bank, and has this to report: "She has purple shoes and red hair." And flying to the Man in the Moon, there's Wally again letting us in on a celestial secret: "The moon is right next to God so he could talk to God." And when the subject is Martin Luther King, the little historians clarify one civil rights issue: "Martin changed all the rules," says Wally. "All the *bad* rules," says Lisa. "But not the one for the bathroom," says Fred. "The girls have to separate from the boys."

There's more to be learned from the Land of Paley's Little People, and it's not all dialogue and not all earth-shattering, though it does suggest how keenly someone is keeping watch over her kingdom.

Paley tells you, almost in passing, that she's noticed these things: Kindergartners draw people from the feet up. They don't color in the faces on their drawings. And they almost always leave a big blank space between the blue sky at the top of the page and the green grass at the bottom. The most vulnerable hero in a kindergartner's story is the one who gets lost in the woods. And you can tell the end of the kindergarten year is nearing, not by some quantitative developmental scale, but when the wall paintings have fewer drips, the labels are in the children's handwriting, and their letters sit more comfortably side by side.

And this, from the gender gap: Boys fly, leap, crash, and dive. Girls have picnics and brush their teeth. The meanest, ugliest character in a girl's story goes on picnics and keeps his teeth clean. Boys animate their drawings of volcanoes and space wars with exploding noises, as if they had jumped inside the pictures—if they sit down to draw at all. Girls sit for hours at the drawing table; flowers, houses and families, three favorite motifs. Boys thrive on blood and mayhem, girls avoid the subject; a character in a girls' story simply dies, no details given. In one particular class, Paley discerned this: You hop to get your milk if you are a boy and skip to the paper shelf if you are a girl. All evidence, she writes, of the "five-year-old's passion for segregation by sex."

Child psychologist Jerome Bruner, himself a master in the domain of deep thought, calls Paley's work "a miracle," and "a rich journey into the mind of a child."

"Blessed Vivian," he calls her, and goes on to say: "She's one of those marvelous characters who has this intuitive gift for knowing how to get into the domain of children. Where did that gift come from? It came from God. But she's not some naive angel. She brings to it a reasoned moral stance that's astonishing. I keep thinking I wish she had taught my children; then I think, I wish she had taught me!"

Dr. Robert Coles, the Harvard child psychiatrist who won a 1973 Pulitzer Prize for two volumes of his "Children of Crisis" series, puts Paley in the company of poets and novelists, "experts on nothing save life itself," and, in particular, says she "belongs in the company of those specially talented novelists who can evoke childhood in all its contradictions and inconsistencies, its never-ending thickness and complexity."

In his foreword to Paley's 1990 book, "The Boy Who Would Be a Helicopter: The Uses of Storytelling in the Classroom," Coles writes: "In an age when ambitious theorists strut across any stage they can find, assaulting us with pronouncements meant to advance careers, here is a teacher who lets life's complexities have their full dignity, who moves ever so gently and thoughtfully from observed life to carefully qualified comment."

Paley has been compared to and, by some, put on the same plane as Jean Piaget, the Swiss cognitive psychologist who broke ground with his studies of how children think at four clearly-defined stages, and Lev Vygotsky, the developmental psychologist referred to as "the Russian Piaget," who took so seriously children's play.

But, of course, this being academia, Paley has her share of critics.

Judith Wells Lindfors, professor of curriculum and instruction at the University of Texas at Austin, remembers being at an academic conference shortly after the publication in a professional journal of her glowing review of Paley's 1984 "Boys & Girls: Superheroes in the Doll Corner," a somewhat controversial examination of the natural separation of the sexes as observed in the nursery school classroom. A "very, very ardent feminist" cornered Lindfors, she recalls, "practically screaming, 'What have you done?' She was absolutely overwhelmed that I'd reviewed it positively. [Paley] really hit an exposed nerve with that one."

And then there is what several academics referred to as, "a wonderful dilemma for researchers," who knot themselves up pondering: "Do you let her in?" As in into the club called Significant Clinical Data Gathering. "Researchers," says Lindfors, "don't know what to do with her."

Lindfors, who is amused by the whole quandary, continues: "There's a funny sort of discomfort. We know she's terribly important, but there's some discomfort with conventions."

It is this bone that they pick: Usually research tapes are transcribed with all the "hmming and hawing and disfluency," says Lindfors. "The sidetracks, overlaps and disciplinary asides are all there." Paley, though, follows the idea of the child, cuts out some of the interruptions, and does not see fit to squib in every last 'Hmm.'

"A researcher gets it down like a photograph; hers is like a painting," says Lindfors, asserting there's nothing dishonest about Paley's "cleaned-up versions" of the script.

And just who is this schoolteacher who has been likened to an anthropologist, armed with her trusty tape recorder (its red "record" button pushed so many times it now dangles from its case), hunkering down with a tribe called Kindergartners, sending out jottings on the heretofore uncharted rites, rituals and beliefs of this naive and as yet unharnessed civilization?

If you'd wanted to catch Paley on her way into the classroom, you'd better have climbed the stairs and rounded the corner by 7:30 a.m. sharp in the Lab Schools' Emmons Blain Hall, a graceful Gothic building looking down on the Midway Plaisance. That's the precise time you'd have bumped into Paley, her beloved husband, Irving, and their yellow Labrador, Cass, bustling in from the daily constitutional that took them first past the neighborhood newsstand and then straight toward Room 284.

Ever since Irving, 70, retired six years ago from the Museum of Science and Industry, where he lived out his "p.r. dream" as head of its public relations department, he had insisted on walking Paley to school each morning and being the one to take down the classroom chairs, worried that his wife of 47 years might wrench her back with all that lifting.

Huffing behind Paley as she cranked into full classroom gear—she'd darted to the sand table, the cubby holes and back to the bookshelves before you could get to the sand table—you wouldn't guess that chiropractic concerns ever crossed her mind.

Nor would you guess that this was the schoolteacher called to Capitol Hill in June of 1994, invited by Sen. Paul Simon to testify at a Senate subcommittee hearing on hate crimes. Paley's name was on a short list that included Hollywood's Steven Spielberg. ("Spielberg had the cameras, she had the credibility," said Sara Bullard of the Southern Poverty Law Center, in Montgomery, Ala., who also was among those testifying in the Senate chambers.)

Paley, known among educators world-wide for her work on the subject, laid out for the senators the social experiment she undertook in her kindergarten to abolish that human foible she says is "older than the Bible"—life's first hate crime, perhaps—the inclination to taunt: "You can't play with us, sit with us, walk with us or join our teams."

The schoolteacher told the senators: "The habit of believing one has the right to demean another classmate publicly can be replaced by an equally powerful notion that everyone owns the classroom in exactly the same way—if we begin early enough without ambivalence."

Paley in person couldn't be more unpretentious. She slops through playground puddles wearing see-through galoshes she calls her "old lady rubbers." She writes in a left-handed scrawl that could be mistaken for a child's. She lays out her lunch—cellophane-wrapped cheese on little rye rolls, a Granny Smith apple, skim milk poured from its little carton into an even littler plastic cup—on a brown paper towel, just like the little people unloading their Lion King lunch boxes all around her. She is forever chasing Snowball, the mischievous white rabbit, lunging boldly for the scruff of his neck, in hopes of staving off his final great escape. And she can't help but chuckle sometimes at the silly rabbit's tricks.

This, the class that would be Paley's last, is a polyglot group from China, Cuba, India, Italy, Mexico, Russia and Scotland, as well as Chicago's Hyde Park—the sons and daughters of a used-car parts salesman, a jeweler, three doctors, a court reporter, a nurse, a recycler, a couple of social workers and the usual smattering of attorneys and academics (this being a neighborhood thick with Ph.D.'s). And many of those parents had to fork over the kindergarten's eye-popping tuition of $7,278 per year (scholarships and tuition breaks for university faculty and staff bring down some bills.)

But, when Paley is talking to the children, no notice is taken of any ethnic or economic difference. There is on her face only the seriousness that heralds her regard for each and every child. She is really, really listening, straining to hear even what they do not say and how they say it all.

It is as in her writing. "Once you've seen the children through her eyes, once you've been given glimpses of the richness of their lives," says Becky New, education professor and coordinator of the graduate program in early childhood education at the University of New Hampshire, "they can't ever again be reduced to ciphers on a screen. They're not just cute or problematic."

To the mother of one of the 21 children in this, Paley's last class, that is the blessing that made it not quite so wrenching to leave her little girl at the kindergarten door. "My daughter is learning how to navigate life outside the home with this extraordinary navigator and friend."

And this is how that navigator, that friend, that scribe of the kindergarten class, has come to map the mind of the 5- or the 6-year-old child:

"Well," she begins in her gravelly voice one spring afternoon, sitting in the sun-drenched den that doubles as her home office, a thermos of decaf coffee within easy reach, "the kindergarten child is first of all filled with lots and lots of stories. There's a continually running internal monologue, which then goes public and has to learn to accommodate to a lot of other people's internal monologues that have gone public. Because, beginning around the kindergarten year, the need to make a friend is so strong that the closer you come to joining your internal stories to their internal stories, you are learning how to create social play.

"The young child wants to play. He wants to play because intuitively he understands that through play he will understand more about who is there for him. The child must really have adults who care about him, are glad to see him, listen to his ideas, give him a hug, make him feel school is a good second place to home.

"What else? Of growing importance, the growing need to feel, 'I am an interesting person. I have interesting ideas. I can pretend things.'

"All of that. I mean this is a very, very lively mind," she says, pausing only for a second before rushing forth with another stream of thought.

"And of course, you have the child-the-philosopher. He's wondering about everything. All the while he's learning to sit in a group and have a discussion and listen to a story and all these things that are important as you begin kindergarten, first grade.

"Yes, this is a very, very busy person."

Time and again in talking to Paley's colleagues—the director of the Lab Schools, the lower school principal, the teachers who work by her side and the ones whose classrooms are down the hall—even to the students, now grown, who've been "Mrs. Paley's kindergarten kids," you hear this about how she comes to know so wholly the children's inner lives: Respect, profound respect, the kind a kid can tell is genuine right away and always.

"Everybody felt they were the greatest kids in the world," remembers Jason Tyler, now 24, and a credit analyst at the American National Bank after graduating from the Lab Schools and Princeton University.

For Tyler, an African-American from the far South Side who was stepping into the predominantly white, middle-class world of the Lab Schools, it was a particularly scary climb up the stairs that first morning of kindergarten, a day he still remembers in vivid detail. Paley swept him in from the start, he says, never batted an eye when there were rough spots. She made him feel proud of his skin color and his neighborhood, first of all simply acknowledging his differences, calling his blackness beautiful and nonchalantly asking about where he lived and wasn't it great that he lived outside Hyde Park.

"You don't necessarily want to have your greatest teachers in high school," Tyler says. "The most important thing is the second they walk in the door to have someone who will really impact the kids. She's the perfect person to have."

Beverly Biggs is now the lower school principal at the Lab Schools, but 15 years ago she was Paley's teaching assistant in a nursery school classroom. (Paley had asked to be transferred there for a year so she could learn the ways of the pre-kindergarten thinker. She stayed six years.)

6. REFLECTIONS

Biggs offers this on her colleague: "She always has the most profound respect for kids. You can see it in every single exchange between her and the kids. When she is talking to them she is talking to just [one] child. Somehow she has antennae that know what the rest of the kids are doing. But she really is focusing on that one child most earnestly.

"That child knows from the way she's looking and listening and attending to him or her that what they're saying is very important. And that whatever they have expressed, she will respond, whether she needs to do something, talk to them, reassure them or empower them."

Watching Paley in her classroom, you see what Biggs is talking about a dozen different ways each day.

You see it when she won't let a music class begin because, en route down the stairs, someone pushed a little girl who then erupts in tears. "Mrs. Wang, excuse me, we have a very serious problem," she says, marching into the room where all but the little girl, who is sobbing at Paley's side, are gearing up to sing. "We can't have any happy singing," Paley says, because the little girl "feels terrible, and I just want to give her a moment to feel better."

And you see it on the way back from music class when, yet again, someone is pushed out of line. There is no scolding (unheard of in Paley's world view, where there is no punishment, only discussion, and certainly not a time-out chair, that latter-day incarnation of the old-fashioned "stand in the corner"). Instead, Paley stops the line and announces that the child pushed out "feels something very unfair has taken place." That's followed by an airing from both sides on what actually has occurred and then a most civilized discourse on what is fair.

Even the simplest infraction inside Paley's four walls becomes fodder for a fairness talk. Nothing is labeled good or bad, only fair or unfair, the lens through which Paley sees all.

Says Paley: "Any classroom—I know the kindergarten best—should develop into a close-knit community of people who care deeply about each other and show it in dozens of ways, who feel free to complain and argue about each other because there is no punishment. It is dialogue. We are attempting to understand why we do the things we do, what we enjoy doing, what other people do not enjoy when we do it. It is a place where ideas, learning how to communicate ideas and listen to the ideas of others, should be among the most exciting activities going on.

"And of course the teacher, above all, models all of this."

Above a dusty blue vinyl phonograph in the corner of Room 284 hangs a sign written in black marker: "You Can't Say You Can't Play." It's the No. 1 rule in Paley's classroom as well as the title of her seventh book, one in which she reported on the year she spent exploring the pain and loneliness of the child who's never asked to play, repeatedly pushed away from the group. That was the year, after much debate with children all the way up to 6th grade, she set down the rule she considers possibly her most lasting contribution to children's lives.

Here is some of that kindergarten debate:

Teacher: Should one child be allowed to keep another child from joining a group? A good rule might be: "You can't say you can't play."

Ben: If you cry people should let you in.

Teacher: What if someone is not crying but feels sad? Should the teacher force children to say yes?

Many voices: No, no.

Sheila: If they don't want you to play they should just go their own way and you should say, "Clara, let's find someone who likes you better."

Angelo: Lisa and her should let Clara in because they like Clara sometimes but not all the time so they should let her in.

A little later in the same debate:

Angelo: Let anybody play if someone asks.

Lisa: Then what's the whole point of playing?

Nelson: You just want Cynthia.

Lisa: I could play alone. Why can't Clare play alone?

Angelo: I think that's pretty sad. People that is alone they has water in their eyes.

Still stinging from the pain of all the children who ever "has water in their eyes," including the one she remembered from her own school days—an overweight girl who always wore the same dress, and was ridiculed by the teacher—Paley set down the rule. She concluded: "Each time a cause for sadness is removed for even one child, the classroom seems nicer. And, by association, we all rise in stature." And the results, even shortly after. "The children are learning that it is far easier to open the doors than to keep people out."

Four years after instituting the anti-rejection rule, Paley is more convinced than ever that the classroom is the laboratory for the moral life of the child: "This is the first place where the morality of life is examined by children, by the teacher, where one can begin to imagine a world that has more fairness, equality and compassion in it. You can do this in a classroom in a way that you really can't do it in the outside society."

As Paley writes and talks abut the "essential loneliness of the child," paying such painstaking attention to the child left out of play, you get the palpable sense she's been there. You're right.

It is stunning to come upon one particular disclosure while reading the works of the woman whose self is so consumed by kindergarten:

"To be accurate," she writes in the opening pages of "You Can't Say," "I didn't really attend kindergarten. Miss Estelle, the teacher, advised my mother to take me out and keep me at home until first grade. 'Your daughter just sits outside the circle and watches,' she said. Much later, when I asked my mother why she didn't insist that I remain and learn how to enter the magic circle, she shrugged. 'But that was the teacher telling me.'"

Paley never mentions that piece of her story in all the hours' talk about kindergarten.

In fact, when asked about her first school memory she responds: "first, last and always, though I myself was not directly affected because I was always very well behaved, to the point of being somewhat shy and quiet, my memories of school were of teachers who were not very nice to a lot of children.

"I never discussed it with anyone—not even at home—but I can remember thinking that there were unnecessarily mean things that were done."

Home for Paley was on Division Street in Humboldt Park where she was one of three children born to Jewish immigrant parents, her father a proctologist—"the doctor in a prayer shawl," she recalls—her mother, now 94, a factory bookkeeper early on.

Theirs was a strictly observant Jewish home, and even today Paley and her husband keep a kosher kitchen, following a strict code of dietary laws. And now, as then, hers is a house filled with books. Shelves and shelves of them. Whole walls, in fact.

Paley remembers being drawn to the stories by Yiddish writers. "I read those stories at an early age and very, very often it was the odd person, the poor person, the cast-aside person who ends up in the role [of] 'best loved by God.' "

In her own growing-up story, Paley's natural-born introspection shadows every page. "I can remember at a very young age, a *very* young age, beginning to wonder if there was really a God. I'd never heard anyone ask that question. I wondered about it all the time and never asked anyone because I knew that it was not a question that was appropriate to ask.

"And I certainly did a lot of wondering about why teachers did what they did, why they behaved so unfairly in so many situations. I'd never talked to anyone about that either.

"I wondered everywhere. Sitting in the classroom, I did a lot of daydreaming."

Any wonder then that she should have found herself back in the classroom daydreaming in the late 1960s?

'This is the first place where the morality of life is examined by children, by the teacher, where one can begin to imagine a world that has more fairness, equality and compassion in it.'—Vivian Paley

---

She'd gotten into teaching she candidly admits because, "Ohhh, I couldn't think of anything else. Sad to say, I hadn't considered anything else either." And for the first 13 years that a bunch of kids called her "Teacher," she did her job the easy way. "I wanted to get through the day as quietly and quickly as possible." She followed the teacher's guides, passed out the mimeographed sheets, even had a time-out chair when it came into vogue.

But then, working on her master's degree in New York, Paley met Professor Piaget, first in textbooks, and once, in person, at a lecture. She was hooked. Here was this guy who didn't just look at kids through a glass wall, scribbling down mysterious notes. He actually talked to children, questioned them, listened to their thoughts, got them doing all sorts of experiments that

showed how they processed ideas. And he didn't jump to conclusions.

Paley tried out Piaget's experiments in her own Long Island classroom. "I was generally beginning to find out what children are like. And little by little I began to listen to conversations that seemed so incredible, so fanciful, that it never occurred to me that children really believed in them."

Not long after that, Irving, who'd graduated from the U. of C., got an offer he wouldn't refuse from his alma mater's public information office. Back to Hyde Park moved the Paleys.

And the schoolteacher in the family settled into one of the kindergartens in the cavernous limestone edifice that houses the Lab Schools' lower school. Still longing for more meaning in her classroom, and beginning what she calls her "awakening," Paley audited a class, "Analysis of Teaching," taught by the esteemed educator Philip W. Jackson, who was then both director of the Lab Schools and dean of the university's graduate school of education.

Paley recalls: "I had *never* thought of myself as a writer. I never wrote so much as an interesting letter. I don't remember the assignment exactly, but I was to think back on the first time I *felt* like a teacher. Now I had been a teacher 13 years and for the very first time I sat myself down and went back in my memory—way, way back—to how I felt the very first time I somehow said to myself, 'I am a teacher.' " She turned in three or four pages.

"I got it back with a note, 'Vivian, see me after school.' He said, 'Look, you didn't follow the assignment, but you have a very interesting voice when you talk about yourself as a teacher.'

"I went home that night—[discovering that voice] had a magical effect—I started writing. It turned out to be 'White Teacher,' " Paley's first and still best selling book. Published in 1979, "White Teacher" examines the ways in which a child's differences—race, religion, even a stutter—are washed over, ignored, never addressed, leaving the child only to feel outcast for that which makes him or her unlike the others.

There've been seven books and some 640 children since then, the moment Paley realized she had, right there before her on the story rug, "an assemblage of truth-tellers" and that the "stuff of children's play is the original Great Books."

She quickly took the role of the ancient Greek chorus, repeating the children's words and phrases, keeping their plots on track. And whenever the Great Ideas of preschool or kindergarten—"birthdays, cooking and eating, going to bed, watching for bad guys, caring for babies," her partial list—were discussed, she would be their Socrates.

That is all over now, now that Paley has packed up her tape recorder and taken it home for the very last time.

But she promised to waste no time transcribing the last classroom voices on the solitary tape she allows herself. (A measure of her discipline: She'd buy only one tape at a time, forcing herself to play back, write down and ponder the previous day's recordings every morning at 4:30, putting in a good two hours' desk work before dawn.)

6. REFLECTIONS

She would be at her desk the very next morning after the very last day, she vowed, penning the first pages of her ninth book, the one that will tie together all her years in the classroom, one that she "must do, emotionally, before I can go on."

And then, on this fine spring afternoon that was losing its light, the schoolroom philosopher drained the very bottom of her flowered-china coffee cup. She offered one last morsel, delivered with full Paley punch:

"I think about the classroom. I figure, 'What the heck, I don't have to think about everything.' How can I? I'll assume other people think about the other things.

"You in your classrooms," she says, her valedictory to the teachers she leaves behind, "are far more powerful to achieve moral changes than you think you are. You don't even need a new curriculum to do it. We have more of an opportunity to change the moral landscape of our little universe than the doctor does in the hospital, than the lawyer does in the court, than the reporter does on the newspaper, than the engineer does in the field.

"I mean, think about it. Twenty, thirty children. What a bonanza we have!"

She paused, only to gather gusto. "I'll miss it. I will miss the kinds of opportunities that come only in the classroom, I swear, and no place else on Earth. I feel sorry for people who work in offices."

And then the teacher rose. Class dismissed.

Families and Children: Who is Responsible?

Sharon L. Kagan

Sharon L. Kagan is Senior Associate at Yale University's Bush Center in Child Development and Social Policy, New Haven, Connecticut. This article is based on her keynote address at the ACEI Study Conference in New Orleans, Louisiana, March 30, 1994.

To people outside the United States, the title of this article must seem unusual. In many other nations, this question was solved long ago. Other nations do not allow national politics to obscure issues of child allowances, paid maternity and paternity leave, voluntary home visitation, quality child care and school age care. Family and child advocates do not have to compete with transportation and defense interests for federal funds. Many countries have established services to children and families as a national priority. Thus, in many nations of the world it is quite clear who is responsible for children and families.

Such commitment to children and families is, however, hardly universal. Furthermore, the increasing needs of youngsters, coupled with global competition and government deficits, make even stronger and broader commitment necessary. We must begin to consider issues of responsibility on an international scale in order to recognize the increasingly complex lifestyles of children and families throughout the world. The United Nations underscored this need by declaring 1994 to be the Year of the Family.

Organization

While no country has perfectly solved the "responsibility" question, this article recognizes that nations have much to teach and learn from each other. Each nation's choices in allocating responsibility for children and families have deep roots in specific cultural values and norms that have developed over time. This article focuses on the United States as a case study, exploring the following issues: the deep roots underlying the nature of responsibility for children and families in America; the deep results, both intended and unintended, of American attitudes toward responsibility for children and families; the deep issues that need to be considered by the United States and all nations when shaping responsibility for children and families; and the deep change that might be possible if we adopt certain concrete strategies for improving services to children and families.

Deep Roots: The American Experience

Historians and social anthropologists note that America developed its notion of social responsibility for children and families from a heritage of English traditions (Cremin, 1987; Lynn, 1980). When the colonists flocked to America, they brought with them a social configuration that separated the household, the church and the school. Each entity "stood in time honored relation to the others, with the nuclear family (an idea transported from England) carrying *by far* the greatest burden" (Cremin, 1987). The family was responsible for framing children's ideas about the world and how they ought to behave in it. The church carried the lesser responsibility of imparting moral teachings and conducting community ceremonials that united individual families. Schools' responsibility was limited mostly to teaching reading and writing.

Framing this tripartite division of responsibility, the colonists reinstituted precedents established in the Poor Laws of 1601 under which families were the line of first provision. The communities (schools and churches) intervened only when families failed and then provided help only for local residents, setting the stage for local and state control of human services and for the

From *Childhood Education*, Fall 1994, pp. 4-8. © 1994 by the Association for Childhood Education International, 11501 Georgia Avenue, Suite 315, Wheaton, MD. Reprinted by permission.

stigmatization of troubled families. From the outset, people regarded a family's need for community support or governmental intervention as a sign of weakness. Colonists attributed poverty to moral indecency and human ineptitude. The colonists did, however, view education as an entitlement for all, presumably to prepare citizens for participation in the great experiment of democracy.

As increasing numbers of immigrants came to the shores of America, social and education services grew. Although funding, professionalization and regulations in these fields increased, the basic nature of human services throughout the nation stayed the same. Social services remained for those who could not provide for themselves; education was for all.

These patterns etched the current nature of responsibility for children and families. Given the history of primarily familial responsibility for child and family well-being and localized community or government intervention only in the case of "failure," federal commitment to families and children in the United States was limited.

Only in the face of national crises have "beneficent" federal legislators accorded temporary support to children and families. The Great Depression, World War II and the War on Poverty inspired federal child care services and Head Start as a means of staving off national disaster. In short, the U.S. government has accepted responsibility for the well-being of children and families only during times of compelling social need. Overall, responsibility for children and families remained with parents and kin and a stigma was attached to government or community help.

Deep Results: What Are the Consequences of America's Deep Roots?

When America's notions of responsibility to children and families were being developed, it was surely difficult to foresee how they would

play out over time. Today, however, we can pinpoint several important consequences of America's ethos of privatized responsibility and deficit-oriented government involvement in child and family issues.

First, services for children and families are not and never have been as abundant as they should be. State and federal child care dollars do not begin to support the need for assistance. A recent Children's Defense Fund report (1994) notes that 31 states and the District of Columbia had waiting lists for child care, with up to 30,000 names and projected waiting periods of over a year. Estimates of homelessness in our nation range from 1.7 million to 3 million per year; families with children account for 43 percent of that population (Children's Defense Fund, 1994). Furthermore, about 45 percent of the nation's children under two are not fully immunized (Children's Defense Fund, 1994). In short, basic needs—child care, housing, immunizations—are not available to all Americans who need them.

A second consequence of America's limited national commitment to children is the severe inequity in who receives the services that exist. Approximately one fourth of America's young children live in poverty. These children need services the most and yet receive them the least. Forty-nine percent of poor children do not have access to preschool programs (U.S. General Accounting Office, 1993).

A third consequence of limited federal responsibility for children and families in the United States is inefficiency, inconsistency and fragmentation of services. The National Academy of Sciences (1990) demonstrated that while scores of disconnected federal supports for child care exist, they are so fragmented that the exact number of these supports has not been formally identified. Some studies (Stephan & Schillmoeller, 1987) identify 22 federal child care programs,

while others (U.S. Department of Labor, 1988) cite 31 programs in 11 federal agencies.

Each program comes with its own unique federal regulations, funding sources and funding patterns, with few incentives for streamlining or collaboration (Kagan, 1991; Sugarman, 1991). Consequently, practitioners compete for children, services, staff and space (Goodman & Brady, 1988). Parents are often forced to piece together services in order to provide full care for their children. Consequently, children are juggled from program to program, rarely experiencing programmatic or philosophic continuity.

Finally, the service system has few quality safeguards. The necessity for quality programming is not adequately recognized by many of those who allocate funds, nor is it supported by state statute. Workers in the child and family service field are unable to command wages much above those of babysitters, and unrestricted access to the field creates an unlimited supply of workers. Therefore, the quality of providers is seriously compromised.

When government has intervened, the resulting child and family services are of high quality. Bereft of federal investments and universal commitments, the quality of child and family services will continue to suffer (Kagan & Newton, 1989; Whitebook, Howes & Phillips, 1989).

In short, the historically rooted national ethos of limited federal responsibility for children and families results in services that are ranked low on every important variable: quantity, equity, continuity and quality. Families do their best to serve their children, but often face untenable odds. They are then forced to turn to an inadequate service system.

Deep Issues: The Who, What and How of Responsibility for Children and Families

Every nation must consider transcendent issues in discerning responsibility for children and families: 1) Who should be targeted for government support and commitment? Should government support mostly children, mostly families or both? 2) Nations must develop a precise focus for government commitment. Should responsibility and support be cultivated for program development only, or for both programs and infrastructure? 3) Nations must discern how different parties should be responsible to children and families. Who should provide direct services and who should determine policy or generate funds? Each of these issues is explored below, using the United States as a case example.

Responsibility for Whom? For centuries, nations have divided their services to children and families. Sometimes the services provided for children are in competition with those provided for families. The early childhood field in the United States has not fallen prey to such dichotomous thinking because of a shared belief that young children cannot be served in isolation from their families. Such beliefs have found expression historically in parenting cooperatives, Head Start and hosts of other programs, including Even Start and the Comprehensive Child Development Program. The growth and expansion of such programs has helped disseminate the notion of public responsibility for both children and families.

But the question of *which* children and *which* families are the nation's responsibility remains largely unanswered in the United States. Despite increased recognition that children and families of all racial and economic backgrounds need supports, public commitment in the United States has been largely limited to poor and minority populations. Indeed, the first National Education Goal—to ready all children for school by the year 2000—may mark the first time that the nation has expressed the clear intention of advancing the health, education and well-being of *all* children.

It is becoming clearer philosophically that nations should be serving families and children together and should be concerned about children and families of all backgrounds. Serving all children, however, requires enormous financial outlays or tax incentives, which in turn depend upon significant changes in political thinking. At the direct service level, working with families and children together also requires change. Staff trained to work primarily with children or with adults question their capacity to deliver high quality programs to both populations simultaneously. In short, the question of whom to support expands the universe of those to be served, bringing with it still unanswered questions of what such expanded responsibility should entail and how it can be achieved.

What Should Be the Focus of Responsibility? Not surprisingly, given the pressing need, responsibility for children and families in the United States has centered on sustaining direct services to children and families rather than focusing on the development of infrastructure—training, regulations, resources and referrals—to support those services. Throughout the 1980s, the policy emphasis on direct services was so strong that lobbying for anything else was considered akin to taking food from the mouths of starving children.

Recently, however, a growing segment of the early childhood field has recognized that direct services to children and families will always be compromised unless the proper supports exist to shore up the service system. We need training mechanisms, an advocacy capacity and data collection. Child and family service providers have come to realize that they must develop a vision extending beyond direct services in order for the field to advance.

This work has begun through the national *Quality 2000* initiative. The leaders have identified not only the characteristics of quality child and family service programs, but also a quality service infrastructure that includes: 1) cross-system collaboration, 2) consumer and public involvement, 3) quality control, 4) adequate levels of financing and 5) the development of the work force (Kagan & *Quality 2000* Essential Functions Task Force, 1993). Therefore, many have recognized that responsibility for children and families must be diversified in focus so that both direct services and service systems can be strengthened.

How Should Responsibility Be Distributed? Apart from issues of who should be covered and what the focus should be, we need to address questions of how responsibility for children and families should be distributed. Osborne and Gaebler (1992), in their work on reinventing government, share the view that the functions of government have been confounded in the United States. The authors contend that government is a blunt instrument for service delivery and therefore should not be in the business of providing direct services to children and families. Rather, government should guide service delivery through policy decisions. Such guidance requires people in government positions who see the universe of options and can balance competing demands for resources.

Direct service, on the other hand, relies on people who are closer to individual consumers and can focus on service missions and perform them well. Theorists have begun to define roles and responsibilities for different parties serving children and families, indicating that without such definition commitment to children and families will have fewer positive effects.

Deep Change—Strategies for Optimal Responsibility
Consideration of these deep issues surrounding responsibility for children and families—the who, the

what and the how—leads to the difficult question of who is really responsible for children and families in America. Given the nation's ideological history, coupled with what we know from research, there is no reason to question that the primary responsibility for child rearing in the United States currently resides first with parents, next with family and kin and then with neighborhood and community. Responsibility for children and families is not shifted wholesale in different stages from one of these groups to another; rather, it is shared among them.

Inherent in this definition of "sharing" is the reality that those closest to the child share more of the responsibility, accompanied by the growing recognition that families need support. Indeed, throughout the nation, an entire new breed of services, called family support programs, are taking root to assist individuals in their parenting roles. Family support programs are designed to serve not just parents in need, but all parents. Such supports are taking the form of parenting education, home visits, center-based services and services that function in mainstream institutions such as schools and hospitals.

Just as important, institutions, including corporations, are adopting family orientations predicated on the belief that in order to secure a better future for children, all of society's institutions must pull together. This family focus will not emerge from installing simple add-on programs that remain separate from mainstream institutions. The adoption of a family focus increasingly results in a reorientation of the very fabric—the institutional culture and beliefs—of an organization. A family-focused institution does not view its employees as workers only; rather, they are workers, parents, community members and partners whose multiple needs and concerns are incorporated into the institution's operating procedures.

Despite these rather robust movements outside of government, the federal government remained quite remote from family support efforts until 1993. Recently, however, the Family Support and Family Preservation Act, the Family Medical Leave Act, new provisions in Head Start and Chapter 1, and Secretary of Education Richard Riley's stated commitment to families, demonstrate that the federal government is recognizing the value of family support and family engagement as prevention and promotion strategies.

This shift in government thinking, however subtle, is important. The recent national legislation reflects government's willingness to carve a role for itself that is more supportive of families than we have ever before seen. Much of the

*t*he recent national legislation reflects government's willingness to carve a role for itself that is more supportive of families than we have ever before seen.

legislation delineates explicit roles for communities, in which communities are considered planning and decision-making entities guided by general frameworks outlined by the federal government. Some call this the top-down/bottom-up approach to shared responsibility.

It is clear that the government perceives itself as the steerer, rather than the rower, in supporting children and families. We should take heart, however, and realize that this perception is an advancement in and of itself. Recognizing this shift in governmental commitment is important. Equally important to

Americans and citizens of other nations is recognizing how the shift came about. Such understanding can guide us in fashioning additional reform. Richmond and Kotelchuck (1984) noted that three things are needed for social reform: 1) a knowledge base, 2) a social strategy and 3) public will.

Fortunately, the knowledge base for family support and for shared commitment to children and families in the United States has been documented in literature and fortified by hundreds of demonstration programs. A social strategy for supporting children and families, however, has been missing in the United States. But as advocates have increasingly come together to pass key legislation, the seeds for a social strategy seem to have been put in place. Indeed, a coalition of multiple organizations participated in framing the ideas for the Family Support and Family Preservation Act.

What seemed to be missing most in that effort was the third necessity for social reform—public will. The strength of public will in the U.S., however, has recently changed. In reviewing polls about child care and family issues, the Child Care Action Campaign and the Communications Consortium Media Center (1994) found that 69 percent of Americans rated child care as either an extremely or a very important priority. In 1993, 55 percent of all Americans stated that government should play a greater role in providing child care assistance to families. This growing concern may be due to the pressure of daily living and to the need for child care and family supports to transcend poverty. In addition, data are unequivocal about the relationship between voter concern and news coverage. Over 200 studies clearly demonstrate that voters' opinions reflect the overall coverage of the preceding week's news. In short, using the media is one way to pique voter support for child and family issues.

Another recently successful strategy has been the forging of coalitions to address specific issues. This approach has been used at the national level to advocate for family support and preservation legislation, and it is also becoming prevalent in states. In Indiana, teams within and outside of government came together to pool resources so that a Healthy Families initiative could be launched. Colorado implemented a similar initiative through the work of advocates outside of government and a combination of public funding streams. Increasingly, strong coalitions of people inside and outside of government are forming to frame action agendas and share responsibility for children and families.

Learning from this deep change taking place in the nation, we can begin to define optimal responsibility. Ideally, who is responsible for children and families? The answer is both simple and complex. We *all* are. Parents, professionals, residents of communities and neighborhoods and taxpayers are all responsible in different ways. The once-prevalent refrain, "Parents first; government when they fail" is slowly being replaced by "Parents are primary; society is willingly supportive."

In a system of shared responsibility, government is responsible for providing incentives and vehicles to empower families in caring for themselves and their children. Government's role includes regulation and the promulgation of new knowledge and information. Government in the United States should not be responsible for actually providing every child with quality early care and education; rather, it must ensure that every child has access to such service.

If government functions in this manner, and if responsibility for and support of children and families is truly shared throughout the nation, significant changes in child and family services may occur by 2010. While child care will still need quality enhancements, it will be available to all children. It is probable that family support as we know it will become institutionalized and that corporations will adopt more family supportive policies. Children may well be fully immunized, and all families will be likely to have a better understanding of child and human development. Overall, the signs indicate that America will become a more caring society, one that is more conducive to children and youth's optimal development.

This change will happen because we will learn from states and other nations, because we will have the knowledge to support the new reality that parenting must be shared, and because we will have energized public will. It will happen because people throughout the nation will see to it that what John Dewey said becomes true: "What every man wants for his own children, a just society has the obligation to deliver for all its children." A poem by Shel Silverstein (Children's Defense Fund, 1991, p. 20) summarizes well where we are with respect to sharing responsibility for children and families:

Listen to the mustn't, child,
Listen to the don'ts
Listen to the shouldn'ts
The impossible, the won'ts
Listen to the never haves
Then listen to me—
Anything can happen, child
ANYTHING can be.

References

Child Care Action Campaign, & Communications Consortium Media Center. (1994). *Polling analysis of child care issues, 1988-1993.* New York: Author.

Children's Defense Fund. (1991). *The state of America's children yearbook, 1991.* Washington, DC: Author.

Children's Defense Fund. (1994). *The state of America's children yearbook, 1994.* Washington, DC: Author.

Cremin, L. (1987). *Traditions of American education.* New York: Basic Books.

Goodman, I. F., & Brady, J. P. (1988). *The challenge of coordination.* Newton, MA: Education Development Center.

Kagan, S. L. (1991). *United we stand: Collaboration for child care and early education services.* New York: Teachers College Press.

Kagan, S. L., & Newton, J. (1989). For-profit and non-profit child care: Similarities and differences. *Young Children, 45*(1), 4-10.

Kagan, S. L., & *Quality 2000* Essential Functions Task Force. (1993). *The essential functions of the early child care and education system: Rationale and definition.* New Haven, CT: Yale University Bush Center.

Lynn, L. (1980). *The state and human services: Organizational change in a political context.* Cambridge, MA: The MIT Press.

National Academy of Sciences. (1990). *Who cares for America's children? Child care policy for the 1990's.* Washington, DC: Author.

Osborne, D., & Gaebler, T. (1992). *Reinventing government: How the entrepreneurial spirit is transforming the public sector.* Reading, MA: Addison-Wesley.

Richmond, J. B., & Kotelchuck, M. (1984). Commentary on changed lives. In J. R. Berrueta-Clement, L. Schweinhart, S. Barnett, A. Epstein, & D. Weikart (Eds.), *Changed lives: The effects of the Perry Preschool Program on youths through age 19.*

Ypsilanti, MI: High/Scope Press.

Stephan, S., & Schillmoeller, S. (1987). *Child day care: Selected federal programs.* Washington, DC: Division of Education and Public Welfare, Congressional Research Services, Library of Congress.

Sugarman, J. M. (1991). *Building early childhood systems: A resource handbook.* Washington, DC: Child Welfare League of America.

U. S. Department of Labor. (1988). *Child care: A workforce issue.* Washington, DC: Author.

U. S. General Accounting Office. (1993). *Poor preschool-aged children.* Washington, DC: Author (GAO/HRD93-111BR).

Whitebook, M., Howes, C., & Phillips, D. (1989). *Who cares? Child care teachers and the quality of care in America* (Executive Summary, National Child Care Staffing Study). Oakland, CA: Child Care Employee Project.

CHOOSING CHILD CARE

From au pairs to centers or family day care,
after-school programs to summer sleepaway camps,
here's a guide to finding what's right for your child

Where to Begin? Try Your Local R & R

Most parents don't know it, but nearly every community in America now has a central source of information about local child care options. These services are called child care resource and referral agencies, or "R&Rs" for short.

An R&R can help you locate licensed child care centers, family day care homes and even in-home caregivers within days, and also give you help in evaluating the quality of care you find. Many also track and help dispense child care subsidies to families who qualify.

Most R&Rs are private nonprofit agencies that often receive some government funds and have close ties to local child care licensing boards. That connection helps them keep tabs on which local caregivers and centers have set up shop and gotten a license—as well as those who have lost theirs.

Many R&Rs also know which local employers offer child care benefits, which agencies in the area sponsor after-school programs, how to find a summer camp and the names of local agencies that place domestic workers. There are now more than 400 R&Rs around the country, covering regions as small as a city and as large as an entire state. They fall generally into one of two categories:
1. **Community R&Rs** serve everyone in their given service area. The fastest way to find yours is to call Child Care Aware (1-800-424-2246)—a tollfree hotline set up by the National Association of Child Care Resource and Referral Agencies.

When you call your local R&R, you can expect to speak with a counselor who is trained to help you explore your options. If you don't know exactly what kind of care you need, she will ask you a series of questions—ranging from where you live and work to whether your child is allergic to any pets—to help you narrow the options. Then your counselor will try to match you with local providers from her R&R database.

In some cases, she will not know whether there are current openings—nor will she be able to guarantee the quality of a particular facility. All she can tell you is that the program is licensed and currently operating.

You can then finish the search on your own, by visiting the centers and checking up on references. Or you can ask for more guidance. Many R&Rs can send you written checklists and brochures to help you evaluate child care. Others, which are well established and well funded, may even have the time to help you develop questions to discuss with potential caregivers or draw up job descriptions for in-home caregivers.

Most services offered by community R&Rs are free, although some charge fees of up to $30 for helping parents secure child care.
2. **Corporate R&R services** are offered as employee benefits, open only to workers at the companies that fund them. If your firm offers such a service, be sure to use it when you are looking for child care! Company-sponsored R&Rs generally offer more in-depth service than

community R&Rs, and many will do a good deal of your legwork. Before giving you a referral, for example, they often check to see if a program actually has an opening for your child.

The best company-sponsored R&Rs have staff trained in child development and sensitive to an individual family's preferences. "Our counselors explore what the parents need, what kind of stresses they face at work and what they are looking for," says Carolyn Stolov-Peters, manager of the Work/Family Directions Early Childhood Team, which provides R&R services for many of the nation's largest corporations. "Each family and situation is unique."

Marian Zytko King, a computer consultant at Johnson & Johnson, learned last year just how valuable her company's R&R could be. King had hoped to use Johnson & Johnson's on-site center for her new baby. But a month before she was to return to work, she learned there was no opening for her child. "One of my co-workers suggested I call our R&R. They really understood my emergency!" says King.

After talking with King, a counselor began an immediate search, and over the next few days kept King posted on her progress until she found a spot in a local family day care home that suited King's needs. King visited it and now she and her baby are happily situated.

"Calling the referral service was one of the best things I have ever done for my baby!" she says. —JENNA SCHNUER

Finding a Family Day Care Home

Many parents like to use a caregiver who runs a program in her own home. This type of care, often called "family day care," is usually more affordable than other options, has a homey atmosphere and may be in your own neighborhood.

How to track one down? Call your local resource and referral agency (see "Where to Begin? Try Your Local R&R") or ask neighbors, friends, coworkers and other parents for leads. You can also look for notices (or post a notice yourself) on bulletin boards at churches, synagogues, community centers, nursery schools, pediatricians' offices, YMCAs, grocery stores and libraries. You can also check out the classified ads under "Child Care" in your local paper.

THE FIRST PHONE CALL

Once you have the names of some potential providers, call them to get basic information (be sure to ask if it's a convenient time to talk—the caregiver may be busy caring for children). Have a piece of paper handy to jot down some notes about the following issues:
- How long has she been caring for children in her home?
- How many children is she currently caring for? How old are they?
- Does she have children of her own? What are their ages? Are they home during the day?
- What hours does she operate?
- Has she had any training in child development? First aid?
- Is she licensed?
- Does she have an assistant?
- What does she do for backup if she or her child gets sick?
- What is her holiday schedule?

After you've spoken to several caregivers, decide which ones sound most promising and arrange to visit them.

WHEN YOU VISIT

When you observe a program, there are a number of things to look for. Here are some guidelines to keep in mind:

You should see children who:
- Seem comfortable and are free to move about and investigate their surroundings the way they would at home.
- Are happily occupied.
- Approach the caregiver easily when they need her help or attention.
- Request food when they're hungry and have appetizing food served to them.
- Have their diapers changed promptly. (The caregiver should wash her hands after every diaper change.)

The caregiver should:
- Help children find enjoyable activities.
- Play directly with the children.
- Respond promptly if a child is in distress or has a question or problem.
- Resolve disputes between children fairly and calmly.

The schedule should include:
- Some active play, such as building with big blocks and playing outdoors.
- Some quiet play, such as looking at books, drawing or pasting.
- Snacks and meals.

You should not see:
- Children ever left unsupervised.
- Children running randomly around the house or bored because there is nothing to do.
- Children hurting each other, with no adult intervention.
- Toys that are inaccessible to the kids, unsafe or not appropriate for their ages.
- Food that can cause choking served to children under three, such as grapes, peanuts or raw carrots.
- Any physical discipline at all—including hitting or shaking children.
- Any verbal reprimand that shames or embarrasses a child.

KEYS TO QUALITY

As every parent knows, kids need a lot of attention. So make sure that any family day care home or child care center has enough adults on hand.

It's also important that the group size be small enough to permit control of the noise and energy level. Here are some guidelines from The National Association for the Education of Young Children (NAEYC) about what to look for, by the age of your child:

Infants (up to 12 months): No more than eight babies per group; one adult for every four.
Young toddlers (12 to 24 months): No more than 12 kids per group; one adult for every four.
Older toddlers (24 to 30 months): No more than 12 children per group; one adult for every six.
Note: Centers accredited by NAEYC are certified as meeting these standards.

THE FINAL DECISION

If everything looks good, be sure to talk to a few parents who have used the program. As you talk to them, listen to the tone of voice they use as well as what is actually said. Do they sound enthusiastic or do they hesitate as they answer your questions? Often people don't like to give negative references unless their experiences were really dreadful.

If parents are enthusiastic, call the provider and tell her that you want to bring your child for a visit. If you like the way the caregiver interacts with your youngster, you have probably found a program that's just right for you and your child!

Choosing a Child Care Center

Over the last decade, a growing number of families have chosen child care centers for many reasons: Centers provide one of the most reliable forms of care, many have stimulating programs, and they are often very affordable.

Many also provide care to children over a wide age span—some even offer after-school care once a child goes on to kindergarten. That means your child can have a long association with the center and many of the caregivers.

If you decide to go this route, you'll want to consider some of the practical issues. Call around to local centers and find out which ones best meet the needs of your family. Be sure to ask about hours, since the definition of "full-time" care can vary widely. Some centers are open from as early as six a.m.; others don't open their doors until eight a.m.

Costs also vary widely, depending on where the centers are located and how well they are staffed. The major expense for the program usually is, and should be, caregivers' salaries. This means that fees may vary according to the age of your child—since more caregivers are needed to care for babies than for preschoolers.

VISITING THE CENTER

The best way to evaluate a day care center is, of course, to observe the program. When you go, talk to the director and spend at least a few hours in the room your child would be in. Here's an age-by-age guide to what you should look for:

With infants, you should see caregivers who:

- Provide lots of physical contact—holding, carrying, rocking on laps.
- Engage in one-to-one interaction with babies, talking and making frequent eye contact with them.
- React quickly and lovingly to babies who are crying or otherwise distressed.
- Feed individual babies when they are hungry.
- Have toys on hand that are both safe and stimulating.
- Diaper babies whenever necessary.
- Allow individual babies to nap when they are tired.
- Encourage attempts at independence by having areas where babies can freely crawl and explore.
- Communicate in a calm voice with the other caregivers in the room.
- Carefully follow health procedures: Wash hands after every diaper change and before feedings. Keep bottles clean and identified for each baby. Store food in the refrigerator. Wash eating utensils thoroughly with soap.

You should not see:

- Infants spending long periods of time confined in playpens, infant seats or cribs unless they are napping.
- Caregivers talking to each other and not attending to the babies.
- Any rough physical handling of babies.
- All babies fed, changed or put to sleep at the same time.
- Babies fed in cribs with their bottles propped up.

With one- and two-year-old children, you should see caregivers who:

- Encourage language development by talking with and listening to kids.
- Understand young children's needs for repetition. (They patiently reread a favorite story when requested.)
- Respond calmly and flexibly to kids who say no repeatedly or test limits constantly. (They make "cleanup" into a

game or give a toddler a few extra minutes to play if he's not ready to tidy up.)
- Encourage children when they try to do something for themselves, such as eating or drinking.
- Offer help when a toddler is frustrated with an activity that's too difficult.
- Have realistic expectations for children—that toddlers may have trouble sharing, for example.
- Actively participate in the games toddlers initiate.
- Frequently read to the children.
- Provide a variety of materials to experiment with—large crayons, Play-Doh, fingerpaints, sand, water.
- Feed toddlers when they are hungry. (There should be enough adults so that no child has to wait too long to be fed.)
- Let children rest when they are tired and sleep when they need to.

You should not see:

- Anybody insisting that toddlers participate in a group activity, unless it is for safety reasons—e.g., a fire drill.
- Caregivers who react angrily when kids say no.
- Children fighting over toys, without adult intervention. (Caregivers should teach children how to take turns and resolve disputes.)
- Caregivers making fun of the way a young child speaks.
- Use of any type of physical punishment or rough handling.
- Caregivers reacting with disgust when children need to be changed.
- Toddlers made to use potties before they are ready for toilet training.
- Children eating foods that can cause choking, such as carrots or nuts.

With preschoolers, you should see:

- A program that is varied, with group activities—meals, stories, music, meetings—as well as individual playtime.
- Plenty of outdoor play, when children can exercise, run, climb and be noisy.
- Times for quiet activities, such as coloring, looking at books or resting.

You should see caregivers who:

- Give children choices about what they want to do.
- Help them find what they need.
- Sit with the kids while they work or play (e.g., at the table with crayons).
- Explain ideas and concepts in language understandable to young children (e.g., using colorful shapes to show the difference between a triangle and a circle).
- Give boys and girls the same opportunities for participation in all activities.
- Offer assistance when needed.

- React with enthusiasm to children's discoveries and accomplishments.
- Help the children to work cooperatively with one another.
- Gear activities to short attention spans.
- Select materials that match the skill levels of the age-group.
- Recognize the strengths of each child; know who needs extra help and provide it.

TALK WITH THE DIRECTOR

At the end of your visit, arrange to chat with the director of the center to discuss the program. It's important that you feel comfortable with her, since she's the one who sets the policy and tone of the center and hires and supervises the staff. Make sure to ask these questions:

1. Will the caregiver you observed actually be the one with your child?
2. How long has each caregiver been with the center? (Make sure there is not a high turnover rate; children are more likely to thrive in consistent care.)
3. What qualifications does the director look for in hiring staff?
4. How many children will be in your child's group? How many caregivers will regularly be present? (See "Keys to Quality" for guidelines on what's best.)
5. What is the policy about illness?
6. Is there anyone on the staff with training in first aid? (There should be.) What physician or hospital emergency room does the center use if immediate action is required?
7. What are the payment policies? Does the center charge additional fees for diapers, milk, etc.?
8. What is the calendar for the year?

CHECK REFERENCES

The last step in making any child care choice is always a careful reference check. Ask the director for the names of some families using the center, and be sure to call them. Keep in mind that the director is most likely to give you only the names of families who have had positive experiences, so ask the parents you call if they know of any families who were less satisfied with the care—and the reasons for that dissatisfaction. If possible, get the names of those parents and follow up with them as well.

You can also call your local R & R agency and any government boards that oversee child care to see if there have been formal complaints about the center.

If everything checks out, then you and your child are off to a great start!

Selecting School-Age Care

When you have a child in school, you know how demanding her day can be. That's why an after-school program should not be just a continuation of the school day, with the same kind of structure or focus on academic activities. Nor should it be a babysitting service, where children just wait around with little to do until their parents are finished working and arrive to take them home. Instead, a quality program should offer:

1. Reliable and qualified staff. After-school programs are frequently staffed by college students, and sometimes by high-school students. These young people probably have no formal training for the job, but if they are energetic and really enjoy being with children, they can be terrific caregivers. However, there should be ongoing training and supervision by a well-qualified director, so that the staff learns to handle a variety of situations and understands what kind of behavior is appropriate for children of different ages.

2. Variety of activities and materials. Children should have a chance to do a wide number of things: art, drama, athletics, music and other activities.

3. Pleasant and safe physical environment. The facility should be clean, well ventilated and well lighted. Walls, floors and ceilings should be in good shape, electric wiring and fixtures safe and in good repair. The kitchen should be clean, with perishable food kept refrigerated.

4. Facilities for active play. Equipment in the outdoor play area should be safe—swings well attached, seesaws securely bolted—and there should be a rubber, sand or grass surface to protect against injuries from falls.

5. Small groups and good adult supervision. Experts suggest that for children between the ages of five and seven, there should be at least one adult for a group of 10 children. For older youngsters, a group size of 13 with at least one adult is workable.

6. Space for quiet activities. After a day at school, children need time alone and a quiet place to daydream, do homework, paint or read a book. Others may want to do things with just one or two friends—play a game of checkers or jacks. There should be a few quiet areas to accommodate them.

7. Good, nutritious food. Healthy and filling snacks like fruit, cheese, peanut butter, milk and juice should be available—rather than junk food.

"FINDING A FAMILY DAY CARE HOME," "CHOOSING A CHILD CARE CENTER," AND "SELECTING SCHOOL-AGE CARE" ARE ALL ADAPTED FROM *THE COMPLETE GUIDE TO CHOOSING CHILD CARE,* BY JUDITH BEREZIN. COPYRIGHT © 1990 BY THE NATIONAL ASSOCIATION OF CHILD CARE RESOURCE AND REFERRAL AGENCIES AND CHILD CARE, INC. PUBLISHED BY RANDOM HOUSE, INC. TO ORDER A COPY FOR $12.95, CALL 1-800-677-7760.

Finding an In-Home Caregiver

Do you want a nanny to come to your home? An au pair from Europe? A part-time caregiver after school? There are several avenues to take:

Placement agencies. Local agencies that specialize in helping families find domestic help are listed in the Yellow Pages under "Child Care" or Domestic Help." Fees range from about $500 to $2,500, if they hook you up with a caregiver. A good agency should offer a refund or replacement if the relationship goes sour in the first few months.

Nanny schools. About 15 schools across the country specialize in training caregivers. For a list, write: American Council of Nanny Schools, Delta College, University Center, MI 48710.

Au pair agencies. The federal government has authorized a limited number of one-year visas to allow legal au pairs into this country. They are allowed to put in 45 hours of child care and light housekeeping each week for a private room, board and a $100-a-week stipend. To get the official list of approved au pair agencies, call the U.S. Information Agency, 202-475-2389.

Advertising: You can advertise in the classified section of your local newspaper, or check out the ads under "Child Care," "Household Help," "Domestic Help" or "Positions Wanted."

INTERVIEWING CANDIDATES

What should you ask a potential caregiver who will work in your home? Here are some ideas:
• Why are you looking for a new job? (Find out if she's truly interested in working with children, and why she left her last job.)
• What do you enjoy about working with children? (Get her to elaborate on her interest in kids.)
• What kinds of activities do you do with children? (Make sure her ideas are appropriate for your children's ages.)
• How did your parents discipline you as a child? (This can indicate what she considers appropriate discipline.)
• How would you handle . . . ? (Fill in situations such as a medical emergency, a tantrum, potty training, sibling conflict, etc.—and see if you are comfortable with her answers.)
• What jobs have you held in the past and what did you like about them?
• Whom may we contact for references? (Get at least two names.)

CHECK REFERENCES

Even if you use a placement agency, check a candidate's references yourself. Here are key questions to ask:
• When and for how long did she work for you? Why did she leave?
• What were her job responsibilities?
• How many children did she care for and what were their ages?
• What activities did she plan?
• How did she handle discipline?
• Was she reliable and prompt?
• Did you find it easy to solve problems together as they arose?
• What are her strengths? Weaknesses?

Many parents also like to check a caregiver's background more thoroughly, especially for live-in positions. You can hire an investigative service (look under "Investigators" in the Yellow Pages) to check for criminal, civil or driving records. Typical charges are $65 to $75.

ADAPTED FROM *THE WORKING PARENTS HELP BOOK,* BY TOM AND SUSAN PRICE. COPYRIGHT © 1994 BY THE AUTHORS. REPRINTED BY PERMISSION OF PETERSON'S. TO ORDER A COPY FOR $12.95, CALL 1-800-677-7760.

Cost, Quality, and Child Outcomes in Child Care Centers: Key Findings and Recommendations

Cost, Quality, and Outcomes Study Team

The *Cost, Quality and Outcomes in Child Care Centers* study combines economic and child development perspectives in a unique examination of the relationships among the costs of child care, the nature of children's child care experiences, and their effects on children. Cost and quality data were collected through visits in 1993 to 400 randomly selected centers in California, Colorado, Connecticut, and North Carolina (50 nonprofit and 50 for-profit programs were selected in each state). In addition, parents were surveyed regarding their perceptions of their child care settings. Data were also collected using individual assessments, teacher ratings, and parent reports on 826 children attending a subsample of participating centers.

In brief, the study found that while child care varies widely between states and within sectors of this industry, most child care—especially for infants and toddlers—is medio-cre in quality and sufficiently poor to interfere with children's emotional and intellectual development. Better quality child care was linked to more positive child outcomes for all children, regardless of background. Market forces—including strong price competition and lack of consumer demand for quality—constrain the cost of child care and at the same time depress the quality of care provided to children.

Major findings

Our findings are grouped as they relate to quality; costs, revenue, and support; sector comparisons; and the economic environment.

Quality

• **Child care at most centers in the United States is poor to mediocre, with 40% of infants and toddlers in rooms having less-than-minimal quality.**

While there is a great deal of variation in the sample, the mean quality score for all centers in the study was 4.0, a full point below the good-quality level. Overall, only 14% of centers were rated as offering developmentally appropriate care, and 12% were rated as poor. As illustrated in Figure 1, child care for infants and toddlers is of particular concern. Of the 225 infant and toddler rooms observed, only 8% were good or excellent, and 40% were rated as poor.

Members of the Cost, Quality, and Child Outcomes Study Team include **Suzanne Helburn** and **Mary L. Culkin**, principal investigators, and **John Morris** and **Naci Moran**, economists, from the University of Colorado at Denver; **Carollee Howes**, principal investigator, and **Leslie Phillipsen**, site coordinator, from the University of California at Los Angeles; **Donna Bryant**, **Richard Clifford**, **Debby Cryer**, and **Ellen Peisner-Feinberg**, principal investigators, and **Margaret Burchinal**, Biostatistician, from the University of North Carolina at Chapel Hill; and **Sharon Lynn Kagan**, principal investigator, and **Jean Rustici**, site coordinator, from Yale University in New Haven, Connecticut.

Quality ratings

We first constructed a seven-point overall index of center quality and then grouped the categories for reporting purposes, as follows: **1:** *Inadequate*—children's needs for health and safety are not met, there is no observed warmth or support from adults, and no learning is encouraged; **3:** *Minimal*—children's basic health and safety needs are met, a little warmth and support is provided by adults, and a few learning experiences are provided; **5:** *Good*—health and safety needs are fully met, warmth and support is provided for all children, and learning is encouraged in many ways through interesting, fun activities; **7:** *Excellent*—all of the characteristics of good care are present, plus children are encouraged to become independent, teachers plan for children's individual learning needs, and adults have close, personal relationships with each child. For reporting purposes, we grouped program scores as follows:

Poor—programs rated below minimal (ratings less than 3)

Mediocre—programs rated between minimal and good (ratings from 3 to less than 5)

Developmentally appropriate—programs rated between good and excellent (ratings of 5 and above)

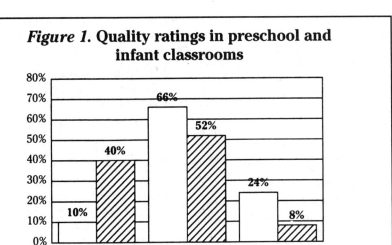

Figure 1. Quality ratings in preschool and infant classrooms

☐ Preschool classroom quality ▨ Infant classroom quality

Note: Data are based on the *Early Childhood Environment Rating Scale* (Harms & Clifford 1980) and the *Infant/Toddler Environment Rating Scale* (Harms & Clifford 1989).

Babies in poor-quality rooms are vulnerable to more illness because basic sanitary conditions for diapering and feeding are not met; they are endangered because of safety problems that exist in the room; they miss warm, supportive relationships with adults; and they lose out on learning because the centers lack the books and toys required for infants' physical and intellectual growth.

• **Children's cognitive and social development are positively related to the quality of their child care experience across all levels of maternal education and child gender and ethnicity.**

Children in higher quality preschool classrooms display greater receptive language ability and pre-mathematics skills, and they have more advanced social skills than children in lower quality classrooms. Children in higher quality centers have more positive self-perceptions and attitudes toward their child care, and their teachers are more likely to have warm, open relationships with them. These relationships were found for all children; quality, however, had an even stronger positive impact for certain children, specifically on the receptive language ability of minority children and on the self-perceptions of children of less educated mothers.

• **Consistent with previous research, the quality of child care is related to specific variables.**

The quality of child care is primarily related to higher staff–child ratios, staff education, and administrators' prior experience. In addition, certain characteristics distinguish poor, mediocre, and good-quality centers, the most important of which are teacher wages, education, and specialized training.

• **States with more stringent licensing standards have fewer poor-quality centers. Centers that comply with additional standards beyond those required for licensing provide higher quality services.**

North Carolina, the state with the least stringent child care standards of the four states in the study, had the most poor-quality centers. At the time of data collection, North Carolina's licensing standards permitted a 1:6 staff–child ratio for infants and a 1:15 ratio for 3-year-olds and had lower staff educational requirements.

Centers that meet higher standards than are required of all centers in their state in order to receive public funding pay higher wages, provide better benefits and working conditions, and have higher overall quality. Finally, accredited centers that voluntarily meet a higher set of standards, such as those set by NAEYC, have higher quality than do nonaccredited centers.

• **Centers provide higher-than-average overall quality when they have access to extra resources that are used to improve quality.**

The 24 publicly operated centers (in public schools, at state colleges and universities, or operated by municipal agencies), the 16 worksite centers, and the 30 centers with public funding tied to higher standards provide higher quality care than other centers. These centers all have higher expended costs and total revenue per child hour, have more donated resources, and are less dependent on parent fees than are other centers; they pay higher wages and provide more staff benefits; they have higher staff–child ratios; and teachers have more education, more specialized training, and longer tenure in the centers.

Costs, revenue, and support

Before discussing costs and revenue, several terms must be defined. *Expended costs* refer to cash costs that are actually incurred to run centers. *Donations* refer to the goods and services that are donated to the center to support child care. *Foregone wages* refer to the difference between the wage a staffperson could earn in another occupation (based on the person's education, gender, age, race, and marital status) and the person's wage as a child care worker.[1] *Full cost* refers to the amount it would take to operate centers if all

[1]*Foregone wages represent another kind of cost. Child care is a labor-intensive industry dependent on female employees who work for wages below those they could earn, even in other female-dominated occupations, all of which pay less than comparable male occupations. Regardless of the reason that child care employees accept jobs in the field, centers are using labor resources that embody human educational investments and work experience that do not show up in center cash outlays. As the industry expands or improves quality, or if the national labor market tightens, it may be naive to expect more and more women to continue working for these lower wages.*

6. REFLECTIONS

costs were included. Finally, *total revenue* refers to the total amount of income received by a center, including parent fees, publicly reimbursed fees, USDA food grants, other public funds, sponsor and other private contributions, and other revenue.

• **Center child care, even mediocre-quality care, is costly to provide. Even so, donations and foregone wages are large, accounting for more than one-fourth of the full cost of care.**

The average expended cost (cash cost) is $95 per week per child, or $2.11 per child hour, to provide mediocre care. Average expended costs, reflecting regional differences in the cost of living, ranged from $1.50 per child hour in North Carolina to $2.88 in Connecticut; in California and Colorado the average expended costs were $2.04 and $2.02 per child care hour, respectively.

Labor costs account for 70% of the total expended costs on the average, with facilities costs contributing an additional 15% and other cash expenses making up the remaining 15%. Expended costs are not higher, because child care employees are primarily female (97% of the sample), who earn even less in child care than they could in other female-dominated occupations. In

this study, the average foregone wage given up by a teacher was $5,238 per year—more than the expended cost per child of $4,940—and each assistant gave up $3,582 per year, on the average.

As depicted in Figure 2, we estimate the average full cost of producing center child care services at $2.83 per child hour ($127 per week), or 72¢ per hour more than expended costs[2]. The difference between expended and full cost reflects foregone wages and benefits (19% of full costs, at 54¢ per child hour); occupancy donations (5%, on the average, of full cost, or 14¢ per child hour); and donated goods and volunteer services (2% of full cost, or 6¢ per child hour).

The amounts of foregone wages and in-kind donations vary by state. Adjusted for regional cost-of-living differences, they are lower in states where overall quality is higher.

A comparison of the expended cost of child care with a typical family's income indicates the high cost of producing even mediocre quality care. The average annual expended cost for centers is $4,940, 8% of the 1993 median before-tax income of a full-time employed dual-earner house-

---
[2]*These figures do not add up to exactly 72¢ because of rounding errors.*

---

hold, and 23% of the average before-tax household income of a full-time employed single parent.

• **Good-quality services cost more than those of mediocre quality, but not a lot more.**

The difference in costs between good to excellent quality and mediocre-to poor-quality programs was about 10%, assuming that the 10% was spent on items related to quality enhancement. Although accurate given *present* conditions, this percentage does not take the full cost of care into consideration, nor does it consider any other *projected* increases, including those related to wages or facilities; hence, the data should not be used for cost-related policy projections.

• **Center enrollment affects costs.**

Two types of enrollment effects were found. First, the larger the number of children served (up to the legal capacity of the center) and/or the longer the hours of service, the lower the cost per child hour for each level of quality. Second, larger centers—those serving a larger number of full-time enrolled (FTE) children—also have lower average total expended costs per child than do centers serving a small number of children, even when quality is constant.

• **Cash payment from government and philanthropies are sources of center revenue that demonstrate a social commitment to sharing the expense of child care. On the average, these cash payments represent 28% of center revenue.**

Child care is an important service that some children need regardless of their family's income or preferences. Economists call such things *merit goods,* because society as a whole, or some groups, believe that all people who need the service merit having it and are willing to pay for it. Cash philanthropic contributions, public funding of centers, and child care tax credits all help reduce the fees paid by parents and other purchasers of child care, as do donations and foregone wages.

For the whole sample, including families whose child care is subsidized, parent payments to centers represent the equivalent of $1.55 per

---

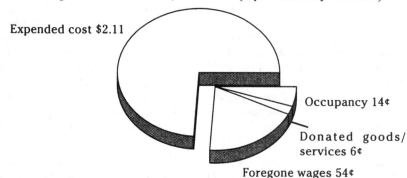

Figure 2. **Average full cost of child care per child hour**

Average full cost = $2.83/child hour

Average hidden cost = 72¢/child hour (represented by cut slice)

Expended cost $2.11

Occupancy 14¢

Donated goods/ services 6¢

Foregone wages 54¢

Note: These full-cost estimates are somewhat lower than estimates based upon NAEYC's Full Cost of Quality *(Willer 1990). NAEYC (1990) recommends that pay reflect professional responsibilities and qualifications, incorporating a pay-equity concept that does not perpetuate pay differentials based on gender or other personal characteristics.*

child hour, or $70 per week, or 71% of center revenue (and 55% of full cost). Among the centers in the sample, the average full tuition payment is $1.92 per child hour, or $86 per week. If a typical family elected to take the federal child care tax credit available to them, their expenses would be reduced by an estimated average of $.21 per child care hour (20% of $200 per month/193 hours per month).

Sector comparisons

Child care centers operate in a mixed market made up of private nonprofit centers, publicly operated nonprofit centers, and centers that are owned and operated for profit. Differences are found between the for-profit and nonprofit sectors, but the overall quality of services is not significantly different between the two sectors except in one state—North Carolina—that has very lax licensing standards. In North Carolina, for-profit centers were found to provide much lower quality care than did other sectors.

Despite the overall similarities in center quality between sectors, some differences were found. In nonprofit centers, staff–child ratios are higher than in for-profit centers; teachers and teacher directors have more specialized training and formal education; assistant teachers and teacher directors have more prior experience; staff have worked more months at the center; and annual turnover rates are lower. Nonprofit centers pay higher wages, and the foregone wages of their staff are lower than in for-profit centers.

Variation by subsector was found in center characteristics and quality, especially in the nonprofit sector. In the for-profit sector, considerable homogeneity was found between the subsectors of independent for-profits, local chains, and national systems with regard to staffing ratios and staff quality, as well as in terms of costs, revenue, and overall quality. National chains offer more staff benefits, such as health insurance, maternity leave, and staff child care discounts, and they pay lower wages in California and Connecticut.

Subsectors in the nonprofit sector—independent, church-affiliated, and publicly operated nonprofit—are less homogeneous. Of these three types of nonprofit centers, centers operated by public agencies have significantly higher costs, revenue, and quality. Church-affiliated centers have lower staff–child ratios, lower levels of trained and educated staff, lower wages, lower cost and revenue per child hour, and, most importantly, lower overall quality than other independent and publicly operated nonprofit programs.

The economic environment

A unique focus of this study was to learn more about the effects of market conditions on the cost and quality of care. Differences in demand and supply conditions faced by different kinds of centers may affect the quality of care provided in the market. Characteristics of the market setting for child care—notably market competition and subsidy dependence—affect center finances. For-profit centers and nonprofit centers face different competitive conditions that can affect their performance.

We found evidence of strong competition in local markets. First, centers in for-profit and nonprofit sectors charge similar fees per child hour. Second, both sectors seem to be equally efficient in their use of resources. Third, both sectors receive similar low rates of profit (surplus) on sales (3.7%).

The composition of costs and the ability to take advantage of scale economies varies somewhat by sector. For-profit centers spend a higher percentage of total costs on facilities and a smaller percent on labor, practices that could lower quality. These centers typically serve a larger number of children and/or provide more hours of service than do nonprofit centers, which allows for-profit centers to operate at a lower average cost per child and enables them to compete successfully with their nonprofit counterparts at a comparable level of quality.

We found evidence of inadequate consumer knowledge, which creates market imperfections and reduces incentives for some centers to provide good-quality care. The study suggests some reasons for the prevalence of low-quality child care, particularly for centers dependent on parent fees. In our parent survey, parents say they value the characteristics of good-quality child care, but they substantially overestimate the quality of services their children are receiving. Ninety percent of parents rate programs as very good, while the ratings of trained observers indicate that most of these same programs are providing care that ranges from poor to mediocre.

There are numerous possible explanations for this discrepancy between parent and observer ratings, some of which the study investigated. For instance, parents are hindered in assessing care by the inherent difficulty of monitoring service. The disparity between scores given by parents and those given by observers assessing quality is higher for aspects of care that are difficult for parents to observe. Also, parents' priorities seem to affect their assessments. The more they value an aspect of care, the greater the disparity between their evaluation and that of the trained observer.

There may be other reasons why parents rate their child care arrangement highly. For instance, they may not think that they have a choice of

> **Given both a competitive market that equalizes fees across centers and parents' difficulty in identifying center quality, centers dependent on parent revenue have no incentive to provide a higher level of quality at higher cost.**

6. REFLECTIONS

care, or they may never have seen good-quality care, giving them no basis for comparison. The inability of parents to recognize good-quality care implies that they do not demand it; the small difference in fees between poor-quality and high-quality centers lends credence to this hypothesis. Given both a competitive market that equalizes fees across centers and parents' difficulty in identifying center quality, centers dependent on parent revenue have no incentive to provide a higher level of quality at higher cost.

Centers appear to be very responsive to consumer demand. Preschool classrooms meet health and safety needs. Centers in the sample are open long hours, 10 to 12 hours per day, enabling parents to work full time. Centers provide part-time care, before- and after-school programs, and summer camps. Parents, however, while they value good-quality services, apparently are not demanding quality. To the extent that government agencies involved in purchasing care for low-income children impose low payments for services or fail to provide higher reimbursement for higher quality, they, too, contribute to lowering the demand for good-quality child care.

Recommendations

The first national education goal states that by the year 2000, all children will enter school ready to learn. The reality of child care in the United States today makes it highly unlikely that we will reach that goal. Unless poor-quality care is curtailed, the development and well-being of large numbers of our nation's children may be jeopardized. To that end, we make one critical recommendation:

The nation must commit to improving the quality of child care services and to ensuring that all children and their families have access to good programs— that is, good-quality child care must become a merit good.

In making this recommendation we assume that child care will re-main voluntary; parents will have the right and responsibility to select the type of child care they wish;

centers will continue to operate in the for-profit, nonprofit, and public sectors; and the financing of quality child care will continue to be shared by families, to the extent feasible, by responsible employers, philanthropic organizations, and the government.

*   *   *

We recommend four action steps.

1. Launch consumer and public education efforts in the public and private sectors to help parents identify high-quality child care programs and to inform the American public of the liability of poor-quality programs.

• Give parents clear information regarding the observable ingredients of good-quality child care.

• Give parents and others information that clearly identifies good-quality programs.

• Initiate a long-term public media campaign, analogous to the one addressing the effect of smoking on health, to raise public awareness of the nature and importance of good-quality child care.

• In collaboration with other private and public agencies, initiate a federally supported program of research to increase understanding of the child care market and to provide an ongoing data base on the status of child care and its effects on children in the United States.

2. Implement higher standards for child care at the state level as a major approach to eliminating poor-quality child care.

• Create higher standards at the state level and improve monitoring of child care as a part of consumer protection. Standards must do more than protect the basic health and safety of children—they must also take into account children's developmental needs.

• Eliminate all exemptions from state licensing standards.

• Encourage centers to seek and maintain voluntary professional center accreditation based on higher standards.

• Give state and federal financial incentives for centers to provide care that meets high standards, eliminating federal regulations that restrict the ability of states to pay higher prices for higher quality care.

3. Increase investments in child care staff to ensure a skilled and stable workforce.

• Invest more federal, state, and local government funds and private-sector funds in the education and training of child care teaching staff and administrators.

• Provide all child care staff compensation appropriate to their training, experience, and responsibility.

4. Ensure adequate financing and support of child care.

• Increase investment in child care by federal, state, and local government, as well as by the private sector, to help families pay the cost of good-quality care.

• Tie all federal and state child care funding to standards that demonstrably produce higher quality care.

• Provide financial incentives that enable centers to hire experienced administrators and skilled staff and to learn how to keep them.

• Tailor employee benefits to provide significant help to employees with young children as part of the private sector's support of child care.

References

Harms, T., & R.M. Clifford. 1980. *Early childhood environment rating scale.* New York: Teachers College Press.

Harms, T., & R.M. Clifford. 1989. *Infant/ toddler environment rating scale.* New York: Teachers College Press.

National Association for the Education of Young Children. 1990. NAEYC position statement on guidelines for compensation of early childhood professionals. In *Reaching the full cost of quality in early childhood programs,* ed. B. Willer. Washington, DC: NAEYC.

Willer, B. , ed. 1990. *Reaching the full cost of quality in early childhood programs.* Washington, DC: NAEYC.

Credits/ Acknowledgments

Cover design by Charles Vitelli

1. Perspectives
Facing overview—Photo by Cheryl Greenleaf.

2. Child Development and Families
Facing overview—Photo by Louis P. Raucci.

3. Educational Practices
Facing overview—Woodfin Camp & Associates photo by Lester Sloan.

4. Guiding and Supporting Young Children
Facing overview—Superstock, Inc., photo.

5. Curricular Issues
Facing overview—Photo by Pamela Carley.

6. Reflections
Facing overview—Photo by Cheryl Greenleaf.

ANNUAL EDITIONS ARTICLE REVIEW FORM

■ NAME: _____ DATE: _____

■ TITLE AND NUMBER OF ARTICLE: _____

■ BRIEFLY STATE THE MAIN IDEA OF THIS ARTICLE: _____

_____

■ LIST THREE IMPORTANT FACTS THAT THE AUTHOR USES TO SUPPORT THE MAIN IDEA:

_____

_____

_____

_____

_____

_____

■ WHAT INFORMATION OR IDEAS DISCUSSED IN THIS ARTICLE ARE ALSO DISCUSSED IN YOUR TEXTBOOK OR OTHER READING YOU HAVE DONE? LIST THE TEXTBOOK CHAPTERS AND PAGE NUMBERS:

_____

_____

_____

_____

_____

_____

■ LIST ANY EXAMPLES OF BIAS OR FAULTY REASONING THAT YOU FOUND IN THE ARTICLE:

_____

_____

_____

_____

■ LIST ANY NEW TERMS/CONCEPTS THAT WERE DISCUSSED IN THE ARTICLE AND WRITE A SHORT DEFINITION:

_____

_____

_____

_____

_____

*Your instructor may require you to use this Annual Editions Article Review Form in any number of ways: for articles that are assigned, for extra credit, as a tool to assist in developing assigned papers, or simply for your own reference. Even if it is not required, we encourage you to photocopy and use this page; you'll find that reflecting on the articles will greatly enhance the information from your text.

ANNUAL EDITIONS: EARLY CHILDHOOD EDUCATION 96/97
Article Rating Form

Here is an opportunity for you to have direct input into the next revision of this volume. We would like you to rate each of the 46 articles listed below, using the following scale:

1. **Excellent: should definitely be retained**
2. **Above average: should probably be retained**
3. **Below average: should probably be deleted**
4. **Poor: should definitely be deleted**

Your ratings will play a vital part in the next revision. So please mail this prepaid form to us just as soon as you complete it.
Thanks for your help!

Annual Editions revisions depend on two major opinion sources: one is our Advisory Board, listed in the front of this volume, which works with us in scanning the thousands of articles published in the public press each year; the other is you—the person actually using the book. Please help us and the users of the next edition by completing the prepaid article rating form on this page and returning it to us. Thank you.

Rating	Article	Rating	Article
	1. Portrait of the American Child		25. Aiming for New Outcomes: The Promise and the Reality
	2. A Call to Action: Improving the Situation of Children Worldwide		26. Misbehavior or Mistaken Behavior?
	3. The Next Baby Boom		27. Behavior Management and "The Five C's"
	4. The World's 5 Best Ideas		28. Encouraging Positive Social Development in Young Children
	5. It's Hard to Do Day Care Right—and Survive		29. Helping Children to Cope with Relocation
	6. Helping Crack-Affected Children Succeed		30. Breaking the Cycle of Violence
	7. Companies Help Solve Day-Care Problems		31. Supporting Victims of Child Abuse
	8. Educational Implications of Developmental Transitions: Revisiting the 5- to 7-Year Shift		32. Diversity: A Program for All Children
	9. The Amazing Minds of Infants		33. Project Work with Diverse Students: Adapting Curriculum Based on the Reggio Emilia Approach
	10. Creativity and the Child's Social Development		34. Curriculum Webs: Weaving Connections from Children to Teachers
	11. Keeping Kids Healthy in Child Care		35. Voice of Inquiry: Possibilities and Perspectives
	12. Why Leave Children with Bad Parents?		36. All about Me
	13. Life without Father		37. A Framework for Literacy
	14. Aiding Families with Referrals		38. Read Me a Story: 101 Good Books Kids Will Love
	15. Homeless Families: Stark Reality of the '90s		39. Early Childhood Physical Education: Providing the Foundation
	16. How Families Are Changing . . . for the Better!		40. Starting Points: Executive Summary of the Report of the Carnegie Corporation of New York Task Force on Meeting the Needs of Young Children
	17. Bringing the DAP Message to Kindergarten and Primary Teachers		
	18. Teaching Young Children: Educators Seek 'Developmental Appropriateness'		41. Sisterhood and Sentimentality— America's Earliest Preschool Centers
	19. Recognizing the Essentials of Developmentally Appropriate Practice		42. The Movers and Shapers of Early Childhood Education
	20. Infants and Toddlers with Special Needs and Their Families		43. Mrs. Paley's Lessons
	21. Fourth-Grade Slump: The Cause and Cure		44. Families and Children: Who Is Responsible?
	22. Strategies for Teaching Children in Multiage Classrooms		45. Choosing Child Care
	23. Nurturing Kids: Seven Ways of Being Smart		46. Cost, Quality, and Child Outcomes in Child Care Centers: Key Findings and Recommendations
	24. The Challenges of Assessing Young Children Appropriately		

(Continued on next page)

ABOUT YOU

Name _____ Date _____

Are you a teacher? ❑   Or student? ❑

Your School Name _____

Department _____

Address _____

City _____ State _____ Zip _____

School Telephone # _____

YOUR COMMENTS ARE IMPORTANT TO US!

Please fill in the following information:

For which course did you use this book? _____

Did you use a text with this Annual Edition? ❑ yes ❑ no

The title of the text? _____

What are your general reactions to the Annual Editions concept?

Have you read any particular articles recently that you think should be included in the next edition?

Are there any articles you feel should be replaced in the next edition? Why?

Are there other areas that you feel would utilize an Annual Edition?

May we contact you for editorial input?

May we quote you from above?

ANNUAL EDITIONS: EARLY CHILDHOOD EDUCATION 96/97

BUSINESS REPLY MAIL		
First Class	Permit No. 84	Guilford, CT

Postage will be paid by addressee

**Dushkin Publishing Group/
Brown & Benchmark Publishers**
Sluice Dock
Guilford, Connecticut 06437